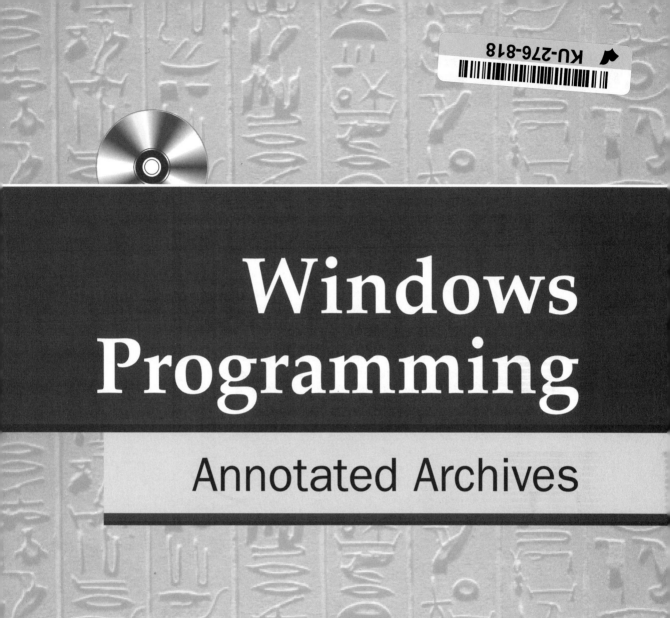

Windows Programming

Annotated Archives

ABOUT THE AUTHOR ...

Herb Schildt is the world's leading programming author. He is an authority on the C and C++ languages, a master Windows programmer, and an expert on Java. His programming books have sold over 2.5 million copies worldwide and have been translated into all major foreign languages. He is the author of numerous best-sellers, including *Windows 2000 Programming from the Ground Up, Windows 98 Programming from the Ground Up, MFC Programming from the Ground Up, C: The Complete Reference, C++: The Complete Reference, C++ from the Ground Up*, and co-author of *Java: The Complete Reference*. Schildt is president of Universal Computing Laboratories, Inc., a software consulting firm in Mahomet, Illinois. He holds a master's degree in computer science from the University of Illinois.

Windows Programming

Annotated Archives

Herbert Schildt

Osborne/**McGraw-Hill**

Berkeley   New York   St. Louis   San Francisco   Auckland Bogotá
Hamburg   London   Madrid   Mexico City   Milan   Montreal   New Delhi
Panama City   Paris   São Paulo   Singapore   Sydney   Tokyo   Toronto

Osborne/**McGraw-Hill**
2600 Tenth Street
Berkeley, California 94710
U.S.A.

For information on translations or book distributors outside the U.S.A., or to arrange
bulk purchase discounts for sales promotions, premiums, or fund-raisers, please
contact Osborne/**McGraw-Hill** at the above address.

Windows Programming Annotated Archives

1234567890 AGM AGM 90198765432109

ISBN 0-07-212123-8

Publisher	**Proofreader**
Brandon A. Nordin	Linda Medoff
Associate Publisher	**Indexer**
and Editor-in-Chief	Sherry Schildt
Scott Rogers	**Computer Designer**
Acquisitions Editor	Gary Corrigan
Wendy Rinaldi	Mickey Galicia
Project Editor	Roberta Steele
Carolyn Welch	**Illustrator**
Editorial Assistant	Robert Hansen
Monika Faltiss	Beth Young
Technical Editor	**Series Design**
Greg Guntle	Roberta Steele
Copy Editor	Peter F. Hancik
Claire Splan	**Cover Design**
	Regan Honda

This book was composed with Corel VENTURA.

Contents at a Glance

Contents

Preface

By any measure, Windows is a challenging programming environment. This statement is true not just for beginners, but for experienced pros, too. Some days it seems like even the simplest new feature will take hours to implement. First, you need to figure out what API functions to use. Then, you must determine the order in which they need to be called and what arguments to pass. Finally, you must handle the appropriate messages. The trouble is that none of this is necessarily self-evident. There are hundreds of API functions, structures, and messages. Finding the right ones — and using them properly — can consume what seems like an inordinate amount of time. Frankly, the whole process can be quite frustrating.

One of the most effective ways to streamline Windows programming (and reduce the frustration) is to have a collection of working code at the ready. As all experienced programmers know, having such a toolkit is indispensable when developing for Windows. When you need to add something to a program, often you can "cut and paste" it from the toolkit, or at least use the toolkit code as a starting point. Either way, a toolkit of debugged Windows code is a necessary part of any programmer's shop. The purpose of this book is to help you expand your Windows toolkit.

Like all books in the *Annotated Archives* series, this book presents code with detailed commentary. It includes everything from major subsystems to simple add-ons, short utility programs to sophisticated, performance boosting techniques. If you want to take command of the Windows programming environment, then you have found the right book. Throughout, you will find the high-powered techniques that help turn a good program into a great program. Along the way, you will see how to use some of Windows' newest, user-pleasing features.

What's Inside

Windows is very large, and covering the entire system would easily fill an entire shelf (or two!) with books. Thus, choosing what to include in this book was a daunting task. To help narrow the list of topics, I used the following criteria.

◆ Practical

◆ Innovative

◆ Interesting

◆ Performance enhancing

◆ Added "pizzaz" to the user interface

Code was included if it fell into one or more of these categories. Not all examples meet all of the criteria, but all meet at least one.

The book begins with a look at advanced menu options. While it is true that menu handling is one of the first things that a beginning Windows programmer learns, menus offer a substantial number of overlooked options. The effective use of these options enhances any program.

Chapter 2 shows how to handle one of the thorniest issues confronting the Window programmer: window repaints. The approach shown in Chapter 2 employs a "virtual window" and this technique is used by several of the other programs in the book. It is a fast, efficient way to repaint a window.

Chapter 3 develops a number of functions that provide simple ways to output text to a window. They are especially useful when debugging, or when developing utility programs for which a sophisticated user interface is not required.

Chapter 4 explores animation and the techniques used to manage it.

Chapter 5 creates a thread control panel that can be used to control the execution and priorities of the individual threads within a multithreaded application. The thread control panel is especially useful when optimizing your multithreaded programs.

Chapter 6 develops a mouse control panel and a keyboard control panel. These control panels can be added, as an amenity to the user, to applications that you create.

Chapter 7 explores messages and message hooks, and develops several programs that allow you to record and replay messages. This is useful when creating automated demos, or for automating a sequence of tasks.

Chapter 8 creates two useful print utilities. The first lets you print the contents of a text file. The second prints the contents of a window, which can contain text and/or graphics. You will find both useful in many programming contexts.

Chapter 9 explores the world of screen savers. It creates a simple, text-based screen saver that displays a clock, and a more sophisticated graphics based one that animates a bitmap. Screen savers are one of the more intriguing Windows applications. I think you will find this chapter quite interesting.

Chapter 10 develops three simple telephone dialing utilities that use the TAPI subsystem. Chapter 11 examines DLLs. The book ends with Chapter 12, which presents three short, but useful utilities: a memory usage monitor, an alarm clock, and a multiple monitor demonstrator.

What Version of Windows

The code in this book was tested with Windows 98, Windows NT, and Windows 2000. In general, the code will work for Windows 95, too. However, no attempt was made to provide compatibility with 16-bit Windows 3.1.

What Compiler Do You Need?

Visual C++ 6 was used to compile and test the programs. Other compilers will probably work, too. However, you must make sure that the compiler is capable of handling modern, Win32 programs. Remember: if it is an older compiler, then it won't know about several of the more modern options and features used by several of the programs.

Watch for the MFC Tips

The code in this book uses the API functions directly. Thus, it is API-based code. It does not use MFC or any other class library. The reason for this is that API-based code is applicable to the widest variety of situations. It also shows all of the details of what is taking place. However, because many programmers use MFC, each chapter contains tips for adapting the examples for use with MFC. Because much of MFC is simply a thin wrapper around the API, converting the code is usually easy, and the MFC tips will help speed the process.

More Books by Herbert Schildt

Windows Programming Annotated Archives is just one of many in the "Herb Schildt" series of programming books. Here is a partial list of Schildt's other books.

If you want to learn more about programming for Windows, we recommend the following:

Windows 2000 Programming from the Ground Up

Windows 98 Programming from the Ground Up

Windows NT 4 from the Ground Up

MFC Programming from the Ground Up

If you want to learn more about C++, you will find these books especially helpful:

C++: The Complete Reference

C++ from the Ground Up

Teach Yourself C++

Expert C++

The C/C++ Annotated Archives (co-authored by Herb Schildt)

If you want to learn more about C, we recommend the following:

Teach Yourself C

C: The Complete Reference

If you will be developing programs for the Web, you will want to read

Java: The Complete Reference

co-authored by Herbert Schildt and Patrick Naughton.

When you need solid answers fast, turn to Herbert Schildt: The recognized authority on programming.

Menu Magic

DynMenu.cpp	Changing menu contents at runtime
ChkRadio.cpp	Using check and radio menu items
Floating.cpp	Using floating context menus
RBMenu.cpp	Processing right mouse button clicks on a menu item
BitMenu.cpp	Adding bitmaps to menu items

This book begins by exploring one of the most fundamental, yet overlooked elements of the Windows user interface: the menu. Menus are the gateway to a Windows program's functionality. It is through menus that most user activity is initiated, and their appearance and usability have a profound effect on how users judge a program. Because menu management is among the first things that one learns about Windows programming, it is easy to take menus for granted, using them in only their most rudimentary forms. Sadly, menus are often the last area to receive attention when a program is being polished. However, this situation is changing.

Many new features and capabilities have been added to the Windows menuing subsystem over the past few years, including some exciting enhancements supplied by Windows 98 and Windows 2000. As you will see, the Windows menuing system now offers the programmer a wide range of options that help put excitement into any application.

This chapter examines the following five techniques that top-notch programmers use to give their menus a stylish, high-quality look that sets their programs apart from the crowd.

◆ Constructing and changing menus at runtime

◆ Using check and radio menu items

◆ Creating floating, popup menus

◆ Handling right button clicks on menu items

◆ Adding bitmaps to menus

Each of these techniques gives you fine-grained control over the contents of your application's menus. But, more importantly, weaving a bit of menu magic into your programs is a good way to improve any Windows program.

As a vehicle for demonstrating menu enhancements, we will use a simple clock application that displays the current system time (updated each second) and, optionally, the current date. While the clock program is fully functional, it intentionally has been kept very simple so as not to get in the way of the menu features being illustrated. It can also serve as an excellent testing environment for your own menu experiments.

PROGRAMMER'S NOTE   *Throughout the course of this book the same general code skeleton is used to create and register the program's window class, create a window, and then start the message loop. These elements of a Windows program should be familiar to any reader of this book and they are not described in the annotations in this or subsequent chapters. However, a detailed description of the skeleton can be found in Appendix A.*

A Short Note About Compatibility

As all Windows programmers know, each new release of Windows brings with it a package of new features. At the time of this writing, Windows 98 and the beta version of Windows 2000 are the latest releases. Throughout this chapter, and throughout this book, we will be taking advantage of the new features supported by these systems. However, where possible, the programs are designed in such a way that they are also backward compatible with Windows 95 and Windows NT 4. Since backward compatibility is a requirement for many applications, it seems only fitting that the code in this book should provide it when possible. With this in mind, unless a program is explicitly described as requiring Windows 98 or Windows 2000, you can assume that it is backward compatible with earlier versions.

One last point: No attempt has been made to provide compatibility with 16-bit Windows, such as Windows 3.1.

Menu API Fundamentals

Although the basic menu structure of most Windows applications is defined within the application's resource file, it is possible to change the content of those menus at runtime. It is also possible to construct a new menu at runtime. These actions allow a program to respond to changing program conditions.

Windows includes several menu management API functions, which allow you to manipulate the contents of a menu during the execution of your program. We will be using several of these functions in the next section and throughout this chapter. Before demonstrating the various menu enhancements, an overview of these functions will be helpful.

Adding an Item to a Menu

To add an item to a menu at runtime, use **InsertMenuItem( )**, shown here:

```
BOOL InsertMenuItem(HMENU hMenu, UINT Where,
                    BOOL How, LPMENUITEMINFO MenuInfo);
```

InsertMenuItem( ) adds an item to the menu whose handle is specified by *hMenu*. The new menu item is inserted into the menu immediately before the item specified by *Where*. The precise meaning of *Where* is determined by the value of *How*. If *How* is nonzero, then *Where* must contain the index at which point the new item is inserted. (Indexing begins at zero.) If *How* is zero, then *Where* must contain the menu ID of an existing item at which point the new item is inserted. The menu item being added is defined by the **MENUITEMINFO** structure pointed to by *MenuInfo*. **MENUITEMINFO** is defined like this:

```
typedef struct tagMENUITEMINFO
{
  UINT cbSize;
  UINT fMask;
  UINT fType;
  UINT fState;
  UINT wID;
  HMENU hSubMenu;
  HBITMAP hbmpChecked;
  HBITMAP hbmpUnchecked;
  DWORD dwItemData;
  LPSTR dwTypeData;
  UINT cch;
  HBITMAP hbmpItem; // requires Windows 98, Windows 2000 or later
} MENUITEMINFO;
```

Here, **cbSize** must contain the size of the **MENUITEMINFO** structure.

The value of **fMask** determines which of the other members of **MENUITEMINFO** contain valid information when setting menu information. That is, it determines which of the other members are active. (It is also used to specify which members will be loaded when menu information is retrieved.) It must be a combination of one or more of these values:

fMask Value	Activates
MIIM_BITMAP	**hbmpItem** (Windows 98 or later)
MIIM_CHECKMARKS	**hbmpChecked** and **hbmpUnchecked**
MIIM_DATA	**dwItemData**
MIIM_FTYPE	**fType** (Windows 98 or later)
MIIM_ID	**wID**
MIIM_STATE	**fstate**
MIIM_STRING	**dwTypeDate** (Windows 98 or later)
MIIM_SUBMENU	**hSubMenu**
MIIM_TYPE	**fType** and **dwTypeData**

The type of the menu item is determined by **fType**. It can be any valid combination of the following values:

fType Value	Meaning
MFT_BITMAP	The low-order word of **dwTypeData** specifies a bitmap handle. The menu item is displayed as a bitmap. (With Windows 98 and later you can specify **MIIM_BITMAP** in **fMask** instead.)
MFT_MENUBARBREAK	For menu bar, causes the item to be put on a new line. For popup menus, causes the item to be put in a different column. In this case, the item is separated using a bar.
MFT_MENUBREAK	Same as **MFT_MENUBARBREAK** except that no separator bar is used.
MF_OWNERDRAW	Owner drawn item.
MFT_RADIOCHECK	Radio button check mark style is used when the item is selected rather than the normal menu check mark. **hbmpChecked** must be **NULL**.
MFT_RIGHTJUSTIFY	For menu bars only. Right justifies the item. Subsequent items are also right justified.
MFT_RIGHTORDER	Menus descend right to left. Supports right-to-left reading languages.
MFT_SEPARATOR	Places a horizontal dividing line between menu items. The values in **dwTypeData** and **cch** are ignored. This type cannot be used for menu bar items.
MFT_STRING	**dwTypeData** is a pointer to a string that describes the menu item. (For Windows 98 and later, you can use **MIIM_STRING** in **fMask** instead.)

The state of the menu item is determined by **fState**. It can be any valid combination of the following values:

fState Value	Meaning
MFS_CHECKED	Item is checked.
MFS_DEFAULT	Item is the default selection.
MFS_DISABLED	Item is disabled.
MFS_ENABLED	Item is enabled. Items are enabled by default.
MFS_GRAYED	Item is disabled and grayed.
MFS_HILITE	Item is highlighted.
MFS_UNCHECKED	Item is unchecked.
MFS_UNHILITE	Item is unhighlighted. Items are unhighlighted by default.

The ID value associated with the menu item is specified in **wID**.

If the item being inserted is a popup submenu, then its handle must be in **hSubMenu**. Otherwise, this value must be **NULL**.

You can specify bitmaps that will be used to indicate a menu item's checked and unchecked state in **hbmpChecked** and **hbmpUnchecked**. To use the default check mark, specify **NULL** for both of these members.

The value of **dwItemData** is application-dependent. If unused, set this value to zero.

The menu item itself is specified in **dwTypeData**. It will be either a pointer to a string or the handle of a bitmap, depending upon the value of **fType**.

When a menu item is being retrieved, **cch** will contain the length of the string if **fType** is **MFT_STRING**. The value of **cch** is ignored when the menu item is being set.

To specify a bitmapped image that will be displayed on the left side of the menu text, assign the handle of the bitmap to **hbmpItem**. This option requires Windows 98, Windows 2000, or later.

InsertMenuItem( ) returns nonzero if successful and zero on failure.

Deleting a Menu Item

To remove a menu item, use the **DeleteMenu( )** function, shown here:

    BOOL DeleteMenu(HMENU *hMenu*, UINT *ItemID*, UINT *How*);

Here, *hMenu* specifies the handle of the menu to be affected. The item to be removed is specified in *ItemID*. The value of *How* determines how *ItemID* is interpreted. If *How* is **MF_BYPOSITION**, then the value in *ItemID* must be the index of the item to be deleted. This index is the position of the item within the menu, with the first menu item being zero. If *How* is **MF_BYCOMMAND**, then *ItemID* is the ID associated with the menu item. **DeleteMenu( )** returns nonzero if successful and zero on failure.

If the menu item deleted is itself a popup submenu, then that popup menu is also destroyed. There is no need to call **DestroyMenu( )**.

Obtaining a Handle to a Menu

As you have just seen, to add or delete a menu item requires a handle to the menu. To obtain the handle of the main menu, use **GetMenu( )**, shown here:

    HMENU GetMenu(HWND *hwnd*);

GetMenu( ) returns the handle of the menu associated with the window specified by *hwnd*. It returns **NULL** on failure.

Given a handle to a window's main menu, you can easily obtain the handles of the popup submenus contained in a menu by using **GetSubMenu( )**. Its prototype is shown here:

HMENU GetSubMenu(HMENU *hMenu*, int *ItemPos*);

Here, *hMenu* is the handle of the parent menu and *ItemPos* is the position of the desired popup (also called *drop-down*) menu within the parent window. (The first position is zero.) The function returns the handle of the specified submenu or **NULL** on failure.

Obtaining the Size of a Menu

Frequently, you will need to know how many items are in a menu. To obtain the number of menu items, use **GetMenuItemCount( )**, shown here:

int GetMenuItemCount(HMENU *hMenu*);

Here, *hMenu* is the handle of the menu in question. The function returns –1 on failure.

Enabling and Disabling a Menu Item

Sometimes a menu item will apply only to certain situations and not to others. In such cases, you may wish to temporarily disable an item, enabling it later. To accomplish this, use the **EnableMenuItem( )** function, shown here:

BOOL EnableMenuItem(HMENU *hMenu*, UINT *ItemID*, UINT *How*);

The handle of the menu is passed in *hMenu*. The item to be enabled or disabled is specified in *ItemID*. The value of *How* determines two things. First, it specifies how *ItemID* is interpreted. If *How* contains **MF_BYPOSITION**, then the value in *ItemID* must be the index of the item to be deleted. This index is the position of the item within the menu, with the first menu item being zero. If *How* contains **MF_BYCOMMAND**, then *ItemID* is the ID associated with the menu item. The value in *How* also determines whether the item will be enabled or disabled, based upon which of the following values are present:

MF_DISABLED	Disables the new menu item.
MF_ENABLED	Enables the new menu item.
MF_GRAYED	Disables the menu item and turns it gray.

To construct the desired value of *How,* OR together the appropriate values.

EnableMenuItem( ) returns the previous state of the item or –1 on failure.

GetMenuItemInfo( ) and SetMenuItemInfo( )

Sometimes you will want to obtain detailed information about or make detailed adjustments to a menu. The easiest way to do this is to use the menu management functions, **GetMenuItemInfo( )** and **SetMenuItemInfo( )**, whose prototypes are shown here:

BOOL GetMenuItemInfo(HMENU *hMenu*, UINT *ItemID*,
                    BOOL *How*, LPMENUITEMINFO *MenuInfo*);

BOOL SetMenuItemInfo(HMENU *hMenu*, UINT *ItemID*,
                    BOOL *How*, LPMENUITEMINFO *MenuInfo*);

These functions get and set all of the information associated with a menu item. The menu containing the item is specified by *hMenu.* The menu item is specified by *ItemID.* The precise meaning of *ItemID* is determined by the value of *How.* If *How* is nonzero, then *ItemID* must contain the index of the item. If *How* is zero, then *ItemID* must contain the menu ID of the item. For **GetMenuItemInfo( )**, the **MENUITEMINFO** structure pointed to by *MenuInfo* will receive the current information about the item. For **SetMenuItemInfo( )**, the contents of the structure pointed to by *MenuInfo* will be used to set the menu item's information.

Both functions return nonzero if successful and zero on failure.

As you can guess, you could use **SetMenuItemInfo( )** to perform relatively simple menu management functions, such as enabling or disabling a menu item. However, using **SetMenuItemInfo( )** and **GetMenuItemInfo( )** for these types of operations is inefficient. They should be reserved for more complex or subtle menu manipulations.

Creating a Popup Menu

In addition to creating new menu items, you can dynamically create an entire popup menu. (That is, you can create a popup menu at runtime.) Once you have created the menu, it can then be added to an existing menu. To dynamically create a popup menu, you first use the API function **CreatePopupMenu( )**, shown here:

HMENU CreatePopupMenu( );

This function creates an empty menu and returns a handle to it. After you have created a menu, add items to it using **InsertMenuItem( )**. Once the menu is fully constructed, you can add it to an existing menu, also using **InsertMenuItem( )**.

Menus created using **CreatePopupMenu( )** must be destroyed. If the menu is attached to a window, then it will be destroyed automatically. A menu is also automatically destroyed when it is removed from a parent menu by a call to **DeleteMenu( )**. Dynamic menus can also be destroyed explicitly by calling **DestroyMenu( )**.

Using Dynamic Menus

One of the first improvements that you will want to make to a program's menuing system is to dynamically control the availability of menu items based upon the current state of the program. You can do this by:

◆ Adding or removing a selection.

◆ Adding or removing a submenu.

◆ Enabling or disabling an item.

The rules for applying these operations are fairly obvious: When an item does not apply to the current state of the program, it should be unavailable; when the item is applicable, it should be available.

Menus that change in response to runtime activity are called *dynamic menus*. The advantage of dynamic menus is that they present the user with a list of options that are appropriate for the current state of the program. One of the marks of a well-written, professional application is that the menus display only those options that are relevant to the operation at hand.

The following program demonstrates dynamic menu management by performing the three types of menu alterations just described.

DynMenu.cpp

Code

The **DynMenu.cpp** program implements a simple clock application that is controlled through its menus. The program always displays the time, but it can also display the date, if the user requests it. The time can be displayed in 12-hour or 24-hour format. The date, if enabled, can be displayed in a long or short form.

The program's top level menu contains the File, Options, and Help selections. The File menu contains three selections: Show Date, Remove Date, and Exit. Initially, Remove Date is grayed and, therefore, may not be selected. To display the date, select Show Date. After selecting Show Date, the Show Date option is disabled (grayed) and Remove Date is enabled. If you select Remove Date, the date is removed from the window, Remove Date is disabled, and Show Date is once again enabled. Thus, the appropriate menu item is enabled only when it can be selected.

Initially, the Options menu contains only one item: the Time submenu. This menu lets you select either a 12-hour or 24-hour format. If the date is also being displayed, then Options contains a second submenu called Date, which allows you to select either a long or a short date format. The Date menu is constructed dynamically when the Show Date option is chosen, and destroyed when the Remove Date option is selected.

Both the Time and Date menus enable and disable the appropriate menu items based upon the format currently being displayed. For example, initially, the time is displayed using a 12-hour format. Therefore, the 12 Hour option is disabled, and the 24 Hour option is enabled. When the user selects the 24 Hour option, the 12 Hour option is enabled and the 24 Hour option is disabled. Thus, all menus in the clock program dynamically adjust to the current state of the program.

Figure 1-1 shows the various states that the clock menus can have.

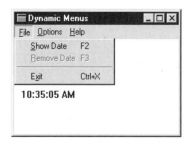
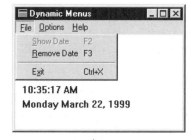
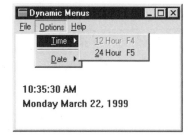
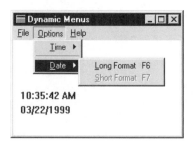

FIGURE 1-1.   The various menu states of **DynMenu.cpp**

Here is code for **DynMenu.cpp**:

```cpp
// DynMenu: A simple clock program that demonstrates dynamic menus.

#include <windows.h>
#include <ctime>
#include "dynmenu.h"

LRESULT CALLBACK WindowFunc(HWND, UINT, WPARAM, LPARAM);

char szWinName[] = "MyWin"; // name of window class

int WINAPI WinMain(HINSTANCE hThisInst, HINSTANCE hPrevInst,
                   LPSTR lpszArgs, int nWinMode)
{
  HWND hwnd;
  MSG msg;
  WNDCLASSEX wcl;
  HACCEL hAccel;

  // Define a window class.
  wcl.cbSize = sizeof(WNDCLASSEX);
  wcl.hInstance = hThisInst;
  wcl.lpszClassName = szWinName;
  wcl.lpfnWndProc = WindowFunc;
  wcl.style = 0; // default style
  wcl.hIcon = LoadIcon(NULL, IDI_APPLICATION); // large icon
  wcl.hIconSm = NULL; // use small version of large icon
  wcl.hCursor = LoadCursor(NULL, IDC_ARROW);
  wcl.hbrBackground = (HBRUSH) GetStockObject(WHITE_BRUSH);
  wcl.cbClsExtra = 0;
  wcl.cbWndExtra = 0;
  wcl.lpszMenuName = "DynMenu"; // specify class menu

  // Register the window class.
  if(!RegisterClassEx(&wcl)) return 0;
```

```
  // Create a window.
  hwnd = CreateWindow(szWinName, "Dynamic Menus",
                      WS_OVERLAPPEDWINDOW,
                      CW_USEDEFAULT, CW_USEDEFAULT,
                      250, 180,
                      NULL, NULL, hThisInst, NULL);

  // Load keyboard accelerators.
  hAccel = LoadAccelerators(hThisInst, "DynMenu");

  // Display the window.
  ShowWindow(hwnd, nWinMode);
  UpdateWindow(hwnd);

  // The message loop.
  while(GetMessage(&msg, NULL, 0, 0))
  {
    if(!TranslateAccelerator(hwnd, hAccel, &msg)) {
      TranslateMessage(&msg);
      DispatchMessage(&msg);
    }
  }
  return msg.wParam;
}

// The window procedure.
LRESULT CALLBACK WindowFunc(HWND hwnd, UINT message,
                            WPARAM wParam, LPARAM lParam)
{
  HDC hdc;
  PAINTSTRUCT ps;
  HMENU hmenu, hsubmenu;
  static HMENU hpopup;
  int response;
  int count;
  MENUITEMINFO miInfo;
  char timestr[80], datestr[80];
  time_t t_t;

  static tm *t;
  static bool twelve_hour = true;
  static bool long_date_format = true;
```

```
static bool date_on = false;

switch(message) {
  case WM_CREATE:
    // start timer
    SetTimer(hwnd, 1, 1000, NULL);

    // get current system time
    t_t = time(NULL);
    t = localtime(&t_t);
    break;
  case WM_TIMER: // update time
    t_t = time(NULL);
    t = localtime(&t_t);
    InvalidateRect(hwnd, NULL, 1);
    break;
  case WM_COMMAND:
    switch(LOWORD(wParam)) {
      case IDM_SHOWDATE: // dynamically add submenu
        // get handle of menu bar
        hmenu = GetMenu(hwnd);

        // get handle of Options menu
        hsubmenu = GetSubMenu(hmenu, 1);

        // get number of items in Options menu
        count = GetMenuItemCount(hsubmenu);

        // create new submenu menu
        hpopup = CreatePopupMenu();

        // add items to dynamic submenu
        miInfo.cbSize = sizeof(MENUITEMINFO);
        miInfo.fMask = MIIM_TYPE | MIIM_ID | MIIM_STATE;
        miInfo.fType = MFT_STRING;
        miInfo.wID = IDM_LONGFORM;
        miInfo.fState = MFS_DISABLED;
        miInfo.hSubMenu = NULL;
        miInfo.hbmpChecked = NULL;
        miInfo.hbmpUnchecked = NULL;
        miInfo.dwItemData = 0;
```

```
miInfo.dwTypeData = "&Long Format\tF6";
InsertMenuItem(hpopup, 0, 1, &miInfo);

miInfo.dwTypeData = "&Short Format\tF7";
miInfo.wID = IDM_SHORTFORM;
miInfo.fState = MFS_ENABLED;
InsertMenuItem(hpopup, 1, 1, &miInfo);

// append a separator
miInfo.cbSize = sizeof(MENUITEMINFO);
miInfo.fMask = MIIM_TYPE;
miInfo.fType = MFT_SEPARATOR;
miInfo.fState = 0;
miInfo.wID = 0;
miInfo.hSubMenu = NULL;
miInfo.hbmpChecked = NULL;
miInfo.hbmpUnchecked = NULL;
miInfo.dwItemData = 0;
InsertMenuItem(hsubmenu, count, 1, &miInfo);

// append dynamic menu to main menu
miInfo.fMask = MIIM_TYPE | MIIM_SUBMENU;
miInfo.fType = MFT_STRING;
miInfo.hSubMenu = hpopup;
miInfo.dwTypeData = "&Date";
InsertMenuItem(hsubmenu, count+1, 1, &miInfo);

// get handle to File menu
hsubmenu = GetSubMenu(hmenu, 0);

// deactivate the Show Date option
EnableMenuItem(hsubmenu, IDM_SHOWDATE,
            MF_BYCOMMAND | MF_GRAYED);

// activate the Remove Date option
EnableMenuItem(hsubmenu, IDM_REMOVEDATE,
            MF_BYCOMMAND | MF_ENABLED);

date_on = true; // turn on date output
InvalidateRect(hwnd, NULL, 1);
break;
```

```
case IDM_REMOVEDATE: // dynamically delete popup menu
  // get handle of menu bar
  hmenu = GetMenu(hwnd);

  // get handle of Options menu
  hsubmenu = GetSubMenu(hmenu, 1);

  // delete the new submenu and the separator
  count = GetMenuItemCount(hsubmenu);
  DeleteMenu(hsubmenu, count-1, MF_BYPOSITION | MF_GRAYED);
  DeleteMenu(hsubmenu, count-2, MF_BYPOSITION | MF_GRAYED);

  // get handle to File menu
  hsubmenu = GetSubMenu(hmenu, 0);

  // reactivate the Show Date option
  EnableMenuItem(hsubmenu, IDM_SHOWDATE,
                 MF_BYCOMMAND | MF_ENABLED);

  // deactivate the Remove Date option
  EnableMenuItem(hsubmenu, IDM_REMOVEDATE,
                 MF_BYCOMMAND | MF_GRAYED);

  date_on = false; // turn off date output
  InvalidateRect(hwnd, NULL, 1);
  break;
case IDM_EXIT:
  response = MessageBox(hwnd, "Quit the Program?",
                        "Exit", MB_YESNO);
  if(response == IDYES) PostQuitMessage(0);
  break;
case IDM_LONGFORM: // display long form of date
  long_date_format = true;

  // switch enabled states for Date menu
  hmenu = GetMenu(hwnd);
  hsubmenu = GetSubMenu(GetSubMenu(hmenu, 1), 2);

  // activate the Short option
  EnableMenuItem(hsubmenu, IDM_SHORTFORM,
                 MF_BYCOMMAND | MF_ENABLED);
```

```
                // deactivate the Long option
                EnableMenuItem(hsubmenu, IDM_LONGFORM,
                            MF_BYCOMMAND | MF_GRAYED);

                InvalidateRect(hwnd, NULL, 1);
                break;
        case IDM_SHORTFORM: // display short form of date
                long_date_format = false;

                // switch enabled states for Date menu
                hmenu = GetMenu(hwnd);
                hsubmenu = GetSubMenu(GetSubMenu(hmenu, 1), 2);

                // activate the Long option
                EnableMenuItem(hsubmenu, IDM_LONGFORM,
                            MF_BYCOMMAND | MF_ENABLED);

                // deactivate the Short option
                EnableMenuItem(hsubmenu, IDM_SHORTFORM,
                            MF_BYCOMMAND | MF_GRAYED);
                InvalidateRect(hwnd, NULL, 1);
                break;
        case IDM_12HOUR: // use 12 hour clock
                twelve_hour = true;

                // switch enabled states for Time menu
                hmenu = GetMenu(hwnd);
                hsubmenu = GetSubMenu(GetSubMenu(hmenu, 1), 0);

                // activate the 24-hour option
                EnableMenuItem(hsubmenu, IDM_24HOUR,
                            MF_BYCOMMAND | MF_ENABLED);

                // deactivate the 12-hour option
                EnableMenuItem(hsubmenu, IDM_12HOUR,
                            MF_BYCOMMAND | MF_GRAYED);

                InvalidateRect(hwnd, NULL, 1);
                break;
        case IDM_24HOUR: // use 24 hour clock
                twelve_hour = false;
```

```
      // switch enabled states for Time menu
      hmenu = GetMenu(hwnd);
      hsubmenu = GetSubMenu(GetSubMenu(hmenu, 1), 0);

      // activate the 12-hour option
      EnableMenuItem(hsubmenu, IDM_12HOUR,
                     MF_BYCOMMAND | MF_ENABLED);

      // deactivate the 24-hour option
      EnableMenuItem(hsubmenu, IDM_24HOUR,
                     MF_BYCOMMAND | MF_GRAYED);

    InvalidateRect(hwnd, NULL, 1);
      break;
    case IDM_ABOUT:
      MessageBox(hwnd, "Demonstrating Dynamic Menus",
                 "About", MB_OK);
      break;
  }
  break;
case WM_PAINT:
  if(twelve_hour)
    strftime(timestr, 79, "%I:%M:%S %p", t);
  else
    strftime(timestr, 79, "%H:%M:%S", t);

  if(long_date_format)
    strftime(datestr, 79, "%A %B %d, %Y", t);
  else
    strftime(datestr, 79, "%m/%d/%Y", t);

  hdc = BeginPaint(hwnd, &ps);

  TextOut(hdc, 10, 70, timestr, strlen(timestr));

  if(date_on)
    TextOut(hdc, 10, 90, datestr, strlen(datestr));

  EndPaint(hwnd, &ps);
  break;
case WM_DESTROY:
  KillTimer(hwnd, 1);
  PostQuitMessage(0);
```

```
      break;
   default:
      return DefWindowProc(hwnd, message, wParam, lParam);
   }
   return 0;
}
```

The resource file **DynMenu.rc** required by the program is shown here:

```
// Dynamic Popup Menus
#include <windows.h>
#include "dynmenu.h"

DynMenu MENU
{
  POPUP "&File"
  {
    MENUITEM "&Show Date\tF2", IDM_SHOWDATE
    MENUITEM "&Remove Date\tF3", IDM_REMOVEDATE, GRAYED
    MENUITEM SEPARATOR
    MENUITEM "E&xit\tCtrl+X", IDM_EXIT
  }
  POPUP "&Options"
  {
    POPUP "&Time" {
      MENUITEM "&12 Hour\tF4", IDM_12HOUR, GRAYED
      MENUITEM "&24 Hour\tF5", IDM_24HOUR
    }
  }
  POPUP "&Help" {
    MENUITEM "&About\tF1", IDM_ABOUT
  }
}


// Define menu accelerators
DynMenu ACCELERATORS
{
  VK_F2, IDM_SHOWDATE, VIRTKEY
  VK_F3, IDM_REMOVEDATE, VIRTKEY
  "^X",  IDM_EXIT
  VK_F4, IDM_12HOUR, VIRTKEY
  VK_F5, IDM_24HOUR, VIRTKEY
  VK_F6, IDM_LONGFORM, VIRTKEY
```

```
    VK_F7, IDM_SHORTFORM, VIRTKEY
    VK_F1, IDM_ABOUT, VIRTKEY
}
```

The **DynMenu.h** header file is shown here:

```
#define IDM_DATE          101
#define IDM_EXIT          102

#define IDM_12HOUR        200
#define IDM_24HOUR        201
#define IDM_SHOWDATE      202
#define IDM_REMOVEDATE    203

#define IDM_ABOUT         304

#define IDM_LONGFORM      400
#define IDM_SHORTFORM     401
```

ANNOTATIONS

WinMain( ) creates and registers the program's window class, creates a main application window, and starts the message loop. The menus and accelerators defined in **DynMenu.rc** are loaded when the program begins. The Time menu is created dynamically, as described below. The primary functionality of the program is controlled by message response code found in **WindowFunc( )**, the details of which are described next.

Handling WM_CREATE

When the program begins, it receives a **WM_CREATE** message, which is handled by the following case:

```
case WM_CREATE:
  // start timer
  SetTimer(hwnd, 1, 1000, NULL);

  // get current system time
  t_t = time(NULL);
  t = localtime(&t_t);
  break;
```

This handler creates a timer with an interval of one second (1,000 milliseconds) and then obtains the current system time. Timers are created by the **SetTimer( )** function, shown here:

UINT SetTimer(HWND *hwnd*, UINT *ID*, UINT *length*, TIMERPROC *lpTFunc*);

Here, *hwnd* is the handle of the window that uses the timer. The value of *ID* specifies a value that will be associated with this timer. (More than one timer can be active.) The value of *length* specifies the length of the period, in milliseconds. That is, *length* specifies how long there is between interrupts. The function pointed to by *lpTFunc* is the timer function that will be called when the timer goes off. However, if the value of *lpTFunc* is **NULL**, as it commonly is, then your program's window function will be used for this purpose. In this case, at the end of each interval, a **WM_TIMER** message is put into the message queue for your program and your program's window function processes it like any other message. This is the approach used by the examples in this chapter. The function returns *ID* if successful. If the timer cannot be allocated, zero is returned. Barring a major system malfunction, **SetTimer( )** will succeed when called with valid arguments.

The system time is obtained using the standard C/C++ time library functions. The current time is held in the static variable **t** for later use by the **WM_PAINT** handler.

Handling WM_TIMER

When the timer goes off, a **WM_TIMER** message is generated. The program responds by updating the time and then requests that the window be repainted by calling **InvalidateRect( )**.

Handling WM_PAINT

The **WM_PAINT** handler, shown next, displays the time and, optionally, the date.

```
case WM_PAINT:
  if(twelve_hour)
    strftime(timestr, 79, "%I:%M:%S %p", t);
  else
    strftime(timestr, 79, "%H:%M:%S", t);

  if(long_date_format)
    strftime(datestr, 79, "%A %B %d, %Y", t);
  else
    strftime(datestr, 79, "%m/%d/%Y", t);

  hdc = BeginPaint(hwnd, &ps);
```

```
TextOut(hdc, 10, 70, timestr, strlen(timestr));

if(date_on)
  TextOut(hdc, 10, 90, datestr, strlen(datestr));

EndPaint(hwnd, &ps);
break;
```

The format of the time is governed by the state of **twelve_hour**. If it is true, then the time is shown using a 12-hour clock. If false, the time is displayed using a 24-hour clock. The format of the date is determined by **long_date_format**. If this variable is true, the date is shown in its long form, with the day and the month spelled out. If false, the date is shown using the standard *mm/dd/yyyy* format. Note also that the date is displayed only if **date_on** is true.

Responding to IDM_SHOWDATE and IDM_REMOVEDATE

The real action of the program, as far as menus are concerned, occurs when the **IDM_SHOWDATE** and **IDM_REMOVEDATE** commands are processed. These commands dynamically alter the menu system of the program and determine whether the current date is displayed in the main window.

When the user selects Show Date from the File menu, a **WM_COMMAND** message is generated that contains the command **IDM_SHOWDATE**. The program responds by performing the following actions:

1. Constructing the Date submenu.
2. Adding the Date submenu to the Options menu.
3. Disabling the Show Date option in the File menu.
4. Enabling the Remove Date option in the File menu.
5. Allowing the date to be displayed in the main window.

Let's examine the process step by step.

To modify a menu at runtime you must have a handle to it. Thus, the first thing that the **IDM_SHOWDATE** handler does is obtain a handle to the Options menu by using this sequence of code:

```
case IDM_SHOWDATE: // dynamically add submenu
  // get handle of menu bar
  hmenu = GetMenu(hwnd);

  // get handle of Options menu
  hsubmenu = GetSubMenu(hmenu, 1);
```

To retrieve the handle of the Options menu, you must first retrieve the handle of its outer menu, which in this case is the program's main menu (i.e., menu bar), using **GetMenu( )**. Next, you must use **GetSubMenu( )** to obtain the handle of its second popup menu, which is Options. Thus, **hsubmenu** is a handle to the Options menu.

Next, the program obtains a count of the number of items in the menu using this statement:

```
// get number of items in Options menu
count = GetMenuItemCount(hsubmenu);
```

This step is technically unnecessary since, in this simple example, we already know this value. However, in a real application, menus might change in many ways and it is often easier to obtain a current count of the number of items in a given menu than to keep track of this number manually.

Next, the program dynamically creates the Date menu using the following statements:

```
// create new submenu menu
hpopup = CreatePopupMenu();


// add items to dynamic submenu
miInfo.cbSize = sizeof(MENUITEMINFO);
miInfo.fMask = MIIM_TYPE | MIIM_ID | MIIM_STATE;
miInfo.fType = MFT_STRING;
miInfo.wID = IDM_LONGFORM;
miInfo.fState = MFS_DISABLED;
miInfo.hSubMenu = NULL;
miInfo.hbmpChecked = NULL;
miInfo.hbmpUnchecked = NULL;
miInfo.dwItemData = 0;
miInfo.dwTypeData = "&Long Format\tF6";
InsertMenuItem(hpopup, 0, 1, &miInfo);


miInfo.dwTypeData = "&Short Format\tF7";
miInfo.wID = IDM_SHORTFORM;
miInfo.fState = MFS_ENABLED;
InsertMenuItem(hpopup, 1, 1, &miInfo);
```

This code creates a new popup menu. (Remember, the terms *popup menu* and *drop-down menu* are used more or less synonymously in Windows.) It then adds two choices to it: Long Format and Short Format. Since the long date format is the way that the date is initially displayed, Long Format is disabled and Short Format is enabled. The command IDs associated with these selections are defined in **DynMenu.rc**.

Next, a separator and then the Date menu are appended to the Options menu by the following code:

```
// append a separator
miInfo.cbSize = sizeof(MENUITEMINFO);
```

```
miInfo.fMask = MIIM_TYPE;
miInfo.fType = MFT_SEPARATOR;
miInfo.fState = 0;
miInfo.wID = 0;
miInfo.hSubMenu = NULL;
miInfo.hbmpChecked = NULL;
miInfo.hbmpUnchecked = NULL;
miInfo.dwItemData = 0;
InsertMenuItem(hsubmenu, count, 1, &miInfo);

// append dynamic menu to main menu
miInfo.fMask = MIIM_TYPE | MIIM_SUBMENU;
miInfo.fType = MFT_STRING;
miInfo.hSubMenu = hpopup;
miInfo.dwTypeData = "&Date";
InsertMenuItem(hsubmenu, count+1, 1, &miInfo);
```

After these statements execute, the Options menu will contain three items: the Time menu, a separator, and the Date menu. Notice that when the Date menu is added to the Options menu, the **MIIM_SUBMENU** flag is set and **hpopop** is passed in the **hSubMenu** field of **miInfo**.

Finally, the Show Date option is disabled, the Remove Date option is enabled, the date display is turned on, and a repaint request is sent by the following code:

```
// get handle to File menu
hsubmenu = GetSubMenu(hmenu, 0);

// deactivate the Show Date option
EnableMenuItem(hsubmenu, IDM_SHOWDATE,
               MF_BYCOMMAND | MF_GRAYED);

// activate the Remove Date option
EnableMenuItem(hsubmenu, IDM_REMOVEDATE,
               MF_BYCOMMAND | MF_ENABLED);

date_on = true; // turn on date output
InvalidateRect(hwnd, NULL, 1);
```

Notice that a handle to the File menu is obtained by calling **GetSubMenu( )** and requesting the first submenu. Since **hmenu** still contains the handle to the menu bar, there is no reason to obtain it again.

To remove the date display, the user selects Remove Date. When this occurs, **IDM_REMOVEDATE** is proccessed by the following code. As you can see, deleting menu items is much easier than adding them.

```
case IDM_REMOVEDATE: // dynamically delete popup menu
  // get handle of menu bar
  hmenu = GetMenu(hwnd);

  // get handle of Options menu
  hsubmenu = GetSubMenu(hmenu, 1);

  // delete the new submenu and the separator
  count = GetMenuItemCount(hsubmenu);
  DeleteMenu(hsubmenu, count-1, MF_BYPOSITION | MF_GRAYED);
  DeleteMenu(hsubmenu, count-2, MF_BYPOSITION | MF_GRAYED);

  // get handle to File menu
  hsubmenu = GetSubMenu(hmenu, 0);

  // reactivate the Show Date option
  EnableMenuItem(hsubmenu, IDM_SHOWDATE,
              MF_BYCOMMAND | MF_ENABLED);

  // deactivate the Remove Date option
  EnableMenuItem(hsubmenu, IDM_REMOVEDATE,
              MF_BYCOMMAND | MF_GRAYED);

  date_on = false; // turn off date output
  InvalidateRect(hwnd, NULL, 1);
```

First, the handle to the Options submenu is obtained by calling **GetMenu( )** followed by **GetSubMenu( )**. Then, the Date submenu and the separator are removed. Next, Show Date in the File menu is enabled and Remove Date is disabled. Finally, the date display is turned off and the window is repainted.

Setting the Time and Date Options

The **IDM_LONGFORM, IDM_SHORTFORM, IDM_12HOUR,** and **IDM_24HOUR** handlers set the time and date options. They perform two functions. First, they set the appropriate flag variable to the appropriate state. Second, they switch the enable/disable states of the items in the affected menu. For example, here is the handler for **IDM_LONGFORM:**

```
case IDM_LONGFORM: // display long form of date
  long_date_format = true;

  // switch enabled states for Date menu
  hmenu = GetMenu(hwnd);
```

```
hsubmenu = GetSubMenu(GetSubMenu(hmenu, 1), 2);

// activate the Short option
EnableMenuItem(hsubmenu, IDM_SHORTFORM,
                MF_BYCOMMAND | MF_ENABLED);

// deactivate the Long option
EnableMenuItem(hsubmenu, IDM_LONGFORM,
                MF_BYCOMMAND | MF_GRAYED);

InvalidateRect(hwnd, NULL, 1);
break;
```

First, the handler sets **long_date_format** to true. It then obtains a handle to the Date submenu. This is done by obtaining a handle to the menu bar, then getting a handle to the Options submenu, and then the handle to the Date menu within the Options submenu. Notice that Date is item 2 in the Options menu because the Time menu is item 0, and the separator counts as item 1. Finally, the enable/disable states of the two options are reversed. The **IDM_SHORTFORM, IDM_12HOUR**, and **IDM_24HOUR** handlers work in a similar fashion.

Check and Radio Menu Items

You can display a check mark next to a menu item. This is useful when a menu item represents an option that can be set. You can also create a set of mutually exclusive menu options that are called *radio menu items*. With radio items, only one item can be selected at any one time. When your program checks one radio menu item, the previously checked item in its group is automatically unchecked. Radio menu items are surprisingly easy to use. The only restriction is that all radio items must be consecutive within a menu. Utilizing check and radio menu items is a way to enhance the functionality and style of many menuing situations. They can also provide a cleaner alternative to enabling/disabling items in many menuing situations.

A check can be placed next to a menu item when it is first created by specifying the **CHECKED** option in the menu item's definition within its resource file. It is also possible to check a menu item later, during execution. There are two ways to do this. One way is to use the **SetMenuItemInfo( )** function described earlier. However, an easier way is to use the **CheckMenuItem( )** function, shown here:

DWORD CheckMenuItem(HMENU *hMenu*, UINT *ItemID*, UINT *How*);

Here, *hMenu* is the handle to the menu. The item to be checked or cleared is specified in *ItemID.* The value of *How* determines two things. First, it specifies how

ItemID is interpreted. If *How* contains **MF_BYPOSITION**, then the value in *ItemID* must be the index of the item. This index is the position of the item within the menu, with the first menu item being zero. If *How* contains **MF_BYCOMMAND**, then *ItemID* is the ID associated with the menu item. The value in *How* also determines whether the item will be checked or cleared, based upon which of the following values are present:

MF_CHECKED	Checks the menu item.
MF_UNCHECKED	Clears the menu item.

To construct the desired value of *How*, OR together the appropriate values. The previous check-state of the item is returned.

You can treat any consecutive group of menu items as radio items by calling **CheckMenuRadioItem( )**, shown here:

```
BOOL CheckMenuRadioItem(HMENU hMenu, UINT StartID,
                    UINT EndID, UINT ItemID, UINT How);
```

Here, *hMenu* is the handle to the menu. The first radio item in the group is specified by *StartID*. The last of the group is passed in *EndID*. The item to be checked is specified in *ItemID*. Any previously selected item is unchecked. If *How* contains **MF_BYPOSITION**, then the values in *StartID*, *EndID*, and *ItemID* must be the indexes of the items. If *How* contains **MF_BYCOMMAND**, these values represent the IDs associated with the menu items. In either case, the items or command IDs must be consecutive. The function returns nonzero if successful and zero on failure.

When you call **CheckMenuRadioItem( )**, it automatically sets the **MFT_RADIOCHECK** flag associated with the item being set. It also clears any check marks associated with any other items within the specified range. Thus, within the range, only the specified item will be checked.

ChkRadio.cpp

Code

The following program demonstrates check and radio menu items by adding them to the clock program. In the process, the program is substantially improved. First, in the File menu, the Show Date option is converted into a check item and Remove Date is eliminated. When Show Date is checked, the date is displayed. When it is unchecked, the date is removed. The entries in the Time and Date submenus are made into radio menu items. For each submenu, the options are mutually exclusive. Thus, they are perfect candidates for radio items. When you try the program you will find that its menus have a cleaner, more sophisticated feel. Sample output is shown in Figure 1-2.

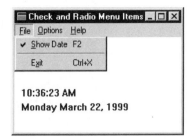

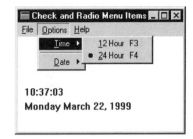

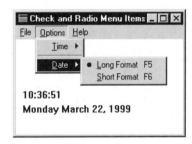

FIGURE 1-2. Using check and radio menu items

```
// ChkRadio.cpp: Add check and radio menu items.

#include <windows.h>
#include <ctime>
#include "chkradio.h"

LRESULT CALLBACK WindowFunc(HWND, UINT, WPARAM, LPARAM);

char szWinName[] = "MyWin"; // name of window class

int WINAPI WinMain(HINSTANCE hThisInst, HINSTANCE hPrevInst,
                   LPSTR lpszArgs, int nWinMode)
{
  HWND hwnd;
  MSG msg;
  WNDCLASSEX wcl;
  HACCEL hAccel;

  // Define a window class.
  wcl.cbSize = sizeof(WNDCLASSEX);
```

```
  wcl.hInstance = hThisInst;
  wcl.lpszClassName = szWinName;
  wcl.lpfnWndProc = WindowFunc;
  wcl.style = 0; // default style
  wcl.hIcon = LoadIcon(NULL, IDI_APPLICATION); // large icon
  wcl.hIconSm = NULL; // use small version of large icon
  wcl.hCursor = LoadCursor(NULL, IDC_ARROW);
  wcl.hbrBackground = (HBRUSH) GetStockObject(WHITE_BRUSH);
  wcl.cbClsExtra = 0;
  wcl.cbWndExtra = 0;
  wcl.lpszMenuName = "CheckRadioMenu"; // specify class menu

  // Register the window class.
  if(!RegisterClassEx(&wcl)) return 0;

  // Create a window.
  hwnd = CreateWindow(szWinName, "Check and Radio Menu Items",
                  WS_OVERLAPPEDWINDOW,
                  CW_USEDEFAULT, CW_USEDEFAULT,
                  250, 180,
                  NULL, NULL, hThisInst, NULL);

  // Load keyboard accelerators.
  hAccel = LoadAccelerators(hThisInst, "CheckRadioMenu");

  // Display the window.
  ShowWindow(hwnd, nWinMode);
  UpdateWindow(hwnd);

  // The message loop.
  while(GetMessage(&msg, NULL, 0, 0))
  {
    if(!TranslateAccelerator(hwnd, hAccel, &msg)) {
      TranslateMessage(&msg);
      DispatchMessage(&msg);
    }
  }
  return msg.wParam;
}
```

```
// The window procedure.
LRESULT CALLBACK WindowFunc(HWND hwnd, UINT message,
                            WPARAM wParam, LPARAM lParam)
{
  HDC hdc;
  PAINTSTRUCT ps;
  HMENU hmenu, hsubmenu;
  static HMENU hpopup;
  int response;
  int count;
  MENUITEMINFO miInfo;
  char timestr[80], datestr[80];
  time_t t_t;

  static tm *t;
  static bool twelve_hour = true;
  static bool long_date_format = true;
  static bool date_on = false;

  switch(message) {
    case WM_CREATE:
      // start timer
      SetTimer(hwnd, 1, 1000, NULL);

      // get current system time
      t_t = time(NULL);
      t = localtime(&t_t);

      // radio check 12-hour time display option
      hmenu = GetMenu(hwnd);
      hsubmenu = GetSubMenu(GetSubMenu(hmenu, 1), 0);
      CheckMenuRadioItem(hsubmenu, IDM_12HOUR, IDM_24HOUR,
                         IDM_12HOUR, MF_BYCOMMAND);
      break;
    case WM_TIMER: // update time
      t_t = time(NULL);
      t = localtime(&t_t);
      InvalidateRect(hwnd, NULL, 1);
      break;
    case WM_COMMAND:
      switch(LOWORD(wParam)) {
        case IDM_SHOWDATE:
          // get handle of menu bar
```

```
hmenu = GetMenu(hwnd);

// get handle of Options menu
hsubmenu = GetSubMenu(hmenu, 1);

if(!date_on) { // add Date menu
  // get number of items in Options menu
  count = GetMenuItemCount(hsubmenu);

  // create new submenu menu
  hpopup = CreatePopupMenu();

  // add items to dynamic submenu
  miInfo.cbSize = sizeof(MENUITEMINFO);
  miInfo.fMask = MIIM_TYPE | MIIM_ID;
  miInfo.fType = MFT_STRING;
  miInfo.fState = 0;
  miInfo.wID = IDM_LONGFORM;
  miInfo.hSubMenu = NULL;
  miInfo.hbmpChecked = NULL;
  miInfo.hbmpUnchecked = NULL;
  miInfo.dwItemData = 0;
  miInfo.dwTypeData = "&Long Format\tF5";
  InsertMenuItem(hpopup, 0, 1, &miInfo);

  miInfo.dwTypeData = "&Short Format\tF6";
  miInfo.wID = IDM_SHORTFORM;
  InsertMenuItem(hpopup, 1, 1, &miInfo);

  // append a separator
  miInfo.cbSize = sizeof(MENUITEMINFO);
  miInfo.fMask = MIIM_TYPE;
  miInfo.fType = MFT_SEPARATOR;
  miInfo.fState = 0;
  miInfo.wID = 0;
  miInfo.hSubMenu = NULL;
  miInfo.hbmpChecked = NULL;
  miInfo.hbmpUnchecked = NULL;
  miInfo.dwItemData = 0;
  InsertMenuItem(hsubmenu, count, 1, &miInfo);

  // append dynamic menu to main menu
  miInfo.fMask = MIIM_TYPE | MIIM_SUBMENU;
```

```
        miInfo.fType = MFT_STRING;
        miInfo.hSubMenu = hpopup;
        miInfo.dwTypeData = "&Date";
        InsertMenuItem(hsubmenu, count+1, 1, &miInfo);

        // get handle to File menu
        hsubmenu = GetSubMenu(hmenu, 0);

        // check Show Date option
        CheckMenuItem(hsubmenu, IDM_SHOWDATE,
                   MF_BYCOMMAND | MF_CHECKED);

        // radio check long form date display option
        long_date_format = true;
        hmenu = GetMenu(hwnd);
        hsubmenu = GetSubMenu(GetSubMenu(hmenu, 1), 2);
        CheckMenuRadioItem(hsubmenu, IDM_LONGFORM, IDM_SHORTFORM,
                      IDM_LONGFORM, MF_BYCOMMAND);

        date_on = true; // turn on date output
      }
    else { // Remove Date menu
      // delete the new submenu and the separator
      count = GetMenuItemCount(hsubmenu);
      DeleteMenu(hsubmenu, count-1, MF_BYPOSITION | MF_GRAYED);
      DeleteMenu(hsubmenu, count-2, MF_BYPOSITION | MF_GRAYED);

      // get handle to File menu
      hsubmenu = GetSubMenu(hmenu, 0);

      // clear Show Date option
      CheckMenuItem(hsubmenu, IDM_SHOWDATE,
                 MF_BYCOMMAND | MF_UNCHECKED);
      date_on = false; // turn off date output
    }
    InvalidateRect(hwnd, NULL, 1);
    break;
  case IDM_EXIT:
    response = MessageBox(hwnd, "Quit the Program?",
                       "Exit", MB_YESNO);
    if(response == IDYES) PostQuitMessage(0);
    break;
```

```
        case IDM_LONGFORM: // display long form of date
          long_date_format = true;
          // radio check long form date display option
          hmenu = GetMenu(hwnd);
          hsubmenu = GetSubMenu(GetSubMenu(hmenu, 1), 2);
          CheckMenuRadioItem(hsubmenu, IDM_LONGFORM, IDM_SHORTFORM,
                          IDM_LONGFORM, MF_BYCOMMAND);
          InvalidateRect(hwnd, NULL, 1);
          break;
        case IDM_SHORTFORM: // display short form of date
          long_date_format = false;
          // radio check short form date display option
          hmenu = GetMenu(hwnd);
          hsubmenu = GetSubMenu(GetSubMenu(hmenu, 1), 2);
          CheckMenuRadioItem(hsubmenu, IDM_LONGFORM, IDM_SHORTFORM,
                          IDM_SHORTFORM, MF_BYCOMMAND);
          InvalidateRect(hwnd, NULL, 1);
          break;
        case IDM_12HOUR: // use 12 hour clock
          twelve_hour = true;
          // radio check 12-hour time display option
          hmenu = GetMenu(hwnd);
          hsubmenu = GetSubMenu(GetSubMenu(hmenu, 1), 0);
          CheckMenuRadioItem(hsubmenu, IDM_12HOUR, IDM_24HOUR,
                          IDM_12HOUR, MF_BYCOMMAND);
          InvalidateRect(hwnd, NULL, 1);
          break;
        case IDM_24HOUR: // use 24 hour clock
          twelve_hour = false;
          // radio check 24-hour time display option
          hmenu = GetMenu(hwnd);
          hsubmenu = GetSubMenu(GetSubMenu(hmenu, 1), 0);
          CheckMenuRadioItem(hsubmenu, IDM_12HOUR, IDM_24HOUR,
                          IDM_24HOUR, MF_BYCOMMAND);
          InvalidateRect(hwnd, NULL, 1);
          break;
        case IDM_ABOUT:
          MessageBox(hwnd, "Demonstrating Check and Radio Items",
                    "About", MB_OK);
          break;
      }
    break;
```

```
    case WM_PAINT:
      if(twelve_hour)
        strftime(timestr, 79, "%I:%M:%S %p", t);
      else
        strftime(timestr, 79, "%H:%M:%S", t);

      if(long_date_format)
        strftime(datestr, 79, "%A %B %d, %Y", t);
      else
        strftime(datestr, 79, "%m/%d/%Y", t);

      hdc = BeginPaint(hwnd, &ps);

      TextOut(hdc, 10, 70, timestr, strlen(timestr));

      if(date_on)
        TextOut(hdc, 10, 90, datestr, strlen(datestr));

      EndPaint(hwnd, &ps);
      break;
    case WM_DESTROY:
      KillTimer(hwnd, 1);
      PostQuitMessage(0);
      break;
    default:
      return DefWindowProc(hwnd, message, wParam, lParam);
  }
  return 0;
}
```

The **ChkRadio.rc** resource file is shown here:

```
// Use check and radio menu items.
#include <windows.h>
#include "chkradio.h"

CheckRadioMenu MENU
{
  POPUP "&File"
  {
    MENUITEM "&Show Date\tF2", IDM_SHOWDATE
```

```
   MENUITEM SEPARATOR
   MENUITEM "E&xit\tCtrl+X", IDM_EXIT
 }
 POPUP "&Options"
 {
   POPUP "&Time" {
     MENUITEM "&12 Hour\tF3", IDM_12HOUR
     MENUITEM "&24 Hour\tF4", IDM_24HOUR
   }
 }
 POPUP "&Help" {
   MENUITEM "&About\tF1", IDM_ABOUT
 }
}

// Define menu accelerators
CheckRadioMenu ACCELERATORS
{
  VK_F2, IDM_SHOWDATE, VIRTKEY
  "^X",  IDM_EXIT
  VK_F3, IDM_12HOUR, VIRTKEY
  VK_F4, IDM_24HOUR, VIRTKEY
  VK_F5, IDM_LONGFORM, VIRTKEY
  VK_F6, IDM_SHORTFORM, VIRTKEY
  VK_F1, IDM_ABOUT, VIRTKEY
}
```

The **ChkRadio.h** header file is shown here:

```
#define IDM_SHOWDATE   100
#define IDM_EXIT       101

#define IDM_12HOUR     200
#define IDM_24HOUR     201

#define IDM_ABOUT      304

#define IDM_LONGFORM   400
#define IDM_SHORTFORM 401
```

ANNOTATIONS

Since much of the program is the same as the preceding version, we will concentrate on the changes. Aside from minor alterations to **WinMain( )**, the main differences from the previous program occur in **WindowFunc( )**. First, there is no handler for **IDM_REMOVEDATE** because this option is no longer needed. Instead, each time Show Date is selected, it toggles between a check and unchecked state, and the flag variable **date_on** also toggles between true and false. When the program begins, **date_on** is false.

As before, when the date is displayed, the Date menu is dynamically constructed and added to the Options menu. The Date menu is removed when the date option is turned off. As you can see, there really is no need for a separate option to remove the date display. The checking or unchecking of Show Date is sufficient. Although quite simple, this is a good example of how a check menu item can streamline a menu and improve its usability at the same time.

Checking a menu is quite easy. For example, here is code that checks the Show Date item.

```
// get handle to File menu
hsubmenu = GetSubMenu(hmenu, 0);


// check Show Date option
CheckMenuItem(hsubmenu, IDM_SHOWDATE,
            MF_BYCOMMAND | MF_CHECKED);
```

First, a handle to the File submenu is obtained and then this handle is used in the call to **CheckMenuItem( )** to check the Show Date option. The code that unchecks Show Date is similar except that **MF_UNCHECKED** is specified.

Managing the radio menu items requires alterations to the **IDM_LONGFORM**, **IDM_SHORTFORM**, **IDM_12HOUR**, and **IDM_24HOUR** handlers. Also, in **WM_CREATE**, the 12-hour option in the Time menu must be checked. Radio-checking a menu item is quite easy. For example, here is the code that radio-checks the Long Format date option:

```
// radio check long form date display option
long_date_format = true;
hmenu = GetMenu(hwnd);
hsubmenu = GetSubMenu(GetSubMenu(hmenu, 1), 2);
CheckMenuRadioItem(hsubmenu, IDM_LONGFORM, IDM_SHORTFORM,
                IDM_LONGFORM, MF_BYCOMMAND);
```

The code first obtains a handle to the menu bar, then it obtains a handle to the Options menu. This handle is not stored, but is used inside the outer call to **GetSubMenu( )** to obtain a handle to the Date menu. Remember that the Date submenu is item 2 within the Options menu. As explained earlier, this is because the separator between Time and Date counts as item number 1.

Using radio menu items is an excellent way to represent mutually exclusive options. Not only does it give immediate, visual feedback to the user that one and only one of these items may be selected, but it also simplifies your code because Windows automatically handles the unchecking process for you.

Using Floating Menus

Although stand-alone, or *floating,* popup menus have been available to Windows programmers for quite some time, they continue to increase in popularity and importance. For example, all current versions of Windows display a floating menu when you click the right mouse button on the desktop. Floating menus are also called *context menus* and *shortcut menus.* This book will use the term "floating menu" because it is the most descriptive. In this section we will convert the clock program's Time and Date submenus into floating menus that are activated by right-clicking the mouse.

Some programmers have been reluctant to employ floating menus because they wrongfully assume that they are difficult to use. Fortunately, such is not the case. A floating menu is activated using **TrackPopupMenuEx( )**. Its prototype is shown here:

BOOL TrackPopupMenuEx(HMENU *hMenu,* UINT *Flags*, int *X*, int *Y*,
　　　　　　　　　　HWND *hwnd*, LPTPMPARMS *OffLimits*);

Here, *hMenu* is the handle of the menu that will be activated.

Various options are specified in *Flags*. This parameter may be any valid (i.e., non-mutually exclusive) combination of the values shown in Table 1-1. If you are writing for Windows 98 or Windows 2000, you can use the menu animation flags, which determine how the popup menu is drawn. Employing the animation flags is an excellent way to customize the feel of your menu system. You can also specify zero for *Flags*. Doing so causes the default configuration to be used.

The location *on the screen* at which to display the menu is specified in *X* and *Y*. Therefore, these coordinates are in terms of screen units, not window or dialog units. To convert between screen and window units, use either the **ClientToScreen( )** or the **ScreenToClient( )** function. In its default configuration, **TrackPopupMenuEx( )** displays the menu with its upper-left corner at the location specified by *X* and *Y*. However, you can use the *Flags* parameter to alter this placement.

The handle of the window that invokes **TrackPopupMenuEx( )** must be passed in *hwnd*.

You may specify a portion of the screen that is off limits to the floating menu. To do so, specify the extent of that region in the **TPMPARAMS** structure pointed to by *OffLimits*. **TPMPARAMS** is defined like this:

```
typedef struct tagTPMPARAMS
{
  UINT cbSize;
  RECT rcExclude;
} TPMPARAMS;
```

Flags Value	Meaning
TPM_BOTTOMALIGN	Floating menu pops up with bottom edge at *Y*.
TPM_CENTERALIGN	Floating menu pops up centered left to right relative to *X*.
TPM_HORIZONTAL	If the menu cannot be fully displayed at the location specified by *X* and *Y*, the horizontal alignment of the menu is given priority.
TPM_HORNEGANIMATION	Right-to-left animation (Windows 98 or later).
TPM_HORPOSANIMATION	Left-to-right animation (Windows 98 or later).
TPM_LEFTALIGN	Floating menu pops up with left side at *X*. (This is the default.)
TPM_LEFTBUTTON	Left mouse button operates the menu. (This is the default.)
TPM_NOANIMATION	No animation (Windows 98 or later).
TPM_NONOTIFY	Menu does not send notification messages.
TPM_RETURNCMD	The ID of the item selected is returned.
TPM_RIGHTALIGN	Floating menu pops up with right side at *X*.
TPM_RIGHTBUTTON	Right mouse button operates the menu.
TPM_TOPALIGN	Floating menu pops up with top edge at *Y*. (This is the default.)
TPM_VCENTERALIGN	Floating menu pops up centered top to bottom relative to *Y*.
TPM_VERNEGANIMATION	Bottom-to-top animation (Windows 98 or later).
TPM_VERNEGANIMATION	Top-to-bottom animation (Windows 98 or later).
TPM_VERTICAL	If the menu cannot be fully displayed at the location specified by *X* and *Y*, the vertical alignment of the menu is given priority.

TABLE 1-1. The Values for the *Flags* Parameter of **TrackPopupMenuEx( )**

Here, **cbSize** must contain the size of the **TPMPARAMS** structure. **rcExclude** must contain the coordinates of the excluded region. The coordinates specified in **rcExclude** must be in terms of screen units. *OffLimits* may be **NULL** if no part of the screen is being excluded.

 TrackPopupMenuEx( ) returns non-zero if successful and zero on failure. However, if **TPM_RETURNCMD** is specified in *Flags*, then the ID of the menu item selected is returned. Zero is returned if no item is chosen.

Floating.cpp

Code

The following clock program modifies the previous version by making the Time and Date drop-down menus into floating, popup menus. Thus, they are no longer part of the menu bar, and the Options menu bar entry is no longer needed. Instead, the floating menus are activated by clicking the right mouse button. If the right button is clicked when the mouse is over the time, the Time menu pops up. If the mouse is right-clicked over the date, the Date menu pops up. Right-clicks over other parts of the program are ignored. When a floating menu is activated, it is displayed at the location of the mouse pointer when the button was pressed. Sample output is shown in Figure 1-3.

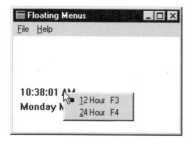 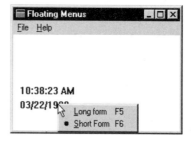

FIGURE 1-3. Sample output from **Floating.cpp**

Here is the code for **Floating.cpp**:

```cpp
// Floating.cpp: Using a floating, popup menu.

#include <windows.h>
#include <ctime>
#include "floating.h"

LRESULT CALLBACK WindowFunc(HWND, UINT, WPARAM, LPARAM);

char szWinName[] = "MyWin"; // name of window class
HINSTANCE hInst; // global instance handle

int WINAPI WinMain(HINSTANCE hThisInst, HINSTANCE hPrevInst,
                   LPSTR lpszArgs, int nWinMode)
{
```

```
HWND hwnd;
MSG msg;
WNDCLASSEX wcl;
HACCEL hAccel;

// Define a window class.
wcl.cbSize = sizeof(WNDCLASSEX);
wcl.hInstance = hThisInst;
wcl.lpszClassName = szWinName;
wcl.lpfnWndProc = WindowFunc;
wcl.style = 0; // default style
wcl.hIcon = LoadIcon(NULL, IDI_APPLICATION); // large icon
wcl.hIconSm = NULL; // use small version of large icon
wcl.hCursor = LoadCursor(NULL, IDC_ARROW);
wcl.hbrBackground = (HBRUSH) GetStockObject(WHITE_BRUSH);
wcl.cbClsExtra = 0;
wcl.cbWndExtra = 0;
wcl.lpszMenuName = "FloatingMenu"; // specify class menu

// Register the window class.
if(!RegisterClassEx(&wcl)) return 0;

// Create a window.
hwnd = CreateWindow(szWinName, "Floating Menus",
                    WS_OVERLAPPEDWINDOW,
                    CW_USEDEFAULT, CW_USEDEFAULT,
                    250, 180,
                    NULL, NULL, hThisInst, NULL);

// Load keyboard accelerators.
hAccel = LoadAccelerators(hThisInst, "FloatingMenu");

hInst = hThisInst; // save instance handle

// Display the window.
ShowWindow(hwnd, nWinMode);
UpdateWindow(hwnd);

// The message loop.
while(GetMessage(&msg, NULL, 0, 0))
{
  if(!TranslateAccelerator(hwnd, hAccel, &msg)) {
    TranslateMessage(&msg);
```

```
      DispatchMessage(&msg);
    }
  }
  return msg.wParam;
}


// The window procedure.
LRESULT CALLBACK WindowFunc(HWND hwnd, UINT message,
                            WPARAM wParam, LPARAM lParam)
{
  HDC hdc;
  PAINTSTRUCT ps;
  HMENU hmenu, hsubmenu;
  static HMENU hpopup;
  int response;
  char timestr[80], datestr[80];
  time_t t_t;
  POINT pt;

  static tm *t;
  static bool twelve_hour = true;
  static bool long_date_format = true;
  static bool date_on = false;

  switch(message) {
    case WM_CREATE:
      // start timer
      SetTimer(hwnd, 1, 1000, NULL);

      // get current system time
      t_t = time(NULL);
      t = localtime(&t_t);

      break;
    case WM_TIMER: // update time
      t_t = time(NULL);
      t = localtime(&t_t);
      InvalidateRect(hwnd, NULL, 1);
      break;
    case WM_COMMAND:
      switch(LOWORD(wParam)) {
        case IDM_SHOWDATE:
```

```
    // get handle of menu bar
    hmenu = GetMenu(hwnd);

    // get handle to File menu
    hsubmenu = GetSubMenu(hmenu, 0);

    if(!date_on) { // check Show Date option
      CheckMenuItem(hsubmenu, IDM_SHOWDATE,
                    MF_BYCOMMAND | MF_CHECKED);

      date_on = true; // turn on date output
    }
    else { // uncheck Show Date option
      // clear Show Date option
      CheckMenuItem(hsubmenu, IDM_SHOWDATE,
                    MF_BYCOMMAND | MF_UNCHECKED);
      date_on = false; // turn off date output
    }
    InvalidateRect(hwnd, NULL, 1);
    break;
  case IDM_EXIT:
    response = MessageBox(hwnd, "Quit the Program?",
                          "Exit", MB_YESNO);
    if(response == IDYES) PostQuitMessage(0);
    break;
  case IDM_LONGFORM: // display long form of date
    long_date_format = true;
    InvalidateRect(hwnd, NULL, 1);
    break;
  case IDM_SHORTFORM: // display short form of date
    long_date_format = false;
    InvalidateRect(hwnd, NULL, 1);
    break;
  case IDM_12HOUR: // use 12 hour clock
    twelve_hour = true;
    InvalidateRect(hwnd, NULL, 1);
    break;
  case IDM_24HOUR: // use 24 hour clock
    twelve_hour = false;
    InvalidateRect(hwnd, NULL, 1);
    break;
  case IDM_ABOUT:
```

```
             MessageBox(hwnd, "Demonstrating Floating Menus",
                     "About", MB_OK);
         break;
    }
    break;
case WM_PAINT:
    if(twelve_hour)
        strftime(timestr, 79, "%I:%M:%S %p", t);
    else
        strftime(timestr, 79, "%H:%M:%S", t);

    if(long_date_format)
        strftime(datestr, 79, "%A %B %d, %Y", t);
    else
        strftime(datestr, 79, "%m/%d/%Y", t);

    hdc = BeginPaint(hwnd, &ps);

    TextOut(hdc, 10, 70, timestr, strlen(timestr));

    if(date_on)
        TextOut(hdc, 10, 90, datestr, strlen(datestr));

    EndPaint(hwnd, &ps);
    break;
case WM_RBUTTONUP: // activate floating menu
    // save mouse location
    pt.x = LOWORD(lParam);
    pt.y = HIWORD(lParam);

    // load appropriate menu
    if(pt.y >= 70 && pt.y < 84) { // Time
        hmenu = LoadMenu(hInst, "Time");
        hsubmenu = GetSubMenu(hmenu, 0);

        // set time menu radio button
        if(twelve_hour)
            CheckMenuRadioItem(hsubmenu, IDM_12HOUR, IDM_24HOUR,
                            IDM_12HOUR, MF_BYCOMMAND);
        else
            CheckMenuRadioItem(hsubmenu, IDM_12HOUR, IDM_24HOUR,
                            IDM_24HOUR, MF_BYCOMMAND);
    } else if(pt.y >= 90 && pt.y < 104 && date_on) { // Date
```

```
            hmenu = LoadMenu(hInst, "Date");
            hsubmenu = GetSubMenu(hmenu, 0);

            // set date menu radio button
            if(long_date_format)
              CheckMenuRadioItem(hsubmenu, IDM_LONGFORM, IDM_SHORTFORM,
                              IDM_LONGFORM, MF_BYCOMMAND);
            else
              CheckMenuRadioItem(hsubmenu, IDM_LONGFORM, IDM_SHORTFORM,
                              IDM_SHORTFORM, MF_BYCOMMAND);
          } else break;

          // convert window coordinates to screen coordinates
          ClientToScreen(hwnd, &pt);

          /* activate floating popup menu */
          TrackPopupMenuEx(hsubmenu, 0, pt.x, pt.y,
                          hwnd, NULL);
          DestroyMenu(hmenu);
          break;
        case WM_DESTROY:
          KillTimer(hwnd, 1);
          PostQuitMessage(0);
          break;
        default:
          return DefWindowProc(hwnd, message, wParam, lParam);
    }
    return 0;
}
```

The **Floating.rc** resource file is shown here:

```
// Demonstrate floating popup menus.
#include <windows.h>
#include "floating.h"

FloatingMenu MENU
{
  POPUP "&File"
  {
    MENUITEM "&Show Date\tF2", IDM_SHOWDATE
    MENUITEM SEPARATOR
```

```
      MENUITEM "E&xit\tCtrl+X", IDM_EXIT
  }
  POPUP "&Help" {
    MENUITEM "&About\tF1", IDM_ABOUT
  }
}


// This menu will popup.
Time MENU
{
  POPUP "&Time" {
    MENUITEM "&12 Hour\tF3", IDM_12HOUR
    MENUITEM "&24 Hour\tF4", IDM_24HOUR
  }
}


// This menu will popup.
Date MENU
{
  POPUP "&Date" {
    MENUITEM "&Long form\tF5", IDM_LONGFORM
    MENUITEM "&Short Form\tF6", IDM_SHORTFORM
  }
}


// Define menu accelerators
FloatingMenu ACCELERATORS
{
  VK_F2, IDM_SHOWDATE, VIRTKEY
  "^X",  IDM_EXIT
  VK_F3, IDM_12HOUR, VIRTKEY
  VK_F4, IDM_24HOUR, VIRTKEY
  VK_F5, IDM_LONGFORM, VIRTKEY
  VK_F6, IDM_SHORTFORM, VIRTKEY
  VK_F1, IDM_ABOUT, VIRTKEY
}
```

Floating.h is shown here:

```
#define IDM_SHOWDATE  100
#define IDM_EXIT      101

#define IDM_12HOUR    200
```

```
#define IDM_24HOUR     201

#define IDM_ABOUT      304

#define IDM_LONGFORM   400
#define IDM_SHORTFORM 401
```

ANNOTATIONS

A number of changes to the clock program are required to incorporate the floating menus. The first thing to notice is that the Date menu is now defined within the resource file rather than being constructed dymamically. While it certainly would have been possible to continue to create the Date menu at runtime, there is no reason to do so. Secondly, the Time menu is now defined as a stand-alone menu rather than as a submenu of the menu bar.

There is a small but important change to **WinMain( )**: The program's instance handle is now saved in the global instance handle **hInst**. This instance handle is required by the **LoadMenu( )** function, which is used to load the floating menus at runtime.

The most important changes to the clock program occur in the **WM_RBUTTONUP** handler. It is here that the Time and Date menus are activated. Let's look at it step by step. The handler begins by saving the coordinates of the mouse when the right click occurs:

```
case WM_RBUTTONUP: // activate floating menu
  // save mouse location
  pt.x = LOWORD(lParam);
  pt.y = HIWORD(lParam);
```

The coordinates are used for two purposes. First, they determine which menu should be displayed. Second, they determine where the menu will be positioned when shown.

Next, the appropriate menu is loaded. If the mouse is located over the row that displays the time, the Time menu is loaded. If the mouse is over the row that displays the date, the Date menu is loaded. Otherwise, nothing happens.

```
  // load appropriate menu
  if(pt.y >= 70 && pt.y < 84) { // Time
    hmenu = LoadMenu(hInst, "Time");
    hsubmenu = GetSubMenu(hmenu, 0);

    // set time menu radio button
    if(twelve_hour)
      CheckMenuRadioItem(hsubmenu, IDM_12HOUR, IDM_24HOUR,
                         IDM_12HOUR, MF_BYCOMMAND);
```

```
      else
         CheckMenuRadioItem(hsubmenu, IDM_12HOUR, IDM_24HOUR,
                            IDM_24HOUR, MF_BYCOMMAND);
   } else if(pt.y >= 90 && pt.y < 104 && date_on) { // Date
     hmenu = LoadMenu(hInst, "Date");
     hsubmenu = GetSubMenu(hmenu, 0);

     // set date menu radio button
     if(long_date_format)
        CheckMenuRadioItem(hsubmenu, IDM_LONGFORM, IDM_SHORTFORM,
                           IDM_LONGFORM, MF_BYCOMMAND);
     else
        CheckMenuRadioItem(hsubmenu, IDM_LONGFORM, IDM_SHORTFORM,
                           IDM_SHORTFORM, MF_BYCOMMAND);
   } else break;
```

As you can see, the position and height of the time and date display are hard-coded into the program. While this is fine for a sample program (and keeps the example uncluttered), you would want to use a different approach for any real application.

Once the appropriate menu is loaded, it is popped up to the screen using the following code. Notice that when **TrackPopupMenuEx( )** returns, the floating menu is destroyed by calling **DestroyMenu( )**.

```
// convert window coordinates to screen coordinates
ClientToScreen(hwnd, &pt);

/* activate floating popup menu */
TrackPopupMenuEx(hsubmenu, 0, pt.x, pt.y,
                 hwnd, NULL);

DestroyMenu(hmenu);
break;
```

The floating menu is displayed with its upper-left corner positioned at the location of the mouse when the right button is pressed. However, since the coordinates specified in **TrackPopupMenuEx( )** are in terms of screen units, the program must convert the mouse's location (which is in window units) into screen units using **ClientToScreen( )**. The prototype for **ClientToScreen( )** is shown here:

BOOL ClientToScreen(HWND *hwnd*, POINT **lpLoc*);

It is called with a window coordinate in the structure pointed to by *lpLoc* and returns the corresponding screen coordinate in that structure. The handle of the window in which the point lies is passed in *hwnd*. The function returns nonzero if successful and zero on failure.

Handling WM_MENURBUTTONUP Messages

Windows 98 and Windows 2000 have added a new dimension to menus that you will want to begin using. As you know, in all modern versions of Windows, a right-click is used to activate a floating context menu or, in some cases, a help window. In the past, this convention applied to all of Windows' interface elements except one: menu items. Fortunately, with the release of Windows 98 this oversight was fixed. Now, when the right button of the mouse is clicked while over a menu item, a **WM_MENURBUTTONUP** message is generated. You can use this message to display help information about the selection, or to pop up a context menu. Handling **WM_MENURBUTTONUP** messages is one of the best ways to give your program a modern, up-to-the-minute feel.

Each time a **WM_MENURBUTTONUP** message is received, **lParam** contains the handle of the menu and **wParam** contains the index of the item that was right-clicked. To see how this information can be used, the clock program will be enhanced so that it displays help information about a menu selection. For example, to receive help about the 12-hour option, position the mouse over the 12 Hour choice and then click the right mouse button.

Code

RBMenu.cpp

The **RBMenu.cpp** illustrates the handling of **WM_MENURBUTTONUP** messages. It uses the same resource file (**Floating.rc**) and header file (**Floating.h**) as the previous clock program. Sample output is shown in Figure 1-4.

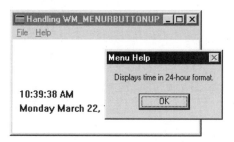

FIGURE 1-4. Sample output from the **RBMenu** program

PROGRAMMER'S NOTE: *Since **WM_MENURBUTTONUP** applies only to Windows 98 and Windows 2000, you may need to define **WINVER** as 0x0500, as the program does. Be careful, however. If you are using an older compiler that does not supply the updated header files and libraries, you might not be able to compile this program.*

```cpp
// RBMenu.cpp: Process right mouse clicks on menu items.

// This program requires Windows 98 or later.
#define WINVER 0x0500

#include <windows.h>
#include <cstring>
#include <ctime>
#include "floating.h"

// menu context help messages
char FileHelp[][80] = {
  "Check to display date.",
  "", // placeholder for separator
  "Terminates clock."
};
char TimeHelp[][80] = {
  "Displays time in 12-hour format.",
  "Displays time in 24-hour format."
};
char DateHelp[][80] = {
  "Displays long form of date.",
  "Displays short form of date.",
};

LRESULT CALLBACK WindowFunc(HWND, UINT, WPARAM, LPARAM);

char szWinName[] = "MyWin"; // name of window class
HINSTANCE hInst; // global instance handle

int WINAPI WinMain(HINSTANCE hThisInst, HINSTANCE hPrevInst,
                   LPSTR lpszArgs, int nWinMode)
{
  HWND hwnd;
  MSG msg;
  WNDCLASSEX wcl;
  HACCEL hAccel;
```

```
// Define a window class.
wcl.cbSize = sizeof(WNDCLASSEX);
wcl.hInstance = hThisInst;
wcl.lpszClassName = szWinName;
wcl.lpfnWndProc = WindowFunc;
wcl.style = 0; // default style
wcl.hIcon = LoadIcon(NULL, IDI_APPLICATION); // large icon
wcl.hIconSm = NULL; // use small version of large icon
wcl.hCursor = LoadCursor(NULL, IDC_ARROW);
wcl.hbrBackground = (HBRUSH) GetStockObject(WHITE_BRUSH);
wcl.cbClsExtra = 0;
wcl.cbWndExtra = 0;
wcl.lpszMenuName = "FloatingMenu"; // specify class menu

// Register the window class.
if(!RegisterClassEx(&wcl)) return 0;

hInst = hThisInst; // save instance handle

// Create a window.
hwnd = CreateWindow(szWinName, "Handling WM_MENURBUTTONUP",
                    WS_OVERLAPPEDWINDOW,
                    CW_USEDEFAULT, CW_USEDEFAULT,
                    250, 180,
                    NULL, NULL, hThisInst, NULL);

// Load keyboard accelerators.
hAccel = LoadAccelerators(hThisInst, "FloatingMenu");

// Display the window.
ShowWindow(hwnd, nWinMode);
UpdateWindow(hwnd);

// The message loop.
while(GetMessage(&msg, NULL, 0, 0))
{
  if(!TranslateAccelerator(hwnd, hAccel, &msg)) {
    TranslateMessage(&msg);
    DispatchMessage(&msg);
  }
}
return msg.wParam;
}
```

```
// The window procedure.
LRESULT CALLBACK WindowFunc(HWND hwnd, UINT message,
                              WPARAM wParam, LPARAM lParam)
{
  HDC hdc;
  PAINTSTRUCT ps;
  HMENU hmenu, hsubmenu;
  static HMENU hpopup;
  int response;
  char timestr[80], datestr[80];
  time_t t_t;
  POINT pt;

  static tm *t;
  static bool twelve_hour = true;
  static bool long_date_format = true;
  static bool date_on = false;

  static HMENU hFileM, hHelpM, hTimeM, hDateM;

  switch(message) {
    case WM_CREATE:
      // start timer
      SetTimer(hwnd, 1, 1000, NULL);

      // get current system time
      t_t = time(NULL);
      t = localtime(&t_t);

      // save handles to menu bar menus
      hFileM = GetSubMenu(GetMenu(hwnd), 0);
      hHelpM = GetSubMenu(GetMenu(hwnd), 1);

      break;
    case WM_TIMER: // update time
      t_t = time(NULL);
      t = localtime(&t_t);
      InvalidateRect(hwnd, NULL, 1);
      break;
    case WM_COMMAND:
      switch(LOWORD(wParam)) {
        case IDM_SHOWDATE:
```

```
  // get handle of menu bar
  hmenu = GetMenu(hwnd);

  // get handle to File menu
  hsubmenu = GetSubMenu(hmenu, 0);

  if(!date_on) { // check Show Date option
    CheckMenuItem(hsubmenu, IDM_SHOWDATE,
                  MF_BYCOMMAND | MF_CHECKED);

    date_on = true; // turn on date output
  }
  else { // uncheck Show Date option
    // clear Show Date option
    CheckMenuItem(hsubmenu, IDM_SHOWDATE,
                  MF_BYCOMMAND | MF_UNCHECKED);
    date_on = false; // turn off date output
  }
  InvalidateRect(hwnd, NULL, 1);
  break;
case IDM_EXIT:
  response = MessageBox(hwnd, "Quit the Program?",
                        "Exit", MB_YESNO);
  if(response == IDYES) PostQuitMessage(0);
  break;
case IDM_LONGFORM: // display long form of date
  long_date_format = true;
  InvalidateRect(hwnd, NULL, 1);
  break;
case IDM_SHORTFORM: // display short form of date
  long_date_format = false;
  InvalidateRect(hwnd, NULL, 1);
  break;
case IDM_12HOUR: // use 12 hour clock
  twelve_hour = true;
  InvalidateRect(hwnd, NULL, 1);
  break;
case IDM_24HOUR: // use 24 hour clock
  twelve_hour = false;
  InvalidateRect(hwnd, NULL, 1);
  break;
case IDM_ABOUT:
  MessageBox(hwnd, "Handling WM_MENURBUTTONUP",
```

```
                         "About", MB_OK);
        break;
    }
    break;
case WM_PAINT:
    if(twelve_hour)
        strftime(timestr, 79, "%I:%M:%S %p", t);
    else
        strftime(timestr, 79, "%H:%M:%S", t);

    if(long_date_format)
        strftime(datestr, 79, "%A %B %d, %Y", t);
    else
        strftime(datestr, 79, "%m/%d/%Y", t);

    hdc = BeginPaint(hwnd, &ps);

    TextOut(hdc, 10, 70, timestr, strlen(timestr));

    if(date_on)
        TextOut(hdc, 10, 90, datestr, strlen(datestr));

    EndPaint(hwnd, &ps);
    break;
case WM_RBUTTONUP: // activate floating menu
    // save mouse location
    pt.x = LOWORD(lParam);
    pt.y = HIWORD(lParam);

    // load appropriate menu
    if(pt.y >= 70 && pt.y < 84) { // Time
        hmenu = LoadMenu(hInst, "Time");
        hsubmenu = GetSubMenu(hmenu, 0);

        // set time menu radio button
        if(twelve_hour)
            CheckMenuRadioItem(hsubmenu, IDM_12HOUR, IDM_24HOUR,
                               IDM_12HOUR, MF_BYCOMMAND);
        else
            CheckMenuRadioItem(hsubmenu, IDM_12HOUR, IDM_24HOUR,
                               IDM_24HOUR, MF_BYCOMMAND);
        // save Time menu handle
        hTimeM = hsubmenu;
```

```
    } else if(pt.y >= 90 && pt.y < 104 && date_on) { // Date
      hmenu = LoadMenu(hInst, "Date");
      hsubmenu = GetSubMenu(hmenu, 0);

      // set date menu radio button
      if(long_date_format)
        CheckMenuRadioItem(hsubmenu, IDM_LONGFORM, IDM_SHORTFORM,
                           IDM_LONGFORM, MF_BYCOMMAND);
      else
        CheckMenuRadioItem(hsubmenu, IDM_LONGFORM, IDM_SHORTFORM,
                           IDM_SHORTFORM, MF_BYCOMMAND);

      // save Date menu handle
      hDateM = hsubmenu;
    } else break;

    // convert window coordinates to screen coordinates
    ClientToScreen(hwnd, &pt);

    /* activate floating popup menu */
    TrackPopupMenuEx(hsubmenu, 0, pt.x, pt.y,
                     hwnd, NULL);
    DestroyMenu(hmenu);
    break;
  case WM_MENURBUTTONUP: // display context-help for menus
    if((HMENU)lParam == hFileM)
      MessageBox(hwnd, FileHelp[wParam], "Menu Help", MB_OK);
    else if((HMENU)lParam == hHelpM)
      MessageBox(hwnd, "Display About box.", "Menu Help", MB_OK);
    else if((HMENU)lParam == hTimeM)
      MessageBox(hwnd, TimeHelp[wParam], "Menu Help", MB_OK);
    else if((HMENU)lParam == hDateM)
      MessageBox(hwnd, DateHelp[wParam], "Menu Help", MB_OK);
    break;
  case WM_DESTROY:
    KillTimer(hwnd, 1);
    PostQuitMessage(0);
    break;
  default:
    return DefWindowProc(hwnd, message, wParam, lParam);
  }
  return 0;
}
```

ANNOTATIONS

Much of the code in **RBMenu.cpp** is the same as it was in **Floating.cpp**, shown earlier. To handle **WM_MENURBUTTONUP** requires additions, but no major restructuring. Let's begin with the code for the **WM_MENURBUTTONUP** message handler, shown here:

```
case WM_MENURBUTTONUP: // display context-help for menus
  if((HMENU)lParam == hFileM)
    MessageBox(hwnd, FileHelp[wParam], "Menu Help", MB_OK);
  else if((HMENU)lParam == hHelpM)
    MessageBox(hwnd, "Display About box.", "Menu Help", MB_OK);
  else if((HMENU)lParam == hTimeM)
    MessageBox(hwnd, TimeHelp[wParam], "Menu Help", MB_OK);
  else if((HMENU)lParam == hDateM)
    MessageBox(hwnd, DateHelp[wParam], "Menu Help", MB_OK);
  break;
```

Each time the user clicks the right mouse button on a menu item, **WM_MENURBUTTONUP** is sent with the menu handle in **lParam** and the index of the menu item in **wParam**. The menu handles **hFileM**, **hHelpM**, **hTimeM**, and **hDateM** are variables that have been added to **WindowFunc( )**. They store the handles to the menus and are used to determine which menu is active when the right button is clicked. After determining which menu is active, the index in **wParam** is used to display a message box that contains information about the menu item. Of course, in a real application you will probably want to use either **WinHelp( )** or **HtmlHelp( )** to present help information, but employing a message box is sufficient for our simple clock program.

The help messages, themselves, are stored in the global character arrays shown here:

```
// menu context help messages
char FileHelp[][80] = {
  "Check to display date.",
  "", // placeholder for separator
  "Terminates clock."
};
char TimeHelp[][80] = {
  "Displays time in 12-hour format.",
  "Displays time in 24-hour format."
};
char DateHelp[][80] = {
  "Displays long form of date.",
  "Displays short form of date.",
};
```

The order of the messages matches the order of the menu items, allowing each array to be indexed by the value contained in **wParam** when **WM_MENURBUTTONUP** is received.

Adding Bitmaps to Menu Items

Another recent addition to the menuing subsystem is the ability to include a bitmap along with a text description of the item. The feature is available only for Windows 98 and later. To add a bitmap, store its handle in the **hbmpItem** field of a **MENUITEMINFO** object, and then call **SetMenuItemInfo( )**. The bitmap will then be displayed to the left of the text.

Code

BitMenu.cpp

BitMenu.cpp

BitMenu.cpp demonstrates bitmap menu items by adding bitmaps to the Time and Date menus used by the preceding example. Sample output is shown in Figure 1-5.

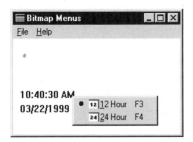

FIGURE 1-5.   Sample output from **BitMenu.cpp**

PROGRAMMER'S NOTE   *Since the **hbmpItem** field is available only in Windows 98 and Windows 2000, you may need to define **WINVER** as 0x0500, as the program does. You may also need to define **_WIN32_WINNT** to be 0x0500 as well. As before, be aware that older compilers may not support the **hbmpItem** field.*

```
// BitMenu.cpp: Adding bitmaps to menu items.

// This program requires Windows 98 or later.
#define WINVER 0x0500
#define _WIN32_WINNT 0x0500
```

```cpp
#include <windows.h>
#include <cstring>
#include <ctime>
#include "bitmenu.h"

// menu context help messages
char FileHelp[][80] = {
  "Check to display date.",
  "", // placeholder for separator
  "Terminates clock."
};
char TimeHelp[][80] = {
  "Displays time in 12-hour format.",
  "Displays time in 24-hour format."
};
char DateHelp[][80] = {
  "Displays long form of date.",
  "Displays short form of date.",
};

LRESULT CALLBACK WindowFunc(HWND, UINT, WPARAM, LPARAM);

char szWinName[] = "MyWin"; // name of window class
HINSTANCE hInst; // global instance handle

int WINAPI WinMain(HINSTANCE hThisInst, HINSTANCE hPrevInst,
                   LPSTR lpszArgs, int nWinMode)
{
  HWND hwnd;
  MSG msg;
  WNDCLASSEX wcl;
  HACCEL hAccel;

  // Define a window class.
  wcl.cbSize = sizeof(WNDCLASSEX);
  wcl.hInstance = hThisInst;
  wcl.lpszClassName = szWinName;
  wcl.lpfnWndProc = WindowFunc;
  wcl.style = 0; // default style
  wcl.hIcon = LoadIcon(NULL, IDI_APPLICATION); // large icon
  wcl.hIconSm = NULL; // use small version of large icon
  wcl.hCursor = LoadCursor(NULL, IDC_ARROW);
  wcl.hbrBackground = (HBRUSH) GetStockObject(WHITE_BRUSH);
```

```
wcl.cbClsExtra = 0;
wcl.cbWndExtra = 0;
wcl.lpszMenuName = "BitmapMenu"; // specify class menu

// Register the window class.
if(!RegisterClassEx(&wcl)) return 0;

hInst = hThisInst; // save instance handle

// Create a window.
hwnd = CreateWindow(szWinName, "Bitmap Menus",
                    WS_OVERLAPPEDWINDOW,
                    CW_USEDEFAULT, CW_USEDEFAULT,
                    250, 180,
                    NULL, NULL, hThisInst, NULL);

// Load keyboard accelerators.
hAccel = LoadAccelerators(hThisInst, "BitmapMenu");

// Display the window.
ShowWindow(hwnd, nWinMode);
UpdateWindow(hwnd);

// The message loop.
while(GetMessage(&msg, NULL, 0, 0))
{
  if(!TranslateAccelerator(hwnd, hAccel, &msg)) {
    TranslateMessage(&msg);
    DispatchMessage(&msg);
  }
}
return msg.wParam;
}


// The window procedure.
LRESULT CALLBACK WindowFunc(HWND hwnd, UINT message,
                            WPARAM wParam, LPARAM lParam)
{
  HDC hdc;
  PAINTSTRUCT ps;
  HMENU hmenu, hsubmenu;
  static HMENU hpopup;
```

```
int response;
char timestr[80], datestr[80];
time_t t_t;
POINT pt;

static tm *t;
static bool twelve_hour = true;
static bool long_date_format = true;
static bool date_on = false;

static HMENU hFileM, hHelpM, hTimeM, hDateM;
MENUITEMINFO miInfo;
HBITMAP hbit1, hbit2;

switch(message) {
  case WM_CREATE:
    // start timer
    SetTimer(hwnd, 1, 1000, NULL);

    // get current system time
    t_t = time(NULL);
    t = localtime(&t_t);

    // save handles to menu bar menus
    hFileM = GetSubMenu(GetMenu(hwnd), 0);
    hHelpM = GetSubMenu(GetMenu(hwnd), 1);

    break;
  case WM_TIMER: // update time
    t_t = time(NULL);
    t = localtime(&t_t);
    InvalidateRect(hwnd, NULL, 1);
    break;
  case WM_COMMAND:
    switch(LOWORD(wParam)) {
      case IDM_SHOWDATE:
        // get handle of menu bar
        hmenu = GetMenu(hwnd);

        // get handle to File menu
        hsubmenu = GetSubMenu(hmenu, 0);
```

```
      if(!date_on) { // check Show Date option
        CheckMenuItem(hsubmenu, IDM_SHOWDATE,
                      MF_BYCOMMAND | MF_CHECKED);

        date_on = true; // turn on date output
      }
      else { // uncheck Show Date option
        // clear Show Date option
        CheckMenuItem(hsubmenu, IDM_SHOWDATE,
                      MF_BYCOMMAND | MF_UNCHECKED);
        date_on = false; // turn off date output
      }
      InvalidateRect(hwnd, NULL, 1);
      break;
    case IDM_EXIT:
      response = MessageBox(hwnd, "Quit the Program?",
                            "Exit", MB_YESNO);
      if(response == IDYES) PostQuitMessage(0);
      break;
    case IDM_LONGFORM: // display long form of date
      long_date_format = true;
      InvalidateRect(hwnd, NULL, 1);
      break;
    case IDM_SHORTFORM: // display short form of date
      long_date_format = false;
      InvalidateRect(hwnd, NULL, 1);
      break;
    case IDM_12HOUR: // use 12 hour clock
      twelve_hour = true;
      InvalidateRect(hwnd, NULL, 1);
      break;
    case IDM_24HOUR: // use 24 hour clock
      twelve_hour = false;
      InvalidateRect(hwnd, NULL, 1);
      break;
    case IDM_ABOUT:
      MessageBox(hwnd, "Demonstrating Bitmap Menus",
                 "About", MB_OK);
      break;
  }
  break;
case WM_PAINT:
```

```
      if(twelve_hour)
        strftime(timestr, 79, "%I:%M:%S %p", t);
      else
        strftime(timestr, 79, "%H:%M:%S", t);

      if(long_date_format)
        strftime(datestr, 79, "%A %B %d, %Y", t);
      else
        strftime(datestr, 79, "%m/%d/%Y", t);

      hdc = BeginPaint(hwnd, &ps);

      TextOut(hdc, 10, 70, timestr, strlen(timestr));

      if(date_on)
        TextOut(hdc, 10, 90, datestr, strlen(datestr));

      EndPaint(hwnd, &ps);
      break;
    case WM_RBUTTONUP: // activate floating menu
      // save mouse location
      pt.x = LOWORD(lParam);
      pt.y = HIWORD(lParam);

      // load appropriate menu
      if(pt.y >= 70 && pt.y < 84) { // Time
        hmenu = LoadMenu(hInst, "Time");
        hsubmenu = GetSubMenu(hmenu, 0);

        // add bitmaps to Time menu
        miInfo.cbSize = sizeof(MENUITEMINFO);
        miInfo.fMask = MIIM_BITMAP;
        miInfo.hbmpItem = hbit1 = LoadBitmap(hInst, "12hour");
        SetMenuItemInfo(hsubmenu, 0, true, &miInfo);

        miInfo.hbmpItem = hbit2 = LoadBitmap(hInst, "24hour");
        SetMenuItemInfo(hsubmenu, 1, true, &miInfo);

         // set time menu radio button
        if(twelve_hour)
          CheckMenuRadioItem(hsubmenu, IDM_12HOUR, IDM_24HOUR,
                          IDM_12HOUR, MF_BYCOMMAND);
```

```
    else
        CheckMenuRadioItem(hsubmenu, IDM_12HOUR, IDM_24HOUR,
                         IDM_24HOUR, MF_BYCOMMAND);

    // save Time menu handle
    hTimeM = hsubmenu;
} else if(pt.y >= 90 && pt.y < 104 && date_on) { // Date
    hmenu = LoadMenu(hInst, "Date");
    hsubmenu = GetSubMenu(hmenu, 0);

    // add bitmaps to Date menu
    miInfo.cbSize = sizeof(MENUITEMINFO);
    miInfo.fMask = MIIM_BITMAP;
    miInfo.hbmpItem = hbit1 = LoadBitmap(hInst, "long");
    SetMenuItemInfo(hsubmenu, 0, true, &miInfo);

    miInfo.hbmpItem = hbit2 = LoadBitmap(hInst, "short");
    SetMenuItemInfo(hsubmenu, 1, true, &miInfo);

    // set date menu radio button
    if(long_date_format)
        CheckMenuRadioItem(hsubmenu, IDM_LONGFORM, IDM_SHORTFORM,
                         IDM_LONGFORM, MF_BYCOMMAND);
    else
        CheckMenuRadioItem(hsubmenu, IDM_LONGFORM, IDM_SHORTFORM,
                         IDM_SHORTFORM, MF_BYCOMMAND);

    // save Date menu handle
    hDateM = hsubmenu;
} else break;

// convert window coordinates to screen coordinates
ClientToScreen(hwnd, &pt);

/* activate floating popup menu */
TrackPopupMenuEx(hsubmenu, 0, pt.x, pt.y,
                 hwnd, NULL);
DestroyMenu(hmenu);
DeleteObject(hbit1);
DeleteObject(hbit2);
break;
case WM_MENURBUTTONUP: // display context-help for menus
```

```
      if((HMENU)lParam == hFileM)
        MessageBox(hwnd, FileHelp[wParam], "Menu Help", MB_OK);
      else if((HMENU)lParam == hHelpM)
        MessageBox(hwnd, "Display About box.", "Menu Help", MB_OK);
      else if((HMENU)lParam == hTimeM)
        MessageBox(hwnd, TimeHelp[wParam], "Menu Help", MB_OK);
      else if((HMENU)lParam == hDateM)
        MessageBox(hwnd, DateHelp[wParam], "Menu Help", MB_OK);
      break;
    case WM_DESTROY:
      KillTimer(hwnd, 1);
      PostQuitMessage(0);
      break;
    default:
      return DefWindowProc(hwnd, message, wParam, lParam);
  }
  return 0;
}
```

The resource file **BitMenu.rc** is shown here:

```
// Demonstrate floating popup menus.
#include <windows.h>
#include "bitmenu.h"

12hour BITMAP "12hour.bmp"
24hour BITMAP "24hour.bmp"
long BITMAP "long.bmp"
short BITMAP "short.bmp"

BitmapMenu MENU
{
  POPUP "&File"
  {
    MENUITEM "&Show Date\tF2", IDM_SHOWDATE
    MENUITEM SEPARATOR
    MENUITEM "E&xit\tCtrl+X", IDM_EXIT
  }
  POPUP "&Help" {
    MENUITEM "&About\tF1", IDM_ABOUT
  }
}
```

```
// This menu will popup.
Time MENU
{
  POPUP "&Time" {
    MENUITEM "&12 Hour\tF3", IDM_12HOUR
    MENUITEM "&24 Hour\tF4", IDM_24HOUR
  }
}

// This menu will popup.
Date MENU
{
  POPUP "&Date" {
    MENUITEM "&Long form\tF5", IDM_LONGFORM
    MENUITEM "&Short Form\tF6", IDM_SHORTFORM
  }
}

// Define menu accelerators
BitmapMenu ACCELERATORS
{
  VK_F2, IDM_SHOWDATE, VIRTKEY
  "^X",  IDM_EXIT
  VK_F3, IDM_12HOUR, VIRTKEY
  VK_F4, IDM_24HOUR, VIRTKEY
  VK_F5, IDM_LONGFORM, VIRTKEY
  VK_F6, IDM_SHORTFORM, VIRTKEY
  VK_F1, IDM_ABOUT, VIRTKEY
}
```

The header file **BitMenu.h** is shown here:

```
#define IDM_SHOWDATE    100
#define IDM_EXIT        101

#define IDM_12HOUR      200
#define IDM_24HOUR      201

#define IDM_ABOUT       304

#define IDM_LONGFORM    400
#define IDM_SHORTFORM 401
```

ANNOTATIONS

The code for **BitMenu.cpp** is the same as for **RBMenu.cpp** except for the addition of the bitmaps. The first change is that four bitmap resources are now specified in **BitMenu.rc**. The other change occurs inside the **WM_MENURBUTTONUP** case, which loads and displays the Time and Date menus. After a menu is loaded, its bitmaps are set. Let's look at this process closely by examining the code that sets the bitmaps for the Time menu. It is shown here:

```
hmenu = LoadMenu(hInst, "Time");
hsubmenu = GetSubMenu(hmenu, 0);

// add bitmaps to Time menu
miInfo.cbSize = sizeof(MENUITEMINFO);
miInfo.fMask = MIIM_BITMAP;
miInfo.hbmpItem = LoadBitmap(hInst, "12hour");
SetMenuItemInfo(hsubmenu, 0, true, &miInfo);

miInfo.hbmpItem = LoadBitmap(hInst, "24hour");
SetMenuItemInfo(hsubmenu, 1, true, &miInfo);
```

First, the handle to the Time submenu is obtained. Then, the **MENUITEMINFO** object **miInfo** has its **fMask** field set to **MIIM_BITMAP**, which allows the **hbmpItem** to be set when **SetMenuItemInfo( )** is called. Next, the **12hour** bitmap is loaded and the first menu item is updated. Then, the **24hour** bitmap is loaded and the second menu item is updated. This same general process is used to set the Date menu bitmaps. Once the bitmaps have been set, they are automatically displayed to the left of the text that describes the menu item.

Things to Try

Here are three other things that you might want to try when working with menus:

♦ Experiment with changing the contents of the menu bar. Items are added to or deleted from the menu bar just as they are from other menus. The only difference is that you will need to redraw the menu bar in order for the changes to be displayed. This is easily accomplished with the **DrawMenuBar( )** function. Try changing the menu bar options based upon the current state of your program.

♦ Try defining your own check mark icons for check menu items. You can set the check mark bitmaps by calling **SetMenuItemBitmaps( )**.

♦ Experiment with the animation flags when using **TrackPopupMenuEx( )**.

Tips for Using MFC

Applying the menuing techniques described in this chapter to MFC is straightforward. The menu functions are members of **CMenu** and most of the **CMenu** functions parallel those defined by the API. For example, to dynamically alter menus, use the following functions:

CMenu::CreatePopupMenu	Creates a new submenu.
CMenu::DeleteMenu	Deletes a menu item.
CMenu::EnableMenuItem	Enables or disables a menu item.
CMenu::GetMenuItemCount	Returns a count of the items in the menu.
CMenu::GetSubMenu	Returns a pointer to a submenu.
CMenu::InsertMenu	Inserts a menu item.
CMenu::TrackPopupMenu	Creates a floating, context menu.

To obtain a pointer to the menu bar, use **CWnd::GetMenu( )**. At the time of this writing, MFC does not provide a wrapper for **InsertMenuItem( )**.

There is, however, one important difference between the way MFC handles menus and the way they are managed using the API: An MFC program uses *menu update handlers*. The menu update handlers determine the display status of items in a menu. Thus, they set or remove check marks, and enable or disable items. Because of the menu update handlers, you will seldom use a function such as **CMenu::EnableMenuItem( )**. It is best to enable or disable menu items through menu update handlers.

Supercharged Repaints

The efficient repainting of a window is important to nearly all Windows applications, but it is especially important when professional, commercial-grade applications need to be produced. When an application does not efficiently handle repaint requests, it appears both sluggish and amateurish to the user. This makes the proper management of **WM_PAINT** one of the most important techniques that a Windows programmer can have in his or her bag of tricks. Properly handling **WM_PAINT** has significant impact on both the performance of your application and the impression it leaves with the user.

This chapter describes three important **WM_PAINT**-related techniques. First, it discusses a general-purpose method by which any program can quickly and efficiently repaint a window when a **WM_PAINT** message is received. This general method is based upon the concept of a *virtual window*. Next, you will see how to use a virtual window to allow a display workspace that is larger than the dimensions of the screen. Finally, the virtual window technology is used to implement a double-buffering mechanism that can construct images in the background and then "snap" them to the screen.

The Repaint Problem

As you know, Windows programs must repaint a window (i.e., redisplay the information contained in the window) each time a **WM_PAINT** message is received. **WM_PAINT** messages are sent to your program whenever the contents of a window need to be restored. For example, when a window is overlayed by another and then uncovered, your program is sent a repaint request. To satisfy this request, your program must redisplay the contents of the window. Windows will not do this for you. It is your responsibility. Of course, this gives rise to the larger question: What mechanism should one use to restore the contents of a window when a **WM_PAINT** message is received? This question has haunted programmers since the early days of Windows. To some extent, its answer depends upon the exact nature of your application. However, over time, three basic methods have emerged.

The first way that your program can repaint a window is by regenerating the output. This method will work only if that output is created by some computational means. For example, a program that displays the square roots of the integers between 1 and 100 could simply recompute the values when a **WM_PAINT** message is received. Unfortunately, few programs fall into this category.

The second way your application can repaint its window is by storing a record of display events and then "replaying" those events when a repaint request is received. For example, such an approach may work for some types of games. For most programs, this approach is not feasible.

The third, and most general, method by which you can repaint a window is by keeping an identical copy of the window (i.e., a virtual window) in memory. Each time a **WM_PAINT** message is received, the contents of the virtual window are copied to the window that is on the screen. One important advantage of this method is that it will work for any and all programs. For this reason, it is the method that will be developed here. As you will see, Windows provides substantial support for this approach to repainting.

Using a Virtual Window

A *virtual window* is a memory device context that is compatible with the display device context defined by your program. Thus, it will behave in the same way as the window that is displayed on the screen, which we will hereafter refer to as the *physical window*. The only difference is that the virtual window exists in memory. In general, here is how a virtual window can be used to respond to a repaint request. All output is written to the virtual window. Of course, you are free to simultaneously write output to the physical window, too. However, at all times, the virtual window must hold a complete copy of whatever is displayed on the screen. This ensures that there is always a record of the current contents of the window. Each time a **WM_PAINT** message is received, the contents of the virtual window are copied into the physical window, restoring its contents. For example, if the physical window is overwritten and then uncovered, a **WM_PAINT** message will be received and the window's contents will be automatically restored.

The advantages to the virtual window approach are many. First, as mentioned earlier, it works for any and all programs. That is, it is a completely general-purpose technique. Second, it is easy to implement. Third, it can be efficiently implemented. Finally, once the virtual window mechanism is in place, it helps solve other output-related problems.

In general, here is how you will create a virtual window. First, create a memory device context (DC) that is compatible with your program's physical device context. This will be done only once, when the program begins execution—typically when the **WM_CREATE** message is received. This compatible device context will stay in existence the entire time the program is executing. Once you have created a compatible DC, you must create a compatible bitmap, which will hold the output directed to the virtual window. The dimensions of this bitmap must be large enough to handle a maximized window. Finally, this bitmap must be selected into the compatible DC and given the same brushes and pens used by the physical window that it is emulating.

VirtWin.cpp

Code

The **VirtWin.cpp** program that follows demonstrates a virtual window. When you run this program, try covering and then uncovering the window. As you will see, the contents of the window are automatically restored. Sample output is shown in Figure 2-1.

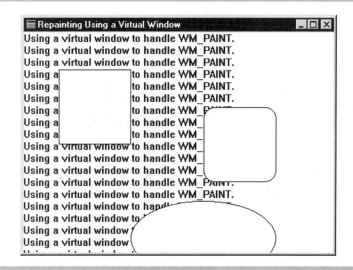

FIGURE 2-1.   Sample output from **VirtWin.cpp**

```cpp
// VirtWin.cpp: Repainting using a virtual window.

#include <windows.h>
#include <cstring>

LRESULT CALLBACK WindowFunc(HWND, UINT, WPARAM, LPARAM);

char szWinName[] = "MyWin"; // name of window class

int WINAPI WinMain(HINSTANCE hThisInst, HINSTANCE hPrevInst,
                   LPSTR lpszArgs, int nWinMode)
{
  HWND hwnd;
  MSG msg;
  WNDCLASSEX wcl;

  // Define a window class.
  wcl.cbSize = sizeof(WNDCLASSEX);
  wcl.hInstance = hThisInst;
  wcl.lpszClassName = szWinName;
  wcl.lpfnWndProc = WindowFunc;
  wcl.style = 0; // default style
  wcl.hIcon = LoadIcon(NULL, IDI_APPLICATION); // large icon
```

```
    wcl.hIconSm = NULL; // use small version of large icon
  wcl.hCursor = LoadCursor(NULL, IDC_ARROW);
  wcl.hbrBackground = (HBRUSH) GetStockObject(WHITE_BRUSH);
  wcl.cbClsExtra = 0;
  wcl.cbWndExtra = 0;
  wcl.lpszMenuName = NULL; // no menu

  // Register the window class.
  if(!RegisterClassEx(&wcl)) return 0;

  // Create a window.
  hwnd = CreateWindow(szWinName,
                      "Repainting Using a Virtual Window",
                      WS_OVERLAPPEDWINDOW,
                      CW_USEDEFAULT, CW_USEDEFAULT,
                      CW_USEDEFAULT, CW_USEDEFAULT,
                      NULL, NULL, hThisInst, NULL);

  // Display the window.
  ShowWindow(hwnd, nWinMode);
  UpdateWindow(hwnd);

  // The message loop.
  while(GetMessage(&msg, NULL, 0, 0))
  {
    TranslateMessage(&msg);
    DispatchMessage(&msg);
  }
  return msg.wParam;
}


// The window procedure.
LRESULT CALLBACK WindowFunc(HWND hwnd, UINT message,
                            WPARAM wParam, LPARAM lParam)
{
  HDC hdc;
  PAINTSTRUCT ps;
  TEXTMETRIC tm;
  char str[255];
  int i;
```

```
static int maxX, maxY; // screen dimensions
int X=0, Y=0;          // current output location
static HDC memdc;      // handle to virtual window context
static HBITMAP hbit;   // handle to virtual window bitmap
HBRUSH hbrush;         // handle to virtual window brush

switch(message) {
  case WM_CREATE:
    // get screen coordinates
    maxX = GetSystemMetrics(SM_CXSCREEN);
    maxY = GetSystemMetrics(SM_CYSCREEN);

    // create the virtual window
    hdc = GetDC(hwnd);
    memdc = CreateCompatibleDC(hdc);
    hbit = CreateCompatibleBitmap(hdc, maxX, maxY);
    SelectObject(memdc, hbit);
    hbrush = (HBRUSH) GetStockObject(WHITE_BRUSH);
    SelectObject(memdc, hbrush);
    PatBlt(memdc, 0, 0, maxX, maxY, PATCOPY);

    // get text metrics
    GetTextMetrics(hdc, &tm);

    // output some text to the virtual window
    for(i=0; i<24; i++) {
      strcpy(str, "Using a virtual window to handle WM_PAINT.");
      TextOut(memdc, X, Y, str, strlen(str)); // output to memory

      // advance to next line
      Y = Y + tm.tmHeight + tm.tmExternalLeading;
    }

    // output some graphics objects to the virtual window
    Rectangle(memdc, 50, 50, 150, 150);
    Ellipse(memdc, 150, 225, 350, 325);
    RoundRect(memdc, 250, 100, 350, 200, 30, 30);

    ReleaseDC(hwnd, hdc);
    InvalidateRect(hwnd, NULL, 0);
    break;
  case WM_PAINT:
    hdc = BeginPaint(hwnd, &ps);
```

```
      // copy virtual window to screen
      BitBlt(hdc, 0, 0, maxX, maxY, memdc, 0, 0, SRCCOPY);

      EndPaint(hwnd, &ps);
      break;
    case WM_DESTROY:
      DeleteDC(memdc);
      DeleteObject(hbit);
      PostQuitMessage(0);
      break;
    default:
      return DefWindowProc(hwnd, message, wParam, lParam);
  }
  return 0;
}
```

ANNOTATIONS

The program begins with the standard Windows skeleton used throughout this book. Notice, however, that no resource or header file is needed. Since the program just displays lines of text and graphics, there is no need for resources or menus. The interesting parts of the program occur when the virtual window is created, when output is written to the virtual window, and when a **WM_PAINT** message is processed. Each is examined in detail.

Creating the Virtual Window

The virtual window is created inside the **WM_CREATE** message handler, using this sequence of code.

```
// get screen coordinates
maxX = GetSystemMetrics(SM_CXSCREEN);
maxY = GetSystemMetrics(SM_CYSCREEN);

// create the virtual window
hdc = GetDC(hwnd);
memdc = CreateCompatibleDC(hdc);
hbit = CreateCompatibleBitmap(hdc, maxX, maxY);
SelectObject(memdc, hbit);
hbrush = (HBRUSH) GetStockObject(WHITE_BRUSH);
SelectObject(memdc, hbrush);
PatBlt(memdc, 0, 0, maxX, maxY, PATCOPY);
```

First, the dimensions of the screen are obtained using **GetSystemMetrics( )**. They will be used to create a compatible bitmap. The prototype for **GetSystemMetrics( )** is shown here:

int GetSystemMetrics(int *what*);

Here, *what* will be a value that specifies the metric that you want to obtain. (It can obtain several different values.) Here is a sampling of some common values:

Value	Metric Obtained
SM_CXFULLSCREEN	Width of maximized client area
SM_CYFULLSCREEN	Height of maximized client area
SM_CXICON	Width of large icon
SM_CYICON	Height of large icon
SM_CXSMICON	Width of small icon
SM_CYSMICON	Height of small icon
SM_CXSCREEN	Width of entire screen
SM_CYSCREEN	Height of entire screen

In the program, the values **SM_CXSCREEN** and **SM_CYSCREEN** are used to obtain the screen extents.

After getting the dimensions of the screen, the current device context is acquired using the function **GetDC( )**. Next, a compatible device context is created in memory, using **CreateCompatibleDC( )**. The handle to this device context is stored in **memdc**, which is a static variable defined within **WindowFunc( )**. The prototype for **CreateCompatibleDC( )** is shown here:

HDC CreateCompatibleDC(HDC *hdc*)

This function returns a handle to a memory device context that is compatible with the device context specified by *hdc* (which, for the program, is the device context of the physical window). The function returns **NULL** if an error occurs.

Next, a compatible bitmap is created using **CreateCompatibleBitmap( )**. This establishes a one-to-one mapping between the virtual window and the physical window. The dimensions of the bitmap are those of the maximum screen size. This ensures that the bitmap will be large enough to fully restore the window even when maximized. (Actually, slightly smaller values could be used, since the borders aren't repainted, but this minor improvement is left to you, as an exercise.) The handle to the bitmap is stored in the static variable **hbit**. The **CreateCompatibleBitmap( )** function creates a bitmap that is compatible with the specified device context. This bitmap can be used by any compatible memory device context. The prototype for **CreateCompatibleBitmap( )** is shown here:

HBITMAP CreateCompatibleBitmap(HDC *hdc*, int *width*, int *height*);

Here, *hdc* is the handle for the device context for which the bitmap will be compatible. The dimensions of the bitmap are specified in *width* and *height*. These values are in pixels. The function returns a handle to the compatible bitmap or **NULL** on failure.

After the bitmap has been created, it must be selected into the memory device context using **SelectObject( )**, which has this prototype:

HGDIOBJ SelectObject(HDC *hdc*, HGDIOBJ *hObject*);

Here, *hdc* specifies the device context and *hObject* is the handle of the object being selected into that context. The function returns the handle of the previously selected object (if there is one), allowing it to be reselected later, if desired. A bitmap can be selected into only one device context at any one time.

Next, a stock white brush is obtained and its handle is stored in the static variable **hbrush**. This brush is selected into the memory device context and then **PatBlt( )** paints the entire virtual window using the brush. Thus, the virtual window will have a white background. Since no pen is selected, the default pen will be used. These choices are arbitrary. In this case, the white background matches the background of the physical window in the **VirtWin.cpp** program. (Remember, these colors are under your control. The colors used here are arbitrary.) The **PatBlt( )** function fills a rectangle with the color and pattern of the currently selected brush. **PatBlt( )** has this prototype:

BOOL PatBlt(HDC *hdc*, int *X*, int *Y*, int *width*, int *height*, DWORD *dwHow*);

Here, *hdc* is the handle of the device context. The coordinates *X* and *Y* specify the upper-left corner of the region to be filled. The width and height of the region are specified in *width* and *height*. The value passed in *dwHow* determines how the brush will be applied. It must be one of these values:

Value	Meaning
BLACKNESS	Region is black (brush is ignored)
WHITENESS	Region is white (brush is ignored)
PATCOPY	Brush is copied to region
PATINVERT	Brush is ORed to region
DSTINVERT	Region is inverted (brush is ignored)

Therefore, if you wish to apply the current brush unaltered, select **PATCOPY** for the value for *dwHow*. The function returns nonzero if successful, zero otherwise.

Outputting to the Virtual Window

After the **WM_CREATE** handler creates the virtual window, some text and graphics are written to it. The code that accomplishes this is shown here:

```
// get text metrics
GetTextMetrics(hdc, &tm);

// output some text to the virtual window
for(i=0; i<24; i++) {
  strcpy(str, "Using a virtual window to handle WM_PAINT.");
  TextOut(memdc, X, Y, str, strlen(str)); // output to memory

  // advance to next line
  Y = Y + tm.tmHeight + tm.tmExternalLeading;
}

// output some graphics objects to the virtual window
Rectangle(memdc, 50, 50, 150, 150);
Ellipse(memdc, 150, 225, 350, 325);
RoundRect(memdc, 250, 100, 350, 200, 30, 30);

ReleaseDC(hwnd, hdc);
InvalidateRect(hwnd, NULL, 0);
```

As this fragment shows, you can output to the virtual window just as you do to a normal window. The only difference is that you must direct the output to the memory device context. In this case, the program outputs only to the virtual window. To cause that output to actually be displayed, **InvalidateRect( )** is called. Of course, you can include a separate output statement that simultaneously writes to the physical window, too, if you also want the output to appear in the physical window prior to a **WM_PAINT** message being received.

Lines of text are output to the screen using **TextOut( )**. When outputting text, you must specify the starting point for each string. Therefore, to write several lines of text, you must manually advance the vertical coordinate to the starting point of each line. However, since Windows allows character fonts of differing sizes, you need to obtain the distance between lines dynamically, at runtime. To do this, the function **GetTextMetrics( )** is used. It obtains a copy of all the information related to text and puts it into a **TEXTMETRIC** structure. The two members of this structure that are needed to compute the starting point of the next line are **tmHeight** and **tmExternalLeading**. These members contain the height of the character set and the space between lines, respectively. Both of these values are in terms of pixels.

Finally, the physical device context is released. However, the memory device context stays in existence until the program ends.

Responding to WM_PAINT

To restore the contents of the window when a **WM_PAINT** message is received, the program simply copies the virtual window to the physical window, as shown here:

```
case WM_PAINT:
  hdc = BeginPaint(hwnd, &ps);

  // copy virtual window to screen
  BitBlt(hdc, 0, 0, maxX, maxY, memdc, 0, 0, SRCCOPY);

  EndPaint(hwnd, &ps);
  break;
```

The actual copying of the bitmaps is done by using the **BitBlt( )** function. **BitBlt( )** copies a bitmap from one device context to another using a very fast bit-block transfer. It has this prototype:

BOOL BitBlt(HDC *hDest*, int *X*, int *Y*, int *Width*, int *Height*,
   HDC *hSource*, int *SourceX*, int *SourceY*,
   DWORD *dwHow*);

Here, *hDest* is the handle of the target device context, and *X* and *Y* are the upper-left coordinates at which point the bitmap will be drawn. The width and height of the bitmap are specified in *Width* and *Height*. The *hSource* parameter contains the handle of the source device context, which in this case will be the memory context obtained using **CreateCompatibleDC( )**. The *SourceX* and *SourceY* specify the upper-left coordinates in the bitmap at which point the copy operation will begin. The value of *dwHow* determines how the bit-by-bit contents of the bitmap will actually be copied. Some of its most common values are shown here:

dwHow	Effect
DSTINVERT	Inverts the bits in the destination bitmap.
SRCAND	ANDs bitmap with current destination.
SRCCOPY	Copies bitmap as is, overwriting previous contents.
SRCERASE	ANDs bitmap with the inverted bits of destination bitmap.
SRCINVERT	XORs bitmap with current destination.
SRCPAINT	ORs bitmap with current destination.

The function returns non-zero if successful and zero otherwise.

In the program, the **BitBlt( )** function copies the image from **memdc** into **hdc**. Remember, the parameter **SRCCOPY** simply means to copy the image as is, without alteration, directly from the source to the target. Because all output has been stored in **memdc**, this statement causes that output to actually be displayed on the screen. More importantly, if the window is covered and then uncovered, **WM_PAINT** will be received and this code causes the contents of that window to be automatically restored.

Optimizing Virtual Window Repaints

In the preceding program, each time a **WM_PAINT** message is received, the entire contents of the window are restored—whether they need to be or not. This is, of course, not the best way. It is important to understand that restoring a window is expensive in terms of time. The larger the window, the longer it takes to restore it. Therefore, it is to your benefit to repaint only those parts of the window that actually need it. For example, it is quite common to cover only a corner of a window. When that corner is uncovered, it will be faster to restore only that portion than to repaint the entire window. Fortunately, Windows provides information that will allow us to do precisely that. By repainting only those parts of a window that actually require it, repaints take less time and your application has a much snappier feel. Frankly, optimizing window repainting is one of the most important performance improvements that you can make to your program.

As all Windows programmers know, when a **WM_PAINT** message is processed, you must call **BeginPaint( )** to obtain a device context. However, what is sometimes overlooked is that **BeginPaint( )** also obtains information about the display state of the window. The prototype for **BeginPaint( )** is shown here:

HDC BeginPaint(HWND *hwnd*, PAINTSTRUCT **lpPS*);

BeginPaint( ) returns a device context if successful or **NULL** on failure. Here, *hwnd* is the handle of the window for which the device context is being obtained. The second parameter is a pointer to a structure of type **PAINTSTRUCT**. The structure pointed to by *lpPS* will contain information that your program can use to repaint the window. **PAINTSTRUCT** is defined like this:

```
typedef struct tagPAINTSTRUCT {
  HDC hdc;                 // handle to device context
  BOOL fErase;             // true if background must be erased
  RECT rcPaint;            // coordinates of region to redraw
  BOOL fRestore;           // reserved
  BOOL fIncUpdate;         // reserved
  BYTE rgbReserved[32];    // reserved
} PAINTSTRUCT;
```

Here, **hdc** will contain the device context of the window that needs to be repainted. This DC is also returned by the call to **BeginPaint( )**. **fErase** will be nonzero if the background of the window needs to be erased. However, as long as you specified a background brush when you created the window, you can ignore the **fErase** member. Windows will erase the window for you.

For the discussion at hand, the element that we are most interested in is **rcPaint**. It contains the coordinates of the region of the window that needs to be repainted. Any part of the window outside that region need not be restored. We can take advantage of this information to reduce the time needed to restore a window. When a **WM_PAINT** message is received, repaint only the portion of the window defined by **rcPaint**.

Utilizing the information in **rcPaint** is easy when using a virtual window. Simply copy the corresponding region of the virtual window to the physical window. Since the two device contexts are identical, so are their coordinate systems. The coordinates that are contained in **rcPaint** can be used for both the physical window and the virtual window.

Code

FastPaint.cpp Here is an improved **WM_PAINT** handler that can be substituted into the VirtWin.cpp program. Because this version copies only the rectangle defined by **rcPaint**, no time is wasted copying information that has not been overwritten.

```
case WM_PAINT: // an improved response to a repaint request
  hdc = BeginPaint(hwnd, &ps);

  //
  BitBlt(hdc, ps.rcPaint.left, ps.rcPaint.top,
         ps.rcPaint.right-ps.rcPaint.left, // width
         ps.rcPaint.bottom-ps.rcPaint.top, // height
         memdc,
         ps.rcPaint.left, ps.rcPaint.top,
         SRCCOPY);

  EndPaint(hwnd, &ps); /* release DC */
  break;
```

ANNOTATIONS

The **BitBlt( )** function uses the information provided in the **PAINTSTRUCT** obtained by **BeginPaint( )** to determine what part of the window should be repainted. As explained, since both the virtual window and the physical window use equivalent coordinate systems, the upper-left corner of the region, which is specified by **ps.rcPaint.top** and **ps.rcPaint.left**, is used as both the source and target locations. The width and height of the region to be copied is found by subtracting the left coordinate from the right, and the top coordinate from the bottom, respectively.

Notice how easy it is to optimize the repainting of a window when using the virtual window method. Almost no additional programming effort is required. As mentioned at the start of this chapter, the virtual window method of repainting is an elegant solution to many repaint-related operations.

Accessing an Oversized Virtual Window

Although the primary purpose of the virtual window technology is to provide a fast and convenient method of repainting a window, it offers substantial benefits in other areas as well. Here we will use it to solve a sometimes frustrating problem: scrolling a large amount of information through a smaller window. This situation can present itself two ways. First, most windows can have their size changed by the user. For example, a user may resize a window by dragging its borders. When a window is reduced in size, it is possible that all of its contents will not fit in the remaining client area. For many applications, it is acceptable to simply allow the information to be clipped. For others, scroll bars are added to the window to allow access to all of the information. In this case, there must be some mechanism to move the information through the remaining portion of the window. The second situation relates to the first. In some cases your application will require a very large workspace for its output. However, because of limits to the size of the screen, only a portion of this workspace will be able to be displayed at any one time. This type of situation is common in computer-aided design programs. The challenge is how best to manage this situation.

The common thread that links these two problems together is the need to access a bitmap that is larger than the physical window. As you will see, by using a virtual window, both of these situations can be dealt with easily.

In principle, accessing a larger virtual window through a smaller physical window is quite easy. The physical window simply displays a subregion of the larger space. That is, the physical window displays whatever portion of the virtual window that it is currently "over." When the physical window is scrolled, it is moved to another location within the virtual window. This process is similar to using a microfilm reader.

BigWin.cpp

Code

BigWin.cpp demonstrates how a large virtual window can be scrolled through a smaller physical window. In general, the program works like this. When the program starts, the portion of the upper-left corner of the virtual window that can fit into the current dimensions of the physical window is displayed. Each time the user changes the position of a scroll bar, the origin of the virtual window is shifted in the appropriate direction, and the window is repainted. This causes the virtual window to scroll through the physical window. Sample output is shown in Figure 2-2.

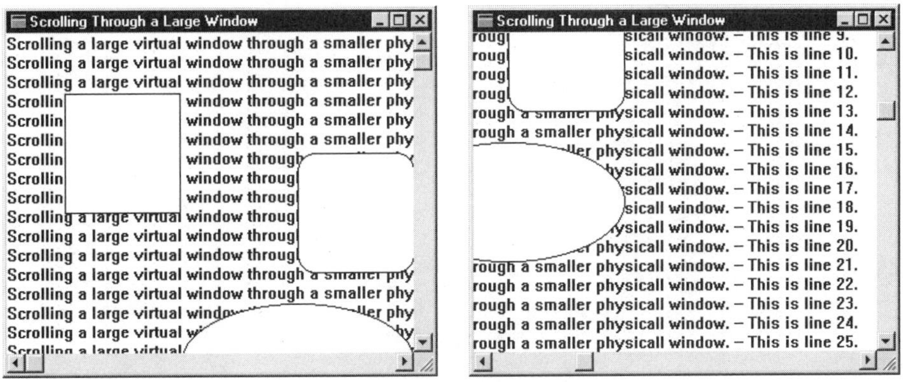

FIGURE 2-2. Sample output from **BigWin.cpp**

```cpp
// BigWin.cpp: Scrolling through a large virtual window.

#include <windows.h>
#include <cstring>
#include <cstdio>

LRESULT CALLBACK WindowFunc(HWND, UINT, WPARAM, LPARAM);

char szWinName[] = "MyWin"; // name of window class

int WINAPI WinMain(HINSTANCE hThisInst, HINSTANCE hPrevInst,
                   LPSTR lpszArgs, int nWinMode)
{
  HWND hwnd;
  MSG msg;
  WNDCLASSEX wcl;

  // Define a window class.
  wcl.cbSize = sizeof(WNDCLASSEX);
  wcl.hInstance = hThisInst;
  wcl.lpszClassName = szWinName;
  wcl.lpfnWndProc = WindowFunc;
  wcl.style = 0; // default style
  wcl.hIcon = LoadIcon(NULL, IDI_APPLICATION); // large icon
  wcl.hIconSm = NULL; // use small version of large icon
  wcl.hCursor = LoadCursor(NULL, IDC_ARROW);
```

```
wcl.hbrBackground = (HBRUSH) GetStockObject(WHITE_BRUSH);
wcl.cbClsExtra = 0;
wcl.cbWndExtra = 0;
wcl.lpszMenuName = NULL; // no menu

// Register the window class.
if(!RegisterClassEx(&wcl)) return 0;

// Create a window.
hwnd = CreateWindow(szWinName,
                    "Scrolling Through a Large Window",
                    WS_OVERLAPPEDWINDOW | WS_HSCROLL | WS_VSCROLL,
                    CW_USEDEFAULT, CW_USEDEFAULT,
                    CW_USEDEFAULT, CW_USEDEFAULT,
                    NULL, NULL, hThisInst, NULL);

// Display the window.
ShowWindow(hwnd, nWinMode);
UpdateWindow(hwnd);

// The message loop.
while(GetMessage(&msg, NULL, 0, 0))
{
  TranslateMessage(&msg);
  DispatchMessage(&msg);
}
return msg.wParam;
}


// The window procedure.
LRESULT CALLBACK WindowFunc(HWND hwnd, UINT message,
                            WPARAM wParam, LPARAM lParam)
{
  HDC hdc;
  PAINTSTRUCT ps;
  TEXTMETRIC tm;
  static SCROLLINFO si;
  char str[255], str2[255];
  int i;
  int inc;
```

```
static int maxX, maxY; // screen dimensions
static int orgX=0, orgY=0; // origin for current display
int X=0, Y=0;           // current output location
static HDC memdc;       // handle to virtual window context
static HBITMAP hbit;    // handle to virtual window bitmap
HBRUSH hbrush;          // handle to virtual window brush
static RECT curdim;     // current size of physical window

switch(message) {
  case WM_CREATE:
    // get screen coordinates
    maxX = GetSystemMetrics(SM_CXSCREEN);
    maxY = GetSystemMetrics(SM_CYSCREEN);

    // create virtual window that is twice as large
    maxX += maxX;
    maxY += maxY;

    // create a virtual window
    hdc = GetDC(hwnd);
    memdc = CreateCompatibleDC(hdc);
    hbit = CreateCompatibleBitmap(hdc, maxX, maxY);
    SelectObject(memdc, hbit);
    hbrush = (HBRUSH) GetStockObject(WHITE_BRUSH);
    SelectObject(memdc, hbrush);
    PatBlt(memdc, 0, 0, maxX, maxY, PATCOPY);

    // initialize scroll bar ranges
    GetClientRect(hwnd, &curdim);

    si.cbSize = sizeof(SCROLLINFO);
    si.fMask = SIF_RANGE;
    si.nMin = 0; si.nMax = maxX-curdim.right;
    SetScrollInfo(hwnd, SB_HORZ, &si, 1);
    si.nMax = maxY-curdim.bottom;
    SetScrollInfo(hwnd, SB_VERT, &si, 1);

    // get text metrics
    GetTextMetrics(hdc, &tm);

    // output lines of text
    for(i=0; i<100; i++) {
      strcpy(str,
```

```
                "Scrolling a large virtual window through ");
      strcat(str, "a smaller physical window.");

      sprintf(str2, " -- This is line %d.", i+1);
      strcat(str, str2);

      TextOut(memdc, X, Y, str, strlen(str)); // output to memory

      // advance to next line
      Y = Y + tm.tmHeight + tm.tmExternalLeading;
    }

    // output some graphics objects to the virtual window
    Rectangle(memdc, 50, 50, 150, 150);
    Ellipse(memdc, 150, 225, 350, 325);
    RoundRect(memdc, 250, 100, 350, 200, 30, 30);

    ReleaseDC(hwnd, hdc);
    InvalidateRect(hwnd, NULL, 0);
    break;
  case WM_PAINT:
    hdc = BeginPaint(hwnd, &ps);

    // copy virtual window onto screen
    BitBlt(hdc, ps.rcPaint.left, ps.rcPaint.top,
           ps.rcPaint.right-ps.rcPaint.left, // width
           ps.rcPaint.bottom-ps.rcPaint.top, // height
           memdc,
           ps.rcPaint.left+orgX, ps.rcPaint.top+orgY,
           SRCCOPY);

    EndPaint(hwnd, &ps);
    break;
  case WM_HSCROLL:
    switch(LOWORD(wParam)) {
      case SB_THUMBTRACK:
        orgX = HIWORD(wParam);
        break;
      case SB_LINERIGHT:
        if(orgX < maxX-curdim.right) orgX++;
        break;
      case SB_LINELEFT:
        if(orgX > 0) orgX--;
        break;
```

```
      case SB_PAGERIGHT:
        if(orgX+5 < maxX-curdim.right) orgX += 5;
        break;
      case SB_PAGELEFT:
        if(orgX-5 > 0) orgX -= 5;
        break;
    }
    si.fMask = SIF_POS;
    si.nPos = orgX;
    SetScrollInfo(hwnd, SB_HORZ, &si, 1);
    InvalidateRect(hwnd, NULL, 0);
    break;
  case WM_VSCROLL:
    switch(LOWORD(wParam)) {
      case SB_THUMBTRACK:
        orgY = HIWORD(wParam);
        break;
      case SB_LINEDOWN:
        if(orgY < maxY-curdim.bottom) orgY++;
        break;
      case SB_LINEUP:
        if(orgY > 0) orgY--;
        break;
      case SB_PAGEDOWN:
        if(orgY+5 < maxY-curdim.bottom) orgY += 5;
        break;
      case SB_PAGEUP:
        if(orgY-5 > 0) orgY -= 5;
        break;
    }
    si.fMask = SIF_POS;
    si.nPos = orgY;
    SetScrollInfo(hwnd, SB_VERT, &si, 1);
    InvalidateRect(hwnd, NULL, 0);
    break;
  case WM_SIZE:
    // update virtual window origins if window size increasing
    inc = HIWORD(lParam)-curdim.bottom;
    if(inc > 0 && orgY >= (maxY-curdim.bottom)) orgY -= inc;
    if(orgY < 0) orgY = 0;

    inc = LOWORD(lParam)-curdim.right;
    if(inc > 0 && orgX >= (maxX-curdim.right)) orgX -= inc;
    if(orgX < 0) orgX = 0;
```

```
     // store new window extents
     curdim.right = LOWORD(lParam);
     curdim.bottom = HIWORD(lParam);

     // reinitialize scroll bar ranges
     si.cbSize = sizeof(SCROLLINFO);
     si.fMask = SIF_RANGE | SIF_POS;
     si.nMin = 0;
     si.nMax = maxX-curdim.right;
     si.nPos = orgX;
     SetScrollInfo(hwnd, SB_HORZ, &si, 1);

     si.nMax = maxY-curdim.bottom;
     si.nPos = orgY;
     SetScrollInfo(hwnd, SB_VERT, &si, 1);

     InvalidateRect(hwnd, NULL, 0);
     break;
   case WM_DESTROY:
     DeleteDC(memdc);
     DeleteObject(hbit);
     PostQuitMessage(0);
     break;
   default:
     return DefWindowProc(hwnd, message, wParam, lParam);
  }
  return 0;
}
```

ANNOTATIONS

BigWin.cpp uses essentially the same virtual window mechanism as **VirtWin.cpp**, described earlier. However, a substantial amount of additional code is required to handle the scrolling of a larger virtual window through a smaller physical window. The first thing to notice is that the window styles **WS_HSCROLL** and **WS_VSCROLL** have been added to the window style parameter in the call to **CreateWindow( )**. This ensures that the standard horizontal and vertical scroll bars will be included in the window. The rest of the changes occur in **WindowFunc( )** as described in the following sections.

The WM_CREATE Handler

The **WM_CREATE** handler performs three functions. It creates the virtual window, initializes the scroll bars, and writes some output to the virtual window. The code that creates the virtual window and writes output to it is similar to that described for the **VirtWin.cpp** program with one notable difference: The virtual window is twice as large as the screen. This is accomplished by the following code sequence:

```
// get screen coordinates
maxX = GetSystemMetrics(SM_CXSCREEN);
maxY = GetSystemMetrics(SM_CYSCREEN);

// create virtual window that is twice as large
maxX += maxX;
maxY += maxY;

// create a virtual window
hdc = GetDC(hwnd);
memdc = CreateCompatibleDC(hdc);
hbit = CreateCompatibleBitmap(hdc, maxX, maxY);
SelectObject(memdc, hbit);
hbrush = (HBRUSH) GetStockObject(WHITE_BRUSH);
SelectObject(memdc, hbrush);
PatBlt(memdc, 0, 0, maxX, maxY, PATCOPY);
```

The dimensions of the screen are obtained and a virtual window is constructed as before, but for demonstration purposes, the values of **maxX** and **maxY** are doubled. This is, of course, an arbitrary size that vividly illustrates the use of a large workspace. Unless you need such a large workspace, you will not generally want to create such a large virtual window.

Next, the scroll bars are initialized using this sequence:

```
// initialize scroll bar ranges
GetClientRect(hwnd, &curdim);

si.cbSize = sizeof(SCROLLINFO);
si.fMask = SIF_RANGE;
si.nMin = 0; si.nMax = maxX-curdim.right;
SetScrollInfo(hwnd, SB_HORZ, &si, 1);
si.nMax = maxY-curdim.bottom;
SetScrollInfo(hwnd, SB_VERT, &si, 1);
```

First, the current dimensions of the physical window are obtained through a call to **GetClientRect( )** and stored in **curdim**, which is a static variable of type **RECT**.

Next, the static variable **si**, which is of type **SCROLLINFO**, is initialized and used to set the range of the scroll bars.

Scroll bar information is set using **SetScrollInfo( )**. Its prototype is shown here:

int SetScrollInfo(HWND *hwnd*, int *which*,
                    LPSCROLLINFO *lpSI*, BOOL *repaint*);

Here, *hwnd* is the handle that identifies the scroll bar. For window scroll bars, this is the handle of the window that owns the scroll bar. For scroll bar controls, this is the handle of the scroll bar itself. The value of *which* determines which scroll bar is affected. If you are setting the attributes of the vertical window scroll bar, then this parameter must be **SB_VERT**. If you are setting the attributes of the horizontal window scroll bar, this value must be **SB_HORZ**. (To set a scroll bar control, this value must be **SB_CTL** and *hwnd* must be the handle of the control.) The attributes are set according to the information pointed to by *lpSI*. If *repaint* is true, then the scroll bar is redrawn. If false, the bar is not redisplayed. The function returns the position of the slider box.

The *lpSI* parameter points to a structure of type **SCROLLINFO**, which is defined like this:

```
typedef struct tagSCROLLINFO
{
  UINT cbSize;     // size of SCROLLINFO
  UINT fMask;      // operation performed
  int nMin;        // minimum range
  int nMax;        // maximum range
  UINT nPage;      // page value
  int nPos;        // slider box position
  int nTrackPos;   // current tracking position
} SCROLLINFO;
```

Here, **cbSize** must contain the size of the **SCROLLINFO** structure. The value or values contained in **fMask** determine which of the remaining members contain valid information. **fMask** must be one or more of these values:

Value	Meaning
SIF_ALL	Same as SIF_PAGE	SIF_POS	SIF_RANGE	SIF_TRACKPOS.
SIF_DISABLENOSCROLL	Scroll bar is disabled rather than removed if its range is set to zero.
SIF_PAGE	**nPage** contains valid information.
SIF_POS	**nPos** contains valid information.
SIF_RANGE	**nMin** and **nMax** contain valid information.
SIF_TRACKPOS	**nTrackPos** contains valid information.

nPage contains the current page setting for proportional scroll bars. **nPos** contains the position of the slider box. **nMin** and **nMax** contain the minimum and maximum range of the scroll bar. **nTrackPos** contains the current tracking position. The tracking position is the current position of the slider box while it is being dragged by the user. This value cannot be set.

The range of the scroll bar determines how many positions there are between one end and the other. By default, window scroll bars have a range of 0 to 100, but this default is not useful to the program. Instead, the scroll bar ranges are set to start at zero and run through to the endpoints of the virtual window, less the amount of the virtual window that will actually fit into the physical window. For example, the vertical scroll bar range begins at zero and ends at **maxX –curdim.bottom**. By subtracting off the height and width of the physical window, the slider boxes of the scroll bars will be at their farthest extremes when the physical window is displaying the lower-right corner of the virtual window.

Next, the **WM_CREATE** handler outputs 100 lines of text. This is actually more text than will fit into either window, but it ensures that the virtual window is filled. Finally, the graphics figures are drawn, the device context for the physical window is released, and the current window is invalidated, causing a **WM_PAINT** message to be sent.

The WM_PAINT Handler

The **WM_PAINT** handler copies that portion of the virtual window that has been scrolled into view onto the physical window using this call to **BitBlt( )**:

```
// copy virtual window onto screen
BitBlt(hdc, ps.rcPaint.left, ps.rcPaint.top,
       ps.rcPaint.right-ps.rcPaint.left, // width
       ps.rcPaint.bottom-ps.rcPaint.top, // height
       memdc,
       ps.rcPaint.left+orgX, ps.rcPaint.top+orgY,
       SRCCOPY);
```

The static variables **orgX** and **orgY** specify the origin of that portion of the virtual window that is currently displayed within the physical window. At the start, both **orgX** and **orgY** are zero. Each time a scroll bar is moved, their values are updated appropriately. Thus, the call to **BitBlt( )** displays only that part of the virtual window that has been scrolled into view. Notice that only the portion of the window that needs to be repainted is actually restored. As explained in the previous sections, this is an efficient way to handle repaint requests.

The Scroll Bar Handlers

When a scroll bar is accessed by the user, it sends either a **WM_VSCROLL** or a **WM_HSCROLL** message, depending upon whether it is the vertical or horizontal scroll bar, respectively. For standard window scroll bars, **lParam** is **NULL**. The value of the low-order word of **wParam** contains a code that describes the activity. Here are values handled by the program.

SB_LINEUP	Scroll bar moved up one unit.
SB_LINEDOWN	Scroll bar moved down one unit.
SB_PAGEUP	Scroll bar moved up one page.
SB_PAGEDOWN	Scroll bar moved down one page.
SB_LINELEFT	Scroll bar moved left one unit.
SB_LINERIGHT	Scroll bar moved right one unit.
SB_PAGELEFT	Scroll bar moved left one page.
SB_PAGERIGHT	Scroll bar moved right one page.
SB_THUMBTRACK	Slider box is being dragged.

The high-order word of **wParam** contains the position of the slider box.

The program handles scroll bar events by changing how the virtual window is mapped to the physical window. When the vertical scroll bar is accessed, **orgY** is updated. When the horizontal scroll bar is changed, **orgX** is adjusted. Thus, changing a scroll bar changes the location of the point within the virtual window that defines the origin of the viewable portion. Once the proper variable has been changed, the scroll bar is updated to reflect the change. Finally, the window is repainted, causing the virtual window to scroll through the physical window. Let's see how this process works in practice by going through the **WM_HSCROLL** handler, in detail. (The **WM_VSCROLL** handler works in the same fashion.)

When a **WM_HSCROLL** message is received, the following **switch** statement adjusts the value of **orgX**.

```
switch(LOWORD(wParam)) {
  case SB_THUMBTRACK:
    orgX = HIWORD(wParam);
    break;
  case SB_LINERIGHT:
    if(orgX < maxX-curdim.right) orgX++;
    break;
  case SB_LINELEFT:
    if(orgX > 0) orgX--;
    break;
```

```
wcl.cbClsExtra = 0;
wcl.cbWndExtra = 0;
wcl.lpszMenuName = NULL; // no menu

// Register the window class.
if(!RegisterClassEx(&wcl)) return 0;

// Create a window.
hwnd = CreateWindow(szWinName,
                    "Demonstrating a Double Buffer",
                    WS_OVERLAPPEDWINDOW,
                    CW_USEDEFAULT, CW_USEDEFAULT,
                    CW_USEDEFAULT, CW_USEDEFAULT,
                    NULL, NULL, hThisInst, NULL);

// Display the window.
ShowWindow(hwnd, nWinMode);
UpdateWindow(hwnd);

// The message loop.
while(GetMessage(&msg, NULL, 0, 0))
{
  TranslateMessage(&msg);
  DispatchMessage(&msg);
}
return msg.wParam;
}


// The window procedure.
LRESULT CALLBACK WindowFunc(HWND hwnd, UINT message,
                           WPARAM wParam, LPARAM lParam)
{
  HDC hdc;
  PAINTSTRUCT ps;
  TEXTMETRIC tm;
  char str[255];
  int i;

  static int maxX, maxY; // screen dimensions
  int X=0, Y=0;          // current output location
  static HDC memdc;      // handle to virtual window context
  static HDC bufdc1, bufdc2;   // handles to buffers
```

```
static HBITMAP hbit1, hbit2;  // handle to bitmaps
HBRUSH hbrush;                // handle to virtual window brush

switch(message) {
  case WM_CREATE:
    // get screen coordinates
    maxX = GetSystemMetrics(SM_CXSCREEN);
    maxY = GetSystemMetrics(SM_CYSCREEN);

    hdc = GetDC(hwnd);

    // create the screen buffers
    bufdc1 = CreateCompatibleDC(hdc);
    hbit1 = CreateCompatibleBitmap(hdc, maxX, maxY);
    SelectObject(bufdc1, hbit1);
    hbrush = (HBRUSH) GetStockObject(WHITE_BRUSH);
    SelectObject(bufdc1, hbrush);
    PatBlt(bufdc1, 0, 0, maxX, maxY, PATCOPY);

    bufdc2 = CreateCompatibleDC(hdc);
    hbit2 = CreateCompatibleBitmap(hdc, maxX, maxY);
    SelectObject(bufdc2, hbit2);
    SelectObject(bufdc2, hbrush);
    PatBlt(bufdc2, 0, 0, maxX, maxY, PATCOPY);

    // get text metrics
    GetTextMetrics(hdc, &tm);

    // output some text to the first buffer
    for(i=0; i<24; i++) {
      strcpy(str, "This is written to the first buffer.");
      TextOut(bufdc1, X, Y, str, strlen(str));

      // advance to next line
      Y = Y + tm.tmHeight + tm.tmExternalLeading;
    }

    // Now, output to second buffer
    strcpy(str, "This is written to the second buffer.");
    TextOut(bufdc2, 0, 0, str, strlen(str));

    Rectangle(bufdc2, 50, 50, 150, 150);
    Ellipse(bufdc2, 150, 225, 350, 325);
```

```
      RoundRect(bufdc2, 250, 100, 350, 200, 30, 30);

   memdc = bufdc1; // start with first buffer

   // start a timer
   SetTimer(hwnd, 1, 1000, NULL);

   ReleaseDC(hwnd, hdc);
   InvalidateRect(hwnd, NULL, 0);
   break;
case WM_TIMER:
   // swap screen buffers once each second
   if(memdc == bufdc1) memdc = bufdc2;
   else memdc = bufdc1;
   InvalidateRect(hwnd, NULL, 0);
   break;
case WM_PAINT:
   hdc = BeginPaint(hwnd, &ps);


   // copy only the necessary portion of the virtual window
   BitBlt(hdc, ps.rcPaint.left, ps.rcPaint.top,
      ps.rcPaint.right-ps.rcPaint.left, // width
      ps.rcPaint.bottom-ps.rcPaint.top, // height
      memdc,
      ps.rcPaint.left, ps.rcPaint.top,
      SRCCOPY);

   EndPaint(hwnd, &ps);
   break;
case WM_DESTROY:
   DeleteDC(bufdc1);
   DeleteDC(bufdc2);
   DeleteObject(hbit1);
   DeleteObject(hbit2);
   KillTimer(hwnd, 1);
   PostQuitMessage(0);
   break;
default:
   return DefWindowProc(hwnd, message, wParam, lParam);
}
return 0;
}
```

ANNOTATIONS

Most of the code in the program will be familiar because it is the same as that used by the earlier programs. Notice, however, that three memory device context handles are created inside **WindowFunc( )**: **memdc**, **bufdc1**, and **bufdc2**. **bufdc1** and **bufdc2** hold the buffered output, and **memdc** holds a handle to the memory buffer that is currently selected for display.

In **WM_CREATE**, two virtual windows (i.e., screen buffers) are created using this code sequence:

```
// create the screen buffers
bufdc1 = CreateCompatibleDC(hdc);
hbit1 = CreateCompatibleBitmap(hdc, maxX, maxY);
SelectObject(bufdc1, hbit1);
hbrush = (HBRUSH) GetStockObject(WHITE_BRUSH);
SelectObject(bufdc1, hbrush);
PatBlt(bufdc1, 0, 0, maxX, maxY, PATCOPY);

bufdc2 = CreateCompatibleDC(hdc);
hbit2 = CreateCompatibleBitmap(hdc, maxX, maxY);
SelectObject(bufdc2, hbit2);
SelectObject(bufdc2, hbrush);
PatBlt(bufdc2, 0, 0, maxX, maxY, PATCOPY);
```

As you can see, two completely separate memory device contexts are created, and both use completely separate and distinct bitmaps. Thus, **bufdc1** and **bufdc2** refer to two different virtual windows.

Next, output is written to the two buffers, as shown here:

```
// output some text to the first buffer
for(i=0; i<24; i++) {
  strcpy(str, "This is written to the first buffer.");
  TextOut(bufdc1, X, Y, str, strlen(str));

  // advance to next line
  Y = Y + tm.tmHeight + tm.tmExternalLeading;
}

// Now, output to second buffer
strcpy(str, "This is written to the second buffer.");
TextOut(bufdc2, 0, 0, str, strlen(str));

Rectangle(bufdc2, 50, 50, 150, 150);
Ellipse(bufdc2, 150, 225, 350, 325);
RoundRect(bufdc2, 250, 100, 350, 200, 30, 30);
```

Then, the following sequence assigns **memdc** the handle to the first buffer, and starts a timer with an interval of one second.

```
memdc = bufdc1; // start with first buffer

// start a timer
SetTimer(hwnd, 1, 1000, NULL);
```

Each time a **WM_TIMER** message is received, the following code executes.

```
case WM_TIMER:
  // swap screen buffers once each second
  if(memdc == bufdc1) memdc = bufdc2;
  else memdc = bufdc1;
  InvalidateRect(hwnd, NULL, 0);
  break;
```

With each click of the timer, the buffer assigned to **memdc** is changed, alternating between **bufdc1** and **bufdc2**. The window is then invalidated, causing a **WM_PAINT** message to be generated.

Inside **WM_PAINT** the device context defined by **memdc** is copied to the screen using **BitBlt( )**. When this occurs, the currently selected buffer is displayed. This causes the contents of that buffer to be "instantly" shown. Thus, you can very quickly switch between the two by simply selecting the desired window. For example, if you have an application that presents two different views of the same information, you could quickly switch between those views by assigning each view to its own virtual window.

Tips for Using MFC

Virtual windows are easily implemented when using MFC. In general, simply substitute the class-based versions of the various bitmap and device-context functions. In MFC, a device context is encapsulated by the **CDC** class. Thus, many of these functions are members of **CDC**, such as **CDC::BitBlt( )**, **CDC::CreateCompatibleDC( )**, and **CDC::PatBlt( )**. Bitmaps are encapsulated by the **CBitmap** class and you will use **CBitmap::CreateCompatibleBitmap( )** to construct a compatible bitmap.

Here is a sequence of MFC-based code that constructs a virtual window.

```
CDC m_memDC;        // virtual window device context
CBitmap m_bmp;      // virtual window bitmap
CBrush m_bkbrush;   // brush for virtual window
CClientDC DC(this); // DC for physical window
```

```
maxX = GetSystemMetrics(SM_CXSCREEN);
maxY = GetSystemMetrics(SM_CYSCREEN);

m_memDC.CreateCompatibleDC(&DC);
m_bmp.CreateCompatibleBitmap(&DC, maxX, maxY);
m_memDC.SelectObject(&m_bmp);
m_bkbrush.CreateStockObject(WHITE_BRUSH);
m_memDC.SelectObject(&m_bkbrush);
m_memDC.PatBlt(0, 0, maxX, maxY, PATCOPY);
```

As you can see, it follows the same general pattern as that used to create a virtual window for an API-based program.

A Text Toolkit

One of the first things that a Windows programmer learns is that the outputting of text is a nontrivial operation in a Windows program. For example, there is no equivalent of the C **printf( )** function, or C++'s I/O operators. For the most part, all text must be manually formatted and positioned in a window by you. Although this requires a bit more work on your part, it does give you detailed control over the way that text is displayed. Windows provides only the most rudimentary support for text output to the client area. The main output function is **TextOut( )**. This function will only display a string beginning at a specified location. It will not format output, perform conversions, or even automatically perform a carriage return/linefeed sequence, for example. Instead, managing output to the client window is completely your job.

Despite these shortcomings, Windows does give you low-level control of text, making it easy to build your own high-level output functions. This chapter develops a toolkit of text output functions, including a Windows version of **printf( )**, a rotated text output function, a scrolling window class, and a multicolumn class. Also included in the toolkit is a function that enumerates the fonts available in a system. This toolkit simplifies the creation of many programs, especially utility programs in which a sophisticated user interface is not required. Such functions are also useful when debugging.

We begin by reviewing the fundamentals of text output management.

Text Output Fundamentals

In Windows, not all characters are the same size. Windows supports many different type fonts, and these fonts can be of different sizes. Also, most text fonts are proportional. Therefore, the character "i" is usually not as wide as the character "w" and the height of each character and the length of descenders vary among fonts. In addition, the amount of space between horizontal lines is also changeable. That these (and other) attributes are variable would not be of too much consequence except for the fact that Windows demands that you, the programmer, manually manage virtually all text output.

The fact that the size of each font may be different (and that fonts may be changed while your program is executing) implies that there must be some way to determine the dimensions and various other attributes of the currently selected font. For example, in order to write one line of text after another you must have some way of knowing how tall the font is and how many pixels are between lines. The API function that obtains information about the current font is called **GetTextMetrics( )**, and it has this prototype:

BOOL GetTextMetrics(HDC *hdc*, LPTEXTMETRIC *lpTAttrib*);

Here, *hdc* is the handle of the output device, which is generally obtained using **GetDC( )** or **BeginPaint( )**, and *lpTAttrib* is a pointer to a structure of type **TEXTMETRIC** that will, upon return, contain the text metrics for the currently selected font. The **TEXTMETRIC** structure is defined as shown here:

```
typedef struct tagTEXTMETRIC
{
  LONG tmHeight;              // total height of font
  LONG tmAscent;             // height above base line
  LONG tmDescent;            // length of descenders
  LONG tmInternalLeading;    // space above characters
  LONG tmExternalLeading;    // blank space between rows
  LONG tmAveCharWidth;       // average width
  LONG tmMaxCharWidth;       // maximum width
  LONG tmWeight;             // weight
  LONG tmOverhang;           // extra width added to special fonts
  LONG tmDigitizedAspectX;   // horizontal aspect
  LONG tmDigitizedAspectY;   // vertical aspect
  BYTE tmFirstChar;          // first character in font
  BYTE tmLastChar;           // last character in font
  BYTE tmDefaultChar;        // default character
  BYTE tmBreakChar;          // character used to separate words
  BYTE tmItalic;             // non-zero if italic
  BYTE tmUnderlined;         // non-zero if underlined
  BYTE tmStruckOut;          // non-zero if struckout
  BYTE tmPitchAndFamily;     // pitch and family of font
  BYTE tmCharSet;            // character set identifier
} TEXTMERIC;
```

Computing the Height of a Line of Text

When outputting text, perhaps the most important value that you will need to know is the height of a line—that is, the vertical distance between lines of text. This value is needed if you want to output more than one line of text to a window. Because each font defines the height of its characters and the amount of space required between lines, it is not possible to know in advance the vertical (Y) coordinate of the next line of text. To determine where the next line of text will begin, you must call **GetTextMetrics( )** to acquire two values: the character height and the amount of space between lines. These values are given in the **tmHeight** and **tmExternalLeading** fields of the **TEXTMETRIC** structure. **tmHeight** contains the height of the font. **tmExternalLeading** contains, in essence, the number of vertical units that should be left blank between lines of text. This value is separate from the height of the font. Thus, both values are needed to compute where the next line of text will begin. By adding them together, you obtain the number of vertical units between lines.

Computing the Length of a String

Windows does not automatically maintain a text cursor or keep track of your current output location. This means that if you wish to display one string after another on the same line, then you will need to remember where the previous output left off. This implies that you have some way of knowing the length of a string in logical units. Because characters in most fonts are not the same size, it is not possible to know the length of a string, in logical units, by simply knowing how many characters it contains. That is, the result returned by **strlen( )** is not meaningful to managing output to a window because characters are of differing widths. To solve this problem, Windows includes the API function **GetTextExtentPoint32( )**, whose prototype is shown here:

>   BOOL GetTextExtentPoint32(HDC *hdc*, LPCSTR *lpszStr*,
>   int *len*, LPSIZE *lpSize*);

Here, *hdc* is the handle of the output device. The string whose length you want is pointed to by *lpszStr*. The number of characters in the string is specified in *len*. The width and height of the string, in logical units, is returned in the **SIZE** structure pointed to by *lpSize*. The **SIZE** structure is defined as shown here:

```
typedef struct tagSIZE {
  LONG cx; // width
  LONG cy; // height
} SIZE;
```

Upon return from a call to **GetTextExtentPoint32( )**, the **cx** field will contain the length of the string. Therefore, this value can be used to determine the starting point for the next string to be displayed if you want to continue on from where the previous output left off.

NEWTEXTMETRIC and NEWTEXTMETRICEX

Before moving on, a small digression is in order. While not used by **GetTextMetrics( )**, there is an enhanced version of **TEXTMETRIC**, called **NEWTEXTMETRIC**.

NEWTEXTMETRIC is exactly the same as **TEXTMETRIC** except that it adds four additional fields at the end. These fields provide support for TrueType fonts. (TrueType fonts have superior scalability features.) The new fields in **NEWTEXTMETRIC** are shown here:

```
DWORD ntmFlags;       // indicates style of font
UINT ntmSizeEM;       // size of an em
UINT ntmCellHeight;   // font height
UINT ntmAvgWidth;     // average character width
```

There has recently been added to Win32 an extension to **NEWTEXTMETRIC**, called **NEWTEXTMETRICEX**. It is defined like this:

```
typedef struct tagNEWTEXTMETRICEX
{
  NEWTEXTMETRIC ntmTm;
  FONTSIGNATURE ntmFontSig; // font signature
} NEWTEXTMETRICEX;
```

As you can see, it includes all of **NEWTEXTMETRIC** and adds the structure **FONTSIGNATURE**, which contains information relating to Unicode and code pages.

For the purposes of this chapter, none of these fields added by **NEWTEXTMETRIC** or **NEWTEXTMETRICEX** are needed. However, they may be of value to applications that you create.

A Windows-Based Version of printf( )

If there is one function that the average Windows programmer wishes were included in the API it would be a Windows-based version of the classic C function **printf( )**. Even though we now have the class-based I/O of C++ with its convenient I/O operators, nothing has yet exceeded **printf( )** in its ability to handle all types of format conversions in a compact, easy-to-use form. The only trouble is that **printf( )** does not work with Windows! Fortunately, it is quite easy to create a Windows-based version.

WinPrint.cpp

Code

The following program contains a function called **WinPrintf( )** that performs the same operations as **printf( )** except that it sends its output to the device context that it is passed. It performs all format conversions and handles the outputting of tabs and new lines. As the following example shows, it is a very useful function to have in your text-management toolkit. Sample output is shown in Figure 3-1.

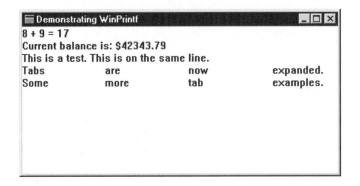

FIGURE 3-1.   Sample output from **WinPrint.cpp**

```cpp
// WinPrint.cpp: Demonstrates the WinPrintf() function.

#include <windows.h>
#include <cstring>
#include <cstdio>

LRESULT CALLBACK WindowFunc(HWND, UINT, WPARAM, LPARAM);

char szWinName[] = "MyWin"; // name of window class

int WinPrintf(HDC hdc, char *str, ...);

int WINAPI WinMain(HINSTANCE hThisInst, HINSTANCE hPrevInst,
                   LPSTR lpszArgs, int nWinMode)
{
  MSG msg;
  WNDCLASSEX wcl;
  HWND hwnd;

  // Define a window class.
  wcl.cbSize = sizeof(WNDCLASSEX);
  wcl.hInstance = hThisInst;
  wcl.lpszClassName = szWinName;
  wcl.lpfnWndProc = WindowFunc;
  wcl.style = 0; // default style
  wcl.hIcon = LoadIcon(NULL, IDI_APPLICATION); // large icon
```

```
    wcl.hIconSm = NULL; // use small version of large icon
    wcl.hCursor = LoadCursor(NULL, IDC_ARROW);
    wcl.hbrBackground = (HBRUSH) GetStockObject(WHITE_BRUSH);
    wcl.cbClsExtra = 0;
    wcl.cbWndExtra = 0;
    wcl.lpszMenuName = NULL; // no menu

    // Register the window class.
    if(!RegisterClassEx(&wcl)) return 0;

    // Create a window.
    hwnd = CreateWindow(szWinName,
                        "Demonstrating WinPrintf",
                        WS_OVERLAPPEDWINDOW,
                        CW_USEDEFAULT, CW_USEDEFAULT,
                        CW_USEDEFAULT, CW_USEDEFAULT,
                        NULL, NULL, hThisInst, NULL);

    // Display the window.
    ShowWindow(hwnd, nWinMode);
    UpdateWindow(hwnd);

    // The message loop.
    while(GetMessage(&msg, NULL, 0, 0))
    {
      TranslateMessage(&msg);
      DispatchMessage(&msg);
    }
    return msg.wParam;
}

// The window procedure.
LRESULT CALLBACK WindowFunc(HWND hwnd, UINT message,
                            WPARAM wParam, LPARAM lParam)
{
  HDC hdc;
  PAINTSTRUCT ps;

  switch(message) {
    case WM_PAINT:
      hdc = BeginPaint(hwnd, &ps);

      WinPrintf(NULL, ""); // reset X and Y
```

```
      WinPrintf(hdc, "%d + %d = %d\n", 8, 9, 8+9);
      WinPrintf(hdc, "Current balance is: $%7.2f\n", 42343.79);
      WinPrintf(hdc, "This is a test. ");
      WinPrintf(hdc, "This is on the same line.\n");
      WinPrintf(hdc, "Tabs\tare \tnow\texpanded.\n");
      WinPrintf(hdc, "Some\tmore\ttab\texamples.\n");

      EndPaint(hwnd, &ps);
      break;
    case WM_DESTROY:
      PostQuitMessage(0);
      break;
    default:
      return DefWindowProc(hwnd, message, wParam, lParam);
  }
  return 0;
}

// A general-purpose, window-based output function.
int WinPrintf(HDC hdc, char *str, ...)
{
  TEXTMETRIC tm; // current text metrics
  SIZE size;     // holds length of line

  char result[1024]; // formatted text
  char chstr[2];     // string-ized character for output
  char *p;           // pointer to result

  int retval;        // holds return value
  int tabwidth;      // width in tab for current font
  int lineheight;    // height of a line of text
  static int X=0, Y=0; // current output location

  if(hdc == NULL) { // reset X and Y
    X = Y = 0;
    return 0;
  }

  va_list ptr; // get arg pointer
```

```
// point ptr to the first arg after str
va_start(ptr, str);

// pass args to vsprintf()
retval = vsprintf(result, str, ptr);

// get text metrics
GetTextMetrics(hdc, &tm);
tabwidth = 8 * tm.tmMaxCharWidth;
lineheight = tm.tmHeight + tm.tmExternalLeading;

chstr[1] = 0; // put a null at end of chstr

// now, output the string
p = result;
while(*p) {
  if(*p == '\n') { // advance to next line
    Y += lineheight;
    X = 0;
    p++;
  }
  else if(*p == '\t') { // process a tab
    X = ((X / tabwidth) * tabwidth) + tabwidth;
    p++;
  }
  else { // handle a normal char
    chstr[0] = *p;
    p++;

    TextOut(hdc, X, Y, chstr, 1); // output each char

    // advance to next character position
    GetTextExtentPoint32(hdc, chstr, 1, &size);
    X += size.cx;
  }
}

return retval;
}
```

ANNOTATIONS

Let's begin by closely examining the **WinPrintf( )** function. This function works just like **printf( )** except that it directs its output to the device context specified as its first parameter. Its prototype is shown here:

```
int WinPrintf(HDC hdc, char *str, ...)
```

Here, **hdc** is the handle to the device context in which the text will be displayed. The second parameter, **str**, is a string that contains either normal characters or format commands. You can use any format command supported by **printf( )** in this string. After the format string, pass the arguments that match the format commands found in **str** (if any).

The function begins by declaring the variables shown here:

```
TEXTMETRIC tm; // current text metrics
SIZE size;      // holds length of line

char result[1024]; // formatted text
char chstr[2];     // string-ized character for output
char *p;           // pointer to result

int retval;     // holds return value
int tabwidth;   // width in tab for current font
int lineheight; // height of a line of text
static int X=0, Y=0; // current output location
```

The **TEXTMETRIC** object **tm** is used in a call to **GetTextMetrics( )** and **size** is used in a call to **GetTextExtentPoint32( )**. The formatted text that is ready for output is held in **result**. Notice that the maximum length of a line of text is 1,024 (including the null). You can change this limit if you like. The array **chstr** holds a "string-ized" character. That is, it will contain a string that consists of only one character. The pointer **p** points into the **result** array. The return value of the function is stored in **retval**, the width of a tab is stored in **tabwidth**, and the height of a line is stored in **lineheight**.

The coordinates at which each character of text is output are specified by the static variables **X** and **Y**. Their values are updated each time a character is displayed. This allows characters to be written consecutively on a line, line after line.

Next, the function checks if **hdc** is **NULL**. If it is, the values of **X** and **Y** are reset using this code:

```
if(hdc == NULL) { // reset X and Y
  X = Y = 0;
  return 0;
}
```

By passing **NULL** for **hdc**, you can restart printing from the top-left corner of the window.

Next, the following code declares a variable-length argument pointer called **ptr**, initializes it to point to the first argument following **str**, and then calls **vsprintf( )** to obtain a formatted string.

```
va_list ptr; // get arg pointer

// point ptr to the first arg after str
va_start(ptr, str);

// pass args to vsprintf()
retval = vsprintf(result, str, ptr);
```

The **vsprintf( )** function formats the string pointed to by **str**, along with the arguments pointed to by **ptr**, and puts the result in **result**. The value returned by **vsprintf( )** is saved and is returned by **WinPrintf( )**. Since **vsprintf( )** performs all of the standard **printf( )** conversions and formatting, placing the result into a string, **WinPrintf( )** need not handle these operations manually.

Next, the current text metrics are obtained, and then the tab width and the line height are computed by the following code:

```
// get text metrics
GetTextMetrics(hdc, &tm);
tabwidth = 8 * tm.tmMaxCharWidth;
lineheight = tm.tmHeight + tm.tmExternalLeading;
```

The tab width is obtained by multiplying the number of characters between tabs, which is hard-coded as 8, by the maximum character width. The line height is computed by adding the height of a line to the distance between lines. Both of these values are in terms of logical units. Since the text metrics may not be the same each time **WinPrintf( )** is called, this information must be computed each time the function is entered.

Next, a null is put into the second character of the **chstr** array, **p** is pointed to the start of **result**, and the **while** loop that will cycle through the characters in **result** is started.

```
chstr[1] = 0; // put a null at end of chstr

// now, output the string
p = result;
while(*p) {
```

Inside the **while** loop, each character in **result** is examined. If it is a new line, then the following code executes:

```
if(*p == '\n') { // advance to next line
  Y += lineheight;
  X = 0;
  p++;
}
```

Here, **Y** is advanced to the next line by adding the height of a line of text, **X** is reset to the start of the next line, and **p** is advanced to the next character.

If the next character is a tab, then this code executes:

```
else if(*p == '\t') { // process a tab
  X = ((X / tabwidth) * tabwidth) + tabwidth;
  p++;
}
```

Here, **X** is advanced to the next tab position by adding the appropriate amount of units. This is computed by first dividing **X** by the tab width and then multiplying this value by the tab width. Because these are integer operations, this yields the position of the previous tab stop. To this value is then added the tab width, which advances output to the next tab stop.

If the next character is a "normal" character, then it is output via this code:

```
else { // handle a normal char
  chstr[0] = *p;
  p++;

  TextOut(hdc, X, Y, chstr, 1); // output each char

  // advance to next character position
  GetTextExtentPoint32(hdc, chstr, 1, &size);
  X += size.cx;
}
```

Here, the character is put into the first element of the **chstr** array and the **TextOut( )** function is called to actually output the character. Then, **X** is advanced by the width of the character as computed by calling **GetTextExtentPoint32( )**.

Finally, the value returned by **vsprintf( )** is returned:

```
return retval;
```

This value will contain the number of characters displayed. It will be –1 if an error occurs.

To demonstrate **WinPrintf( )**, the program executes this sequence each time **WM_PAINT** is received:

```
hdc = BeginPaint(hwnd, &ps);

WinPrintf(NULL, ""); // reset X and Y

WinPrintf(hdc, "%d + %d = %d\n", 8, 9, 8+9);
WinPrintf(hdc, "Current balance is: $%7.2f\n", 42343.79);
WinPrintf(hdc, "This is a test. ");
WinPrintf(hdc, "This is on the same line.\n");
WinPrintf(hdc, "Tabs\tare \tnow\texpanded.\n");
WinPrintf(hdc, "Some\tmore\ttab\texamples.\n");

EndPaint(hwnd, &ps);
```

Notice that the first call to **WinPrintf( )** passes a null for the device context. This causes **X** and **Y** to be reset to 0. Then, several lines are displayed that demonstrate the function.

WinPrintf( ) is especially useful for debugging because it is an easy way to display complicated information without a lot of effort. It is also useful for simple utility programs in which a more sophisticated user interface is not required.

Here is something that you might like to try: Using techniques similar to those employed by **WinPrintf( )**, you could create overloaded C++-style I/O operators that directed their output to a device context. Doing so would allow you to use the I/O operators to output text to a window.

A Scrolling Window Class

If you have ever wanted a simple way to create a window that acts more like a console session than a GUI-based window, then you will find the **ScrollWin** class described here especially helpful. Nearly all Windows programmers have, from time to time, wanted to have at their disposal a window that would simply scroll its contents when the end of the window was reached. Such a window would act much like an old-style terminal or a console-session window. A scrolling window is useful in many situations. For example, during program development you often need to observe a stream of data when the programming is running. A scrolling window is perfect for this type of situation because it has little overhead. You simply output information and it will scroll that information up when the end of the window is reached. The scrolling window class developed here gives you an easy way to display line after line of text in a window without having to worry about exceeding the size of the window.

Code

ScrlPrnt.cpp

The following program defines the **ScrollWin** class, which maintains a scrolling window. The scrolling window uses an underlying bitmap to help manage scrolling, adapting the virtual window technology developed in Chapter 2. To demonstrate the scrolling window, the program starts a timer and outputs a new line of text once each second. You can also output lines of text by pressing the right mouse button. Pressing the left mouse button clears the window and restarts output from the upper-left corner. Sample output is shown in Figure 3-2.

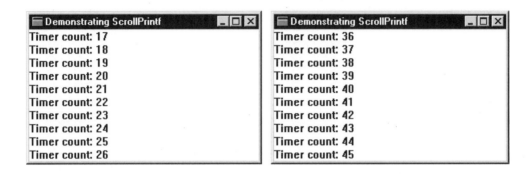

FIGURE 3-2. Sample output from **ScrlPrnt.cpp**

```cpp
// ScrlPrnt.cpp: Demonstrating the ScrollWin class.

#include <windows.h>
#include <cstring>
#include <cstdio>

LRESULT CALLBACK WindowFunc(HWND, UINT, WPARAM, LPARAM);

char szWinName[] = "MyWin"; // name of window class

class ScrollWin {
  HWND hwnd;
  HDC memdc;
  int maxX, maxY;
  int X, Y;
  HBITMAP hbit;
public:
  ScrollWin(HWND wnd) {
    HDC hdc;
    HBRUSH hbrush;
```

```
    hwnd = wnd;

    // get screen coordinates
    maxX = GetSystemMetrics(SM_CXSCREEN);
    maxY = GetSystemMetrics(SM_CYSCREEN);

    // create the virtual window
    hdc = GetDC(hwnd);
    memdc = CreateCompatibleDC(hdc);
    hbit = CreateCompatibleBitmap(hdc, maxX, maxY);
    SelectObject(memdc, hbit);
    hbrush = (HBRUSH) GetStockObject(WHITE_BRUSH);
    SelectObject(memdc, hbrush);
    PatBlt(memdc, 0, 0, maxX, maxY, PATCOPY);

    ReleaseDC(hwnd, hdc);
    X = Y = 0;
  }

  ~ScrollWin() {
    DeleteDC(memdc);
    DeleteObject(hbit);
  }

  // get handle to memDC
  HDC GetmemDC() { return memdc; }

  // display output
  int ScrollPrintf(char *str, ...);

  // reset output
  void reset() {
    X = Y = 0;
    PatBlt(memdc, 0, 0, maxX, maxY, PATCOPY);
  }
};

int WINAPI WinMain(HINSTANCE hThisInst, HINSTANCE hPrevInst,
                   LPSTR lpszArgs, int nWinMode)
{
  MSG msg;
  WNDCLASSEX wcl;
  HWND hwnd;
```

```
  // Define a window class.
  wcl.cbSize = sizeof(WNDCLASSEX);
  wcl.hInstance = hThisInst;
  wcl.lpszClassName = szWinName;
  wcl.lpfnWndProc = WindowFunc;
  wcl.style = 0; // default style
  wcl.hIcon = LoadIcon(NULL, IDI_APPLICATION); // large icon
  wcl.hIconSm = NULL; // use small version of large icon
  wcl.hCursor = LoadCursor(NULL, IDC_ARROW);
  wcl.hbrBackground = (HBRUSH) GetStockObject(WHITE_BRUSH);
  wcl.cbClsExtra = 0;
  wcl.cbWndExtra = 0;
  wcl.lpszMenuName = NULL; // no menu

  // Register the window class.
  if(!RegisterClassEx(&wcl)) return 0;

  // Create a window.
  hwnd = CreateWindow(szWinName,
                      "Demonstrating ScrollPrintf",
                      WS_OVERLAPPEDWINDOW,
                      CW_USEDEFAULT, CW_USEDEFAULT,
                      CW_USEDEFAULT, CW_USEDEFAULT,
                      NULL, NULL, hThisInst, NULL);

  // Display the window.
  ShowWindow(hwnd, nWinMode);
  UpdateWindow(hwnd);

  // The message loop.
  while(GetMessage(&msg, NULL, 0, 0))
  {
    TranslateMessage(&msg);
    DispatchMessage(&msg);
  }
  return msg.wParam;
}

// The window procedure.
LRESULT CALLBACK WindowFunc(HWND hwnd, UINT message,
                            WPARAM wParam, LPARAM lParam)
```

```
{
  HDC hdc;
  PAINTSTRUCT ps;

  static ScrollWin swin(hwnd); // create a ScrollWin
  static int count = 0;   // counter for timer

  switch(message) {
    case WM_CREATE:
      SetTimer(hwnd, 1, 1000, NULL);
      break;
    case WM_LBUTTONUP:
      swin.reset();
      break;
    case WM_RBUTTONUP:
      swin.ScrollPrintf("A console-style scrolling window.\n");
      break;
    case WM_TIMER:
      swin.ScrollPrintf("Timer count: %d\n", count++);
      break;
    case WM_PAINT:
      hdc = BeginPaint(hwnd, &ps);


      // copy only the necessary portion of the virtual window
      BitBlt(hdc, ps.rcPaint.left, ps.rcPaint.top,
          ps.rcPaint.right-ps.rcPaint.left, // width
          ps.rcPaint.bottom-ps.rcPaint.top, // height
          swin.GetmemDC(),
          ps.rcPaint.left, ps.rcPaint.top,
          SRCCOPY);


      EndPaint(hwnd, &ps);
      break;
    case WM_DESTROY:
      KillTimer(hwnd, 1);
      PostQuitMessage(0);
      break;
    default:
      return DefWindowProc(hwnd, message, wParam, lParam);
  }
  return 0;
```

```
}

// A scrolling, general-purpose, window-based output function.
int ScrollWin::ScrollPrintf(char *str, ...)
{
  TEXTMETRIC tm;
  SIZE size;
  RECT r;

  char result[1024]; // formatted text
  char chstr[2];     // string-ized character for output
  char *p;           // pointer to result

  int retval;     // holds return value
  int tabwidth;   // width in tab for current font
  int lineheight; // height of a line of text

  va_list ptr; // get arg pointer

  // point ptr to the first arg after str
  va_start(ptr, str);

  // pass args to vsprintf()
  retval = vsprintf(result, str, ptr);

  // get text metrics
  GetTextMetrics(memdc, &tm);
  tabwidth = 8 * tm.tmMaxCharWidth;
  lineheight = tm.tmHeight + tm.tmExternalLeading;

  // get dimensions of window
  GetClientRect(hwnd, &r);

  chstr[1] = 0; // put a null at end of chstr

  // now, output the string
  p = result;
  while(*p) {
    if(*p == '\n') { // advance to next line
      Y += lineheight;
      while(Y > r.bottom) { // scroll window if at end
        // scroll window up one line
        BitBlt(memdc, 0, 0, maxX, maxY,
```

```
                    memdc, 0, lineheight, SRCCOPY);

        Y -= lineheight; // reset line counter

        // clear scrolled-out text
        PatBlt(memdc, 0, Y, maxX, maxY, PATCOPY);
      }
      X = 0;
      p++;
    }
    else if(*p == '\t') { // process a tab
      X = ((X / tabwidth) * tabwidth) + tabwidth;
      p++;
    }
    else { // handle a normal char
      chstr[0] = *p;
      p++;

      TextOut(memdc, X, Y, chstr, 1); // output each char

      // advance to next character position
      GetTextExtentPoint32(memdc, chstr, 1, &size);
      X += size.cx;
    }
  }

  InvalidateRect(hwnd, NULL, 1);
  return retval;
}
```

ANNOTATIONS

The **ScrollWin** class encapsulates a scrolling window. Its class declaration is shown here:

```
class ScrollWin {
  HWND hwnd;
  HDC memdc;
  int maxX, maxY;
  int X, Y;
  HBITMAP hbit;
public:
  ScrollWin(HWND wnd) {
```

```
        HDC hdc;
        HBRUSH hbrush;

        hwnd = wnd;

        // get screen coordinates
        maxX = GetSystemMetrics(SM_CXSCREEN);
        maxY = GetSystemMetrics(SM_CYSCREEN);

        // create the virtual window
        hdc = GetDC(hwnd);
        memdc = CreateCompatibleDC(hdc);
        hbit = CreateCompatibleBitmap(hdc, maxX, maxY);
        SelectObject(memdc, hbit);
        hbrush = (HBRUSH) GetStockObject(WHITE_BRUSH);
        SelectObject(memdc, hbrush);
        PatBlt(memdc, 0, 0, maxX, maxY, PATCOPY);

        ReleaseDC(hwnd, hdc);
        X = Y = 0;
    }

    ~ScrollWin() {
      DeleteDC(memdc);
      DeleteObject(hbit);
    }

    // get handle to memDC
    HDC GetmemDC() { return memdc; }

    // display output
    int ScrollPrintf(char *str, ...);

    // reset output
    void reset() {
      X = Y = 0;
      PatBlt(memdc, 0, 0, maxX, maxY, PATCOPY);
    }
};
```

The first thing to notice is that **ScrollWin** defines several private members. Here, **hwnd** is the handle to the application's window and **memdc** is the handle to the memory device context that supports the virtual window. The length and width of the underlying bitmap (that is, the virtual window) are stored in **maxX** and **maxY**.

The **X** and **Y** members hold the coordinates of the current output location. The **hbit** member holds a handle to the virtual window bitmap.

Most of **ScrollWin**'s member functions are defined in-line. Its constructor creates a virtual window using the methods described in Chapter 2. The destructor frees the memory device context handle and bitmap handle when a **ScrollWin** object is destroyed. **GetmemDC( )** returns the handle of the device context. **reset( )** resets output coordinates to 0, 0 and clears the virtual window.

The scrolling capabilities of **ScrollWin** are implemented by **ScrollPrintf( )**, which is a variation on the **WinPrintf( )** function described in the preceding section. Let's examine it closely. **ScrollPrintf( )** begins like this:

```
int ScrollWin::ScrollPrintf(char *str, ...)
{
  TEXTMETRIC tm;
  SIZE size;
  RECT r;

  char result[1024]; // formatted text
  char chstr[2];     // string-ized character for output
  char *p;           // pointer to result

  int retval;     // holds return value
  int tabwidth;   // width in tab for current font
  int lineheight; // height of a line of text
```

As you can see, since **ScrollPrintf( )** is a member of **ScrollWin**, there is no need to pass it the device context—it can simply use the one stored in the **memdc** member. Most of the variables have essentially the same meaning as they did in **WinPrintf( )**. The **RECT** variable **r** receives the current dimensions of the client area when **GetClientRect( )** is called later in the function.

Next, the following code initializes the variable-length argument pointer **ptr**, makes a call to **vsprintf( )** to obtain a formatted string, and obtains the text metrics.

```
va_list ptr; // get arg pointer

// point ptr to the first arg after str
va_start(ptr, str);

// pass args to vsprintf()
retval = vsprintf(result, str, ptr);

// get text metrics
GetTextMetrics(memdc, &tm);
tabwidth = 8 * tm.tmMaxCharWidth;
lineheight = tm.tmHeight + tm.tmExternalLeading;
```

Using the following code, **ScrollPrintf( )** next obtains the current dimensions of the client area of the window by calling **GetClientRect( )**. It then puts a null at the end of the **chstr** array, assigns **p** the address of the start of **result**, and then starts the **while** loop that outputs the text one character at a time.

```
// get dimensions of window
GetClientRect(hwnd, &r);

chstr[1] = 0; // put a null at end of chstr

// now, output the string
p = result;
while(*p) {
```

As with **WinPrintf( )**, the characters are output one at a time. If the next character is a new line, then the following code executes:

```
if(*p == '\n') { // advance to next line
  Y += lineheight;
  while(Y > r.bottom) { // scroll window if at end
    // scroll window up one line
    BitBlt(memdc, 0, 0, maxX, maxY,
           memdc, 0, lineheight, SRCCOPY);

    Y -= lineheight; // reset line counter

    // clear scrolled-out text
    PatBlt(memdc, 0, Y, maxX, maxY, PATCOPY);
  }
  X = 0;
  p++;
}
```

First, the Y coordinate is advanced by the height of a line. If this yields a value that is greater than the height of the client area (stored in **r**), then the contents of the window must be scrolled up one line. This is done by the **BitBlt( )** function, which operates on the virtual window whose device context is specified by **memdc**. The value Y is then reset to its previous value and the last line in the window is cleared. If the Y coordinate is not greater than the height of the client area, then there is no need to scroll the virtual window. In either event, the X coordinate is set to 0 and **p** is advanced to the next character.

Tab characters are processed as they were in **WinPrintf( )**, using the following code:

arcs that make up each glyph, as well as instructions on how to draw the character. This approach gives TrueType fonts excellent scalability. They are also the most faithfully translated from screen to printer. For this reason, TrueType fonts are quite popular for desktop publishing applications. OpenType fonts are essentially TrueType fonts that support Postscript-style glyphs.

Creating Custom Fonts

As you will see, the easiest way to rotate text through an angle is to create a custom font. Although it may sound complex, it is actually very easy to create a custom font because you are not defining a new typeface. Instead, you will be tailoring an existing typeface so that it meets the specifications that you desire. (That is, you don't need to define the shape of each character in the font that you create.) In the process, you can specify an angle of rotation for the font. This angle is then used by functions such as **TextOut( )** when displaying text. Thus, a rotated font causes text to be automatically displayed at an angle.

To create your own font, use the **CreateFont( )** API function, whose prototype is shown here:

```
HFONT CreateFont(int Height, int Width, int Escapement,
                 int Orientation, int Weight,
                 DWORD Ital, DWORD Underline,
                 DWORD StrikeThru, DWORD Charset,
                 DWORD Precision, DWORD ClipPrecision,
                 DWORD Quality, DWORD PitchFam,
                 LPCSTR TypefaceName);
```

The height of the font is passed in *Height*. If *Height* is zero, then a default size is used. The width of the font is specified in *Width*. If *Width* is zero, then Windows chooses an appropriate value based upon the current aspect ratio. Both *Height* and *Width* are in terms of logical units.

When creating the font, you can specify the angle at which a line of text will be displayed. This angle is determined by the *Escapement* parameter. For normal, horizontal text, this value should be 0. Otherwise, it specifies the number of 1/10 degree increments through which the text should be rotated in a counterclockwise direction. For example, a value of 900 causes the text to be rotated 90 degrees, causing output to be vertical. The angle of each individual character can also be specified using the *Orientation* parameter. It, too, uses 1/10 degree increments to specify the angle of each character relative to a horizontal line in a counterclockwise direction. In general, when rotating a font, both *Escapement* and *Orientation* will be set to the same angle.

Weight specifies the preferred weight of the font in the range of 0 to 1,000. A value of 0 specifies the default weight. To specify a normal weight, use 400. For bold, use 700. You can also use any of these macros to specify the font weight:

FW_DONTCARE
FW_THIN
FW_EXTRALIGHT
FW_LIGHT
FW_NORMAL
FW_MEDIUM
FW_SEMIBOLD
FW_BOLD
FW_EXTRABOLD
FW_HEAVY

To create an italic font, specify *Ital* as non-zero. Otherwise, this parameter should be zero. To create an underlined font, specify *Underline* as non-zero. Otherwise, this parameter should be zero. To create a strikethrough font, specify *StrikeThru* as non-zero. Otherwise, this parameter should be zero.

Charset indicates which character set is desired. The example that follows uses **ANSI_CHARSET**. *Precision* specifies the preferred output precision. This determines just how closely the output must match the requested font's characteristics. The examples in this chapter use **OUT_DEFAULT_PRECIS**. *ClipPrecision* specifies the preferred clipping precision. Clipping precision determines how each character that extends beyond the clipping region is to be "clipped." The value used by the example in this chapter is **CLIP_DEFAULT_PRECIS**.

Quality determines how closely the logical font will be matched with the actual physical fonts provided for the requested output device. Its most commonly used values are shown here:

DEFAULT_QUALITY	DRAFT_QUALITY	PROOF_QUALITY

PitchFam specifies the pitch and family of the font. There are three pitch choices:

DEFAULT_PITCH	FIXED_PITCH	VARIABLE_PITCH

There are six possible font family values:

FF_DECORATIVE	FF_DONTCARE	FF_MODERN
FF_ROMAN	FF_SCRIPT	FF_SWISS

The **FF_DONTCARE** family is used when you don't care what font family is used. The font family is meaningful only if the typeface you specify is not available on the system. To create the value for *PitchFam*, OR together one pitch value and one font family value.

A pointer to the name of the typeface is passed in *TypefaceName*. This name cannot be longer than 32 characters. The font you specify must be installed in your system. Alternatively, you can specify **NULL** for this parameter and Windows will automatically select a font that is compatible with the characteristics that you specify in the other parameters. (You will see how to obtain a list of available fonts later in this chapter.)

If successful, **CreateFont( )** returns a handle to the font. On failure, **NULL** is returned. Fonts created using **CreateFont( )** must be deleted before your program ends. To delete a font, call **DeleteObject( )**.

Code

Rotate.cpp

The following program defines the **RotPrintf( )** function, which outputs lines of text in a window at a given angle. The **RotPrintf( )** function is adapted from **WinPrintf( )**, but it has several differences because of its rotational capabilities. The program displays text in each of the four corners of a window and then rotates text through 360 degrees at the center of the window. Sample output is shown in Figure 3-3.

FIGURE 3-3. Sample output from **Rotate.cpp**

```cpp
// Rotate.cpp: Demonstrating RotPrintf().

#include <windows.h>
#include <cstring>
#include <cstdio>
#include <cmath>

LRESULT CALLBACK WindowFunc(HWND, UINT, WPARAM, LPARAM);

char szWinName[] = "MyWin"; // name of window class

int RotPrintf(HDC hdc, char *str, int startX, int startY,
              int theta, char *fontname, ...);

char cornerText[] = "Rotating\n"
                    "text is easy\n"
                    "with Windows.";
char centerText[] = "This rotates\n"
                    "once a second.\n"
                    "Angle is: %d.";

int WINAPI WinMain(HINSTANCE hThisInst, HINSTANCE hPrevInst,
                   LPSTR lpszArgs, int nWinMode)
{
  MSG msg;
  WNDCLASSEX wcl;
  HWND hwnd;

  // Define a window class.
  wcl.cbSize = sizeof(WNDCLASSEX);
  wcl.hInstance = hThisInst;
  wcl.lpszClassName = szWinName;
  wcl.lpfnWndProc = WindowFunc;
  wcl.style = 0; // default style
  wcl.hIcon = LoadIcon(NULL, IDI_APPLICATION); // large icon
  wcl.hIconSm = NULL; // use small version of large icon
  wcl.hCursor = LoadCursor(NULL, IDC_ARROW);
  wcl.hbrBackground = (HBRUSH) GetStockObject(WHITE_BRUSH);
  wcl.cbClsExtra = 0;
  wcl.cbWndExtra = 0;
  wcl.lpszMenuName = NULL; // no menu
```

```
  // Register the window class.
  if(!RegisterClassEx(&wcl)) return 0;

  // Create a window.
  hwnd = CreateWindow(szWinName,
                      "Demonstrating RotPrintf",
                      WS_OVERLAPPEDWINDOW,
                      CW_USEDEFAULT, CW_USEDEFAULT,
                      CW_USEDEFAULT, CW_USEDEFAULT,
                      NULL, NULL, hThisInst, NULL);

  // Display the window.
  ShowWindow(hwnd, nWinMode);
  UpdateWindow(hwnd);

  // The message loop.
  while(GetMessage(&msg, NULL, 0, 0))
  {
    TranslateMessage(&msg);
    DispatchMessage(&msg);
  }
  return msg.wParam;
}

// The window procedure.
LRESULT CALLBACK WindowFunc(HWND hwnd, UINT message,
                            WPARAM wParam, LPARAM lParam)
{
  HDC hdc;
  PAINTSTRUCT ps;

  static int theta = 0;  // angle of rotation

  switch(message) {
    case WM_CREATE:
      SetTimer(hwnd, 1, 1000, NULL);
      break;
    case WM_TIMER:
      InvalidateRect(hwnd, NULL, 1);
      break;
    case WM_PAINT:
      hdc = BeginPaint(hwnd, &ps);
```

```
      // display rotated text in the four corners
      RotPrintf(hdc, cornerText, 0, 50, 400,
              "Times New Roman");
      RotPrintf(hdc, cornerText, 350, 0, -450,
              "Times New Roman");
      RotPrintf(hdc, cornerText, 50, 350, 1350,
              "Times New Roman");
      RotPrintf(hdc, cornerText, 400, 300, -1350,
              "Times New Roman");

      // rotate text in the center of the window
      RotPrintf(hdc, centerText, 200, 180, theta,
              "Century Gothic", theta/10);
      theta += 150;
      if(theta >= 3600) theta = 0;

      EndPaint(hwnd, &ps);
      break;
    case WM_DESTROY:
      KillTimer(hwnd, 1);
      PostQuitMessage(0);
      break;
    default:
      return DefWindowProc(hwnd, message, wParam, lParam);
  }
  return 0;
}

// A window-based output function with rotation.
int RotPrintf(HDC hdc, char *str, int startX, int startY, int theta,
            char *fontname, ...)
{
  HFONT hrotFont, hFtemp; // font handles
  TEXTMETRIC tm;

  char result[1024]; // formatted text
  char line[1024];   // one line of text
  char *p, *lp;       // pointers to result and line

  int retval;      // holds return value
  int lineheight; // height of a line of text
  int X=0, Y=0;   // current output location
  int rX, rY;      // rotated coordinates
  double rads;     // holds theta converted to radians
```

```
int tabcnt = 0; // tab position counter
int i;

// create a font at the specified angle of rotation
hrotFont = CreateFont(20, 0, theta, theta, FW_NORMAL,
                    0, 0, 0, ANSI_CHARSET,
                    OUT_DEFAULT_PRECIS,
                    CLIP_DEFAULT_PRECIS,
                    DEFAULT_QUALITY,
                    DEFAULT_PITCH | FF_DONTCARE,
                    fontname);


hFtemp = (HFONT) SelectObject(hdc, hrotFont); // select font

// convert degrees to radians
rads = theta/10 * 3.1416/180;

va_list ptr; // get arg pointer

// point ptr to the first arg after str
va_start(ptr, fontname);

// pass args to vsprintf()
retval = vsprintf(result, str, ptr);

// get text metrics
GetTextMetrics(hdc, &tm);
lineheight = tm.tmHeight + tm.tmExternalLeading;

// now, output the string one line at a time
p = result;
lp = line;
while(*p) {
  if(*p == '\n') { // advance to next line
    *lp = 0; // null terminate line

    // compute rotated starting position
    rX = (int) (X * cos(rads) + Y * sin(rads));
    rY = (int) (-X * sin(rads) + Y * cos(rads));
    rX += startX; // translate coordinates
    rY += startY; // translate coordinates

    TextOut(hdc, rX, rY, line, strlen(line)); // output line
```

```
    Y += lineheight;
    X = 0;
    p++;
    lp = line; // start new line
    tabcnt = 0;
  }
  else if(*p == '\t') { // process a tab
    for(i=(tabcnt % 8); i < 8; i++) {
      *lp = ' ';
      lp++;
      tabcnt++;
    }
    p++;
  }
  else { // handle a normal char
    *lp = *p;
    p++;
    lp++;
    tabcnt++;
  }
}

// output the last line
rX = (int) (X * cos(rads) + Y * sin(rads));
rY = (int) (-X * sin(rads) + Y * cos(rads));
rX += startX;
rY += startY;
*lp = 0; // null-terminate line
TextOut(hdc, rX, rY, line, strlen(line));

SelectObject(hdc, hFtemp); // restore old font
DeleteObject(hrotFont);
return retval;
}
```

ANNOTATIONS

The **RotPrintf( )** function displays text in the specified device context, at the specified angle, using the specified font. It is adapted from the **WinPrintf( )** function described in the previous section. The prototype for **RotPrintf( )** is shown here:

```
int RotPrintf(HDC hdc, char *str, int startX, int startY,
              int theta, char *fontname, ...);
```

The device context is passed in **hdc**, the string to be displayed is passed in **str**, and the starting point for the string is passed in **startX** and **startY**. The angle of rotation, specified in tenths of degrees is passed in **theta**. The name of the font in which to display the text is passed in **fontname**.

Next, these variables are declared:

```
HFONT hrotFont, hFtemp; // font handles
TEXTMETRIC tm;

char result[1024]; // formatted text
char line[1024];   // one line of text
char *p, *lp;      // pointers to result and line

int retval;        // holds return value
int lineheight; // height of a line of text
int X=0, Y=0;      // current output location
int rX, rY;        // rotated coordinates
double rads;       // holds theta converted to radians
int tabcnt = 0; // tab position counter
int i;
```

Here, **tm**, **result**, **p**, **retval**, and **lineheight** are used the same as they are in **WinPrintf( )**. The variable **hrotFont** will hold the handle to the rotated font and **hFtemp** will hold the handle to the previously selected font. The character array **line** will hold a formatted line of text. As you will see, because of the rotation, it is best to output an entire line of text at a time, rather than one character at a time the way **WinPrintf( )** does. The pointer **lp** will point into **line**. The variables **rX** and **rY** hold the coordinates of the starting point of a line of text after it has been rotated. The angle of rotation converted into radians is held in **rads**. Because of the need to construct a complete line of text prior to outputting it, **RotPrintf( )** handles tabs slightly differently than **WinPrintf( )** does. It keeps a character count in **tabcnt** and uses this value to output the proper number of spaces each time that a tab is encountered.

Next, the specified font is created using this call to **CreateFont( )**:

```
hrotFont = CreateFont(20, 0, theta, theta, FW_NORMAL,
                      0, 0, 0, ANSI_CHARSET,
                      OUT_DEFAULT_PRECIS,
                      CLIP_DEFAULT_PRECIS,
                      DEFAULT_QUALITY,
                      DEFAULT_PITCH | FF_DONTCARE,
                      fontname);

hFtemp = (HFONT) SelectObject(hdc, hrotFont); // select font
```

Here, the font size is hard-coded as 20, but you can change this, or parameterize it, if you like. The default font width is used. Notice that the font is created with the angle of escapement and orientation both being **theta**. Thus, when the font is created, it will be rotated to the angle specified by **theta**. The specific font to create is specified by **fontname**. If this font does not exist, then the closest match is used. Later in this chapter you will see how to determine which fonts are available in a given system. After the font is created, it is selected in the device context passed via **hdc** and the previously selected font is stored in **hFtemp**.

Next, the angle of rotation specified by **theta** is converted into radians using this statement:

```
// convert degrees to radians
rads = theta/10 * 3.1416/180;
```

Since **theta** is in tenths of degrees, it is first divided by 10 to obtain the number of degrees. Then it is multiplied by the degrees-to-radians conversion factor. This conversion is necessary because later in **RotPrintf( )** the angle of rotation is passed to the **sin( )** and **cos( )** functions, which require that angles be in terms of radians.

RotPrintf( ) then intializes the variable-length argument pointer **ptr** and calls **vsprintf( )** to obtain a formatted string. Then, the text metrics are obtained and the height of a line is computed.

Now we are ready to actually begin outputting text. This is done on a line-by-line basis. Because the text is rotated through an angle, it is best to pass an entire line to **TextOut( )** rather than outputting a series of characters as **WinPrintf( )** did. Displaying an entire line produces a slightly smoother look. Before a line is output, it must be constructed. The function reads characters from **result** and puts them into **line** until a newline character is encountered. When this happens, the line is displayed, and the process repeats until there are no more characters in **result**. This takes place within the following **while** loop:

```
// now, output the string one line at a time
p = result;
lp = line;
while(*p) {
  if(*p == '\n') { // advance to next line
    *lp = 0; // null terminate line

    // compute rotated starting position
    rX = (int) (X * cos(rads) + Y * sin(rads));
    rY = (int) (-X * sin(rads) + Y * cos(rads));
    rX += startX; // translate coordinates
    rY += startY; // translate coordinates

    TextOut(hdc, rX, rY, line, strlen(line)); // output line
```

```
      Y += lineheight;
      X = 0;
      p++;
      lp = line; // start new line
      tabcnt = 0;
    }
    else if(*p == '\t') { // process a tab
      for(i=(tabcnt % 8); i < 8; i++) {
        *lp = ' ';
        lp++;
        tabcnt++;
      }
      p++;
    }
    else { // handle a normal char
      *lp = *p;
      p++;
      lp++;
      tabcnt++;
    }
  }
}
```

Inside the loop, if the next character in **result** (pointed to by **p**) is a newline, then the string in **line** (pointed to by **lp**) is null-terminated. Next, the starting location for the rotated line is computed. This step is necessary because more than one line of text might be contained within a single call to **RotPrintf( )**. As lines advance "down" the screen, the starting point of the next line is needed. Since the text is rotated, this point must be computed. It must also be translated relative to the starting location specified by **startX** and **startY**. The standard algebraic formulas for rotation and translation are used. Once the starting point of the line has been computed, the line is output by calling **TextOut( )**. Then, **Y** is advanced by the line height, **X** is reset to 0, the tab counter is reset, and a new line is begun.

If the next character in **result** is a tab, then the appropriate number of spaces are copied into **line**.

If the next character is a "normal" character, then it is stored in **line**, and the tab counter is increased.

Before the function ends, the last line of text is displayed. This code is needed only when the last line does not end with a newline. Just prior to returning, the previously selected font contained in **hFtemp** is restored by the call to **SelectObject( )**, and **hrotFont** is freed by calling **DeleteObject( )**.

Inside **WindowFunc( )**, each time a **WM_PAINT** message is received, text is displayed in the four corners of the window and in the center of the window. The text in the center is rotated by 15 degrees each time the window is repainted. The program creates a timer with an interval of one second. At the conclusion of each interval, the window is repainted. This causes the text in the center to rotate continuously.

Enumerating Fonts

The preceding program simply assumed that a desired font was available when creating a rotated font. However, it is usually not a good idea to assume anything when programming for Windows! For example, it is possible to add or remove fonts to or from a system. Fortunately, there is a relatively easy way to determine what fonts are available for use.

To enumerate the available fonts, you will use the **EnumFontFamiliesEx( )** API function, shown here:

int EnumFontFamiliesEx(HDC *hdc*, LPLOGFONT *lpFontInfo*,
                               FONTENUMPROC *EnumFunc*,
                               LPARAM *lParam*, DWORD *NotUsed*);

Here, *hdc* is the device context from which the fonts are being obtained. Different device contexts may support different fonts. Various characteristics that define the type of fonts that you want enumerated are passed in the **LOGFONT** structure pointed to by *lpFontInfo*. *EnumFunc* is a pointer to a callback function that will be called once for each font enumerated. You can use *lParam* to pass any application-dependent information to the callback function pointed to by *EnumProc*. *NotUsed* is unused and must be zero. The function returns the last value returned by *EnumProc*.

The **LOGFONT** structure encapsulates logical information about a font. It is defined like this:

```
typedef struct tagLOGFONT
{
  LONG lfHeight;        // height of font
  LONG lfWidth;         // width of font
  LONG lfEscapement;    // angle of text
  LONG lfOrientation;   // angle of character
  LONG lfWeight;        // darkness
  BYTE lfItalic;        // 1 if ital
  BYTE lfUnderline;     // 1 if underline
  BYTE lfStrikeOut;     // 1 if strike-through
  BYTE lfCharSet;       // character set
  BYTE lfOutPrecision;  // output precision
  BYTE lfClipPrecision; // clipping precision
  BYTE lfQuality;       // display quality
  BYTE lfPitchAndFamily; // pitch and family
  CHAR lfFaceName[LF_FACESIZE]; // name
} LOGFONT;
```

The fields in **LOGFONT** have the same meaning and use the same values as the parameters to **CreateFont( )**, described earlier.

Before calling **EnumFontFamiliesEx( )**, you must initialize three fields in the **LOGFONT** structure pointed to by *FontInfo*: **lfCharSet**, **lfPitchAndFamily**, and **lfFaceName**. To enumerate fonts with a particular character set, specify the name of that set in **lfCharSet**. To enumerate fonts with any type of character set, use **DEFAULT_CHARSET**. To enumerate all fonts of a particular typeface, specify the name of the typeface in **lfFaceName**. To enumerate a representative font for all typefaces, initialize this member using the null string. Finally, for most applications, **lfPitchAndFamily** must be set to zero. (For Hebrew or Arabic, set this field to **MONO_FONT**.)

Each time Windows enumerates a font, it calls the function pointed to by *EnumFunc*. This function processes the enumerated font and then returns non-zero if it wants to process another font or zero to stop. This function must have this general form.

> int CALLBACK EnumFunc(ENUMLOGFONTEX *lpLFInfo,
>   NEWTEXTMETRICEX *lpTMInfo,
>   int *type*, LPARAM *lParam*);

Here, *lpLFInfo* is a pointer to an **ENUMLOGFONTEX** structure that contains logical information about the enumerated font. *lpTMInfo* is a pointer to a **NEWTEXTMETRICEX** structure that contains physical information about the font. Non-TrueType fonts receive a pointer to a **TEXTMETRIC** structure, instead. The value of *type* indicates the font type. It can be one of these:

RASTER_FONTTYPE	TRUETYPE_FONTTYPE	DEVICE_FONTTYPE

lParam receives the value passed in *lParam* by **EnumFontFamiliesEx( )**.

The **ENUMLOGFONTEX** structure is defined as shown here:

```
typedef struct tagENUMLOGFONTEX
{
  LOGFONT elfLogFont;
  BYTE elfFullName[LF_FULLFACESIZE]; // full name of font
  BYTE elfStyle[LF_FACESIZE];        // style of font
  BYTE elfScript[LF_FACESIZE];       // script used by font
} ENUMLOGFONTEX;
```

elfLogFont is a **LOGFONT** structure that contains most of the logical font information. The information in this structure could be used in a call to **CreateFont( )** or **CreateFontIndirect( )**. The full name of the font is contained in **elfFullName**. The style (such as bold, italics, and so on) is contained in **elfStyle**. This field is not valid for non-TrueType fonts. The name of the script is found in **elfScript**.

EnumFont.cpp

Code

The following program shows how to enumerate fonts two different ways. First, when you select Available Fonts from the Enumerate menu, you obtain representative fonts for all of the supported typefaces. By choosing Selected Typeface, you will obtain all fonts for the typeface that you specify. Sample output is shown in Figure 3-4.

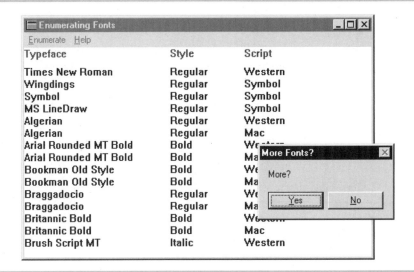

FIGURE 3-4. Sample output from **EnumFont.cpp**

```cpp
// EnumFont.cpp: Enumerating Fonts

#include <windows.h>
#include <cstring>
#include <cstdio>
#include "enumfont.h"

LRESULT CALLBACK WindowFunc(HWND, UINT, WPARAM, LPARAM);
int CALLBACK FontFunc(ENUMLOGFONTEX *lpLF,
                      NEWTEXTMETRICEX *lpTM,
                      int type, LPARAM lParam);
```

```
BOOL CALLBACK FontDialog(HWND hdwnd, UINT message,
                         WPARAM wParam, LPARAM lParam);

char szWinName[] = "MyWin"; // name of window class

char fontstr[255]; // holds user-entered font name

int X=0, Y=0;     // current output location
int maxX, maxY; // screen dimensions
int lineheight; // spacing between lines

HDC memdc;        // store the virtual device handle

HINSTANCE hInst;

int WINAPI WinMain(HINSTANCE hThisInst, HINSTANCE hPrevInst,
                   LPSTR lpszArgs, int nWinMode)
{
  HWND hwnd;
  MSG msg;
  WNDCLASSEX wcl;
  HACCEL hAccel;

  // Define a window class.
  wcl.cbSize = sizeof(WNDCLASSEX);
  wcl.hInstance = hThisInst;
  wcl.lpszClassName = szWinName;
  wcl.lpfnWndProc = WindowFunc;
  wcl.style = 0; // default style
  wcl.hIcon = LoadIcon(NULL, IDI_APPLICATION); // large icon
  wcl.hIconSm = NULL; // use small version of large icon
  wcl.hCursor = LoadCursor(NULL, IDC_ARROW);
  wcl.hbrBackground = (HBRUSH) GetStockObject(WHITE_BRUSH);
  wcl.cbClsExtra = 0;
  wcl.cbWndExtra = 0;
  wcl.lpszMenuName = "FontEnumMenu"; // main menu

  // Register the window class.
  if(!RegisterClassEx(&wcl)) return 0;
```

```
  // Create a window.
  hwnd = CreateWindow(szWinName,
                      "Enumerating Fonts",
                      WS_OVERLAPPEDWINDOW,
                      CW_USEDEFAULT, CW_USEDEFAULT,
                      CW_USEDEFAULT, CW_USEDEFAULT,
                      NULL, NULL, hThisInst, NULL);

  hInst = hThisInst;

  // Load accelerators.
  hAccel = LoadAccelerators(hThisInst, "FontEnumMenu");

  // Display the window.
  ShowWindow(hwnd, nWinMode);
  UpdateWindow(hwnd);

  // The message loop.
  while(GetMessage(&msg, NULL, 0, 0))
  {
    if(!TranslateAccelerator(hwnd, hAccel, &msg)) {
      TranslateMessage(&msg);
      DispatchMessage(&msg);
    }
  }
  return msg.wParam;
}

// The window procedure.
LRESULT CALLBACK WindowFunc(HWND hwnd, UINT message,
                            WPARAM wParam, LPARAM lParam)
{
  HDC hdc;
  static TEXTMETRIC tm;
  PAINTSTRUCT paintstruct;
  LOGFONT lf;
  static HBITMAP hbit;
  HBRUSH hbrush;
  int result;
  int response;

  switch(message) {
    case WM_CREATE:
```

```
        // get screen coordinates
        maxX = GetSystemMetrics(SM_CXSCREEN);
        maxY = GetSystemMetrics(SM_CYSCREEN);

        // create a virtual window
        hdc = GetDC(hwnd);
        memdc = CreateCompatibleDC(hdc);
        hbit = CreateCompatibleBitmap(hdc, maxX, maxY);
        SelectObject(memdc, hbit);
        hbrush = (HBRUSH) GetStockObject(WHITE_BRUSH);
        SelectObject(memdc, hbrush);
        PatBlt(memdc, 0, 0, maxX, maxY, PATCOPY);

        // get text metrics
        GetTextMetrics(memdc, &tm);
        // compute line height
        lineheight = tm.tmHeight + tm.tmExternalLeading;

        // display header in bright red/orange
        SetTextColor(memdc, RGB(255, 100, 0));
        TextOut(memdc, X, 0, "Typeface", strlen("Typeface"));
        TextOut(memdc, X+200, 0, "Style", strlen("Style"));
        TextOut(memdc, X+300, 0, "Script", strlen("Script"));
        SetTextColor(memdc, RGB(0, 0, 0));

        ReleaseDC(hwnd, hdc);
        break;
    case WM_COMMAND:
        switch(LOWORD(wParam)) {
          case IDM_FONTS: // display fonts
            Y = lineheight + lineheight/2;
            PatBlt(memdc, 0, lineheight, maxX, maxY, PATCOPY);

            lf.lfCharSet = DEFAULT_CHARSET;
            strcpy(lf.lfFaceName, "");
            lf.lfPitchAndFamily = 0;

            // enumerate fonts
            hdc = GetDC(hwnd);
            EnumFontFamiliesEx(hdc, &lf,
                (FONTENUMPROC) FontFunc, (LPARAM)hwnd, 0);
            ReleaseDC(hwnd, hdc);
```

```
        break;
      case IDM_TYPEFACE: // display selected typeface
        // get name of font
        result = DialogBox(hInst, "FontDB", hwnd,
                        (DLGPROC) FontDialog);

        if(!result) break; // user cancelled

        Y = lineheight + lineheight/2;
        PatBlt(memdc, 0, lineheight, maxX, maxY, PATCOPY);

        lf.lfCharSet = DEFAULT_CHARSET;
        strcpy(lf.lfFaceName, fontstr);
        lf.lfPitchAndFamily = 0;

        // enumerate all styles for given font
        hdc = GetDC(hwnd);
        EnumFontFamiliesEx(hdc, &lf,
            (FONTENUMPROC) FontFunc, (LPARAM) hwnd, 0);
        ReleaseDC(hwnd, hdc);

        break;
      case IDM_EXIT:
        response = MessageBox(hwnd, "Quit the Program?",
                        "Exit", MB_YESNO);
        if(response == IDYES) PostQuitMessage(0);
        break;
      case IDM_ABOUT:
        MessageBox(hwnd, "Enumerating Fonts\n",
                        "About", MB_OK);
        break;
    }
    break;
  case WM_PAINT:
    hdc = BeginPaint(hwnd, &paintstruct);

    // copy virtual window onto the screen
    BitBlt(hdc, 0, 0, maxX, maxY, memdc, 0, 0, SRCCOPY);
    EndPaint(hwnd, &paintstruct);
    break;
  case WM_DESTROY:
    DeleteDC(memdc);
    DeleteObject(hbit);
        PostQuitMessage(0);
```

```
            break;
     default:
       return DefWindowProc(hwnd, message, wParam, lParam);
   }
   return 0;
}


// Enumerate Fonts
int CALLBACK FontFunc(ENUMLOGFONTEX *lpLF,
                       NEWTEXTMETRICEX *lpTM,
                       int type, LPARAM lParam)
{
   int response;
   RECT rect;

   // display font info
   TextOut(memdc, X, Y, lpLF->elfLogFont.lfFaceName,
           strlen(lpLF->elfLogFont.lfFaceName)); // font name

   if(type == TRUETYPE_FONTTYPE)
     TextOut(memdc, X+200, Y, (char *)lpLF->elfStyle,
             strlen((char *)lpLF->elfStyle)); // style
   else
     TextOut(memdc, X+200, Y, "N/A", 3);

   TextOut(memdc, X+300, Y, (char *)lpLF->elfScript,
           strlen((char *)lpLF->elfScript)); // script style


   Y += lineheight;

   InvalidateRect((HWND)lParam, NULL, 0);

   GetClientRect((HWND)lParam, &rect);

   // pause at bottom of window
   if( (Y + lineheight) >= rect.bottom) {
     Y = lineheight + lineheight/2; // reset to top
     response = MessageBox((HWND)lParam, "More?",
                           "More Fonts?", MB_YESNO);
     if(response == IDNO) return 0;
     PatBlt(memdc, 0, lineheight, maxX, maxY, PATCOPY);
   }
```

```
  return 1;
}

// Enumerate font dialog box.
BOOL CALLBACK FontDialog(HWND hdwnd, UINT message,
                         WPARAM wParam, LPARAM lParam)
{
  switch(message) {
    case WM_COMMAND:
      switch(LOWORD(wParam)) {
        case IDCANCEL:
          EndDialog(hdwnd, 0);
          return 1;
        case IDD_ENUM:
          // get typeface name
          GetDlgItemText(hdwnd, IDD_EB1, fontstr, 80);
          EndDialog(hdwnd, 1);
          return 1;
      }
      break;
  }
  return 0;
}
```

EnumFont.cpp uses the **EnumFont.rc** resource file, shown here:

```
#include <windows.h>
#include "enumfont.h"

FontEnumMenu MENU
{
  POPUP "&Enumerate" {
    MENUITEM "Available &Fonts\tF2", IDM_FONTS
    MENUITEM "Selected &Typeface\tF3", IDM_TYPEFACE
    MENUITEM "E&xit\tCtrl+X", IDM_EXIT
  }
  POPUP "&Help" {
    MENUITEM "&About", IDM_ABOUT
  }
}
```

```
FontEnumMenu ACCELERATORS
{
  VK_F2, IDM_FONTS, VIRTKEY
  VK_F3, IDM_TYPEFACE, VIRTKEY
  "^X", IDM_EXIT
  VK_F1, IDM_ABOUT, VIRTKEY
}

FontDB DIALOG 10, 10, 100, 60
CAPTION "Enumerate Typeface"
STYLE WS_POPUP | WS_CAPTION | WS_SYSMENU | WS_VISIBLE
{
  CTEXT "Enter Typeface", 300, 10, 10, 80, 12
  EDITTEXT IDD_EB1, 10, 20, 80, 12, ES_LEFT |
           WS_VISIBLE | WS_BORDER | ES_AUTOHSCROLL |
           WS_TABSTOP
  DEFPUSHBUTTON "Enumerate" IDD_ENUM, 30, 40, 40, 14,
           WS_CHILD | WS_VISIBLE | WS_TABSTOP
}
```

The **EnumFont.h** header file is shown here:

```
#define IDM_FONTS      100
#define IDM_TYPEFACE   101
#define IDM_EXIT       102
#define IDM_ABOUT      103

#define IDD_EB1        200
#define IDD_ENUM       201
```

ANNOTATIONS

Notice that **EnumFont.cpp** defines several global variables. They are global because they are used by more than one function in the program. The purpose of these variables should be clear from the comments.

When the program receives a **WM_CREATE** message, it creates a virtual window that will store output. It then computes the height of a line of text and outputs column headers for the font information that will be enumerated.

When you select Available Fonts, the **IDM_FONTS** handler is executed. It is shown here:

```
case IDM_FONTS: // display fonts
  // clear window
```

```
Y = lineheight + lineheight/2;
PatBlt(memdc, 0, lineheight, maxX, maxY, PATCOPY);

lf.lfCharSet = DEFAULT_CHARSET;
strcpy(lf.lfFaceName, "");
lf.lfPitchAndFamily = 0;

// enumerate fonts
hdc = GetDC(hwnd);
EnumFontFamiliesEx(hdc, &lf,
    (FONTENUMPROC) FontFunc, (LPARAM)hwnd, 0);
ReleaseDC(hwnd, hdc);

break;
```

First, the part of the window beneath the header line is cleared by calling **PatBlt( )**. Recall that **PatBlt( )** paints the specified region using the currently selected brush. In this case, the entire window is repainted white (except for the header line). Next, the call to **EnumFontFamiliesEx( )** is set up. In this case, **lf.lfFaceName** is given a null string, which causes a representative font from each typeface supported by the system to be returned.

Choosing Selected Typeface executes the **IDM_TYPEFACE** handler shown here:

```
case IDM_TYPEFACE: // display selected typeface
  // get name of font
  result = DialogBox(hInst, "FontDB", hwnd,
                     (DLGPROC) FontDialog);

  if(!result) break; // user cancelled

  // clear window
  Y = lineheight + lineheight/2;
  PatBlt(memdc, 0, lineheight, maxX, maxY, PATCOPY);

  lf.lfCharSet = DEFAULT_CHARSET;
  strcpy(lf.lfFaceName, fontstr);
  lf.lfPitchAndFamily = 0;

  // enumerate all styles for given font
  hdc = GetDC(hwnd);
  EnumFontFamiliesEx(hdc, &lf,
      (FONTENUMPROC) FontFunc, (LPARAM) hwnd, 0);
  ReleaseDC(hwnd, hdc);

  break;
```

First, a small dialog box is activated in which you can enter the name of the desired typeface. This string is then used for the **lf.lfFaceName** field. This causes all fonts of only that typeface to be enumerated. After clearing the window (less the header line), the call to **EnumFontFamiliesEx( )** is set up and the desired font is enumerated.

The **FontDialog( )** function handles input from the font dialog box. It contains two items: the typeface edit box and the Enumerate push button. When the user presses the Enumerate button, the name of the font is obtained from the edit box and copied into **fontstr**. This string is then used by the **IDM_TYPEFACE** handler to enumerate the desired font.

The callback function **FontFunc( )** receives each enumerated font and displays it. The function begins with the following declarations:

```
// Enumerate Fonts
int CALLBACK FontFunc(ENUMLOGFONTEX *lpLF,
                      NEWTEXTMETRICEX *lpTM,
                      int type, LPARAM lParam)
{
  int response;
  RECT rect;
```

Each time **FontFunc( )** is called, information about the font is pointed to by **lpLF** and **lpTM**.

Next, **FontFunc( )** displays some of this information using the following code:

```
// display font info
TextOut(memdc, X, Y, lpLF->elfLogFont.lfFaceName,
        strlen(lpLF->elfLogFont.lfFaceName)); // font name

if(type == TRUETYPE_FONTTYPE)
  TextOut(memdc, X+200, Y, (char *)lpLF->elfStyle,
          strlen((char *)lpLF->elfStyle)); // style
else
  TextOut(memdc, X+200, Y, "N/A", 3);

TextOut(memdc, X+300, Y, (char *)lpLF->elfScript,
        strlen((char *)lpLF->elfScript)); // script style

Y += lineheight;

InvalidateRect((HWND)lParam, NULL, 0);
```

Notice that the style is displayed only for TrueType fonts.

For simplicity, the function displays a window full of fonts and then pops up a message box, asking if you want to see more. If you do, the next window's worth is shown. To determine the current size of the window, **FontFunc( )** calls

GetClientRect( ). The value in **rect.bottom** is used to determine if there is sufficient room to display another line of text within the current height of the window. This is accomplished by the following code:

```
GetClientRect((HWND)lParam, &rect);

// pause at bottom of window
if( (Y + lineheight) >= rect.bottom) {
  Y = lineheight + lineheight/2; // reset to top
  response = MessageBox((HWND)lParam, "More?",
                        "More Fonts?", MB_YESNO);
  if(response == IDNO) return 0;
  PatBlt(memdc, 0, lineheight, maxX, maxY, PATCOPY);
}

return 1;
}
```

If you want to see more fonts, then 1 is returned. Otherwise, 0 is returned and the enumeration is stopped.

Displaying Multiple Columns of Text

Sometimes you will want to display text within a column. While you can do this using **TextOut( )**, and handling clipping and line wrapping manually, Windows provides the function **DrawText( )**, which automates much of the process. Unlike **TextOut( )**, the **DrawText( )** function automatically expands tabs and handles new lines. However, **DrawText( )** requires that you define a rectangular region in which the text will be displayed, rather than just a starting point. This is why **TextOut( )** is much more frequently used when outputting text. However, with a little work, we can take advantage of **DrawText( )** to create a class that supports output of text to a column. Using this class, it is possible to define and manage several columns of text.

The **DrawText( )** function is shown here:

int DrawText(HDC *hdc*, LPCSTR *Str*, int *Len*, LPRECT *Rect*, UINT *Flags*);

Here, the device context in which the text is displayed in passed in *hdc*. The string to be displayed is passed in *Str*, and the number of characters in that string is passed in *Len*. If *Str* is a null-terminated string, then *Len* can be –1. The coordinates of the rectangular region (column) in which the text will be displayed is passed in *Rect*. The value of *Flags* determines precisely how the text is displayed. Here are some commonly used values:

Value	Meaning
DT_CENTER	Centers the text.
DT_LEFT	Left-justifies text.
DT_RIGHT	Right-justifies text.
DT_SINGLELINE	New lines are not recognized.
DT_WORDBREAK	Wraps line at word boundaries.

For our purposes, the most important flag is **DT_WORDBREAK**. By including this flag, long lines of text are automatically broken at the end of a word and wrapped to fit within the bounding rectangle.

DrawText( ) returns the height of the text, or 0 on failure.

MultiCol.cpp

Code

The **MultiCol.cpp** program that follows creates a class called **MultiColumn** that makes it easy to output a column of text. Each **MultiColumn** object defines its own column. Thus, you can create as many columns as you like and each is completely independent of the others. Sample output is shown in Figure 3-5.

```
Demonstrating MultiColumn                        _ □ ×
This is the first column.          This is the second column.
The sum of the squares of the      The sum of the squares of the
two opposing sides is equal to     two opposing sides is equal to
the square of the hypotenuse       the square of the hypotenuse




            This is the
            third column.
            DrawText          This is the fourth
            makes working     column.
            with multiple     You might try
            columns easy.     adding scrolling
                              features to a
                              region using the
                              techniques shown
                              in Chapter 2.
```

FIGURE 3-5. Sample output from **MultiCol.cpp**

```cpp
// MultiCol.cpp: An easy way to create multiple columns of text.

#include <windows.h>
#include <cstring>
#include <cstdio>

LRESULT CALLBACK WindowFunc(HWND, UINT, WPARAM, LPARAM);

char szWinName[] = "MyWin"; // name of window class

class MultiColumn {
  RECT region;
public:
  MultiColumn() {
    region.top = region.left =
      region.right = region.bottom = 0;
  }

  MultiColumn(int top, int left,
              int bottom, int right);

  bool MultiColOut(HDC hdc, char *str);
};

char str[][255] = {
  "This is the first column.\n"
  "The sum of the squares of the"
  " two opposing sides is equal to"
  " the square of the hypotenuse",

  "This is the second column.\n"
  "The sum of the squares of the"
  " two opposing sides is equal to"
  " the square of the hypotenuse",

  "This is the third column.\n"
  "DrawText makes working with multiple"
  " columns easy.",

  "This is the fourth column.\n"
  "You might try adding scrolling features"
  " to a region using the techniques shown"
```

```
   " in Chapter 2."
};

int WINAPI WinMain(HINSTANCE hThisInst, HINSTANCE hPrevInst,
                   LPSTR lpszArgs, int nWinMode)
{
  MSG msg;
  WNDCLASSEX wcl;
  HWND hwnd;

  // Define a window class.
  wcl.cbSize = sizeof(WNDCLASSEX);
  wcl.hInstance = hThisInst;
  wcl.lpszClassName = szWinName;
  wcl.lpfnWndProc = WindowFunc;
  wcl.style = 0; // default style
  wcl.hIcon = LoadIcon(NULL, IDI_APPLICATION); // large icon
  wcl.hIconSm = NULL; // use small version of large icon
  wcl.hCursor = LoadCursor(NULL, IDC_ARROW);
  wcl.hbrBackground = (HBRUSH) GetStockObject(WHITE_BRUSH);
  wcl.cbClsExtra = 0;
  wcl.cbWndExtra = 0;
  wcl.lpszMenuName = NULL; // no menu

  // Register the window class.
  if(!RegisterClassEx(&wcl)) return 0;

  // Create a window.
  hwnd = CreateWindow(szWinName,
                      "Demonstrating MultiColumn",
                      WS_OVERLAPPEDWINDOW,
                      CW_USEDEFAULT, CW_USEDEFAULT,
                      CW_USEDEFAULT, CW_USEDEFAULT,
                      NULL, NULL, hThisInst, NULL);

  // Display the window.
  ShowWindow(hwnd, nWinMode);
  UpdateWindow(hwnd);

  // The message loop.
  while(GetMessage(&msg, NULL, 0, 0))
  {
    TranslateMessage(&msg);
```

```
      DispatchMessage(&msg);
  }
  return msg.wParam;
}


// The window procedure.
LRESULT CALLBACK WindowFunc(HWND hwnd, UINT message,
                               WPARAM wParam, LPARAM lParam)
{
  HDC hdc;
  PAINTSTRUCT ps;
  static MultiColumn mcol[4];
  int i;

  switch(message) {
    case WM_CREATE:
      mcol[0] = MultiColumn(0, 0, 100, 200);
      mcol[1] = MultiColumn(0, 250, 100, 450);
      mcol[2] = MultiColumn(120, 50, 250, 150);
      mcol[3] = MultiColumn(150, 175, 300, 300);
      break;
    case WM_PAINT:
      hdc = BeginPaint(hwnd, &ps);

      for(i=0; i<4; i++)
        mcol[i].MultiColOut(hdc, str[i]);

      EndPaint(hwnd, &ps);
      break;
    case WM_DESTROY:
      PostQuitMessage(0);
      break;
    default:
      return DefWindowProc(hwnd, message, wParam, lParam);
  }
  return 0;
}


// Output text to a column.
bool MultiColumn::MultiColOut(HDC hdc, char *str)
{
  DrawText(hdc, str, -1, &region, DT_WORDBREAK);
  return true;
```

```
}

// Create a column.
MultiColumn::MultiColumn(int top, int left,
                         int bottom, int right)
{
  region.top = top;
  region.left = left;
  region.bottom = bottom;
  region.right = right;
}
```

ANNOTATIONS

Let's begin with the **MultiColumn** class. It is shown here:

```
class MultiColumn {
  RECT region;
public:
  MultiColumn() {
    region.top = region.left =
      region.right = region.bottom = 0;
  }

  MultiColumn(int top, int left,
              int bottom, int right);

  bool MultiColOut(HDC hdc, char *str);
};
```

It has only one data member, **region**, which is private to the class. This structure holds the coordinates of the column in which text will be displayed. **MultiCol**'s default constructor simply initializes **region** to zero dimensions. The parameterized constructor is shown here:

```
// Create a column.
MultiColumn::MultiColumn(int top, int left,
                         int bottom, int right)
{
  region.top = top;
  region.left = left;
  region.bottom = bottom;
  region.right = right;
}
```

As you can see, it sets the dimensions of **region** as specified by the parameters.

Once a **MultiColumn** object has been created, you can output text to it by calling **MultiColOut( )**, shown here:

```
// Output text to a column.
bool MultiColumn::MultiColOut(HDC hdc, char *str)
{
  DrawText(hdc, str, -1, &region, DT_WORDBREAK);
  return true;
}
```

This function must be called with the device context in which you want the text displayed and the null-terminated string that contains the text. Notice that word-wrapping is turned on.

When the program begins, **WM_CREATE** creates four columns. Each time **WM_PAINT** is received, text is output to the columns.

Tips for Using MFC

The techniques in this chapter can be easily implemented in MFC. Here is a mapping of the API functions to their MFC counterparts.

API	MFC
CreateFont	CFont::CreateFont
GetTextMetrics	CDC::GetTextMetrics
GetTextExtentPoint32	CDC::GetTextExtent
DrawText	CDC::DrawText
TextOut	CDC::TextOut

For information on creating a virtual window using MFC, see Chapter 2.

Animation

I t is very likely that some form of animation will be part of your programming future. Whether used in computer games, virtual reality applications, or to display video, animation is becoming an increasingly important part of many Windows applications. All modern versions of Windows provide some built-in support for animation. For example, if you want to view a video clip, you can use the Animation common control (or its MFC equivalent, the **CAnimateCtrl** class). However, for other types of animation, you will need to handle the process yourself. Techniques that help you do this are the subject of this chapter.

The chapter begins with two versions of a simple animated banner program (that is, a program that displays a moving text message). It then explains how to animate a sprite (a small bitmapped image). The chapter concludes with a discussion of foregrounds and backgrounds.

Animation Fundamentals

As you almost certainly know, animation is accomplished by drawing, erasing, and redrawing an object. Between the two drawings, the object is either moved or changed, or both. If this process is performed fast enough, the object appears to be moving and animation is achieved. While this general process is easy to understand, it may not be completely clear how animation is actually performed on a computer—specifically one running Windows.

To begin, let's define two terms. The draw-erase-redraw sequence completes one *animation cycle.* At the end of each cycle, a new *frame* has been produced. The rapid sequencing of frames produces the illusion of motion.

In the most general sense, animation is achieved on a computer through the use of bit manipulations. For example, a screen image can be moved leftward by left-shifting the bits that make up that image. Animation can also be achieved by rapidly erasing and redrawing an object using a bit-block transfer.

One of the greatest problems with computer animation is flicker. Flicker is produced when one or both of the following conditions occurs:

◆ The drawing-erasing-redrawing sequence is performed too slowly.

◆ The animation process is performed incorrectly.

Fortunately, Windows provides the means by which images can be rapidly drawn and, as you will soon see, it is relatively easy to correctly animate an image.

Animation makes extensive use of bitmaps, memory device contexts, and various bit-manipulation functions. These items are discussed in Chapter 2 and those discussions are not repeated here. All of the examples in this chapter make use of the virtual window technology, also developed in Chapter 2. Refer there for details.

Driving the Animation

Because animation requires that the draw-erase-redraw cycle be repeated evenly and regularly, there must be some way to drive this process. That is, your program must provide a mechanism that repeatedly causes the next cycle to take place in a regular fashion. At first, you might think that this is a trivial problem. However, this is not the case because a Windows application program is message driven. This means that, in general, your program is active only when it is responding to a message. Put differently, a Windows program cannot enter a "mode" of operation. For example, a Windows program cannot simply enter a loop that draws, erases, and redraws images. Instead, it must return control to Windows as soon as it has finished processing a message. The question then becomes "How do I force each animation cycle to occur?" There are three ways in which this can be done. The first way is to use a timer. Each time the timer goes off, your program performs one animation cycle. The second way is to take advantage of the idle time that occurs when your program is not processing any other messages. The third way is to use multithreaded multitasking, with each animated object driven by its own thread of execution. In this chapter, the first two ways are examined. In the following chapter, the multithreaded example is presented.

Animating a Banner Using a Timer

To begin our examination of animation, we will begin with a simple, but useful program. This program animates a line of text from right to left. That is, the program displays a moving banner. As the text moves off the left end, it wraps around to the right end. Although this example is quite simple, it introduces all of the basic elements found in any animation situation. The animation is driven by the timer.

Code

Here is the code for **Banner1.cpp**. Sample output is shown in Figure 4-1.

Banner1.cpp

FIGURE 4-1.   Sample output from **Banner1.cpp**

```
// A simple animated banner that is driven by a timer.

#include <windows.h>
#include <cstring>
#include <cstdio>

LRESULT CALLBACK WindowFunc(HWND, UINT, WPARAM, LPARAM);

char szWinName[] = "MyWin";

int WINAPI WinMain(HINSTANCE hThisInst, HINSTANCE hPrevInst,
                   LPSTR lpszArgs, int nWinMode)
{
  HWND hwnd;
  MSG msg;
  WNDCLASSEX wcl;

  // Define a window class.
  wcl.cbSize = sizeof(WNDCLASSEX);
  wcl.hInstance = hThisInst;
  wcl.lpszClassName = szWinName;
  wcl.lpfnWndProc = WindowFunc;
  wcl.style = 0; // default style
  wcl.hIcon = LoadIcon(NULL, IDI_APPLICATION); // large icon
  wcl.hIconSm = NULL; // use small version of large icon
  wcl.hCursor = LoadCursor(NULL, IDC_ARROW);
  wcl.hbrBackground = (HBRUSH) GetStockObject(WHITE_BRUSH);
  wcl.cbClsExtra = 0;
  wcl.cbWndExtra = 0;
  wcl.lpszMenuName = NULL; // no main

  // Register the window class.
```

```
  if(!RegisterClassEx(&wcl)) return 0;

  // Create a window.
  hwnd = CreateWindow(szWinName,
                      "Animating a Banner",
                      WS_OVERLAPPEDWINDOW,
                      CW_USEDEFAULT, CW_USEDEFAULT,
                      CW_USEDEFAULT, CW_USEDEFAULT,
                      NULL, NULL, hThisInst, NULL);

  // Display the window.
  ShowWindow(hwnd, nWinMode);
  UpdateWindow(hwnd);

  // The message loop.
  while(GetMessage(&msg, NULL, 0, 0))
  {
    TranslateMessage(&msg);
    DispatchMessage(&msg);
  }

  return msg.wParam;
}

// The window procedure.
LRESULT CALLBACK WindowFunc(HWND hwnd, UINT message,
                            WPARAM wParam, LPARAM lParam)
{
  HDC hdc;
  PAINTSTRUCT ps;

  static int X=0, Y=20; // current output location
  static int maxX, maxY;// screen dimensions
  static TEXTMETRIC tm; // font information
  static RECT animdim;  // size of area to animate

  static HDC memdc;     // virtual window handle
  static HBITMAP hbit;  // virtual window bitmap
  HBRUSH hbrush;        // brush

  char str[] = "This is an animated message.";

  switch(message) {
```

```
case WM_CREATE:
  // start a timer
  if(!SetTimer(hwnd, 1, 50, NULL))
    MessageBox(hwnd, "Timer Error", "Error", MB_OK);

  // create virtual window
  maxX = GetSystemMetrics(SM_CXSCREEN);
  maxY = GetSystemMetrics(SM_CYSCREEN);
  hdc = GetDC(hwnd);
  memdc = CreateCompatibleDC(hdc);
  hbit = CreateCompatibleBitmap(hdc, maxX, maxY);
  SelectObject(memdc, hbit);
  hbrush = (HBRUSH) GetStockObject(WHITE_BRUSH);
  SelectObject(memdc, hbrush);
  PatBlt(memdc, 0, 0, maxX, maxY, PATCOPY);

  GetTextMetrics(hdc, &tm);

  animdim.left = X; animdim.top = Y;
  animdim.right = maxX + X;
  animdim.bottom = tm.tmHeight + Y;

  TextOut(memdc, X, Y, str, strlen(str));

  ReleaseDC(hwnd, hdc);
  InvalidateRect(hwnd, NULL, 1);
  break;
case WM_PAINT:
  hdc = BeginPaint(hwnd, &ps);

  // copy virtual window to screen
  BitBlt(hdc, ps.rcPaint.left, ps.rcPaint.top,
         ps.rcPaint.right-ps.rcPaint.left, // width
         ps.rcPaint.bottom-ps.rcPaint.top, // height
         memdc,
         ps.rcPaint.left, ps.rcPaint.top,
         SRCCOPY);

  EndPaint(hwnd, &ps);
  break;
case WM_TIMER: // timer went off - update display

  // move left edge to the right end
  BitBlt(memdc, maxX-1, Y, 1, tm.tmHeight,
```

```
                memdc, 0, Y, SRCCOPY);

      // move remaining image left
      BitBlt(memdc, 0, Y, maxX-1, tm.tmHeight,
             memdc, 1, Y, SRCCOPY);

      // update
      InvalidateRect(hwnd, &animdim, 0);
      break;
    case WM_DESTROY:
      DeleteDC(memdc);
      DeleteObject(hbit);
      PostQuitMessage(0);
      break;
    default:
      return DefWindowProc(hwnd, message, wParam, lParam);
  }
  return 0;
}
```

ANNOTATIONS

To begin, let's examine what occurs inside the **WM_CREATE** handler. First, a timer is started. The length of the period determines how fast the message is scrolled across the screen. As written, the timer goes off once every 50 milliseconds. (The **SetTimer( )** function is described in Chapter 1.) Next, a virtual window is created. The virtual window is used for two purposes: to refresh the window when a **WM_PAINT** message is received and to prepare the next frame for animation.

Next, the following code is executed:

```
GetTextMetrics(hdc, &tm);

animdim.left = X; animdim.top = Y;
animdim.right = maxX + X;
animdim.bottom = tm.tmHeight + Y;

TextOut(memdc, X, Y, str, strlen(str));
```

GetTextMetrics( ) is called so that the current height of the font can be obtained. Next, **animdim** is initialized. This structure defines the size of the area that contains the text that will be scrolled across the screen. It will be used in calls to **InvalidateRect( )** when the text is moved. The width of the animation area is the maximum width of the screen. The area's height is set to the height of the currently selected font. Thus, the area is tall enough to hold a line of text. The entire animation area is offset by the values located in **X** and **Y**. Next, the string to be animated is output to the virtual window at the location specified by **X** and **Y**. As the program is written, **X** is 0 and **Y** is 20. This means that the text is displayed (and scrolled) in a line slightly below the top of the client area.

Before the **WM_CREATE** handler ends, a call is made to **InvalidateRect( )**, which causes the first frame to be displayed.

On the conclusion of each timing interval a **WM_TIMER** message is received. This causes a two-step process to occur. First, the leftmost bits of the text region are moved to the far right side using this call to **BitBlt( )**:

```
// move left edge to the right end
BitBlt(memdc, maxX-1, Y, 1, tm.tmHeight,
       memdc, 0, Y, SRCCOPY);
```

Next, the remaining portion of the text region is moved left one position by this call to **BitBlt( )**:

```
// move remaining image left
BitBlt(memdc, 0, Y, maxX-1, tm.tmHeight,
       memdc, 1, Y, SRCCOPY);
```

After these lines execute, the animated line will have advanced by one frame. This process is depicted in Figure 4-2.

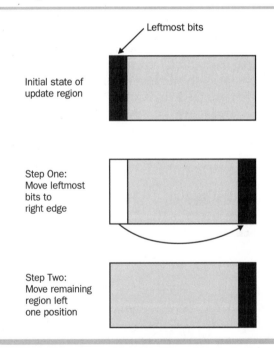

Leftmost bits

Initial state of
update region

Step One:
Move leftmost
bits to
right edge

Step Two:
Move remaining
region left
one position

FIGURE 4-2.   How the animated banner program works

To actually display the next frame, this call to **InvalidateRect( )** is executed:

```
InvalidateRect(hwnd, &animdim, 0);
```

Notice that the **animdim** structure is passed as the second parameter. This region specifies the part of the window that you want repainted. Since **animdim** defines the part of the window that holds the animated banner, it causes only that portion of the window to be redrawn. This is much more efficient than repainting the entire window with each animation cycle.

When you run **Banner1.cpp**, you will notice that the message scrolls rather slowly. This is not because Windows is slow. Instead, it is caused by inherent limitations in how fast timer messages can be produced and processed through the system. The next program demonstrates how your animations can be driven at substantially faster speeds.

Using Idle Cycles for Animation

While using a timer to drive animation will work for some applications, it is far too slow for many others. Most animation applications require that the animation take place at rates approximating real-time activities. To accomplish this, you need a way to "nudge" the animation subsystem as frequently as possible. One way is to take advantage of the idle time that is present in most Windows applications. Consider the following message loop, which is common in Windows programs.

```
while(GetMessage(&msg, NULL, 0, 0))
{
  TranslateMessage(&msg);
  DispatchMessage(&msg);
}
```

This piece of code repeatedly obtains and dispatches messages. When your application is not processing a message in its window procedure, it is running this message loop. Put differently, this loop is running whenever your application is not doing anything else and is, thus, idle. By adding code to the message loop that cycles the animation system, you can achieve fast motion.

Banner2.cpp

Code

Banner2.cpp, shown next, animates a text banner by taking advantage of the idle time present in the program.

```
// An animated banner that runs during idle cycles.

#include <windows.h>
#include <cstring>
```

```
#include <cstdio>

void run(HWND hwnd, HDC memdc);

LRESULT CALLBACK WindowFunc(HWND, UINT, WPARAM, LPARAM);

char szWinName[] = "MyWin";

HDC memdc;        // virtual window handle
int X=0, Y=20;    // current output location
int maxX, maxY;   // screen dimensions
TEXTMETRIC tm;    // font information
RECT animdim;     // size of area to animate

int WINAPI WinMain(HINSTANCE hThisInst, HINSTANCE hPrevInst,
                   LPSTR lpszArgs, int nWinMode)
{
  HWND hwnd;
  MSG msg;
  WNDCLASSEX wcl;

  // Define a window class.
  wcl.cbSize = sizeof(WNDCLASSEX);
  wcl.hInstance = hThisInst;
  wcl.lpszClassName = szWinName;
  wcl.lpfnWndProc = WindowFunc;
  wcl.style = 0; // default style
  wcl.hIcon = LoadIcon(NULL, IDI_APPLICATION); // large icon
  wcl.hIconSm = NULL; // use small version of large icon
  wcl.hCursor = LoadCursor(NULL, IDC_ARROW);
  wcl.hbrBackground = (HBRUSH) GetStockObject(WHITE_BRUSH);
  wcl.cbClsExtra = 0;
  wcl.cbWndExtra = 0;
  wcl.lpszMenuName = NULL; // no main

  // Register the window class.
  if(!RegisterClassEx(&wcl)) return 0;

  // Create a window.
```

```
  hwnd = CreateWindow(szWinName,
                      "Using Idle Cycles for Animation",
                      WS_OVERLAPPEDWINDOW,
                      CW_USEDEFAULT, CW_USEDEFAULT,
                      CW_USEDEFAULT, CW_USEDEFAULT,
                      NULL, NULL, hThisInst, NULL);

  // Display the window.
  ShowWindow(hwnd, nWinMode);
  UpdateWindow(hwnd);

  // The message loop.
  while(GetMessage(&msg, NULL, 0, 0))
  {
    TranslateMessage(&msg);
    DispatchMessage(&msg);
    run(hwnd, memdc); // cycle the animation
  }

  return msg.wParam;
}

// The window procedure.
LRESULT CALLBACK WindowFunc(HWND hwnd, UINT message,
                            WPARAM wParam, LPARAM lParam)
{
  HDC hdc;
  PAINTSTRUCT ps;

  static HBITMAP hbit; // virtual window bitmap
  HBRUSH hbrush;       // brush

  char str[] = "This is an animated message.";

  switch(message) {
    case WM_CREATE:
      // create virtual window
      maxX = GetSystemMetrics(SM_CXSCREEN);
      maxY = GetSystemMetrics(SM_CYSCREEN);
```

```
      hdc = GetDC(hwnd);
      memdc = CreateCompatibleDC(hdc);
      hbit = CreateCompatibleBitmap(hdc, maxX, maxY);
      SelectObject(memdc, hbit);
      hbrush = (HBRUSH) GetStockObject(WHITE_BRUSH);
      SelectObject(memdc, hbrush);
      PatBlt(memdc, 0, 0, maxX, maxY, PATCOPY);

      GetTextMetrics(hdc, &tm);

      animdim.left = X; animdim.top = Y;
      animdim.right = maxX + X;
      animdim.bottom = tm.tmHeight + Y;

      TextOut(memdc, X, Y, str, strlen(str));

      ReleaseDC(hwnd, hdc);
      InvalidateRect(hwnd, NULL, 1);
      break;
    case WM_PAINT:
      hdc = BeginPaint(hwnd, &ps);

      // copy virtual window to screen
      BitBlt(hdc, ps.rcPaint.left, ps.rcPaint.top,
            ps.rcPaint.right-ps.rcPaint.left, // width
            ps.rcPaint.bottom-ps.rcPaint.top, // height
            memdc,
            ps.rcPaint.left, ps.rcPaint.top,
            SRCCOPY);

      EndPaint(hwnd, &ps);
      break;
    case WM_DESTROY:
      DeleteDC(memdc);
      DeleteObject(hbit);
      PostQuitMessage(0);
      break;
    default:
      return DefWindowProc(hwnd, message, wParam, lParam);
  }
  return 0;
}
```

```
// Animate the banner during idle time.
void run(HWND hwnd, HDC memdc)
{
  // move left edge to the right end
  BitBlt(memdc, maxX-1, Y, 1, tm.tmHeight,
         memdc, 0, Y, SRCCOPY);

  // move remaining image left
  BitBlt(memdc, 0, Y, maxX-1, tm.tmHeight,
         memdc, 1, Y, SRCCOPY);

//  Sleep(10); // use this to slow animation

  InvalidateRect(hwnd, &animdim, 0);
}
```

ANNOTATIONS

There are three main differences between **Banner2.cpp** and **Banner1.cpp**. First, several variables, such as **memdc** and **animdim**, that had previously been static local variables in **WindowFunc( )** have been made global. This was necessary because they are now needed by both the **WindowFunc( )** and **run( )** functions.

Second, a call to **run( )** has been added to the message loop inside **WinMain( )** as shown here:

```
// The message loop.
while(GetMessage(&msg, NULL, 0, 0))
{
  TranslateMessage(&msg);
  DispatchMessage(&msg);
  run(hwnd, memdc); // cycle the animation
}
```

Thus, **run( )** is called whenever the program is idle (that is, between messages).

Third, the **run( )** function now handles the animation. It is shown here:

```
// Animate the banner during idle time.
void run(HWND hwnd, HDC memdc)
{
  // move left edge to the right end
  BitBlt(memdc, maxX-1, Y, 1, tm.tmHeight,
         memdc, 0, Y, SRCCOPY);

  // move remaining image left
```

```
BitBlt(memdc, 0, Y, maxX-1, tm.tmHeight,
       memdc, 1, Y, SRCCOPY);

//  Sleep(10); // use this to slow animation

InvalidateRect(hwnd, &animdim, 0);
}
```

Each time that **run( )** is called, it cycles the animation and then calls
InvalidateRect( ) to update the screen. It performs the same bit manipulations as the
WM_TIMER handler in **Banner1.cpp**. When you try this version of the program,
you will see a remarkable improvement in speed. However, it might even run too
fast. To handle this situation, remove the comments from the call to **Sleep( )** at the
end of **run( )**. You will need to experiment a bit with the precise length of the delay,
but usually a few milliseconds are sufficient.

Since the use of idle time produces much faster animation, it will be used by the
subsequent examples in this chapter.

Animating Sprites

A *sprite* is a small, animated object. Usually, a sprite is a bitmapped image, but it
could be any animated object no matter how it is drawn. For the purposes of this
chapter, all sprites are bitmapped images. As you will see, the general method used
to animate a sprite is straightforward. Of course, complexity increases as your
animated landscape grows.

The remainder of this chapter develops three sample programs that animate
bitmaps. The first presents the easiest animation case: A single bitmap is moved
over a solid background. The second animates three slightly different versions of the
bitmap, enhancing the illusion of movement. The third creates a foreground and
background aspect.

Although the techniques developed in this chapter can be used to animate any
size bitmap, the examples use bitmaps that are 64 × 64 pixels square. On the CD you
will find all of the bitmaps necessary for the examples in this chapter. The bitmap
used by the first example is the cat shown in Figure 4-3 while being edited. You can
also create your own bitmaps if you like by using an image editor. (One is usually
supplied by your compiler.) Just be sure that your bitmap is 64 × 64 pixels square. If
you choose to create your own, then for the first example, you will need one bitmap
called **BP1.BMP**.

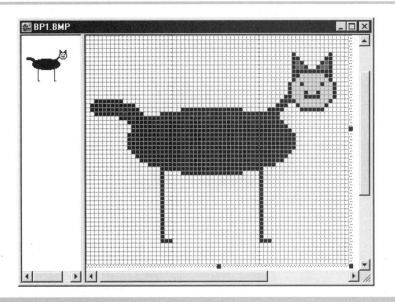

FIGURE 4-3. The **BP1.BMP** bitmap while being edited

A Simple Example of Sprite Animation

The simplest case of sprite animation occurs when the following two conditions are met:

◆ The bitmap is moved over a solid background.

◆ The bitmap contains a border that is at least one pixel thick and has the same color as the background color.

In this case, to animate a bitmap, all you have to do is repeatedly redraw the image, shifting it slightly with each cycle. As each new image is drawn, it overwrites the old image. Because the colors of the background and of the bitmap's border are the same, there is no need for an explicit erase operation. Of course, using this scheme, you must not move the sprite farther than the width of its border in any single animation cycle. While this approach may at first seem very limiting, it is actually quite useful in a variety of situations and is very efficient. The following program demonstrates it.

Code

Sprite1.cpp, shown here, animates a bitmapped sprite.

```cpp
// Animating a bitmapped sprite.

#include <windows.h>
#include <cstring>
#include <cstdio>

#define BITMAPSIZE 64

void run(HWND hwnd, HDC memdc);

LRESULT CALLBACK WindowFunc(HWND, UINT, WPARAM, LPARAM);

char szWinName[] = "MyWin";

HDC memdc;        // virtual window handle
HDC bmpdc;        // store bitmap device handle
int X=0, Y=20;    // current output location
int maxX, maxY;   // screen dimensions
TEXTMETRIC tm;    // font information
RECT animdim;     // size of area to animate

HBITMAP hAnBit1;  // animation bitmap

int WINAPI WinMain(HINSTANCE hThisInst, HINSTANCE hPrevInst,
                   LPSTR lpszArgs, int nWinMode)
{
  HWND hwnd;
  MSG msg;
  WNDCLASSEX wcl;

  // Define a window class.
  wcl.cbSize = sizeof(WNDCLASSEX);
  wcl.hInstance = hThisInst;
  wcl.lpszClassName = szWinName;
```

```
  wcl.lpfnWndProc = WindowFunc;
  wcl.style = 0; // default style
  wcl.hIcon = LoadIcon(NULL, IDI_APPLICATION); // large icon
  wcl.hIconSm = NULL; // use small version of large icon
  wcl.hCursor = LoadCursor(NULL, IDC_ARROW);
  wcl.hbrBackground = (HBRUSH) GetStockObject(WHITE_BRUSH);
  wcl.cbClsExtra = 0;
  wcl.cbWndExtra = 0;
  wcl.lpszMenuName = NULL; // no main

  // Register the window class.
  if(!RegisterClassEx(&wcl)) return 0;

  // load the bitmap
  hAnBit1 = LoadBitmap(hThisInst, "MYBP1");

  // Create a window.
  hwnd = CreateWindow(szWinName,
                      "Animating a Sprite",
                      WS_OVERLAPPEDWINDOW,
                      CW_USEDEFAULT, CW_USEDEFAULT,
                      CW_USEDEFAULT, CW_USEDEFAULT,
                      NULL, NULL, hThisInst, NULL);

  // Display the window.
  ShowWindow(hwnd, nWinMode);
  UpdateWindow(hwnd);

  // The message loop.
  while(GetMessage(&msg, NULL, 0, 0))
  {
    TranslateMessage(&msg);
    DispatchMessage(&msg);
    run(hwnd, memdc); // cycle the animation
  }

  return msg.wParam;
}

// The window procedure.
LRESULT CALLBACK WindowFunc(HWND hwnd, UINT message,
                            WPARAM wParam, LPARAM lParam)
{
  HDC hdc;
```

```
PAINTSTRUCT ps;

static HBITMAP hbit; // virtual window bitmap
HBRUSH hbrush;          // brush

switch(message) {
  case WM_CREATE:
    // create virtual window
    maxX = GetSystemMetrics(SM_CXSCREEN);
    maxY = GetSystemMetrics(SM_CYSCREEN);
    hdc = GetDC(hwnd);
    memdc = CreateCompatibleDC(hdc);
    hbit = CreateCompatibleBitmap(hdc, maxX, maxY);
    SelectObject(memdc, hbit);
    hbrush = (HBRUSH) GetStockObject(WHITE_BRUSH);
    SelectObject(memdc, hbrush);
    PatBlt(memdc, 0, 0, maxX, maxY, PATCOPY);

    animdim.left = X; animdim.top = Y;
    animdim.right = X + BITMAPSIZE;
    animdim.bottom = Y + BITMAPSIZE;

    bmpdc = CreateCompatibleDC(hdc);

    SelectObject(bmpdc, hAnBit1);

    // copy bitmap to virtual window
    BitBlt(memdc, X, Y, BITMAPSIZE, BITMAPSIZE,
           bmpdc, 0, 0, SRCCOPY);

    ReleaseDC(hwnd, hdc);
    InvalidateRect(hwnd, NULL, 1);
    break;
  case WM_PAINT:
    hdc = BeginPaint(hwnd, &ps);

    // copy virtual window to screen
    BitBlt(hdc, ps.rcPaint.left, ps.rcPaint.top,
           ps.rcPaint.right-ps.rcPaint.left, // width
           ps.rcPaint.bottom-ps.rcPaint.top, // height
           memdc,
           ps.rcPaint.left, ps.rcPaint.top,
           SRCCOPY);
```

```
      EndPaint(hwnd, &ps);
      break;
    case WM_SIZE:
      // clear window when resizing
      PatBlt(memdc, 0, 0, maxX, maxY, PATCOPY);
      InvalidateRect(hwnd, NULL, 0);
      break;
    case WM_DESTROY:
      DeleteDC(memdc);
      DeleteDC(bmpdc);
      DeleteObject(hbit);
      DeleteObject(hAnBit1);
      PostQuitMessage(0);
      break;
    default:
      return DefWindowProc(hwnd, message, wParam, lParam);
  }
  return 0;
}

// Animate during idle time.
void run(HWND hwnd, HDC memdc)
{
  RECT r;

  X++;

  // get size of client area
  GetClientRect(hwnd, &r);
  if(X+1 > r.right) X = 0;

  // copy bitmap to virtual window
  BitBlt(memdc, X, Y, BITMAPSIZE, BITMAPSIZE,
         bmpdc, 0, 0, SRCCOPY);

  animdim.left = X;
  animdim.top = Y;
  animdim.right = X + BITMAPSIZE;
  animdim.bottom = Y + BITMAPSIZE;

  Sleep(5); // use this to slow animation

  InvalidateRect(hwnd, &animdim, 0);
}
```

The resource file **Sprite1.rc** is shown here:

```
MYBP1 BITMAP BP1.BMP
```

ANNOTATIONS

Sprite1.cpp has many similarities to the banner programs, but there are also several important differences. The first thing to notice is that inside **WinMain( )**, the program loads the sprite bitmap and puts its handle into **hAnBit1**. As explained, this bitmap contains the image that will be animated.

Inside **WM_CREATE** a virtual window is created and then **animdim** is initialized using this code:

```
animdim.left = X; animdim.top = Y;
animdim.right = X + BITMAPSIZE;
animdim.bottom = Y + BITMAPSIZE;
```

Here, the region of the window that will be animated is the size of the bitmap plus the offsets supplied by **X** and **Y**. Unlike the banner programs, which manipulated an entire row of pixels, the sprite animation programs manipulate only the area covered by the sprite.

Next, the **WM_CREATE** handler creates a compatible device context that is used to hold the sprite, and then the sprite bitmap is selected into this device context. This is accomplished by these lines of code:

```
bmpdc = CreateCompatibleDC(hdc);

SelectObject(bmpdc, hAnBit1);
```

Here, **bmpdc** holds the bitmap's device context.

Next, the bitmap is initially drawn to the virtual window using this call to **BitBlt( )**:

```
// copy bitmap to virtual window
BitBlt(memdc, X, Y, BITMAPSIZE, BITMAPSIZE,
       bmpdc, 0, 0, SRCCOPY);
```

Before ending, **WM_CREATE** requests a repaint by calling **InvalidateRect( )**, causing the bitmap to be displayed on the screen.

The actual animation is performed by the **run( )** function. It begins with the following sequence:

```
X++;

// get size of client area
GetClientRect(hwnd, &r);
if(X+1 > r.right) X = 0;
```

In this and subsequent examples, the sprite is repeatedly moved across the window, left to right. To accomplish this, **X** is incremented. When the rightmost extent is reached, **X** is reset to 0. However, since the size of the window may change, the first thing that **run( )** does is obtain the current dimensions of the client area. This provides the current rightmost coordinate no matter what size the window is.

After the coordinates have been updated, the next image is copied into the virtual window specified by **memdc** using this call to **BitBlt( )**:

```
// copy bitmap to virtual window
BitBlt(memdc, X, Y, BITMAPSIZE, BITMAPSIZE,
       bmpdc, 0, 0, SRCCOPY);
```

Next, the **animdim** structure is updated to reflect the new location of the bitmap, as shown here:

```
animdim.left = X;
animdim.top = Y;
animdim.right = X + BITMAPSIZE;
animdim.bottom = Y + BITMAPSIZE;
```

This structure is then used in the following call to **InvalidateRect( )** to actually update the screen.

```
InvalidateRect(hwnd, &animdim, 0);
```

Thus, only the region of the window actually covered by the bitmap is repainted. This is much more efficient than repainting the entire window with each animation cycle. Because the bitmap has the same color border as the background of the window over which it is animated, and because its position is shifted by only one pixel with each cycle, there is no need for a separate erase operation. The trailing edge of the redrawn bitmap overwrites any residual part of the previous image.

If the animation runs too fast or too slow, you can change or eliminate the call to **Sleep( )** within **run( )**.

As mentioned earlier, the approach to animation used by **Sprite1.cpp** is limited for two reasons. First, it moves only a single bitmap. Second, it will work only with a solid background. In the next two sections, these two limitations will be removed.

Sprite-Level Animation

If you think about it, there are really two types of animation. The first is screen-based. This is the type of animation implemented by the preceding program. In screen-based animation, a fixed object is moved about the screen, but the object itself is unchanging. The second type of animation is sprite-based. In this case, the sprite itself changes form as it is animated. For example, to effectively animate an image of a cat walking, you will need to move the entire cat, but you will also need to show its legs moving. The movement of the legs occurs within the sprite itself.

The point here is that to achieve lifelike animation, both screen-level and sprite-level animation are required.

As with most other things, there are various ways to perform sprite-level animation. One of the easiest is to simply create multiple sprites, each slightly different from the next. When the sprite is animated, the images are sequenced with each animation cycle. This is the method of sprite-level animation used by the following example.

The following program requires two additional 64 × 64 pixel sprites, called **BP2.BMP** and **BP3.BMP**. The ones used in this book are present on the CD and are shown in Figure 4-4 (while being edited). Of course, you can also create your own bitmaps. Just make sure that they show slightly different versions of your original bitmap in **BP1.BMP**. Also, remember to leave a one-pixel border around your image.

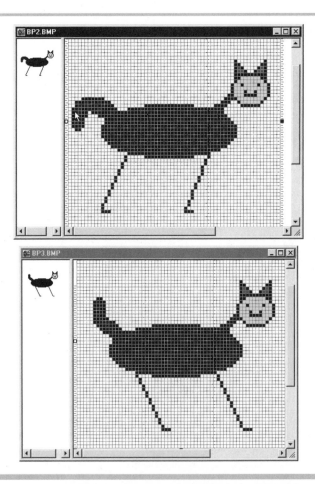

FIGURE 4-4.   The two additional sprites (**BP2.BMP** and **BP3.BMP**) required for the sprite-level animation example

Code

The **Sprite2.cpp** program is shown here. It is an enhanced version of **Sprite1.cpp** that performs both screen-level and sprite-level animation.

```cpp
// Adding sprite-level animation.

#include <windows.h>
#include <cstring>
#include <cstdio>

#define BITMAPSIZE 64

void run(HWND hwnd, HDC memdc);

LRESULT CALLBACK WindowFunc(HWND, UINT, WPARAM, LPARAM);

char szWinName[] = "MyWin";

HDC memdc;          // virtual window handle
HDC bmpdc;          // store bitmap device handle
int X=0, Y=20;      // current output location
int maxX, maxY;     // screen dimensions
TEXTMETRIC tm;      // font information
RECT animdim;       // size of area to animate

HBITMAP hAnBit1, hAnBit2, hAnBit3; // animation bitmaps

int WINAPI WinMain(HINSTANCE hThisInst, HINSTANCE hPrevInst,
                   LPSTR lpszArgs, int nWinMode)
{
  HWND hwnd;
  MSG msg;
  WNDCLASSEX wcl;

  // Define a window class.
  wcl.cbSize = sizeof(WNDCLASSEX);
  wcl.hInstance = hThisInst;
  wcl.lpszClassName = szWinName;
  wcl.lpfnWndProc = WindowFunc;
  wcl.style = 0; // default style
  wcl.hIcon = LoadIcon(NULL, IDI_APPLICATION); // large icon
  wcl.hIconSm = NULL; // use small version of large icon
```

```
wcl.hCursor = LoadCursor(NULL, IDC_ARROW);
wcl.hbrBackground = (HBRUSH) GetStockObject(WHITE_BRUSH);
wcl.cbClsExtra = 0;
wcl.cbWndExtra = 0;
wcl.lpszMenuName = NULL; // no main

// Register the window class.
if(!RegisterClassEx(&wcl)) return 0;

// load the bitmaps
hAnBit1 = LoadBitmap(hThisInst, "MYBP1");
hAnBit2 = LoadBitmap(hThisInst, "MYBP2");
hAnBit3 = LoadBitmap(hThisInst, "MYBP3");

// Create a window.
hwnd = CreateWindow(szWinName,
                    "Animating Multiple Sprites",
                    WS_OVERLAPPEDWINDOW,
                    CW_USEDEFAULT, CW_USEDEFAULT,
                    CW_USEDEFAULT, CW_USEDEFAULT,
                    NULL, NULL, hThisInst, NULL);

// Display the window.
ShowWindow(hwnd, nWinMode);
UpdateWindow(hwnd);

// The message loop.
while(GetMessage(&msg, NULL, 0, 0))
{
  TranslateMessage(&msg);
  DispatchMessage(&msg);
  run(hwnd, memdc); // cycle the animation
}

return msg.wParam;
}

// The window procedure.
LRESULT CALLBACK WindowFunc(HWND hwnd, UINT message,
                            WPARAM wParam, LPARAM lParam)
{
  HDC hdc;
  PAINTSTRUCT ps;
```

```
static HBITMAP hbit; // virtual window bitmap
HBRUSH hbrush;         // brush

switch(message) {
  case WM_CREATE:
    // create virtual window
    maxX = GetSystemMetrics(SM_CXSCREEN);
    maxY = GetSystemMetrics(SM_CYSCREEN);
    hdc = GetDC(hwnd);
    memdc = CreateCompatibleDC(hdc);
    hbit = CreateCompatibleBitmap(hdc, maxX, maxY);
    SelectObject(memdc, hbit);
    hbrush = (HBRUSH) GetStockObject(WHITE_BRUSH);
    SelectObject(memdc, hbrush);
    PatBlt(memdc, 0, 0, maxX, maxY, PATCOPY);

    animdim.left = X; animdim.top = Y;
    animdim.right = X + BITMAPSIZE;
    animdim.bottom = Y + BITMAPSIZE;

    bmpdc = CreateCompatibleDC(hdc);

    // select and copy first bitmap to virtual window
    SelectObject(bmpdc, hAnBit1);
    BitBlt(memdc, X, Y, BITMAPSIZE, BITMAPSIZE,
           bmpdc, 0, 0, SRCCOPY);

    ReleaseDC(hwnd, hdc);
    InvalidateRect(hwnd, NULL, 1);
    break;
  case WM_PAINT:
    hdc = BeginPaint(hwnd, &ps);

    // copy virtual window to screen
    BitBlt(hdc, ps.rcPaint.left, ps.rcPaint.top,
           ps.rcPaint.right-ps.rcPaint.left, // width
           ps.rcPaint.bottom-ps.rcPaint.top, // height
           memdc,
           ps.rcPaint.left, ps.rcPaint.top,
           SRCCOPY);

    EndPaint(hwnd, &ps);
```

```
        break;
    case WM_SIZE:
      // clear window when resizing
      PatBlt(memdc, 0, 0, maxX, maxY, PATCOPY);
      InvalidateRect(hwnd, NULL, 0);
      break;
    case WM_DESTROY:
      DeleteDC(memdc);
      DeleteDC(bmpdc);
      DeleteObject(hbit);
      DeleteObject(hAnBit1);
      DeleteObject(hAnBit2);
      DeleteObject(hAnBit3);
      PostQuitMessage(0);
      break;
    default:
      return DefWindowProc(hwnd, message, wParam, lParam);
  }
  return 0;
}

// Animate during idle time.
void run(HWND hwnd, HDC memdc)
{
  RECT r;

  static int map = 0;

  X++;

  // get size of client area
  GetClientRect(hwnd, &r);
  if(X+1 > r.right) X = 0;

  map++;
  if(map>2) map = 0;

  // switch between sprites
  switch(map) {
```

```
   case 0:
     SelectObject(bmpdc, hAnBit1);
     break;
   case 1:
     SelectObject(bmpdc, hAnBit2);
     break;
   case 2:
     SelectObject(bmpdc, hAnBit3);
     break;
 }

 // copy bitmap to virtual window
 BitBlt(memdc, X, Y, BITMAPSIZE, BITMAPSIZE,
        bmpdc, 0, 0, SRCCOPY);

 animdim.left = X;
 animdim.top = Y;
 animdim.right = X + BITMAPSIZE;
 animdim.bottom = Y + BITMAPSIZE;

 Sleep(5); // use this to slow down animation
 InvalidateRect(hwnd, &animdim, 0);
}
```

The **Sprite2.rc** resource file is shown here:

```
MYBP1 BITMAP BP1.BMP
MYBP2 BITMAP BP2.BMP
MYBP3 BITMAP BP3.BMP
```

▌**ANNOTATIONS**

Notice that **WinMain( )** now loads three bitmaps, storing their handles in **hAnBit1** through **hAnBit3**, using the following code:

```
// load the bitmaps
hAnBit1 = LoadBitmap(hThisInst, "MYBP1");
hAnBit2 = LoadBitmap(hThisInst, "MYBP2");
hAnBit3 = LoadBitmap(hThisInst, "MYBP3");
```

As explained, each bitmap contains a slightly different image and each will be used in turn when the animation cycles.

To support sprite-level animation, some important changes to **run( )** have been made. First, the static variable **map** is declared and initialized to 0. This variable controls which bitmap is displayed by each animation cycle. Each time the function is called, **map** is incremented using the following code:

```
map++;
if(map>2) map = 0;
```

Next, the following code executes:

```
// switch between sprites
switch(map) {
  case 0:
    SelectObject(bmpdc, hAnBit1);
    break;
  case 1:
    SelectObject(bmpdc, hAnBit2);
    break;
  case 2:
    SelectObject(bmpdc, hAnBit3);
    break;
}

// copy bitmap to virtual window
BitBlt(memdc, X, Y, BITMAPSIZE, BITMAPSIZE,
       bmpdc, 0, 0, SRCCOPY);
```

The **switch** statement determines which bitmap will be displayed by selecting the proper bitmap into the **bmpdc** device context. The call to **BitBlt( )** outputs the bitmap to the virtual window. Since **map** is incremented with each call to **run( )**, each animation cycle displays a different bitmap. For the bitmaps supplied for this example, this causes the legs of the cat to move as it runs across the window.

Working with Foregrounds and Backgrounds

Up to this point, all animation has taken place against a solid background. However, for more sophisticated animation, you will be animating a sprite in the foreground against some sort of background scene. Working with foregrounds and backgrounds adds complexity and overhead to any animation system. However, this is the price that must be paid for more lifelike animation.

When working against a background scene, another step is added to the animation cycle because the background must be restored. Thus, each time an animation cycle occurs, the following two-step procedure must be followed:

1. The background of the region currently occupied by the sprite must be restored, erasing the sprite in the process.

2. The sprite must be redrawn in its new location, preserving any part of the background that is not part of the sprite itself.

Step 2 is potentially non-trivial. If the sprite is contained in a bitmap, then some means of drawing the sprite will need to be worked out so that only those portions of the background that are actually covered by the sprite are overwritten.

Typically, the background is held in its own bitmap, which means that another bitmap will be added to the animation program. It is important to understand that only those parts of the background that need to be restored should be restored. The reason for this is speed. It takes much less time to restore a small region than it does to restore the entire screen.

Handling the Transparency Problem

When working with a foreground and a background, the most troubling problem is the issue of transparency. For example, if we want to animate a cat walking alongside a fence and if the cat is contained in a bitmap, then when the cat bitmap is copied onto the background, we want only the cat itself and not the entire rectangular region to appear in the final scene. Exactly how this is achieved will vary depending upon exactly what effect you are trying to achieve. For example, if you can color-code your background and foreground so that both use different color sets, then you can write very fast animation code using XOR operations. However, it is also possible to write "generic" code that will allow you to add a sprite over any background. This method is described here and used in the example at the end of this section.

To begin, let's restate the problem a bit more formally. As you know, in Windows, bitmaps are rectangular objects. That is, it is not possible to create an irregularly shaped bitmap. Most often, the sprite is contained within the confines of its bitmap, but does not utilize every pixel in the map. For example, the cat shown in

Figure 4-3 is a representative example. The cat itself occupies a relatively small portion of the entire map. The remainder of the map is simply unused. In the preceding examples, this situation did not cause a problem because the background of the screen was the same solid color as that of the background of the bitmap. However, when you want to animate a bitmapped sprite over a background scene containing several different shapes and colors, there must be some mechanism to prevent the unused portions of the bitmap from overwriting the background. Put differently, when you animate a sprite over a background scene, you want to see only the sprite, not the entire rectangular bitmap. Thus, there must be some means by which the unused background surrounding the sprite is rendered transparent.

The most general method by which the desired result can be achieved is through the use of a sequence of logical bitwise operations using the **BitBlt( )** function. In general terms, here is what will occur. First, you need to decide upon a transparent color. For the purposes of this chapter, white is used. Next, a monochrome (that is, black and white) image of each sprite in the animation sequence must be generated. These monochrome images will serve as masking bitmaps. Construct each mask so that the entire sprite is black on a white background. Once you have created each mask, the following steps are required to transparently write a sprite over an existing background scene.

1. Redraw the background, if necessary—that is, start with an untouched background.

2. AND the mask onto the background. This causes the area that will be occupied by the sprite to be cut out of the scene. (It will look like a sprite-shaped cookie cutter was used.)

3. Invert the mask. This produces a negative (black and white reversed) image of the mask.

4. AND the inverted mask with the sprite and save the result.

5. Invert the mask a second time to restore it to its original appearance so that it is ready for the next animation cycle.

6. OR the result of step 4 onto the background created in step 2.

After following these steps, the sprite portion of the bitmap will have been copied to the screen, but the surrounding background will have been left as-is. This process is depicted in Figure 4-5.

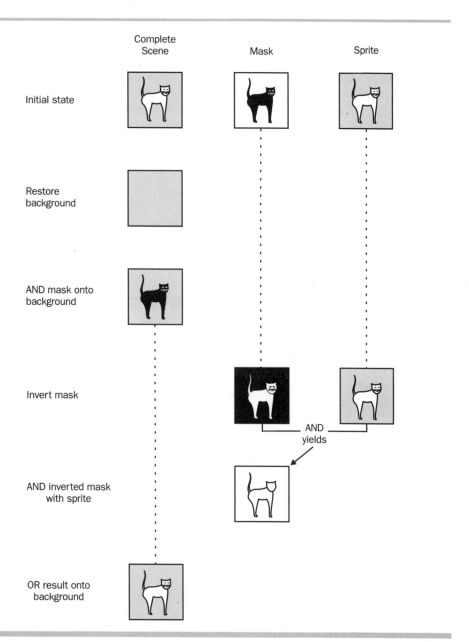

FIGURE 4-5.   Transparently drawing a sprite over a background scene

Creating the Masks

The CD contains the three masking bitmaps required by the following example in the files **BP4.BMP**, **BP5.BMP**, and **BP6.BMP**. If you are working with your own bitmaps, then you must create the three masks that correspond to the images contained in **BP1.BMP**, **BP2.BMP**, and **BP3.BMP**. The easiest way to do this is to create monochrome versions of each sprite. Depending upon what compiler you are using, you might be able to do this by loading the original image, changing its property to monochrome, and then saving it as the masking image.

Code

BckGrdAn.cpp

Here is the **BckGrdAn.cpp** program that illustrates animating a sprite against a background. In this case, the background is a picket fence. Thus, the program animates the cat running alongside the fence. Sample output is shown in Figure 4-6.

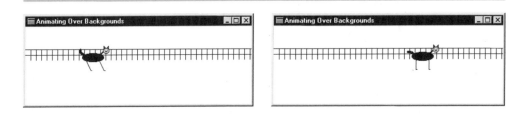

FIGURE 4-6.   Sample output from **BckGrdAn.cpp**

```
// Working with foregrounds and backgrounds.

#include <windows.h>
#include <cstring>
#include <cstdio>

#define BITMAPSIZE 64

void run(HWND hwnd, HDC memdc);

LRESULT CALLBACK WindowFunc(HWND, UINT, WPARAM, LPARAM);

char szWinName[] = "MyWin";

HDC memdc;          // virtual window handle
```

```
HDC bmpdc;          // store bitmap device handle
HDC backgroundDC;   // background DC
HDC tempdc1, tempdc2; // temporary DCs
int X=0, Y=20;      // current output location
int maxX, maxY;     // screen dimensions
TEXTMETRIC tm;      // font information
RECT animdim;       // size of area to animate

HBITMAP hAnBit1, hAnBit2, hAnBit3;   // animation bitmaps
HBITMAP hbit2, hbittemp1, hbittemp2; // bitmap handles
HBITMAP hmaskbit1, hmaskbit2, hmaskbit3; // masks

int WINAPI WinMain(HINSTANCE hThisInst, HINSTANCE hPrevInst,
                   LPSTR lpszArgs, int nWinMode)
{
  HWND hwnd;
  MSG msg;
  WNDCLASSEX wcl;

  // Define a window class.
  wcl.cbSize = sizeof(WNDCLASSEX);
  wcl.hInstance = hThisInst;
  wcl.lpszClassName = szWinName;
  wcl.lpfnWndProc = WindowFunc;
  wcl.style = 0; // default style
  wcl.hIcon = LoadIcon(NULL, IDI_APPLICATION); // large icon
  wcl.hIconSm = NULL; // use small version of large icon
  wcl.hCursor = LoadCursor(NULL, IDC_ARROW);
  wcl.hbrBackground = (HBRUSH) GetStockObject(WHITE_BRUSH);
  wcl.cbClsExtra = 0;
  wcl.cbWndExtra = 0;
  wcl.lpszMenuName = NULL; // no main

  // Register the window class.
  if(!RegisterClassEx(&wcl)) return 0;

  // load the bitmaps
  hAnBit1 = LoadBitmap(hThisInst, "MYBP1");
  hAnBit2 = LoadBitmap(hThisInst, "MYBP2");
  hAnBit3 = LoadBitmap(hThisInst, "MYBP3");

  // load the masks
  hmaskbit1 = LoadBitmap(hThisInst, "MASKBIT1");
```

```
      hmaskbit2 = LoadBitmap(hThisInst, "MASKBIT2");
      hmaskbit3 = LoadBitmap(hThisInst, "MASKBIT3");

      // Create a window.
      hwnd = CreateWindow(szWinName,
                          "Animating Over Backgrounds",
                          WS_OVERLAPPEDWINDOW,
                          CW_USEDEFAULT, CW_USEDEFAULT,
                          CW_USEDEFAULT, CW_USEDEFAULT,
                          NULL, NULL, hThisInst, NULL);

      // Display the window.
      ShowWindow(hwnd, nWinMode);
      UpdateWindow(hwnd);

      // The message loop.
      while(GetMessage(&msg, NULL, 0, 0))
      {
        TranslateMessage(&msg);
        DispatchMessage(&msg);
        run(hwnd, memdc); // cycle the animation
      }

      return msg.wParam;
}

// The window procedure.
LRESULT CALLBACK WindowFunc(HWND hwnd, UINT message,
                            WPARAM wParam, LPARAM lParam)
{
  HDC hdc;
  PAINTSTRUCT ps;

  static HBITMAP hbit; // virtual window bitmap
  HBRUSH hbrush;       // brush

  int i;

  switch(message) {
    case WM_CREATE:
      // create virtual window
      maxX = GetSystemMetrics(SM_CXSCREEN);
      maxY = GetSystemMetrics(SM_CYSCREEN);
```

```
hdc = GetDC(hwnd);
memdc = CreateCompatibleDC(hdc);
hbit = CreateCompatibleBitmap(hdc, maxX, maxY);
SelectObject(memdc, hbit);
hbrush = (HBRUSH) GetStockObject(WHITE_BRUSH);
SelectObject(memdc, hbrush);
PatBlt(memdc, 0, 0, maxX, maxY, PATCOPY);

// create the background DC
backgroundDC = CreateCompatibleDC(hdc);
hbit2 = CreateCompatibleBitmap(hdc, maxX, maxY);
SelectObject(backgroundDC, hbit2);
SelectObject(backgroundDC, hbrush);
PatBlt(backgroundDC, 0, 0, maxX, maxY, PATCOPY);

// draw the fence to background
for(i=40; i<60; i += 10) {
  MoveToEx(backgroundDC, 0, i, NULL);
  LineTo(backgroundDC, maxX, i);
}
for(i=10; i<maxX; i += 10) {
  MoveToEx(backgroundDC, i, 40, NULL);
  LineTo(backgroundDC, i, 60);
}

// copy background
BitBlt(memdc, 0, 0, maxX, maxY,
       backgroundDC, 0, 0, SRCCOPY);

// create temporary DCs
tempdc1 = CreateCompatibleDC(hdc);
tempdc2 = CreateCompatibleDC(hdc);
hbittemp2 = CreateCompatibleBitmap(hdc,
                  BITMAPSIZE, BITMAPSIZE);
SelectObject(tempdc2, hbittemp2);

animdim.left = X; animdim.top = Y;
animdim.right = X + BITMAPSIZE;
animdim.bottom = Y + BITMAPSIZE;

bmpdc = CreateCompatibleDC(hdc);

ReleaseDC(hwnd, hdc);
```

```
        InvalidateRect(hwnd, NULL, 1);
        break;
    case WM_PAINT:
        hdc = BeginPaint(hwnd, &ps);

        // copy virtual window to screen
        BitBlt(hdc, ps.rcPaint.left, ps.rcPaint.top,
                ps.rcPaint.right-ps.rcPaint.left, // width
                ps.rcPaint.bottom-ps.rcPaint.top,  // height
                memdc,
                ps.rcPaint.left, ps.rcPaint.top,
                SRCCOPY);

        EndPaint(hwnd, &ps);
        break;
    case WM_SIZE:
        // clear window when resizing
        PatBlt(memdc, 0, 0, maxX, maxY, PATCOPY);

        // copy background
        BitBlt(memdc, 0, 0, maxX, maxY,
                backgroundDC, 0, 0, SRCCOPY);

        InvalidateRect(hwnd, NULL, 0);
        break;
    case WM_DESTROY:
        DeleteDC(memdc);
        DeleteDC(bmpdc);
        DeleteDC(backgroundDC);
        DeleteDC(tempdc1);
        DeleteDC(tempdc2);
        DeleteObject(hAnBit1);
        DeleteObject(hAnBit2);
        DeleteObject(hAnBit3);
        DeleteObject(hbit);
        DeleteObject(hbit2);
        DeleteObject(hbittemp1);
        DeleteObject(hbittemp2);
        DeleteObject(hmaskbit1);
        DeleteObject(hmaskbit2);
        DeleteObject(hmaskbit3);
```

```
      PostQuitMessage(0);
      break;
    default:
      return DefWindowProc(hwnd, message, wParam, lParam);
  }
  return 0;
}

// Animate during idle time.
void run(HWND hwnd, HDC memdc)
{
  RECT r;

  static int map = 0;

  // restore the background
  BitBlt(memdc, X, Y, BITMAPSIZE, BITMAPSIZE,
          backgroundDC, X, Y, SRCCOPY);

  X++;

  // get size of client area
  GetClientRect(hwnd, &r);
  if(X+1 > r.right) X = 0;

  map++;
  if(map>2) map = 0;

  switch(map) {
    case 0:
      SelectObject(bmpdc, hAnBit1);
      SelectObject(tempdc1, hmaskbit1);
      break;
    case 1:
      SelectObject(bmpdc, hAnBit2);
      SelectObject(tempdc1, hmaskbit2);
      break;
    case 2:
      SelectObject(bmpdc, hAnBit3);
      SelectObject(tempdc1, hmaskbit3);
      break;
  }
```

```
   // AND masking image on background
   BitBlt(memdc, X, Y, BITMAPSIZE, BITMAPSIZE,
          tempdc1, 0, 0, SRCAND);

   // invert mask
   BitBlt(tempdc1, 0, 0, BITMAPSIZE, BITMAPSIZE,
          tempdc1, 0, 0, DSTINVERT);

   // copy sprite to work area
   BitBlt(tempdc2, 0, 0, BITMAPSIZE, BITMAPSIZE,
          bmpdc, 0, 0, SRCCOPY);

   // AND sprite with inverted mask
   BitBlt(tempdc2, 0, 0, BITMAPSIZE, BITMAPSIZE,
          tempdc1, 0, 0, SRCAND);

   // restore mask
   BitBlt(tempdc1, 0, 0, BITMAPSIZE, BITMAPSIZE,
          tempdc1, 0, 0, DSTINVERT);

   // OR resulting image onto background
   BitBlt(memdc, X, Y, BITMAPSIZE, BITMAPSIZE,
          tempdc2, 0, 0, SRCPAINT);

   animdim.left = X;
   animdim.top = Y;
   animdim.right = X + BITMAPSIZE;
   animdim.bottom = Y + BITMAPSIZE;

   Sleep(5); // use this to slow down animation

   InvalidateRect(hwnd, &animdim, 0);
}
```

Here is the **BckGrdAn.rc** resource file:

```
MYBP1 BITMAP BP1.BMP
MYBP2 BITMAP BP2.BMP
MYBP3 BITMAP BP3.BMP
MASKBIT1 BITMAP BP4.BMP
MASKBIT2 BITMAP BP5.BMP
MASKBIT3 BITMAP BP6.BMP
```

ANNOTATIONS

As you can see, this program is substantially more complex than the others in this chapter. The reason for this is, of course, because of all the extra bit manipulations needed to handle the foreground and background. For example, the program requires the use of two bitmaps that will act simply as scratch work areas. The handles to these areas are specified by **hbittemp1** and **hbittemp2**. The device contexts used by the scratch bitmaps are **tempdc1** and **tempdc2**. The handles to the masking bitmaps are held in **hmaskbit1**, **hmaskbit2**, and **hmaskbit3**. The background scene is held in the bitmap whose handle is **hbit2** and whose device context is specified by **backgroundDC**.

Inside **WinMain( )**, the following statements load the bitmaps and their masks:

```
// load the bitmaps
hAnBit1 = LoadBitmap(hThisInst, "MYBP1");
hAnBit2 = LoadBitmap(hThisInst, "MYBP2");
hAnBit3 = LoadBitmap(hThisInst, "MYBP3");

// load the masks
hmaskbit1 = LoadBitmap(hThisInst, "MASKBIT1");
hmaskbit2 = LoadBitmap(hThisInst, "MASKBIT2");
hmaskbit3 = LoadBitmap(hThisInst, "MASKBIT3");
```

Inside the **WM_CREATE** handler, the virtual window is created as before. After that, the following code creates a second memory device context that will hold the background image:

```
// create the background DC
backgroundDC = CreateCompatibleDC(hdc);
hbit2 = CreateCompatibleBitmap(hdc, maxX, maxY);
SelectObject(backgroundDC, hbit2);
SelectObject(backgroundDC, hbrush);
PatBlt(backgroundDC, 0, 0, maxX, maxY, PATCOPY);
```

Then, the background (which is a fence) is drawn onto the background bitmap using this code:

```
// draw the fence to background
for(i=40; i<60; i += 10) {
  MoveToEx(backgroundDC, 0, i, NULL);
  LineTo(backgroundDC, maxX, i);
}
for(i=10; i<maxX; i += 10) {
  MoveToEx(backgroundDC, i, 40, NULL);
  LineTo(backgroundDC, i, 60);
}
```

Then, the background is copied to the virtual window by this call to **BitBlt( )**:

```
// copy background
BitBlt(memdc, 0, 0, maxX, maxY,
       backgroundDC, 0, 0, SRCCOPY);
```

Next, **WM_CREATE** creates the two temporary DCs, **tempdc1** and **tempdc2**, with the following statements:

```
// create temporary DCs
tempdc1 = CreateCompatibleDC(hdc);
tempdc2 = CreateCompatibleDC(hdc);
```

The **tempdc1** is used by **run( )** to hold the currently selected mask. **tempdc2** is used as a work area for the various bit manipulations.

Then, a compatible bitmap is created and selected into **tempdc2** using the following sequence.

```
hbittemp2 = CreateCompatibleBitmap(hdc,
                   BITMAPSIZE, BITMAPSIZE);
SelectObject(tempdc2, hbittemp2);
```

tempdc2 can be given a bitmap when the window is created since it will not change over the course of the program. (Of course, the *contents* of the bitmap will change.)

As before, the **run( )** function cycles the animation, cycling through the sprite bitmaps and masks in the process. Much of the code is similar to that described for **Sprite2.cpp**. However, notice that the following **switch** statement selects both the proper image and mask.

```
switch(map) {
  case 0:
    SelectObject(bmpdc, hAnBit1);
    SelectObject(tempdc1, hmaskbit1);
    break;
  case 1:
    SelectObject(bmpdc, hAnBit2);
    SelectObject(tempdc1, hmaskbit2);
    break;
  case 2:
    SelectObject(bmpdc, hAnBit3);
    SelectObject(tempdc1, hmaskbit3);
    break;
}
```

Next, the bit manipulations take place, using these statements:

```
// invert mask
BitBlt(tempdc1, 0, 0, BITMAPSIZE, BITMAPSIZE,
       tempdc1, 0, 0, DSTINVERT);

// copy sprite to work area
BitBlt(tempdc2, 0, 0, BITMAPSIZE, BITMAPSIZE,
       bmpdc, 0, 0, SRCCOPY);

// AND sprite with inverted mask
BitBlt(tempdc2, 0, 0, BITMAPSIZE, BITMAPSIZE,
       tempdc1, 0, 0, SRCAND);

// restore mask
BitBlt(tempdc1, 0, 0, BITMAPSIZE, BITMAPSIZE,
       tempdc1, 0, 0, DSTINVERT);

// OR resulting image onto background
BitBlt(memdc, X, Y, BITMAPSIZE, BITMAPSIZE,
       tempdc2, 0, 0, SRCPAINT);
```

These operations are described in the comments and simply implement the procedures described earlier.

Something to Try

If you want to use a lifelike background for your animation, try scanning one in from a photograph. This is usually easier than trying to create one by hand. If you don't have a scanner, try this trick: Fax a copy of the photograph to your computer. Remember, fax machines contain scanners. The faxed image will be stored in a bitmap, which you should be able to use.

Tips for Using MFC

To implement bitmapped animation in an MFC program, follow the same procedures described in this chapter. The bit manipulations are not dependent upon either the API or the MFC approach to creating a Windows application. As explained at the end of Chapter 2, functions such as **BitBlt( )**, **PatBlt( )**, and **CreateCompatibleDC( )** are encapsulated by the **CDC** class. The bitmap functions, such as **CreateCompatibleBitmap( )** and **LoadBitmap( )**, are encapsulated by the **CBitmap** class. Suggestions for implementing a virtual window using MFC are also given at the end of Chapter 2.

Even though you don't actually see it in your MFC source code, all Windows programs, including those written using MFC, contain message loops. If you want to take advantage of the idle time available in an MFC application's message loop, you must override the **CWinApp::OnIdle( )** handler. In your override, implement the functionality contained in the **run( )** function in the examples.

A Thread Control Panel

Panel.h	A thread control panel
DemoPan.cpp	Demonstrates the thread control panel

All 32-bit versions of Windows support two forms of multitasking. The first type is process-based. This is the type of multiprocessing that Windows has supported from its inception. A process is, essentially, a program that is executing. In process-based multitasking, two or more processes can execute concurrently. The second type of multitasking is thread-based. A *thread* is a path of execution within a process. Every process has at least one thread, but it may have two or more. Thread-based multitasking allows two or more parts of a single program to execute concurrently. This added multitasking dimension allows extremely efficient programs to be written because you, the programmer, can define the separate threads of execution, and thus manage the way that your program executes.

In this chapter we will develop a useful tool that will help you when developing, debugging, and tuning multithreaded programs: a *thread control panel*. Using this control panel, you can change the priority of a thread, suspend a thread, resume a thread, or terminate a thread. Thus, the thread control panel lets you dynamically alter the execution characteristics of a multithreaded program while the program is running. Several of my introductory books on Windows programming have described a simplified version of this panel. The one developed here is substantially more sophisticated and is a good addition to your programmer's toolkit.

To illustrate the thread control panel, a multithreaded animation program (adapted from the animation examples in Chapter 4) is created. The control panel is included, allowing you to experiment with different priority settings and to see the effects of suspending and resuming thread execution.

If multithreading is new territory for you, then you will need to read the next few sections before moving on to the control panel. If you are already familiar with multithreading, then you can jump ahead.

Thread Fundamentals

Multithreaded multitasking adds a new dimension to your programming because it lets you, the programmer, more fully control how pieces of your program execute. This enables you to implement more efficient programs. For example, you could assign one thread of a program the job of sorting a file, another thread the job of gathering information from some remote source, and still another thread the task of performing user input. Because of multithreaded multitasking, each thread could execute concurrently and no CPU time would be wasted.

It is important to understand that all processes have at least one thread of execution. For the sake of discussion, this is called the *main thread*. However, it is possible to create one or more other threads of execution within the same process. In general, once a new thread is created, it also begins execution. Thus, each process starts with one thread of execution and may create one or more additional threads.

Creating a Thread

To create a thread, use the API function **CreateThread( )**. Its prototype is shown here:

```
HANDLE CreateThread(LPSECURITY_ATTRIBUTES lpSecAttr,
                    DWORD dwStackSize,
                    LPTHREAD_START_ROUTINE lpThreadFunc,
                    LPVOID lpParam,
                    DWORD dwFlags,
                    LPDWORD lpdwThreadID);
```

Here, *lpSecAttr* is a pointer to a set of security attributes pertaining to the thread. If *lpSecAttr* is **NULL**, then the default security descriptor is used. Because security is ignored by Windows 95/98, *lpSecAttr* should be **NULL** for those environments. In general, security attributes apply only to Windows NT/2000.

Each thread has its own stack. You can specify the size of the new thread's stack, in bytes, using the *dwStackSize* parameter. If this value is zero, then the thread will be given a stack that is the same size as the main thread of the process that creates it. (Specifying zero is the common approach taken to thread stack size.) The stack will be expanded, if necessary.

Each thread of execution begins with a call to a function, called the *thread function*, within the process. Execution of the thread continues until the thread function returns. The address of this function (that is, the entry point to the thread) is specified in *lpThreadFunc*. All thread functions must have this prototype:

```
DWORD WINAPI threadfunc(LPVOID param);
```

Any argument that you need to pass to the new thread is specified in **CreateThread( )**'s *lpParam*. This 32-bit value is recieved by the thread function in its parameter. This parameter may be used for any purpose. The function returns its exit status.

The *dwFlags* parameter determines the execution state of the thread. If it is zero, the thread begins execution immediately. If it is **CREATE_SUSPEND**, the thread is created in a suspended state, awaiting execution. (It may be started using a call to **ResumeThread( )**, discussed later.)

The identifier associated with a thread is returned in the double word pointed to by *lpdwThreadID*.

The function returns a handle to the thread if successful or **NULL** if a failure occurs. The thread handle can be explicitly destroyed by calling **CloseHandle( )**.

Terminating a Thread

As stated, a thread of execution terminates when its thread function returns. The process may also terminate the thread manually, using either **TerminateThread( )** or **ExitThread( )**, whose prototypes are shown here:

> BOOL TerminateThread(HANDLE *hThread*, DWORD *dwStatus*);
> VOID ExitThread(DWORD *dwStatus*);

For **TerminateThread( )**, *hThread* is the handle of the thread to be terminated. **ExitThread( )** can only be used to terminate the thread that calls **ExitThread( )**. For both functions, *dwStatus* is the termination status. **TerminateThread( )** returns nonzero if successful and zero otherwise.

Calling **ExitThread( )** is functionally equivalent to allowing a thread function to return normally. This means that the stack is properly reset. When a thread is terminated using **TerminateThread( )**, it is stopped immediately and does not perform any special cleanup activities. Also, **TerminateThread( )** may stop a thread during an important operation. For these reasons, it is usually best (and easiest) to let a thread terminate normally when its entry function returns.

Suspending and Resuming a Thread

A thread of execution may be suspended by calling **SuspendThread( )**. It may be resumed by calling **ResumeThread( )**. The prototypes for these functions are shown here:

> DWORD SuspendThread(HANDLE *hThread*);
> DWORD ResumeThread(HANDLE *hThread*);

For both functions, the handle to the thread is passed in *hThread*.

Each thread of execution has associated with it a *suspend count*. If this count is zero, then the thread is not suspended. If it is nonzero, the thread is in a suspended state. Each call to **SuspendThread( )** increments the suspend count. Each call to **ResumeThread( )** decrements the suspend count. A suspended thread will only resume after its suspend count has reached zero. Therefore, to resume a suspended thread implies that there must be the same number of calls to **ResumeThread( )** as there have been calls to **SuspendThread( )**.

Both functions return the thread's previous suspend count or –1 if an error occurs.

Sometimes you will want to suspend execution of a thread for only a short period of time and then have it resume. The easiest way to accomplish this is with the **Sleep( )** function, shown here:

> VOID Sleep(DWORD *Duration*);

Duration specifies the length of time, in milliseconds, that the calling thread will suspend. When this time has passed, the thread will automatically resume execution.

Sleep( ) has two main uses. First, it can be used to create a short time delay. You saw an example of this use in the preceding chapter. There, it was used to slow the animation cycle. Its second use is to force a task-switch. When a thread calls **Sleep( )**, the execution of the calling task is suspended and the next ready-to-run thread resumes. You can use **Sleep( )** to give up the remainder of the calling thread's time slice by specifying a zero duration.

Thread Priorities

Each thread has associated with it a priority setting. A thread's priority determines how much CPU time a thread receives. Low priority threads receive little. High priority threads receive a lot. Of course, how much CPU time a thread receives has profound impact on its execution characteristics and its interaction with other threads currently executing in the system.

A thread's priority setting is the combination of two values: the overall priority class of the process and the priority setting of the individual thread relative to that priority class. That is, a thread's actual priority is determined by combining the process' priority class with the thread's individual priority level. Each priority component is examined next.

PRIORITY CLASSES

You can obtain the current priority class by calling **GetPriorityClass( )** and you can set the priority class by calling **SetPriorityClass( )**. The prototypes for these functions are shown here:

DWORD GetPriorityClass(HANDLE *hApp*);
BOOL SetPriorityClass(HANDLE *hApp*, DWORD *dwPriority*);

Here, *hApp* is the handle of the process. **GetPriorityClass( )** returns the priority class of the application or zero on failure. For **SetPriorityClass( )**, *dwPriority* specifies the process' new priority class. The priority class values that are valid for all 32-bit versions of Windows are shown here, in order of highest to lowest priority:

REALTIME_PRIORITY_CLASS
HIGH_PRIORITY_CLASS
NORMAL_PRIORITY_CLASS
IDLE_PRIORITY_CLASS

SetPriorityClass( ) returns nonzero on success and zero on failure.

Programs are given the **NORMAL_PRIORITY_CLASS**, by default. Usually, you won't need to alter the priority class of your program. In fact, changing a process' priority class can have negative consequences on the overall performance of the computer system. For example, if you increase a program's priority class to **REALTIME_PRIORITY_CLASS**, it will dominate the CPU. For some specialized applications, you may need to increase an application's priority class, but usually you won't. For the purposes of this chapter, the default priority setting of a process will be used.

THREAD PRIORITIES

For any given priority class, each individual thread's priority determines how much CPU time it receives within its process. When a thread is first created, it is given normal priority. However, you can change a thread's priority—even while it is executing.

You can obtain a thread's priority setting by calling **GetThreadPriority( )**. You can increase or decrease a thread's priority using **SetThreadPriority( )**. The prototypes for these functions are shown here:

BOOL SetThreadPriority(HANDLE *hThread*, int *Priority*);
int GetThreadPriority(HANDLE *hThread*);

For both functions, *hThread* is the handle of the thread. For **SetThreadPriority( )**, *Priority* is the new priority setting. For **GetThreadPriority( )**, the current priority setting is returned. The priority settings are shown here, in order of highest to lowest:

Thread Priority	Value
THREAD_PRIORITY_TIME_CRITICAL	15
THREAD_PRIORITY_HIGHEST	2
THREAD_PRIORITY_ABOVE_NORMAL	1
THREAD_PRIORITY_NORMAL	0
THREAD_PRIORITY_BELOW_NORMAL	−1
THREAD_PRIORITY_LOWEST	−2
THREAD_PRIORITY_IDLE	−15

These values are actually increments or decrements that are applied to the priority class of the process. Through the combination of a process' priority class and thread priority, Windows supports 31 different priority settings for application programs.

GetThreadPriority( ) returns **THREAD_PRIORITY_ERROR_RETURN** if an error occurs. **SetThreadPriority( )** returns nonzero if successful and zero on failure.

A Thread Control Panel

When developing multithreaded programs, it is often useful to experiment with various thread attributes while your program is running. For example, you will want to try different priority settings, see the effects of suspending or resuming a thread, or even terminate a thread. Such experimentation can help you tune a program for maximum performance or test for thread-related bugs. The thread control panel developed in this section allows you to do these things. Using the control panel, you can easily change the execution profile of a thread and immediately observe the results.

The thread control panel is capable of controlling up to five threads. For the sake of simplicity, the control panel is implemented as a modal dialog box that is executed as part of the program's main thread. The thread control panel is capable of performing the following actions:

- Setting a thread's priority
- Suspending a thread
- Resuming a thread
- Terminating a thread

It also displays the current priority setting of each thread.

As stated, the control panel is implemented as a modal dialog box. As you know, when a modal dialog box is activated, it usually implies that the rest of the application is suspended until the user closes the box. However, in a multithreaded program, it is possible for a modal dialog box to run in its own thread. When this is the case, the other threads in the program remain active. As mentioned, the thread control panel will be executed by the main thread of any program that uses it. Therefore, it will be executing in its own thread of execution. The advantage of this approach is that modal dialog boxes are a little easier to create than are modeless ones. Also, since the dialog box may run in its own thread, there is no particular advantage, in this case, of using a modeless dialog box.

Panel.h

Code

The thread control panel is contained within a header file called **Panel.h**, shown here. The panel, itself, is defined by the **ThreadCtlPanel** class. To use the panel, follow these three steps:

1. Create a **ThreadCtlPanel** object.
2. Using **AddThread( )**, add to the panel the threads that you want to monitor. As the code is currently written, up to five threads can be monitored.
3. Activate the panel by calling **Activate( )**.

When activated, the panel looks like the one shown in Figure 5-1. Later in this chapter, you will see an example that uses the panel to control the execution of two threads.

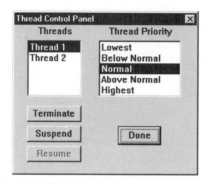

FIGURE 5-1.   The thread control panel

```
// Panel.h: A thread control panel class.

#include <windows.h>
#include "panelIDs.h"

#define NUMPRIORITIES 5
#define MAXTHREADS 5
#define OFFSET 2

class ThreadCtlPanel {
  static bool instantiated; // panel object exists
  static int numThreads; // number of threads monitored
  static HANDLE Threads[MAXTHREADS]; // thread handles
  static char thrdName[MAXTHREADS][80]; // thread names
  static bool suspended[MAXTHREADS]; // suspended?
  static bool terminated[MAXTHREADS]; // terminated?
  static char priorities[NUMPRIORITIES][80]; // priority
  HINSTANCE hInst; // instance handle of owner
  HWND hwnd; // window handle of owner
public:
  ThreadCtlPanel(HINSTANCE hI, HWND hw) {
    if(instantiated) {
      MessageBox(hwnd, "Panel already created.",
                 "Error", MB_OK);
```

```cpp
HANDLE ThreadCtlPanel::Threads[MAXTHREADS];
char ThreadCtlPanel::thrdName[MAXTHREADS][80];
bool ThreadCtlPanel::suspended[MAXTHREADS];
bool ThreadCtlPanel::terminated[MAXTHREADS];
char ThreadCtlPanel::priorities[NUMPRIORITIES][80] = {
  "Lowest",
  "Below Normal",
  "Normal",
  "Above Normal",
  "Highest"
};

// Thread control panel dialog box.
LRESULT CALLBACK ThreadCtlPanel::ThreadPanel(HWND hdwnd, UINT message,
                    WPARAM wParam, LPARAM lParam)
{
  int i;
  HWND hpb;
  static int ThPriority = 0;
  static int curThrd = 0;

  switch(message) {
    case WM_INITDIALOG:
      // initialize thread names list box
      for(i=0; i<numThreads; i++)
        SendDlgItemMessage(hdwnd, IDD_LB1,
            LB_ADDSTRING, 0, (LPARAM) thrdName[i]);

      // initialize thread priorities list box
      for(i=0; i<NUMPRIORITIES; i++)
        SendDlgItemMessage(hdwnd, IDD_LB2,
            LB_ADDSTRING, 0, (LPARAM) priorities[i]);

      // get current priority
      ThPriority = GetThreadPriority(Threads[curThrd]) + OFFSET;

      // update priority list box
      SendDlgItemMessage(hdwnd, IDD_LB2, LB_SETCURSEL,
                    (WPARAM) ThPriority, 0);

      // update thread selection list box
      SendDlgItemMessage(hdwnd, IDD_LB1, LB_SETCURSEL,
                    (WPARAM) curThrd, 0);
```

```
      return;
    }
    instantiated = true;
    hInst = hI;
    hwnd = hw;
    numThreads = 0;
    for(int i=0; i<MAXTHREADS; i++) {
      suspended[i] = false;
      terminated[i] = true;
    }
  }

  ~ThreadCtlPanel() {
    instantiated = false;
  }

  // add a thread to the panel
  bool AddThread(HANDLE hThrd, char *name) {
    if(numThreads >= MAXTHREADS) {
      MessageBox(HWND_DESKTOP, "Too many threads.",
                 "Error", MB_OK);
      return false;
    }
    Threads[numThreads] = hThrd;
    strcpy(thrdName[numThreads], name);
    terminated[numThreads] = false;
    numThreads++;
    return true;
  }

  // activate the panel
  int Activate() {
    return DialogBox(hInst, "THREADDB", hwnd,
                     (DLGPROC) ThreadPanel);
  }

  static LRESULT CALLBACK ThreadPanel(HWND hdwnd, UINT message,
                        WPARAM wParam, LPARAM lParam);
};

// declare static members for ThreadCtlPanel
bool ThreadCtlPanel::instantiated = false;
int ThreadCtlPanel::numThreads;
```

```
   // disable suspend button if necessary
   if(suspended[curThrd]) {
     hpb = GetDlgItem(hdwnd, IDD_SUSPEND);
     EnableWindow(hpb, 0); // disable suspend
   }
   else { // disable resume button
     hpb = GetDlgItem(hdwnd, IDD_RESUME);
     EnableWindow(hpb, 0); // disable resume
   }


   // disable terminate button if necessary
   if(!terminated[curThrd]) {
     hpb = GetDlgItem(hdwnd, IDD_TERMINATE);
     EnableWindow(hpb, 1); // enable terminate
   }
   else {
     hpb = GetDlgItem(hdwnd, IDD_TERMINATE);
     EnableWindow(hpb, 0); // disable terminate
   }

   return 1;
case WM_COMMAND:
   // get currently selected thread
   curThrd = SendDlgItemMessage(hdwnd, IDD_LB1,
                                LB_GETCURSEL, 0, 0);

   switch(LOWORD(wParam)) {
     case IDD_TERMINATE:
       // terminate selected thread
       TerminateThread(Threads[curThrd], 0);
       hpb = GetDlgItem(hdwnd, IDD_TERMINATE);
       EnableWindow(hpb, 0); // disable terminate
       terminated[curThrd] = true; // thread killed
       return 1;
     case IDD_SUSPEND:
       // suspend selected thread
       SuspendThread(Threads[curThrd]);
       suspended[curThrd] = true;
       hpb = GetDlgItem(hdwnd, IDD_SUSPEND);
       EnableWindow(hpb, 0); // disable suspend
       hpb = GetDlgItem(hdwnd, IDD_RESUME);
       EnableWindow(hpb, 1); // enable resume
       return 1;
```

```
case IDD_RESUME:
  // resume selected thread
  ResumeThread(Threads[curThrd]);
  suspended[curThrd] = false;
  hpb = GetDlgItem(hdwnd, IDD_SUSPEND);
  EnableWindow(hpb, 1); // enable suspend
  hpb = GetDlgItem(hdwnd, IDD_RESUME);
  EnableWindow(hpb, 0); // disable resume
  return 1;
case IDD_LB1:
  if(HIWORD(wParam)==LBN_SELCHANGE) {
    // selection in thread box is changing
    curThrd = SendDlgItemMessage(hdwnd, IDD_LB1,
                  LB_GETCURSEL, 0, 0);
    // set suspend/resume button state appropriately
    if(suspended[curThrd]) {
      hpb = GetDlgItem(hdwnd, IDD_SUSPEND);
      EnableWindow(hpb, 0); // disable suspend
      hpb = GetDlgItem(hdwnd, IDD_RESUME);
      EnableWindow(hpb, 1); // enable resume
    }
    else {
      hpb = GetDlgItem(hdwnd, IDD_SUSPEND);
      EnableWindow(hpb, 1); // enable suspend
      hpb = GetDlgItem(hdwnd, IDD_RESUME);
      EnableWindow(hpb, 0); // disable resume
    }

    // set terminate button state appropriately
    if(!terminated[curThrd]) {
      hpb = GetDlgItem(hdwnd, IDD_TERMINATE);
      EnableWindow(hpb, 1); // enable terminate
    }
    else {
      hpb = GetDlgItem(hdwnd, IDD_TERMINATE);
      EnableWindow(hpb, 0); // disable terminate
    }

    // update priority list box
    ThPriority =
      GetThreadPriority(Threads[curThrd]) + OFFSET;
    SendDlgItemMessage(hdwnd, IDD_LB2, LB_SETCURSEL,
                  (WPARAM) ThPriority, 0);
  }
```

```
        return 1;
    case IDD_LB2:
      if(HIWORD(wParam)==LBN_SELCHANGE) {
        // change thread's priority
        ThPriority = SendDlgItemMessage(hdwnd, IDD_LB2,
                        LB_GETCURSEL, 0, 0);
        SetThreadPriority(Threads[curThrd], ThPriority-OFFSET);
      }
      return 1;
    case IDCANCEL:
      EndDialog(hdwnd, 0);
      return 1;
  }
}

return 0;
}
```

The thread control panel requires the resource file **Panel.rc**, shown here. You will need to include this file in the resource file for any application that uses the thread control panel.

```
#include <windows.h>
#include "panelIDs.h"


THREADDB DIALOG 20, 20, 140, 110
CAPTION "Thread Control Panel"
STYLE DS_MODALFRAME | WS_POPUP | WS_CAPTION | WS_SYSMENU
{
  DEFPUSHBUTTON "Done", IDCANCEL, 80, 75, 33, 14,
                WS_CHILD | WS_VISIBLE | WS_TABSTOP
  LISTBOX IDD_LB1, 10, 11, 42, 42, LBS_NOTIFY | WS_CHILD |
             WS_VISIBLE | WS_BORDER | WS_VSCROLL | WS_TABSTOP
  PUSHBUTTON "Terminate", IDD_TERMINATE, 10, 60, 42, 12,
                WS_CHILD | WS_VISIBLE | WS_TABSTOP
  PUSHBUTTON "Suspend", IDD_SUSPEND, 10, 75, 42, 12,
                WS_CHILD | WS_VISIBLE | WS_TABSTOP
  PUSHBUTTON "Resume", IDD_RESUME, 10, 90, 42, 12,
                WS_CHILD | WS_VISIBLE | WS_TABSTOP
  LISTBOX IDD_LB2, 65, 11, 63, 42, LBS_NOTIFY |
           WS_VISIBLE | WS_BORDER | WS_VSCROLL | WS_TABSTOP
  CTEXT "Threads", IDD_TEXT1, 0, 0, 64, 10
  CTEXT "Thread Priority", IDD_TEXT2, 65, 0, 64, 10
}
```

The header file **PanelIDs.h** is shown next:

```
#define IDD_LB1        200
#define IDD_LB2        201
#define IDD_TERMINATE  202
#define IDD_SUSPEND    204
#define IDD_RESUME     206
#define IDD_TEXT1      208
#define IDD_TEXT2      209
```

ANNOTATIONS

Panel.h begins by defining the following macros:

```
#define NUMPRIORITIES 5
#define MAXTHREADS 5
#define OFFSET 2
```

MAXTHREADS determines the number of threads the panel can monitor. You can increase this if you like. **NUMPRIORITIES** defines the number of priorities that a thread may have. Using the control panel, you can set a thread to one of the following priorities.

    THREAD_PRIORITY_HIGHEST
    THREAD_PRIORITY_ABOVE_NORMAL
    THREAD_PRIORITY_NORMAL
    THREAD_PRIORITY_BELOW_NORMAL
    THREAD_PRIORITY_LOWEST

The other two thread priority settings

    THREAD_PRIORITY_TIME_CRITICAL
    THREAD_PRIORITY_IDLE

are not supported because, relative to the control panel, they are of little practical value. For example, if you want to create a time-critical application, you are better off making its priority class time-critical. However, you may want to try adding these settings on your own.

OFFSET defines an offset that will be used to translate between list box indexes and thread priorities. You should recall that normal priority has the value zero. In this example, the highest priority is **THREAD_PRIORITY_HIGHEST**, which is 2. The lowest priority is **THREAD_PRIORITY_LOWEST**, which is –2. Since list box indexes begin at zero, the offset is used to convert between indexes and priority settings.

The following sections examine the contents of **ThreadCtlPanel** in detail.

The ThreadCtlPanel Member Variables

The thread control panel is encapsulated by the **ThreadCtlPanel** class. The class defines the following member variables:

```
static bool instantiated; // panel object exists
static int numThreads; // number of threads monitored
static HANDLE Threads[MAXTHREADS]; // thread handles
static char thrdName[MAXTHREADS][80]; // thread names
static bool suspended[MAXTHREADS]; // suspended?
static bool terminated[MAXTHREADS]; // terminated?
static char priorities[NUMPRIORITIES][80]; // priority
HINSTANCE hInst; // instance handle of owner
HWND hwnd; // window handle of owner
```

The **instantiated** variable is used to ensure that one and only one instance of **ThreadCtlPanel** is created at any given time. This is necessary since the control panel is a global mechanism that affects the entire program that it is monitoring. The number of threads being controlled are stored in **numThreads**. The handles of the threads are stored in **Threads** and the names of those threads are stored in **thrdName**. The thread names are completely arbitrary and simply identify the threads in the panel. The suspended/running state of each thread is contained in **suspended**. A **true** value indicates that the thread is suspended. The terminated/alive state of each thread is stored in **terminated**. A **true** value indicates that the thread has been terminated. The current priority of each thread is stored in **priorities**. The instance handle and window handle of the application are stored in **hInst** and **hwnd**, respectively.

Notice that most of the member variables are static. The reason for this is that the window function for the control panel is, itself, static. As you should recall, a static member function can operate only upon static data members. Static member variables must be declared separately from their declarations within a class. The declarations for the static member variables are shown here:

```
// declare static members for ThreadCtlPanel
bool ThreadCtlPanel::instantiated = false;
int ThreadCtlPanel::numThreads;
HANDLE ThreadCtlPanel::Threads[MAXTHREADS];
char ThreadCtlPanel::thrdName[MAXTHREADS][80];
bool ThreadCtlPanel::suspended[MAXTHREADS];
bool ThreadCtlPanel::terminated[MAXTHREADS];
char ThreadCtlPanel::priorities[NUMPRIORITIES][80] = {
  "Lowest",
  "Below Normal",
  "Normal",
  "Above Normal",
  "Highest"
};
```

The ThreadCtlPanel Constructor

The constructor for **ThreadCtlPanel** is shown here. It must be passed the instance
and window handles of the application.

```
ThreadCtlPanel(HINSTANCE hI, HWND hw) {
  if(instantiated) {
    MessageBox(hwnd, "Panel already created.",
               "Error", MB_OK);
    return;
  }
  instantiated = true;
  hInst = hI;
  hwnd = hw;
  numThreads = 0;
  for(int i=0; i<MAXTHREADS; i++) {
    suspended[i] = false;
    terminated[i] = true;
  }
}
```

Let's examine this constructor line by line. First, if **instantiated** is **true**, then an error
is displayed and the constructor returns.

The next line sets **instantiated** to **true**. As mentioned, only one **ThreadCtlPanel**
object can be in existence at any one time. The **instantiated** member is initialized to
false. When an object is created, it is set to **true**.

Next, the instance handle **hInst** and the window handle **hwnd** are assigned the
values passed to the constructor. These handles will be used when the thread panel
dialog box is activated.

Next, **numThreads** is set to zero. This member will be incremented each time
a thread is added to the panel. Finally, the **suspended** and **terminated** arrays
are initialized.

The ThreadCtlPanel Destructor

The **ThreadCtlPanel** destructor is shown here:

```
~ThreadCtlPanel() {
  instantiated = false;
}
```

As you can see, it simply sets **instantiated** to **false**. Remember, only one object of
type **ThreadCtlPanel** can be active at any one time, so setting **instantiated** to **false**
allows a new panel to be instantiated.

AddThread( )

Once you have created a **ThreadCtlPanel** object, you add the threads that you want to control by calling **AddThread( )**, shown here. You must pass the handle to the thread in the first parameter and a pointer to the name that you want associated with the thread in the second parameter.

```
// add a thread to the panel
bool AddThread(HANDLE hThrd, char *name) {
  if(numThreads >= MAXTHREADS) {
    MessageBox(HWND_DESKTOP, "Too many threads.",
               "Error", MB_OK);
    return false;
  }
  Threads[numThreads] = hThrd;
  strcpy(thrdName[numThreads], name);
  terminated[numThreads] = false;
  numThreads++;
  return true;
}
```

First, the function determines if there is room for another thread. If not, an error is reported and **false** is returned. The variable **numThreads** keeps track of the number of threads. It also serves as the index number associated with the new thread. Next, the thread handle is assigned to the **Threads** array, the name is copied into the **thrdName** array, and the new thread's termination status is set to **false**. Next, **numThreads** is incremented and then **true** is returned. Your program can check the return value of **AddThread( )** to determine if the new thread was successfully added.

Activate( )

To activate the panel and display it on the screen, call **Activate( )**, shown here:

```
// activate the panel
int Activate() {
  return DialogBox(hInst, "THREADDB", hwnd,
                   (DLGPROC) ThreadPanel);
}
```

Activate( ) simply calls the Windows API function **DialogBox( )**, which creates and displays a modal dialog box. The window function for the box is **ThreadPanel( )**, described in the next section.

ThreadPanel( )

The **ThreadPanel( )** function is **ThreadCtlPanel**'s window function. It handles all of the user interaction with the panel. It is a long function and we will examine each message handler individually.

WM_INITDIALOG   When the panel is first displayed, **ThreadPanel( )** receives a **WM_INITDIALOG** message. The handler begins by initializing the list boxes that hold the names of the threads being controlled and the thread priorities using the code shown here:

```
// initialize thread names list box
for(i=0; i<numThreads; i++)
  SendDlgItemMessage(hdwnd, IDD_LB1,
      LB_ADDSTRING, 0, (LPARAM) thrdName[i]);


// initialize thread priorities list box
for(i=0; i<NUMPRIORITIES; i++)
  SendDlgItemMessage(hdwnd, IDD_LB2,
      LB_ADDSTRING, 0, (LPARAM) priorities[i]);
```

The **SendDlgItemMessage( )** function sends a message to a control that is contained within a dialog box. In this case, the messages are sent to the Threads and Thread Priority list boxes. The message **LB_ADDSTRING** tells the specified list box to add the string pointed to by the last argument to the end of the list.

Next, the priority setting of the currently selected thread (which is thread 0 by default) is obtained, and that entry in the Thread Priority list box is highlighted by the following code:

```
// get current priority
ThPriority = GetThreadPriority(Threads[curThrd]) + OFFSET;


// update priority list box
SendDlgItemMessage(hdwnd, IDD_LB2, LB_SETCURSEL,
                    (WPARAM) ThPriority, 0);
```

Here, the priority of the currently selected thread is obtained by calling **GetThreadPriority( )**. Notice that **OFFSET** is added to the value obtained from **GetThreadPriority( )**. This translates the priority setting into a zero-based index. This index is used by the call to **SendDlgItemMessage( )** to highlight the corresponding priority in the Threads Priority list box. In this call, **LB_SETCURSEL** tells the list box to set its current selection to the index specified by **ThPriority**.

The next line of code highlights the name of the currently selected thread in the Threads list box.

```
// update thread selection list box
SendDlgItemMessage(hdwnd, IDD_LB1, LB_SETCURSEL,
                   (WPARAM) curThrd, 0);
```

Although **curThrd** will be 0 the first time that the panel is activated, it might
be set to a different value on a subsequent activation. The preceding code ensures
that the settings for the currently selected thread are always shown when the panel
is activated.

Finally, the Resume, Suspend, and Terminate pushbuttons are enabled or
disabled as required by this code:

```
// disable suspend button if necessary
if(suspended[curThrd]) {
  hpb = GetDlgItem(hdwnd, IDD_SUSPEND);
  EnableWindow(hpb, 0); // disable suspend
}
else { // disable resume button
  hpb = GetDlgItem(hdwnd, IDD_RESUME);
  EnableWindow(hpb, 0); // disable resume
}

// disable terminate button if necessary
if(!terminated[curThrd]) {
  hpb = GetDlgItem(hdwnd, IDD_TERMINATE);
  EnableWindow(hpb, 1); // enable terminate
}
else {
  hpb = GetDlgItem(hdwnd, IDD_TERMINATE);
  EnableWindow(hpb, 0); // disable terminate
}

return 1;
```

Although it requires several steps, this code should be easy to follow. It simply
enables or disables the pushbuttons for the currently selected thread based upon the
values in the **suspended** and **terminated** arrays.

IDD_TERMINATE   When the user presses the Terminate button, the currently
selected thread is terminated by the following code:

```
case IDD_TERMINATE:
  // terminate selected thread
  TerminateThread(Threads[curThrd], 0);
  hpb = GetDlgItem(hdwnd, IDD_TERMINATE);
```

```
EnableWindow(hpb, 0); // disable terminate
terminated[curThrd] = true; // thread killed
return 1;
```

First, the API function **TerminateThread( )** is called to end the thread. Next, the Terminate button is disabled and the thread's entry in the **terminated** array is set to true. Once a thread has been terminated, it cannot be restarted.

As explained earlier, **TerminateThread( )** is not the safest way to stop a thread. It is, however, the only way that the thread control panel can stop a thread since the control panel is outside of the thread that it is terminating. (Recall that the better option, **ExitThread( )**, can be called only from within the thread itself.) You should terminate threads with caution since it is possible to stop a thread while it is in the middle of some important operation. For example, if you stop a thread while it holds a lock on a resource, that lock will never be released and the other threads in the program may suspend forever.

IDD_SUSPEND AND IDD_RESUME   When the user presses the Suspend button, the currently selected thread is suspended. The **IDD_SUSPEND** handler is shown here.

```
case IDD_SUSPEND:
  // suspend selected thread
  SuspendThread(Threads[curThrd]);
  suspended[curThrd] = true;
  hpb = GetDlgItem(hdwnd, IDD_SUSPEND);
  EnableWindow(hpb, 0); // disable suspend
  hpb = GetDlgItem(hdwnd, IDD_RESUME);
  EnableWindow(hpb, 1); // enable resume
  return 1;
```

The thread is suspended by calling the API function **SuspendThread( )**. Next, the thread's entry in the **suspended** array is set to **true**. Then, the Suspend button is disabled and the Resume button is enabled.

To resume a suspended thread, the user presses the Resume button. This causes an **IDD_RESUME** command message to be sent, which is handled by this code.

```
case IDD_RESUME:
  // resume selected thread
  ResumeThread(Threads[curThrd]);
  suspended[curThrd] = false;
  hpb = GetDlgItem(hdwnd, IDD_SUSPEND);
  EnableWindow(hpb, 1); // enable suspend
  hpb = GetDlgItem(hdwnd, IDD_RESUME);
  EnableWindow(hpb, 0); // disable resume
  return 1;
```

The thread is resumed by calling the API function **ResumeThread( )**. Next, the thread's entry in the **suspended** array is set to **true**. Then the Resume button is disabled and the Suspend button is enabled.

The handlers for **IDD_SUSPEND** and **IDD_RESUME** enable or disable the Suspend and Resume buttons so that for the selected thread, only the applicable button is available. For example, when a thread is running, the Suspend button is enabled and the Resume button is disabled. When you suspend the thread, the button states reverse.

You will need to exercise some caution when suspending a thread because it is possible to interrupt an important operation. For example, if the thread is holding a lock on a resource, then that resource will not be released until the suspended thread is resumed.

IDD_LB1 When the user interacts with the Threads list box, an **IDD_LB1** command message is generated. For list boxes, the high-order word of **wParam** contains the notification code associated with this message. List boxes can generate several different notification codes. The only one that we are interested in is **LBN_SELCHANGE**, which means that the user has changed the selection. As it relates to an **IDD_LB1** command message, this means that the user has changed the thread. This event is handled by the following code:

```
case IDD_LB1:
  if(HIWORD(wParam)==LBN_SELCHANGE) {
    // selection in thread box is changing
    curThrd = SendDlgItemMessage(hdwnd, IDD_LB1,
                  LB_GETCURSEL, 0, 0);
    // set suspend/resume button state appropriately
    if(suspended[curThrd]) {
      hpb = GetDlgItem(hdwnd, IDD_SUSPEND);
      EnableWindow(hpb, 0); // disable suspend
      hpb = GetDlgItem(hdwnd, IDD_RESUME);
      EnableWindow(hpb, 1); // enable resume
    }
    else {
      hpb = GetDlgItem(hdwnd, IDD_SUSPEND);
      EnableWindow(hpb, 1); // enable suspend
      hpb = GetDlgItem(hdwnd, IDD_RESUME);
      EnableWindow(hpb, 0); // disable resume
    }

    // set terminate button state appropriately
    if(!terminated[curThrd]) {
```

```
      hpb = GetDlgItem(hdwnd, IDD_TERMINATE);
      EnableWindow(hpb, 1); // enable terminate
    }
    else {
      hpb = GetDlgItem(hdwnd, IDD_TERMINATE);
      EnableWindow(hpb, 0); // disable terminate
    }

    // update priority list box
    ThPriority =
      GetThreadPriority(Threads[curThrd]) + OFFSET;
    SendDlgItemMessage(hdwnd, IDD_LB2, LB_SETCURSEL,
                  (WPARAM) ThPriority, 0);
  }
  return 1;
```

After confirming that an **LBN_SELCHANGE** message has been received, the **IDD_LB1** handler obtains the index of the newly selected thread by sending the box the **LB_GETCURSEL** message via the **SendDlgItemMessage( )** API function. The list box responds by returning the index of the selected item.

Next, the Suspend, Resume, and Terminate buttons are set according to the state of the newly selected thread. Then the Thread Priorities list box is updated to reflect the priority setting of the newly selected thread. Remember, each thread is separate from the others. Thus, the settings in the panel must be updated each time a new thread is selected.

IDD_LB2   When the user interacts with the Thread Priority list box, an **IDD_LB2** command message is sent. As just explained, the high-order word of **wParam** contains the notification code associated with this message and, again, the only one that we are interested in is **LBN_SELCHANGE**. In this case, it means that the user has changed a thread's priority. This event is handled by the following code.

```
case IDD_LB2:
  if(HIWORD(wParam)==LBN_SELCHANGE) {
    // change thread's priority
    ThPriority = SendDlgItemMessage(hdwnd, IDD_LB2,
                  LB_GETCURSEL, 0, 0);
    SetThreadPriority(Threads[curThrd], ThPriority-OFFSET);
  }
  return 1;
```

After confirming that an **LBN_SELCHANGE** message has been received, the **IDD_LB2** handler obtains the index of the new priority by sending the box the **LB_GETCURSEL** message. The handler then sets the currently selected thread to that priority. Thus, the thread's priority is changed immediately after a new priority has been chosen.

Demonstrating the Thread Control Panel

To add the thread control panel to a program, follow these three steps.

1. Include the header **Panel.h** in your program.

2. Include the file **Panel.rc** in your program's resource file.

3. Include in your program some way to add the threads to the panel and to activate the panel when it is needed.

Although using the thread control panel does require the addition of a minor amount of code to an application, this effort is easily offset by the benefit of being able to dynamically experiment with the runtime characteristics of the program's threads.

To demonstrate the thread control panel, we will create a multithreaded animation program that is adapted from those shown in Chapter 4. As mentioned in Chapter 4, one way that animation can be driven is by dedicating a thread of execution to each animated object. Each time an animation thread receives a time slice, the object being animated is moved. There is no longer a need for any additional means of cycling the animation. The multitasking system does this for you automatically. The program will animate two images, each driven by its own thread of execution. The thread control panel will be used to control the execution of each thread. Thus, you will be able to readily see the effects of changing a thread's priority, suspending/resuming a thread, or terminating a thread.

Code

DemoPan.cpp

The **DemoPan.cpp** program shown here creates two threads of animation and uses the thread control panel to alter their execution characteristics. Notice that it includes **Panel.h**. To activate the control panel, click the left mouse button. Sample output is shown in Figure 5-2.

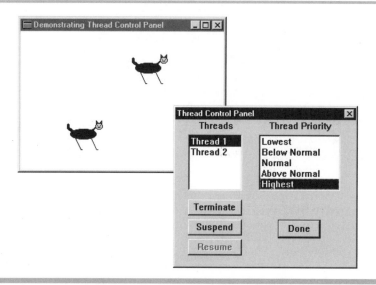

FIGURE 5-2. Sample output from **DemoPan.cpp**

```
// DemoPan.cpp: Demonstrating a thread control panel.

#include <windows.h>
#include "panel.h"

#define BITMAPSIZE 64

DWORD run1(LPVOID param);
DWORD run2(LPVOID param);

LRESULT CALLBACK WindowFunc(HWND, UINT, WPARAM, LPARAM);

char szWinName[] = "MyWin";

HDC memdc;          // virtual window handle
HDC bmpdc;          // store the bitmap device handle
int X=0, Y=20;      // current output location of object 1
int X2=0, Y2=120;   // current output location of object 2
int maxX, maxY;     // screen dimensions
TEXTMETRIC tm;      // font information

RECT animdim1, animdim2; // size of areas to animate

HBITMAP hAnBit1, hAnBit2, hAnBit3;    // animation bitmaps
```

```
HINSTANCE hInst;
int WINAPI WinMain(HINSTANCE hThisInst, HINSTANCE hPrevInst,
                   LPSTR lpszArgs, int nWinMode)
{
  HWND hwnd;
  MSG msg;
  WNDCLASSEX wcl;

  // Define a window class.
  wcl.cbSize = sizeof(WNDCLASSEX);
  wcl.hInstance = hThisInst;
  wcl.lpszClassName = szWinName;
  wcl.lpfnWndProc = WindowFunc;
  wcl.style = 0; // default style
  wcl.hIcon = LoadIcon(NULL, IDI_APPLICATION); // large icon
  wcl.hIconSm = NULL; // use small version of large icon
  wcl.hCursor = LoadCursor(NULL, IDC_ARROW);
  wcl.hbrBackground = (HBRUSH) GetStockObject(WHITE_BRUSH);
  wcl.cbClsExtra = 0;
  wcl.cbWndExtra = 0;
  wcl.lpszMenuName = NULL; // no main

  // Register the window class.
  if(!RegisterClassEx(&wcl)) return 0;

  // load the bitmaps
  hAnBit1 = LoadBitmap(hThisInst, "MYBP1");
  hAnBit2 = LoadBitmap(hThisInst, "MYBP2");
  hAnBit3 = LoadBitmap(hThisInst, "MYBP3");

  // Create a window.
  hwnd = CreateWindow(szWinName,
                      "Demonstrating Thread Control Panel",
                      WS_OVERLAPPEDWINDOW,
                      CW_USEDEFAULT, CW_USEDEFAULT,
                      CW_USEDEFAULT, CW_USEDEFAULT,
                      NULL, NULL, hThisInst, NULL);

  // Display the window.
  ShowWindow(hwnd, nWinMode);
  UpdateWindow(hwnd);
```

```
   // The message loop.
   while(GetMessage(&msg, NULL, 0, 0))
   {
     TranslateMessage(&msg);
     DispatchMessage(&msg);
   }

   return msg.wParam;
}

// The window procedure.
LRESULT CALLBACK WindowFunc(HWND hwnd, UINT message,
                           WPARAM wParam, LPARAM lParam)
{
  HDC hdc;
  PAINTSTRUCT ps;

  static HBITMAP hbit; // virtual window bitmap
  HBRUSH hbrush;        // brush

  DWORD Tid1, Tid2; // thread IDs
  static HANDLE hThread1, hThread2; // thread handles

  // create a thread control panel
  static ThreadCtlPanel panel(hInst, hwnd);

  switch(message) {
    case WM_CREATE:
      // create a virtual window
      maxX = GetSystemMetrics(SM_CXSCREEN);
      maxY = GetSystemMetrics(SM_CYSCREEN);
      hdc = GetDC(hwnd);
      memdc = CreateCompatibleDC(hdc);
      hbit = CreateCompatibleBitmap(hdc, maxX, maxY);
      SelectObject(memdc, hbit);
      hbrush = (HBRUSH) GetStockObject(WHITE_BRUSH);
      SelectObject(memdc, hbrush);
      PatBlt(memdc, 0, 0, maxX, maxY, PATCOPY);

      bmpdc = CreateCompatibleDC(hdc);

      ReleaseDC(hwnd, hdc);
      InvalidateRect(hwnd, NULL, 1);
```

```
  // start threads

  hThread1 = CreateThread(NULL, 0, (LPTHREAD_START_ROUTINE) run1,
                 (LPVOID) hwnd, 0, &Tid1);


  hThread2 = CreateThread(NULL, 0, (LPTHREAD_START_ROUTINE) run2,
                 (LPVOID) hwnd, 0, &Tid2);


  // add threads to panel
  panel.AddThread(hThread1, "Thread 1");
  panel.AddThread(hThread2, "Thread 2");
  break;
case WM_LBUTTONDOWN:
  // start thread control panel
  panel.Activate();
  break;
case WM_PAINT:
  hdc = BeginPaint(hwnd, &ps);

  // copy virtual window to screen
  BitBlt(hdc, ps.rcPaint.left, ps.rcPaint.top,
       ps.rcPaint.right-ps.rcPaint.left, // width
       ps.rcPaint.bottom-ps.rcPaint.top, // height
       memdc,
       ps.rcPaint.left, ps.rcPaint.top,
       SRCCOPY);


  EndPaint(hwnd, &ps);
  break;
case WM_DESTROY:
  DeleteDC(memdc);
  DeleteDC(bmpdc);
  DeleteObject(hAnBit1);
  DeleteObject(hAnBit2);
  DeleteObject(hAnBit3);
  DeleteObject(hbit);
  CloseHandle(hThread1);
  CloseHandle(hThread2);
  PostQuitMessage(0);
  break;
default:
  return DefWindowProc(hwnd, message, wParam, lParam);
}
```

```
    return 0;
}

// Animation thread #1.
DWORD run1(LPVOID param)
{
  RECT r;
  HWND hwnd;

  static int map = 0;

  hwnd = (HWND) param;

  for(;;) {
    X++;

    // get size of client area
    GetClientRect(hwnd, &r);
    if(X+1 > r.right) X = 0;

    map++;
    if(map>2) map = 0;

    // switch between sprites
    switch(map) {
      case 0:
        SelectObject(bmpdc, hAnBit1);
        break;
      case 1:
        SelectObject(bmpdc, hAnBit2);
        break;
      case 2:
        SelectObject(bmpdc, hAnBit3);
        break;
    }

    // copy bitmap to virtual window
    BitBlt(memdc, X, Y, BITMAPSIZE, BITMAPSIZE,
           bmpdc, 0, 0, SRCCOPY);

    animdim1.left = X;
    animdim1.top = Y;
```

```
      animdim1.right = X + BITMAPSIZE;
      animdim1.bottom = Y + BITMAPSIZE;

      InvalidateRect(hwnd, &animdim1, 0);
      Sleep(2); // use to slow animation
    }
  return 0;
}

// Animation thread #2.
DWORD run2(LPVOID param)
{
  RECT r;
  HWND hwnd;

  static int map = 0;

  hwnd = (HWND) param;

  for(;;) {
    X2++;

    // get size of client area
    GetClientRect(hwnd, &r);
    if(X2 > r.right) X2 = 0;

    map++;
    if(map>2) map = 0;

    // switch between sprites
    switch(map) {
      case 0:
        SelectObject(bmpdc, hAnBit1);
        break;
      case 1:
        SelectObject(bmpdc, hAnBit2);
        break;
      case 2:
        SelectObject(bmpdc, hAnBit3);
        break;
    }
```

```
    // copy bitmap to virtual window
    BitBlt(memdc, X2, Y2, BITMAPSIZE, BITMAPSIZE,
            bmpdc, 0, 0, SRCCOPY);
    animdim2.left = X2;
    animdim2.top = Y2;
    animdim2.right = X2 + BITMAPSIZE;
    animdim2.bottom = Y2 + BITMAPSIZE;

    InvalidateRect(hwnd, &animdim2, 0);
    Sleep(2); // use to slow animation
  }
  return 0;
}
```

The resource file **DemoPan.rc** is shown here. It declares the animation bitmaps, which are the same as those used in Chapter 4. Notice that it includes **Panel.rc**, which contains the dialog box used by the thread control panel.

```
#include "panel.rc"

MYBP1 BITMAP BP1.BMP
MYBP2 BITMAP BP2.BMP
MYBP3 BITMAP BP3.BMP
```

ANNOTATIONS

The animation aspects of the program are fully described in Chapter 4 and those discussions are not duplicated here. Notice, however, that the animation code has been moved into the two **run** functions.

Inside **WindowFunc( )**, variables that will hold the handles and IDs of the threads are created by these declarations:

```
DWORD Tid1, Tid2; // thread IDs
static HANDLE hThread1, hThread2; // thread handles
```

Next, a thread control panel object is created by this line of code.

```
// create a thread control panel
static ThreadCtlPanel panel(hInst, hwnd);
```

This creates an empty, inactive panel. After the threads are created, they will be added to the panel.

After creating the necessary bitmaps and DCs, the **WM_CREATE** handler creates two threads of execution, as shown here:

```
// start threads
hThread1 = CreateThread(NULL, 0, (LPTHREAD_START_ROUTINE) run1,
                 (LPVOID) hwnd, 0, &Tid1);

hThread2 = CreateThread(NULL, 0, (LPTHREAD_START_ROUTINE) run2,
                 (LPVOID) hwnd, 0, &Tid2);
```

The first call to **CreateThread( )** starts a thread of execution, specifying **run1( )** as the thread function. The second call to **CreateThread( )** creates a thread that uses **run2( )** as the thread function. The thread handles **hThread1** and **hThread2** receives the handles of the newly created threads. By default, each thread is created with a normal priority setting.

Next, the **WM_CREATE** handler adds the two threads of execution to the panel using this code sequence:

```
// add threads to panel
panel.AddThread(hThread1, "Thread 1");
panel.AddThread(hThread2, "Thread 2");
```

Remember, the names that you give to the threads are arbitrary. They simply identify the threads inside the Threads list box.

To activate the panel, click the left mouse button anywhere inside the main program window. This causes the **WM_LBUTTONDOWN** handler, shown next, to execute.

```
case WM_LBUTTONDOWN:
  // start thread control panel
  panel.Activate();
  break;
```

Once the panel is displayed, you can use it to control the execution of the two animation threads.

PROGRAMMER'S NOTE   *At the time of this writing, the effects of changing the thread priorities in DemoPan.cpp are most apparent when running Windows 95/98. When running the program under Windows NT/2000, you may need to remove or alter the calls to Sleep( ) to see any effects. You may also need to remove or alter the calls to Sleep( ) depending upon the speed of your computer's processor. Finally, increasing the priority of a thread to Highest might cause it to dominate the system. If this happens, just reduce its priority. You might have to be patient, however, because the other threads won't be getting much CPU time.*

Alternatives to CreateThread( ) and ExitThread( )

Before ending our discussion of the thread control panel, it is worthwhile to mention a potential problem. Depending upon what C/C++ compiler you are using and what C standard library functions are employed in your program, you may need to avoid the use of **CreateThread( )** and **ExitThread( )** because they may result in small memory leaks. A *memory leak* is the loss of a small amount of memory. It is usually caused when a portion of memory allocated by a program is not released when the program terminates. For many C/C++ compilers, including Microsoft Visual C++, if a multithreaded program utilizes standard C/C++ library functions and uses **CreateThread( )** and **ExitThread( )**, then small amounts of memory will be lost. (If your program does not use the C/C++ standard library, then no such losses will occur.) To eliminate this problem, you can use functions defined by the C/C++ runtime library to start and stop threads rather than those specified by the Win32 API. The ones provided by Visual C++ are described here.

The Visual C++ Thread Functions

The Microsoft Visual C++ alternatives to **CreateThread( )** and **ExitThread( )** are **_beginthreadex( )** and **_endthreadex( )**. They use the header file PROCESS.H. Here is the prototype for **_beginthreadex( )**.

```
unsigned long _beginthreadex(void *secAttr, unsigned stackSize,
                        unsigned (__stdcall *threadFunc)(void *),
                        void *param, unsigned flags,
                        unsigned *threadID);
```

As you can see, the parameters to **_beginthreadex( )** parallel those of **CreateThread( )**. Furthermore, they have the same meaning as those specified by **CreateThread( )**. *secAttr* is a pointer to a set of security attributes pertaining to the thread. However, for Windows 95/98, *secAttr* should be **NULL** because the security descriptor is ignored. The size of the new thread's stack, in bytes, is passed in *stackSize* parameter. If this value is zero, then the thread will be given a stack that is the same size as the main thread of the process that creates it. The stack will be expanded, if necessary.

The address of the thread function (that is, the entry point to the thread) is specified in *threadFunc*. For **_beginthreadex( )**, thread functions must have this prototype:

```
unsigned __stdcall threadfunc(void * param);
```

This prototype is functionally equivalent to the one for **CreateThread( )**, but uses different type names. Any argument that you need to pass to the new thread is specified in **_beginthreadex( )**'s *param* parameter.

The *flags* parameter determines the execution state of the thread. If it is zero, the thread begins execution immediately. If it is **CREATE_SUSPEND**, the thread is created in a suspended state, awaiting execution. (It may be started using a call to **ResumeThread( )**.) The identifier associated with a thread is returned in the variable pointed to by *threadID*.

The function returns a handle to the thread if successful or zero if a failure occurs. The prototype for **_endthreadex( )** is shown here:

void _endthreadex(unsigned *status*);

It functions just like **ExitThread( )** by stopping the thread and returning the exit code specified in *status*.

When using **_beginthreadex( )** and **_endthreadex( )**, you must remember to link in the multithreaded library.

PROGRAMMER'S NOTE *Microsoft supplies the functions **_beginthread( )** and **_endthread( )**, which can also be used to create and terminate a thread. However, **_beginthread( )** is a generic thread function that does not provide the detailed level of control available in **CreateThread( )**.*

Avoiding the C Library Functions

For many multithreaded programs, it is possible to avoid the use of the C/C++ standard library. In this case, you can use **CreateThread( )** and **ExitThread( )** without the potential for incurring memory leaks. For example, many of the programs in this book only use two C/C++ library functions: **sprintf( )** and **strlen( )**. Win32 contains substitutes for these functions called **wsprintf( )** and **lstrlen( )**, respectively. These functions contain some additional functionality that allows them to handle Unicode characters, but for the most part they work the same as their C/C++ library relatives.

Win32 also contains substitutes for several other C/C++ string handling functions. For example, **lstrcat( )**, **lstrcmp( )**, and **lstrcpy( )**. Various character functions are also provided, such as **CharUpper( )**, **CharLower( )**, **IsCharAlpha( )**, and **IsCharAlphaNumeric( )**. In general, if you are using the C/C++ standard library only for simple character handling, you can probably bypass it by using the functions built into Win32.

Tips for Using MFC

MFC defines two types of threads: *interface* and *worker*. An interface thread is capable of receiving and processing messages. In the language of MFC, interface threads contain a *message pump*. For this reason, the main thread of an MFC application (which is started when you declare an object of type **CWinApp**) is an interface thread. Worker threads do not receive or process messages. Instead, they exist to provide additional paths of execution within an interface thread. When creating multithreaded programs, you will most often add worker threads. The reason for this is that few applications need more than one message pump, but many applications benefit from additional threads of execution, which provide background processing. For example, the threads that run the animation in **DemoPan.cpp** would be translated into worker threads in an MFC program.

The thread functions are encapsulated by the **CWinThread** class. Although you can use **CWinThread::CreateThread( )**, most often you will use the **AfxBeginThread( )** function to create a thread. To terminate a thread, use **AfxEndThread( )**. Here are the mappings of the API to **CWinThread** members for the other thread functions used in this chapter:

SuspendThread	CWinThread::SuspendThread
ResumeThread	CWinThread::ResumeThread
GetThreadPriority	CWinThread::GetThreadPriority
SetThreadPriority	CWinThread::SetThreadPriority

Managing the Mouse and the Keyboard

| Mouse.cpp | A mouse control panel |
| Keyboard.cpp | A keyboard control panel |

A resource is said to be system wide when its operation or attributes affect the entire system, not just a single program. In general, when a program manages the system, it does so by changing the characteristics of system-wide resources. This chapter develops subsystems that manage two system-wide resources: the mouse and the keyboard. The subsystems are organized into control panels, which enable a user to easily change the attributes of these important input devices.

A Mouse Control Panel

The mouse is, of course, the most fundamental Windows control device. The handling of messages such as **WM_LBUTTONDOWN** is something that all beginning Windows programmers learn early on. Thus, most programmers are experienced at processing input from the mouse. What is sometimes overlooked, however, is that the mouse has various attributes that can be set under program control. For example, you can swap the left and right buttons, or set the double-click interval. While it is true that these and other attributes can be set using the Windows Control Panel, they can also be set by your application.

Taking control of the mouse offers significant benefits for some types of programs. For example, a program might want to allow the user to swap the left and right mouse buttons, allowing the mouse to be used in the weak hand, freeing the strong hand for keyboard input. Another program may want to change the double-click interval to simplify some complex selection process. Whatever the reason, it is easy for an application to set the mouse parameters.

The code in this section develops a mouse control panel that allows the user to

◆ Swap the mouse buttons

◆ Turn on and set the number of mouse trails

◆ Set the threshold double-click interval

Remember, however, that the mouse is a system-wide resource and the changes that you make via the control panel will affect other programs.

We will begin by reviewing the mouse-related API functions that we will be using.

Swapping the Mouse Buttons

It is an easy matter to reverse the meaning of the left and right mouse buttons. When reversed, the right button selects objects, such as a menu item, and the left button activates help and context menus. This is the opposite of their normal usage. Swapping the buttons is especially useful for left-handed users and for certain specialized input situations.

To swap the mouse buttons, call **SwapMouseButton( )**. Its prototype is shown here:

BOOL SwapMouseButton(BOOL *How*);

If *How* is non-zero, the meaning of the left and right mouse buttons will be reversed. To return the buttons to their default state, pass zero in *How*. The previous setting is returned.

Setting the Double-Click Interval

As you know, a double-click is two presses of a mouse button in quick succession. You can obtain and/or set the time interval in which two presses of a mouse button must occur in order for a double-click message to be generated. To obtain the double-click interval, use the API function **GetDoubleClickTime( )**, whose prototype is shown here:

UINT GetDoubleClickTime(void);

This function returns the interval of time (specified in milliseconds) in which a double-click must occur.

To set the double-click interval, use **SetDoubleClickTime( )**. Its prototype is shown here:

BOOL SetDoubleClickTime(UINT *Interval*);

Here, *Interval* specifies the number of milliseconds in which two presses of a mouse button must occur in order for a double-click to be generated. If you specify zero, then the default double-click time is used. (The default interval is approximately half a second.) The function returns non-zero if successful and zero on failure.

Here is a related point: To allow a window to receive double-click messages, you will need to specify **CS_DBLCLKS** in the **style** member of the **WNDCLASSEX** structure prior to registering the window class. That is, you must use a line of code like that shown here:

```
wcl.style = CS_DBLCLKS; // allow double-clicks
```

After you have enabled double-clicks, your program can receive double-click messages, including **WM_LBUTTONDBLCLK** and **WM_RBUTTONDBLCLK**.

Using Mouse Trails

Mouse trails are ghost images of the mouse pointer that persist on the screen for a short time and then fade. Mouse trails are helpful in a variety of situations, such as when using certain types of low-contrast display monitors, nonstandard color schemes, or custom mouse cursors.

To turn on and control mouse trails, you will need to use the **SystemParametersInfo( )** function, shown here:

BOOL SystemParametersInfo(UINT *What*, UINT *Param*,
                          VOID **pParam*, UINT *Update*);

Here, *What* specifies the system-wide parameter that you want to obtain or change. The meanings of *Param* and *pParam* vary depending upon the value of *What*. The *Update* parameter determines if the user profile is to be changed. If it is 0, as it is in the examples in this chapter, then the user profile is unchanged.

To turn on mouse trails, pass the value **SPI_SETMOUSETRAILS** in *What*. The value of *Param* determines the number of trails that will be shown. For example, to show five images, pass the value 5 in *Param*. If *Param* is 0 or 1, then no trails are displayed. The *pParam* parameter is not used.

To obtain the current mouse trails setting, pass the value **SPI_GETMOUSETRAILS** in *What* and pass a pointer to an integer variable in *pParam*. On return, that variable will contain the number of trails displayed. A value of 0 or 1 means that no trails are displayed. The *Param* parameter is not used.

Mouse.cpp

Code

The mouse control panel is contained in the **Mouse.cpp** program shown here. To activate the panel, select Options | Mouse Manager. To test the double-click interval, try double-clicking in the client area of the main window. If a double-click is generated, the message "double-click" will be displayed. Otherwise, the message "single-click" will be shown. Sample output is shown in Figure 6-1.

FIGURE 6-1. Sample output from **Mouse.cpp**

PROGRAMMER'S NOTE: *The **Mouse.cpp** program uses a trackbar common control. This means that you must include **ComCtl32.lib** in the link.*

```
// Mouse.cpp -- A mouse manager.

#include <windows.h>
#include <commctrl.h>
#include <cstring>
#include <cstdio>
#include "mouse.h"

LRESULT CALLBACK WindowFunc(HWND, UINT, WPARAM, LPARAM);
BOOL CALLBACK MousePanel(HWND, UINT, WPARAM, LPARAM);

char szWinName[] = "MyWin";

HINSTANCE hInst;

int WINAPI WinMain(HINSTANCE hThisInst, HINSTANCE hPrevInst,
                   LPSTR lpszArgs, int nWinMode)
{
  MSG msg;
  HWND hwnd;
  WNDCLASSEX wcl;
  HACCEL hAccel;
  INITCOMMONCONTROLSEX cc;

  // Define a window class.
  wcl.cbSize = sizeof(WNDCLASSEX);
  wcl.hInstance = hThisInst;
  wcl.lpszClassName = szWinName;
  wcl.lpfnWndProc = WindowFunc;
  wcl.style = CS_DBLCLKS; // enable double-clicks
  wcl.hIcon = LoadIcon(NULL, IDI_APPLICATION); // large icon
  wcl.hIconSm = NULL; // use small version of large icon
  wcl.hCursor = LoadCursor(NULL, IDC_ARROW);
  wcl.hbrBackground = (HBRUSH) GetStockObject(WHITE_BRUSH);
  wcl.cbClsExtra = 0;
  wcl.cbWndExtra = 0;
  wcl.lpszMenuName = "MouseMenu";
```

```
  // Register the window class.
  if(!RegisterClassEx(&wcl)) return 0;

  // Create a window.
  hwnd = CreateWindow(szWinName,
                      "Demonstrating The Mouse Control Panel",
                      WS_OVERLAPPEDWINDOW,
                      CW_USEDEFAULT, CW_USEDEFAULT,
                      CW_USEDEFAULT, CW_USEDEFAULT,
                      NULL, NULL, hThisInst, NULL);

  hInst = hThisInst; // save the current instance handle

  // Load accelerators.
  hAccel = LoadAccelerators(hThisInst, "MouseMenu");

  // Initialize the common controls.
  cc.dwSize = sizeof(INITCOMMONCONTROLSEX);
  cc.dwICC = ICC_BAR_CLASSES;
  InitCommonControlsEx(&cc);

  // Display the window.
  ShowWindow(hwnd, nWinMode);
  UpdateWindow(hwnd);

  // The message loop.
  while(GetMessage(&msg, NULL, 0, 0))
  {
    if(!TranslateAccelerator(hwnd, hAccel, &msg)) {
      TranslateMessage(&msg);
      DispatchMessage(&msg);
    }
  }

  return msg.wParam;
}

// The window procedure.
LRESULT CALLBACK WindowFunc(HWND hwnd, UINT message,
                           WPARAM wParam, LPARAM lParam)
{
  int response;
  HDC hdc;
```

```
char str[80];

switch(message) {
  case WM_COMMAND:
    switch(LOWORD(wParam)) {
      case IDM_DIALOG:
        DialogBox(hInst, "MouseDB", hwnd,
                  (DLGPROC) MousePanel);
        break;
      case IDM_EXIT:
        response = MessageBox(hwnd, "Quit the Program?",
                             "Exit", MB_YESNO);
        if(response == IDYES) PostQuitMessage(0);
        break;
      case IDM_ABOUT:
        MessageBox(hwnd, "Mouse Control Panel, V1.0",
                  "Mouse Control Panel", MB_OK);
        break;
    }
    break;
  case WM_LBUTTONDBLCLK:
    hdc = GetDC(hwnd);

    strcpy(str, "double-click");
    TextOut(hdc, 1, 1, str, strlen(str));

    ReleaseDC(hwnd, hdc);
    break;
  case WM_LBUTTONDOWN:
    hdc = GetDC(hwnd);

    strcpy(str, "single-click ");
    TextOut(hdc, 1, 1, str, strlen(str));

    ReleaseDC(hwnd, hdc);
    break;
  case WM_DESTROY:
    PostQuitMessage(0);
    break;
  default:
    return DefWindowProc(hwnd, message, wParam, lParam);
}
return 0;
```

```
}

// Mouse Manager
BOOL CALLBACK MousePanel(HWND hdwnd, UINT message,
                         WPARAM wParam, LPARAM lParam)
{
  char str[80];
  HDC hdc;
  PAINTSTRUCT paintstruct;

  static unsigned orgDblClk;
  static unsigned orgTrails;
  static int orgBswap;

  static HWND hTrackTrails;
  static HWND hTrackDblClk;

  unsigned trackpos;
  int low=1, high=10;

  switch(message) {
    case WM_INITDIALOG:
      // create double-click track bar
      orgDblClk = GetDoubleClickTime();
      hTrackDblClk = CreateWindow(TRACKBAR_CLASS,
                  "",
                  WS_CHILD | WS_VISIBLE | WS_TABSTOP |
                  TBS_AUTOTICKS | WS_BORDER,
                  2, 2,
                  200, 28,
                  hdwnd,
                  NULL,
                  hInst,
                  NULL
      );
      SendMessage(hTrackDblClk, TBM_SETRANGE,
                  1, MAKELONG(low, high));
      SendMessage(hTrackDblClk, TBM_SETPOS,
                  1, orgDblClk / 100);


      // create mouse trails track bar
      SystemParametersInfo(SPI_GETMOUSETRAILS,
```

```
                       NULL, &orgTrails, 0);
  if(orgTrails==0) orgTrails = 1;
  hTrackTrails = CreateWindow(TRACKBAR_CLASS,
               "",
               WS_CHILD | WS_VISIBLE | WS_TABSTOP |
               TBS_AUTOTICKS | WS_BORDER,
               2, 62,
               200, 28,
               hdwnd,
               NULL,
               hInst,
               NULL
  );
  SendMessage(hTrackTrails, TBM_SETRANGE,
             1, MAKELONG(low, high));
  SendMessage(hTrackTrails, TBM_SETPOS,
             1, orgTrails);


  // set double-click time in edit box
  SetDlgItemInt(hdwnd, IDD_EB1, orgDblClk, 1);

  // set mouse trails in edit box
  SetDlgItemInt(hdwnd, IDD_EB2, orgTrails-1, 1);

  // determine original swap-state of buttons
  orgBswap = SwapMouseButton(false);
  SwapMouseButton(orgBswap);

  // set button swap check box
  SendDlgItemMessage(hdwnd, IDD_CB1, BM_SETCHECK,
                    orgBswap, 0);

  return 1;
case WM_HSCROLL: // a track bar was activated
  if(hTrackTrails == (HWND)lParam) {
    switch(LOWORD(wParam)) {
      case TB_TOP:
      case TB_BOTTOM:        // For this program
      case TB_LINEUP:        // all messages will be
      case TB_LINEDOWN:      // processed in the same
      case TB_THUMBPOSITION: // way.
      case TB_THUMBTRACK:
```

```
            case TB_PAGEUP:
            case TB_PAGEDOWN:
              trackpos = SendMessage(hTrackTrails,
                            TBM_GETPOS, 0, 0);
              SetDlgItemInt(hdwnd, IDD_EB2, trackpos-1, 1);
              SystemParametersInfo(SPI_SETMOUSETRAILS,
                                  trackpos, 0, 0);

              return 1;
          }
        }
      else if(hTrackDblClk == (HWND)lParam) {
        switch(LOWORD(wParam)) {
          case TB_TOP:
          case TB_BOTTOM:        // For this program
          case TB_LINEUP:        // all messages will be
          case TB_LINEDOWN:      // processed in the same
          case TB_THUMBPOSITION: // way.
          case TB_THUMBTRACK:
          case TB_PAGEUP:
          case TB_PAGEDOWN:
            trackpos = SendMessage(hTrackDblClk,
                          TBM_GETPOS, 0, 0);
            SetDlgItemInt(hdwnd, IDD_EB1,
                          trackpos * 100, 1);
            SetDoubleClickTime(trackpos * 100);
            return 1;
        }
      }
      break;
    case WM_COMMAND:
      switch(LOWORD(wParam)) {
        case IDOK:
          EndDialog(hdwnd, 0);
          return 1;
        case IDCANCEL:
          SystemParametersInfo(SPI_SETMOUSETRAILS,
                              orgTrails, 0, 0);
          SetDoubleClickTime(orgDblClk);

          if(orgBswap)
            SwapMouseButton(true);
          else
```

```
                    SwapMouseButton(false);

                  EndDialog(hdwnd, 1);
                  return 1;
                case IDD_CB1:
                  if(SendDlgItemMessage(hdwnd,
                       IDD_CB1, BM_GETCHECK, 0, 0) == BST_CHECKED)
                    SwapMouseButton(true);
                  else
                    SwapMouseButton(false);

                  return 1;
                case IDD_EB1:
                  // update double-click trackbar
                  trackpos = GetDlgItemInt(hdwnd, IDD_EB1, NULL, 1) / 100;
                  SendMessage(hTrackDblClk, TBM_SETPOS, 1, trackpos);
                  SetDoubleClickTime(trackpos * 100);
                  return 1;
                case IDD_EB2:
                  // update mouse trails trackbar
                  trackpos = GetDlgItemInt(hdwnd, IDD_EB2, NULL, 1);
                  SendMessage(hTrackTrails, TBM_SETPOS, 1, trackpos+1);
                  SystemParametersInfo(SPI_SETMOUSETRAILS,
                                       trackpos+1, 0, 0);
                  return 1;
              }
              break;
          case WM_PAINT:
            hdc = BeginPaint(hdwnd, &paintstruct);
            SetBkMode(hdc, TRANSPARENT);

            sprintf(str, "Set Double-Click Time");
            TextOut(hdc, 30, 34, str, strlen(str));

            sprintf(str, "Set Number of Trails");
            TextOut(hdc, 30, 92, str, strlen(str));

            EndPaint(hdwnd, &paintstruct);
            return 1;
        }
      return 0;
    }
```

The **Mouse.rc** resource file is shown here:

```
#include <windows.h>
#include "mouse.h"

MouseMenu MENU
{
  POPUP "&Options"
  {
    MENUITEM "&Mouse Manager\tF2", IDM_DIALOG
    MENUITEM "&Exit\tF3", IDM_EXIT
  }
  POPUP "&Help" {
    MENUITEM "&About\tF1", IDM_ABOUT
  }
}


MouseMenu ACCELERATORS
{
  VK_F2, IDM_DIALOG, VIRTKEY
  VK_F3, IDM_EXIT, VIRTKEY
  VK_F1, IDM_ABOUT, VIRTKEY
}


MouseDB DIALOG 18, 18, 126, 100
CAPTION "Mouse Manager"
STYLE DS_MODALFRAME | WS_POPUP | WS_CAPTION | WS_SYSMENU
{
  PUSHBUTTON "OK", IDOK, 30, 80, 30, 14,
            WS_CHILD | WS_VISIBLE | WS_TABSTOP
  PUSHBUTTON "Cancel", IDCANCEL, 70, 80, 30, 14,
            WS_CHILD | WS_VISIBLE | WS_TABSTOP
  EDITTEXT IDD_EB1, 105, 2, 20, 12, ES_LEFT | WS_CHILD |
          WS_VISIBLE | WS_BORDER
  EDITTEXT IDD_EB2, 105, 31, 12, 12, ES_LEFT | WS_CHILD |
          WS_VISIBLE | WS_BORDER
  AUTOCHECKBOX "Swap Buttons", IDD_CB1, 1, 60, 60, 10
}
```

The header file **Mouse.h** is shown next:

```
#define IDM_DIALOG    100
#define IDM_EXIT      101
#define IDM_ABOUT     102
```

```
#define IDD_CB1        400

#define IDD_EB1        500
#define IDD_EB2        501
```

ANNOTATIONS

Although it has the same basic skeleton as that used by most of the other examples in this book, **WinMain( )** has two important differences. First, the style field of its window class is assigned the value **CS_DBLCLKS**. As explained earlier, this enables the main window to receive double-click messages. The ability to receive double-clicks is needed to allow you to try the double-click interval after you have changed it.

The second difference in **WinMain( )** is the code that initializes the common controls. As you probably know, there are a number of common controls, such as toolbars, trackbars, tree views, and tooltips. Any program that uses a common control must do three things. First, it must include the **CommCtrl.h** header file. Second, it must include **ComCtl32.lib** in the link process. Third, it must initialize the common controls by calling **InitCommonControlsEx( )**, specifying the control(s) that it will be using. The mouse control panel uses a trackbar and this is initialized by the following sequence:

```
// Initialize the common controls.
cc.dwSize = sizeof(INITCOMMONCONTROLSEX);
cc.dwICC = ICC_BAR_CLASSES;
InitCommonControlsEx(&cc);
```

Here, **cc** is a structure of type **INITCOMMONCONTROLSEX**. Its **dwICC** field specifies the controls that you want initialized. Here, **ICC_BAR_CLASSES** is used, which initializes the bar-based common controls, including the trackbar. For other types of common controls, other values will need to be passed.

MousePanel( )

The main action of the program takes place in **MousePanel( )**, which is the dialog box function that handles user input from the mouse control panel. This is a long function and each part is examined separately.

THE VARIABLES   **MousePanel( )** begins by defining the following variables:

```
char str[80];
HDC hdc;
PAINTSTRUCT paintstruct;
```

```
static unsigned orgDblClk;
static unsigned orgTrails;
static int orgBswap;

static HWND hTrackTrails;
static HWND hTrackDblClk;

unsigned trackpos;
int low=1, high=10;
```

The **str**, **hdc**, and **paintstruct** variables are used when outputting text to the dialog box. The double-click interval, the mouse trails setting, and the button reversal status that were in place when the mouse control panel was activated are stored in **orgDblClk**, **orgTrails**, and **orgBswap**, respectively. The handles to the double-click and mouse trails trackbars are stored in **hTrackDblClk** and **hTrackTrails**, respectively. The **trackpos** variable is used to hold the current position of a trackbar. The **low** and **high** variables simply store the trackbar extents. You can change these values if you like.

THE WM_INITDIALOG HANDLER   When the mouse control panel dialog box is first displayed, it must initialize its various controls. This occurs when **WM_INITDIALOG** is handled. We will examine it piece by piece. First, the trackbar that allows the user to set the double-click interval is initialized by the following code:

```
case WM_INITDIALOG:
  // create double-click track bar
  orgDblClk = GetDoubleClickTime();
  hTrackDblClk = CreateWindow(TRACKBAR_CLASS,
              "",
              WS_CHILD | WS_VISIBLE | WS_TABSTOP |
              TBS_AUTOTICKS | WS_BORDER,
              2, 2,
              200, 28,
              hdwnd,
              NULL,
              hInst,
              NULL
  );
  SendMessage(hTrackDblClk, TBM_SETRANGE,
            1, MAKELONG(low, high));
  SendMessage(hTrackDblClk, TBM_SETPOS,
            1, orgDblClk / 100);
```

The current double-click interval is obtained and stored in **orgDblClk**. This value is used to reset the interval if the user exits the control panel by pressing the Cancel button. Next, the trackbar is created by calling **CreateWindow( )**, specifying the **TRACKBAR_CLASS**. Notice the inclusion of the **TBS_AUTOTICKS** style. This causes "tick" marks to be displayed at uniform intervals, providing a scale for the bar.

Once the trackbar has been created, its range is set by sending it a **TBM_SETRANGE** message via the **SendMessage( )** function. Recall that **SendMessage( )** has this prototype:

LRESULT SendMessage(HWND *hwnd*, UINT *msg*,
                        WPARAM *wParam*, LPARAM *lParam*);

For **TBM_SETRANGE**, the *wParam* parameter determines if the bar should be redrawn after setting the range. If it is non-zero (as it is in the program), then the bar will be redrawn. The *lParam* parameter contains the range encoded into a long integer, with the low-order word specifying the minimum and the high-order word specifying the maximum. Notice that the range is set using the macro **MAKELONG( )**. This macro assembles two integers into a long integer. It has this general form:

DWORD MAKELONG(WORD *low*, WORD *high*);

The low-order part of the double word value is specified in *low* and the high-order portion is specified in *high*. **MAKELONG( )** is quite useful whenever you need to encode two word values into a long integer and it is frequently used when sending messages to the common controls.

Next, the position of the trackbar is set to reflect the current double-click interval. This is done by sending a **TBM_SETPOS** message. Again, the *wParam* parameter determines if the trackbar will be redrawn. The *lParam* parameter specifies the position. In this case, the trackbar value contained in **orgDblClk** is divided by 100. Thus, each position on the bar (that is, each tick mark) represents 100 milliseconds.

The following code creates the mouse trails trackbar:

```
// create mouse trails track bar
SystemParametersInfo(SPI_GETMOUSETRAILS,
                     NULL, &orgTrails, 0);
if(orgTrails==0) orgTrails = 1;
hTrackTrails = CreateWindow(TRACKBAR_CLASS,
              "",
              WS_CHILD | WS_VISIBLE | WS_TABSTOP |
              TBS_AUTOTICKS | WS_BORDER,
              2, 62,
              200, 28,
```

```
                        hdwnd,
                        NULL,
                        hInst,
                        NULL
        );
        SendMessage(hTrackTrails, TBM_SETRANGE,
                    1, MAKELONG(low, high));
        SendMessage(hTrackTrails, TBM_SETPOS,
                    1, orgTrails);
```

First, the original mouse trails setting is obtained by calling **SystemParametersInfo( )**, specifying **SPI_GETMOUSETRAILS**, and storing the result in **orgTrails**. As explained, no mouse trails are shown if the setting is either 0 or 1. For simplicity, the program uses the value 1 to indicate no mouse trails; so if the original value is 0, it is set to 1. Next, the trackbar is created and initialized with a range of 1 through 10, and its initial position is set.

Next, the edit boxes associated with the double-click and mouse trails trackbars are initialized by calling **SetDlgItemInt( )**. The code that performs these functions is shown here:

```
// set double-click time in edit box
SetDlgItemInt(hdwnd, IDD_EB1, orgDblClk, 1);


// set mouse trails in edit box
SetDlgItemInt(hdwnd, IDD_EB2, orgTrails-1, 1);
```

Here, the values in **orgDlbClk** and **orgTrails–1** are converted into their string equivalents and displayed in their corresponding edit boxes.

Finally, the original swap-state of the mouse buttons is obtained and the Swap Buttons check box is set accordingly by the following code:

```
// determine original swap-state of buttons
orgBswap = SwapMouseButton(false);
SwapMouseButton(orgBswap);

// set button swap check box
SendDlgItemMessage(hdwnd, IDD_CB1, BM_SETCHECK,
                    orgBswap, 0);
```

Notice how the determination about the swap-status of the mouse buttons is achieved. **SwapMouseButton( )** is called once to obtain the original setting. This setting is stored in **orgBswap** and then used to restore the swap-state by calling **SwapMouseButton( )** a second time.

THE WM_HSCROLL HANDLER   When a trackbar is accessed, it generates either a **WM_HSCROLL** or a **WM_VSCROLL** scroll message, depending upon whether the

Message	Meaning
TB_BOTTOM	END key is pressed. Slider is moved to minimum value.
TB_ENDTRACK	End of trackbar activity.
TB_LINEDOWN	Right arrow or down arrow key is pressed.
TB_LINEUP	Left arrow or up arrow key is pressed.
TB_PAGEDOWN	PAGE DOWN key is pressed or mouse is clicked before slider.
TB_PAGEUP	PAGE UP key is pressed or mouse is clicked ahead of slider.
TB_THUMBPOSITION	Slider is moved using the mouse.
TB_THUMBTRACK	Slider is dragged using the mouse.
TB_TOP	HOME key is pressed. Slider is moved to maximum value.

TABLE 6-1.   Common Trackbar Notification Messages

trackbar is horizontal or vertical. Since both of the trackbars in the mouse control panel are horizontal, only **WM_HSCROLL** messages need be handled. A notification message describing the nature of the activity is passed in the low-order word of **wParam**. The handle of the trackbar that generated the message is in **lParam**. Common trackbar notification messages are shown in Table 6-1. Trackbars are fully automated. For example, the trackbar will move itself when its position is changed by the user. Your program does not need to do this manually.

The **WM_HSCROLL** handler used by the mouse control panel is shown here:

```
case WM_HSCROLL: // a track bar was activated
  if(hTrackTrails == (HWND)lParam) {
    switch(LOWORD(wParam)) {
      case TB_TOP:
      case TB_BOTTOM:         // For this usage
      case TB_LINEUP:         // all messages will be
      case TB_LINEDOWN:       // processed in the same
      case TB_THUMBPOSITION:  // way.
      case TB_THUMBTRACK:
      case TB_PAGEUP:
      case TB_PAGEDOWN:
        trackpos = SendMessage(hTrackTrails,
                   TBM_GETPOS, 0, 0);
        SetDlgItemInt(hdwnd, IDD_EB2, trackpos-1, 1);
        SystemParametersInfo(SPI_SETMOUSETRAILS,
                   trackpos, 0, 0);
        return 1;
```

```
        }
      }
      else if(hTrackDblClk == (HWND)lParam) {
        switch(LOWORD(wParam)) {
          case TB_TOP:
          case TB_BOTTOM:        // For this usage
          case TB_LINEUP:        // all messages will be
          case TB_LINEDOWN:      // processed in the same
          case TB_THUMBPOSITION: // way.
          case TB_THUMBTRACK:
          case TB_PAGEUP:
          case TB_PAGEDOWN:
            trackpos = SendMessage(hTrackDblClk,
                         TBM_GETPOS, 0, 0);
            SetDlgItemInt(hdwnd, IDD_EB1,
                         trackpos * 100, 1);
            SetDoubleClickTime(trackpos * 100);
            return 1;
        }
      }
     break;
```

Since there are two trackbars, the value of **lParam** must be tested to determine
which trackbar was changed. If it contains **hTrackTrails**, then the mouse trails
trackbar was activated. In this case, the new position is obtained by sending the
trackbar a **TBM_GETPOS** message, which causes the trackbar to return its position.
Next, the edit box is updated to display the current setting. This is accomplished by
calling **SetDlgItemInt( )**. Thus, when the user changes the trackbar, the value
displayed in the edit box is also changed. Then, **SystemParametersInfo( )** is called
with **SPI_SETMOUSETRAILS** to set the number of mouse trails.

If the double-click trackbar was altered, then **lParam** contains **hTrackDblClk**. In
this case, the new setting of the trackbar is obtained and this value is used to set the
double-click interval, by calling **SetDoubleClickTime( )**. The value in the
double-click edit box is also updated to reflect the new setting. Notice that the
position of the trackbar is multiplied by 100 when setting and displaying the
interval. This is necessary because each unit in the double-click trackbar represents
100 milliseconds.

PROGRAMMER'S NOTE: *When a **WM_VSCROLL** or **WM_HSCROLL** message is received from a
trackbar, the value in **HIWORD(wParam)** will be zero unless the notification message is either
TB_THUMBPOSITION or **TB_THUMBTRACK**. In this case, it will contain the current position
of the bar. In general, to obtain the current trackbar position, you can always send a **TBM_GETPOS**
message, as the program does.*

THE EDIT BOX HANDLERS   The user can bypass the mouse trails and double-click trackbars, setting these values manually by entering the desired value into the corresponding edit boxes. When this is done, an **IDD_EB1** or an **IDD_EB2** command message is generated. The code that handles these messages is shown here:

```
case IDD_EB1:
  // update double-click trackbar
  trackpos = GetDlgItemInt(hdwnd, IDD_EB1, NULL, 1) / 100;
  SendMessage(hTrackDblClk, TBM_SETPOS, 1, trackpos);
  SetDoubleClickTime(trackpos * 100);
  return 1;
case IDD_EB2:
  // update mouse trails trackbar
  trackpos = GetDlgItemInt(hdwnd, IDD_EB2, NULL, 1);
  SendMessage(hTrackTrails, TBM_SETPOS, 1, trackpos+1);
  SystemParametersInfo(SPI_SETMOUSETRAILS,
                        trackpos+1, 0, 0);
  return 1;
```

Both handlers work in the same way. First, the new value is obtained by calling **GetDlgItemInt( )**, which returns the integer equivalent of the value shown in the edit box. Next, this value is used to update the position of the slider within the trackbar. Finally, the appropriate setting is changed. Notice, however, that for the double-click box, the value returned by **GetDlgItemInt( )** is divided by 100 to obtain the corresponding trackbar position.

THE CHECK BOX HANDLER   To reverse the meaning of the mouse buttons, the user checks the Swap Buttons check box. When this happens, an **IDD_CB1** command message is sent. Its handler is shown here:

```
case IDD_CB1:
  if(SendDlgItemMessage(hdwnd,
      IDD_CB1, BM_GETCHECK, 0, 0) == BST_CHECKED)
    SwapMouseButton(true);
  else
    SwapMouseButton(false);

  return 1;
```

The current state of the check box is obtained by sending a **BM_GETCHECK** message via **SendDlgItemMessage( )**. If the button is checked, then **BST_CHECKED** is returned. In this case, **SwapMouseButton( )** is called to reverse the button meanings. If the button is cleared, then **SwapMouseButton( )** is called to restore the meanings of the button.

CANCELING THE MOUSE CONTROL PANEL   If the user presses the Cancel button, then the standard command identifier **IDCANCEL** is sent to the control panel. It is handled by the following code:

```
case IDCANCEL:
  SystemParametersInfo(SPI_SETMOUSETRAILS,
                        orgTrails, 0, 0);
  SetDoubleClickTime(orgDblClk);

  if(orgBswap)
    SwapMouseButton(true);
  else
    SwapMouseButton(false);

  EndDialog(hdwnd, 1);
  return 1;
```

This handler resets the double-click interval, the mouse trails setting, and the button meanings to what they were when the control panel was first activated. Thus, pressing Cancel nullifies any changes to these items.

HANDLING WM_PAINT   The **WM_PAINT** handler, shown here, displays captions under the two trackbars. While this could have been done using resource commands in the resource file, it just seemed more convenient to do it inside the **WM_PAINT** handler.

```
case WM_PAINT:
  hdc = BeginPaint(hdwnd, &paintstruct);
  SetBkMode(hdc, TRANSPARENT);

  sprintf(str, "Set Double-Click Time");
  TextOut(hdc, 30, 34, str, strlen(str));

  sprintf(str, "Set Number of Trails");
  TextOut(hdc, 30, 92, str, strlen(str));

  EndPaint(hdwnd, &paintstruct);
  return 1;
```

WindowFunc( )

In addition to providing the standard clerical functionality common to all top-level windows, **WindowFunc( )** serves two main purposes. First, it activates the mouse control panel when the user selects Options | Mouse Manager. This causes an

IDM_DIALOG command message to be generated. The handler for this message simply activates the mouse control panel.

The second important function performed by **WindowFunc( )** is to allow the user to test the double-click rate. Recall that when the left mouse button is pressed, a **WM_LBUTTONDOWN** message is generated. However, when the left mouse button is double-clicked, a **WM_LBUTTONDBLCLK** is generated. By handling both of these messages, the program can provide feedback indicating which event occurred. This enables the user to confirm that the double-click rate suits his or her preferences. The handlers for these messages are shown here:

```
case WM_LBUTTONDBLCLK:
  hdc = GetDC(hwnd);

  strcpy(str, "double-click");
  TextOut(hdc, 1, 1, str, strlen(str));

  ReleaseDC(hwnd, hdc);
  break;
case WM_LBUTTONDOWN:
  hdc = GetDC(hwnd);

  strcpy(str, "single-click ");
  TextOut(hdc, 1, 1, str, strlen(str));

  ReleaseDC(hwnd, hdc);
  break;
```

When a single-click is received, the message "single-click" is displayed. When a double-click is received, "double-click" is shown.

A Keyboard Control Panel

All Windows programmers know how to handle input from the keyboard, which comes via messages such as **WM_CHAR**, **WM_KEYDOWN**, and **WM_KEYUP**. However, like the mouse, the keyboard itself has various attributes that can be set under program control. The two that we will utilize in this chapter are the auto-repeat delay interval and the auto-repeat rate (also called the auto-repeat speed). Although these features can be set using the Windows Control Panel, it is easy to offer the users of your programs this convenience without having to launch another application.

Taking control of the keyboard offers advantages for many types of programs. For example, the user of a word processor may want a slower auto-repeat rate when working with tables than he or she does when laying out figures. Also, some users will find that the optimal delay and repeat rates differ from program to program.

Setting and Retrieving the Keyboard Delay and Repeat Settings

The delay and repeat settings for the keyboard are obtained and set by calling the **SystemParametersInfo( )** function described earlier in this chapter (where it was used to set the mouse trails). Its prototype is shown again, here, for your convenience:

BOOL SystemParametersInfo(UINT *What*, UINT *Param*,
                          VOID **pParam*, UINT *Update*);

To obtain the current keyboard delay, pass **SPI_GETKEYBOARDDELAY** in *What* and in *pParam* pass a pointer to an integer that will receive the current delay. This value will be between 0 and 3, inclusive. Each unit represents a delay of approximately 250 milliseconds.

To set the keyboard delay, pass **SPI_SETKEYBOARDDELAY** in *What* and pass the new delay setting, which must be a value between 0 and 3, in *Param*.

To obtain the current keyboard auto-repeat rate, pass **SPI_GETKEYBOARDSPEED** in *What* and in *pParam* pass a pointer to an integer that will receive the current repeat rate. This will be a value between 0 and 31, inclusive.

To set the keyboard auto-repeat rate, pass **SPI_SETKEYBOARDSPEED** in *What* and pass the new repeat settting, which must be a value between 0 and 31, in *Param*.

Keyboard.cpp

Code

The keyboard control panel is contained in **Keyboard.cpp**, shown here. To activate the panel, select Options | Keyboard Manager. You can test the auto-repeat delay and speed settings by typing characters, which will be shown in the main window of the program. Sample output is shown in Figure 6-2.

FIGURE 6-2.   Sample output from **Keyboard.cpp**

PROGRAMMER'S NOTE: *The Keyboard.cpp program uses a trackbar common control. This means that you must include ComCtl32.lib in the link.*

```cpp
// Keyboard.cpp -- A keyboard manager.

#include <windows.h>
#include <commctrl.h>
#include <cstring>
#include <cstdio>
#include "keyboard.h"

LRESULT CALLBACK WindowFunc(HWND, UINT, WPARAM, LPARAM);
BOOL CALLBACK KeyboardPanel(HWND, UINT, WPARAM, LPARAM);

char szWinName[] = "MyWin";

HINSTANCE hInst;

int WINAPI WinMain(HINSTANCE hThisInst, HINSTANCE hPrevInst,
                   LPSTR lpszArgs, int nWinMode)
{
  MSG msg;
  HWND hwnd;
  WNDCLASSEX wcl;
  HACCEL hAccel;
  INITCOMMONCONTROLSEX cc;

  // Define a window class.
  wcl.cbSize = sizeof(WNDCLASSEX);
  wcl.hInstance = hThisInst;
  wcl.lpszClassName = szWinName;
  wcl.lpfnWndProc = WindowFunc;
  wcl.style = 0; // default style
  wcl.hIcon = LoadIcon(NULL, IDI_APPLICATION); // large icon
  wcl.hIconSm = NULL; // use small version of large icon
  wcl.hCursor = LoadCursor(NULL, IDC_ARROW);
  wcl.hbrBackground = (HBRUSH) GetStockObject(WHITE_BRUSH);
  wcl.cbClsExtra = 0;
  wcl.cbWndExtra = 0;
  wcl.lpszMenuName = "KeyboardMenu";

  // Register the window class.
  if(!RegisterClassEx(&wcl)) return 0;
```

```
  // Create a window.
  hwnd = CreateWindow(szWinName,
                      "Demonstrating the Keyboard Control Panel",
                      WS_OVERLAPPEDWINDOW,
                      CW_USEDEFAULT, CW_USEDEFAULT,
                      CW_USEDEFAULT, CW_USEDEFAULT,
                      NULL, NULL, hThisInst, NULL);

  hInst = hThisInst; // save the current instance handle

  // Load accelerators.
  hAccel = LoadAccelerators(hThisInst, "KeyboardMenu");

  // Initialize the common controls.
  cc.dwSize = sizeof(INITCOMMONCONTROLSEX);
  cc.dwICC = ICC_BAR_CLASSES | ICC_UPDOWN_CLASS;
  InitCommonControlsEx(&cc);

  // Display the window.
  ShowWindow(hwnd, nWinMode);
  UpdateWindow(hwnd);

  // The message loop.
  while(GetMessage(&msg, NULL, 0, 0))
  {
    if(!TranslateAccelerator(hwnd, hAccel, &msg)) {
      TranslateMessage(&msg);
      DispatchMessage(&msg);
    }
  }

  return msg.wParam;
}

// The window procedure.
LRESULT CALLBACK WindowFunc(HWND hwnd, UINT message,
                            WPARAM wParam, LPARAM lParam)
{
  int response;
  static int X=0, Y=0;
  HDC hdc;
  TEXTMETRIC tm;
```

```
SIZE size;
char str[80];

switch(message) {
  case WM_COMMAND:
    switch(LOWORD(wParam)) {
      case IDM_DIALOG:
        DialogBox(hInst, "KeyboardDB", hwnd,
                  (DLGPROC) KeyboardPanel);
        break;
      case IDM_EXIT:
        response = MessageBox(hwnd, "Quit the Program?",
                             "Exit", MB_YESNO);
        if(response == IDYES) PostQuitMessage(0);
        break;
      case IDM_ABOUT:
        MessageBox(hwnd, "Keyboard Control Panel, V1.0",
                   "Keyboard Control Panel", MB_OK);
        break;
    }
    break;
  case WM_CHAR:
    // let user test delay and repeat speed
    hdc = GetDC(hwnd);
    GetTextMetrics(hdc, &tm);
    if(wParam != '\r') {
      sprintf(str, "%c", (char) wParam);
      TextOut(hdc, X, Y, str, strlen(str));
      GetTextExtentPoint32(hdc, str, strlen(str), &size);
      X += size.cx;
    } else {
      X = 0;
      Y = Y + tm.tmHeight + tm.tmExternalLeading;
    }
    ReleaseDC(hwnd, hdc);
    break;
  case WM_DESTROY:
    PostQuitMessage(0);
    break;
  default:
    return DefWindowProc(hwnd, message, wParam, lParam);
}
return 0;
```

```
}

// Keyboard Manager
BOOL CALLBACK KeyboardPanel(HWND hdwnd, UINT message,
                            WPARAM wParam, LPARAM lParam)
{
  char str[80];
  HDC hdc;
  PAINTSTRUCT paintstruct;

  static unsigned orgDelay;
  static unsigned orgRepeat;

  static HWND hTrackDelay;
  static HWND hTrackRepeat;

  long trackpos;
  int repeatLow=0, repeatHigh=31;
  int delayLow=0, delayHigh=3;

  switch(message) {
    case WM_INITDIALOG:
      // create delay track bar
      SystemParametersInfo(SPI_GETKEYBOARDDELAY,
                           NULL, &orgDelay, 0);
      hTrackDelay = CreateWindow(TRACKBAR_CLASS,
                    "",
                    WS_CHILD | WS_VISIBLE | WS_TABSTOP |
                    TBS_AUTOTICKS | WS_BORDER,
                    2, 2,
                    200, 28,
                    hdwnd,
                    NULL,
                    hInst,
                    NULL
      );
      SendMessage(hTrackDelay, TBM_SETRANGE,
                  1, MAKELONG(delayLow, delayHigh));
      SendMessage(hTrackDelay, TBM_SETPOS,
                  1, orgDelay);

      // create repeat-speed track bar
      SystemParametersInfo(SPI_GETKEYBOARDSPEED,
```

```
                        NULL, &orgRepeat, 0);
  hTrackRepeat = CreateWindow(TRACKBAR_CLASS,
               "",
               WS_CHILD | WS_VISIBLE | WS_TABSTOP |
               TBS_AUTOTICKS | WS_BORDER,
               2, 62,
               200, 28,
               hdwnd,
               NULL,
               hInst,
               NULL
);
SendMessage(hTrackRepeat, TBM_SETRANGE,
            1, MAKELONG(repeatLow, repeatHigh));
SendMessage(hTrackRepeat, TBM_SETPOS,
            1, orgRepeat);


  // set delay time in edit box
  SetDlgItemInt(hdwnd, IDD_EB1,
               orgDelay, 1);


  // set repeat speed in edit box
  SetDlgItemInt(hdwnd, IDD_EB2, orgRepeat, 1);


  return 1;
case WM_HSCROLL: // a track bar was activated
  if(hTrackRepeat == (HWND)lParam) {
    switch(LOWORD(wParam)) {
      case TB_TOP:
      case TB_BOTTOM:          // For this program
      case TB_LINEUP:          // all messages will be
      case TB_LINEDOWN:        // processed in the same
      case TB_THUMBPOSITION: // way.
      case TB_THUMBTRACK:
      case TB_PAGEUP:
      case TB_PAGEDOWN:
        trackpos = SendMessage(hTrackRepeat,
                   TBM_GETPOS, 0, 0);
        SetDlgItemInt(hdwnd, IDD_EB2, trackpos, 1);
        SystemParametersInfo(SPI_SETKEYBOARDSPEED,
                        trackpos, 0, 0);
        return 1;
```

```
        }
      }
    else if(hTrackDelay == (HWND)lParam) {
      switch(LOWORD(wParam)) {
        case TB_TOP:
        case TB_BOTTOM:        // For this program
        case TB_LINEUP:        // all messages will be
        case TB_LINEDOWN:      // processed in the same
        case TB_THUMBPOSITION: // way.
        case TB_THUMBTRACK:
        case TB_PAGEUP:
        case TB_PAGEDOWN:
          trackpos = SendMessage(hTrackDelay,
                          TBM_GETPOS, 0, 0);
          SetDlgItemInt(hdwnd, IDD_EB1,
                          trackpos, 1);
          SystemParametersInfo(SPI_SETKEYBOARDDELAY,
                                  trackpos, 0, 0);


          return 1;
      }
    }
    break;
  case WM_COMMAND:
    switch(LOWORD(wParam)) {
      case IDOK:
        EndDialog(hdwnd, 0);
        return 1;
      case IDCANCEL:
        SystemParametersInfo(SPI_SETKEYBOARDSPEED,
                                orgRepeat, 0, 0);
        SystemParametersInfo(SPI_SETKEYBOARDDELAY,
                                orgDelay, 0, 0);
        EndDialog(hdwnd, 1);
        return 1;
      case IDD_EB1:
        // update delay trackbar
        trackpos = GetDlgItemInt(hdwnd, IDD_EB1, NULL, 1);
        SendMessage(hTrackDelay, TBM_SETPOS, 1, trackpos);
        SystemParametersInfo(SPI_SETKEYBOARDDELAY,
                                trackpos, 0, 0);
        return 1;
      case IDD_EB2:
```

```
            // update repeat speed trackbar
            trackpos = GetDlgItemInt(hdwnd, IDD_EB2, NULL, 1);
            SendMessage(hTrackRepeat, TBM_SETPOS, 1, trackpos);
            SystemParametersInfo(SPI_SETKEYBOARDSPEED,
                                 trackpos, 0, 0);

            return 1;
      }
      break;
    case WM_PAINT:
      hdc = BeginPaint(hdwnd, &paintstruct);
      SetBkMode(hdc, TRANSPARENT);

      sprintf(str, "Set Auto-Repeat Delay");
      TextOut(hdc, 30, 34, str, strlen(str));

      sprintf(str, "Set Auto-Repeat Speed");
      TextOut(hdc, 30, 92, str, strlen(str));

      EndPaint(hdwnd, &paintstruct);
      return 1;
  }
  return 0;
}
```

The **Keyboard.rc** resource file is shown here:

```
#include <windows.h>
#include "keyboard.h"

KeyboardMenu MENU
{
  POPUP "&Options"
  {
    MENUITEM "&Keyboard Manager\tF2", IDM_DIALOG
    MENUITEM "&Exit\tF3", IDM_EXIT
  }
  POPUP "&Help" {
    MENUITEM "&About\tF1", IDM_ABOUT
  }
}


KeyboardMenu ACCELERATORS
```

```
{
  VK_F2, IDM_DIALOG, VIRTKEY
  VK_F3, IDM_EXIT, VIRTKEY
  VK_F1, IDM_ABOUT, VIRTKEY
}

KeyboardDB DIALOG 18, 18, 126, 90
CAPTION "Keyboard Manager"
STYLE DS_MODALFRAME | WS_POPUP | WS_CAPTION | WS_SYSMENU
{
  PUSHBUTTON "OK", IDOK, 28, 66, 30, 14,
             WS_CHILD | WS_VISIBLE | WS_TABSTOP
  PUSHBUTTON "Cancel", IDCANCEL, 68, 66, 30, 14,
             WS_CHILD | WS_VISIBLE | WS_TABSTOP
  EDITTEXT IDD_EB1, 105, 2, 12, 12, ES_LEFT | WS_CHILD |
           WS_VISIBLE | WS_BORDER
  EDITTEXT IDD_EB2, 105, 31, 12, 12, ES_LEFT | WS_CHILD |
           WS_VISIBLE | WS_BORDER
}
```

The header file **Keyboard.h** is shown next:

```
#define IDM_DIALOG    100
#define IDM_EXIT      101
#define IDM_ABOUT     102

#define IDD_EB1       500
#define IDD_EB2       501
```

ANNOTATIONS

The general skeleton code for **Keyboard.cpp** is the same as for most of the other programs in this book. However, like the mouse control panel, **Keyboard.cpp** makes use of a trackbar common control, so the common controls must be initialized. This takes place within **WinMain( )**.

KeyboardPanel( )

The main action of the program occurs within **KeyboardPanel( )**. This is the dialog function that handles input from the keyboard control panel. Much of the code is similar to that found in **MousePanel( )**, described earlier, so we will concentrate on the differences.

THE VARIABLES   KeyboardPanel( ) defines the following variables:

```
char str[80];
HDC hdc;
PAINTSTRUCT paintstruct;

static unsigned orgDelay;
static unsigned orgRepeat;

static HWND hTrackDelay;
static HWND hTrackRepeat;

long trackpos;
int repeatLow=0, repeatHigh=31;
int delayLow=0, delayHigh=3;
```

The **str**, **hdc**, and **paintstruct** variables are used when outputting text to the dialog box. The auto-repeat delay and speed settings that were in place when the keyboard control panel was activated are stored in **orgDelay** and **orgRepeat**, respectively. The handles to the delay and repeat-speed trackbars are stored in **hTrackDelay** and **hTrackRepeat**, respectively. The **trackpos** variable is used to hold the current position of a trackbar. The **repeatLow** and **repeatHigh** variables hold the extents for the repeat-speed trackbar. The **delayLow** and **delayHigh** variables hold the extents for the delay trackbar.

THE WM_INITDIALOG HANDLER   When the keyboard control panel dialog box is first displayed, it must initialize the delay and repeat-speed trackbars and edit boxes when **WM_INITDIALOG** is received. It must also save the current delay and speed settings so that they can be restored if the user cancels the keyboard control panel.

The **WM_INITDIALOG** handler begins by creating and initializing the delay trackbar, as shown here:

```
case WM_INITDIALOG:
  // create delay track bar
  SystemParametersInfo(SPI_GETKEYBOARDDELAY,
                   NULL, &orgDelay, 0);
  hTrackDelay = CreateWindow(TRACKBAR_CLASS,
             "",
             WS_CHILD | WS_VISIBLE | WS_TABSTOP |
             TBS_AUTOTICKS | WS_BORDER,
             2, 2,
             200, 28,
             hdwnd,
```

```
                NULL,
                hInst,
                NULL
    );
    SendMessage(hTrackDelay, TBM_SETRANGE,
                1, MAKELONG(delayLow, delayHigh));
    SendMessage(hTrackDelay, TBM_SETPOS,
                1, orgDelay);
```

The current delay setting is obtained by calling **SystemParametersInfo( )** and this value is stored in **orgDelay**. Next, the trackbar is created, its range is initialized, and its position is set to reflect the current delay setting. (A complete description of setting a trackbar is given earlier in this chapter.)

Next, the repeat-speed trackbar is created and initialized by the following code:

```
// create repeat-speed track bar
SystemParametersInfo(SPI_GETKEYBOARDSPEED,
                    NULL, &orgRepeat, 0);
hTrackRepeat = CreateWindow(TRACKBAR_CLASS,
            "",
            WS_CHILD | WS_VISIBLE | WS_TABSTOP |
            TBS_AUTOTICKS | WS_BORDER,
            2, 62,
            200, 28,
            hdwnd,
            NULL,
            hInst,
            NULL
);
SendMessage(hTrackRepeat, TBM_SETRANGE,
            1, MAKELONG(repeatLow, repeatHigh));
SendMessage(hTrackRepeat, TBM_SETPOS,
            1, orgRepeat);
```

First, the current auto-repeat speed is obtained and stored in **orgRepeat**. Then the trackbar is created, its range is set, and its position is initialized.

Next, the edit boxes that correspond to the trackbars are set by the following sequence:

```
// set delay time in edit box
SetDlgItemInt(hdwnd, IDD_EB1,
            orgDelay, 1);

// set repeat speed in edit box
SetDlgItemInt(hdwnd, IDD_EB2, orgRepeat, 1);
```

THE WM_HSCROLL HANDLER   When the user changes one of the trackbars, a
WM_HSCROLL message is received. The handler for these messages is shown here:

```
case WM_HSCROLL: // a track bar was activated
  if(hTrackRepeat == (HWND)lParam) {
    switch(LOWORD(wParam)) {
      case TB_TOP:
      case TB_BOTTOM:        // For this program
      case TB_LINEUP:        // all messages will be
      case TB_LINEDOWN:      // processed in the same
      case TB_THUMBPOSITION: // way.
      case TB_THUMBTRACK:
      case TB_PAGEUP:
      case TB_PAGEDOWN:
        trackpos = SendMessage(hTrackRepeat,
                    TBM_GETPOS, 0, 0);
        SetDlgItemInt(hdwnd, IDD_EB2, trackpos, 1);
        SystemParametersInfo(SPI_SETKEYBOARDSPEED,
                          trackpos, 0, 0);

        return 1;
    }
  }
  else if(hTrackDelay == (HWND)lParam) {
    switch(LOWORD(wParam)) {
      case TB_TOP:
      case TB_BOTTOM:        // For this program
      case TB_LINEUP:        // all messages will be
      case TB_LINEDOWN:      // processed in the same
      case TB_THUMBPOSITION: // way.
      case TB_THUMBTRACK:
      case TB_PAGEUP:
      case TB_PAGEDOWN:
        trackpos = SendMessage(hTrackDelay,
                    TBM_GETPOS, 0, 0);
        SetDlgItemInt(hdwnd, IDD_EB1,
                    trackpos, 1);
        SystemParametersInfo(SPI_SETKEYBOARDDELAY,
                          trackpos, 0, 0);

        return 1;
```

This code is similar to that described for the mouse control panel. Recall
that the handle of the trackbar is contained in **lParam**. This value is used to
determine which trackbar was accessed by the user. When the auto-repeat speed

trackbar is changed, the speed is set by calling **SystemParametersInfo( )** with **SPI_SETKEYBOARDSPEED** and specifying the new speed. When the delay trackbar is changed, the delay is set by calling **SystemParametersInfo( )** with **SPI_SETKEYBOARDDELAY** and specifying the new delay.

THE EDIT BOX HANDLERS   The delay and repeat rate can be set manually, by entering the desired value into the appropriate edit box. When this is done, an **IDD_EB1** or an **IDD_EB2** command message is generated. The code that handles these messages is shown here:

```
case IDD_EB1:
  // update delay trackbar
  trackpos = GetDlgItemInt(hdwnd, IDD_EB1, NULL, 1);
  SendMessage(hTrackDelay, TBM_SETPOS, 1, trackpos);
  SystemParametersInfo(SPI_SETKEYBOARDDELAY,
                       trackpos, 0, 0);
  return 1;
case IDD_EB2:
  // update repeat speed trackbar
  trackpos = GetDlgItemInt(hdwnd, IDD_EB2, NULL, 1);
  SendMessage(hTrackRepeat, TBM_SETPOS, 1, trackpos);
  SystemParametersInfo(SPI_SETKEYBOARDSPEED,
                       trackpos, 0, 0);
  return 1;
```

Both handlers work in the same way. First, the new value is obtained by calling **GetDlgItemInt( )**, which returns the integer equivalent of the value shown in the edit box. Next, this value is used to update the position of the slider within the trackbar. Finally, the appropriate setting is changed.

CANCELING THE KEYBOARD CONTROL PANEL   If the user presses the Cancel button, then the standard command identifier **IDCANCEL** is sent to the control panel.

This causes the delay and speed settings to be reset to their original values. The **IDCANCEL** handler is shown here:

```
case IDCANCEL:
  SystemParametersInfo(SPI_SETKEYBOARDSPEED,
                       orgRepeat, 0, 0);
  SystemParametersInfo(SPI_SETKEYBOARDDELAY,
                       orgDelay, 0, 0);
  EndDialog(hdwnd, 1);
  return 1;
```

WindowFunc( )

As it relates to the keyboard control panel, **WindowFunc( )** performs two functions. First, it allows you to activate the control panel. Second, it handles **WM_CHAR** messages by displaying each charater in the main window. This enables you to see the effects of changing the auto-repeat delay and speed settings. Simply press and hold a key. The **WM_CHAR** handler uses the techniques described in Chapter 3 to position each character in the window and to start a new line when the user presses ENTER. Its operation is straightforward.

Tips for Using MFC

SystemParametersInfo( ), **SwapMouseButtons( )**, **GetDoubleClickTime( )**, and **SetDoubleClickTime( )** do not have MFC equivalents. Because they affect system-wide resources, there is no reason for MFC to wrap them within a class. The trackbar common control is encapsulated by the **CSliderCtrl** MFC class.

Recording Messages and Using Hooks

I f you have ever wanted to create an automated demo for a program, add a macro facility to your application, or keep a record of program events, then this chapter is for you. What these items have in common is the recording and playing back of messages. Toward this end, this chapter shows various ways to accomplish these operations. In the process, it describes one of Windows' more interesting and unique API subsystems: *hooks*.

At first, the recording and replaying of messages may seem to be a trivial task. As you will see, however, it requires some careful thought and planning. Fortunately, Windows provides substantial support for this activity.

There are many reasons why you might want to monitor, record, or play back a series of window messages. First, recording messages is one way to implement a macro facility in your application program. For example, to create a macro, you turn on the recorder, manually perform the procedure, and then stop the recorder. To use the macro, simply play back the prerecorded messages. A second reason for recording messages is to allow them to be examined, possibly during debugging. A third reason is to create and maintain a journal of program activity. Such a journal could be used to analyze and optimize your program's input features. It could also be used to maintain a log to help detect unauthorized accesses. A fourth reason for recording messages is to allow the creation of automated program demos. Finally, you might want to monitor the message stream so that a new hardware device can be tested.

In this chapter, three sample programs are developed that monitor, record, and play back messages. Each implements a different strategy. The first simply records messages received by the program. The second intercepts messages using a hook function. The third implements a system-wide message journal using two hook functions. You will find that one of these approaches will satisfy most message monitoring, recording, or playback needs.

A Simple Message Recorder

In this section you will see the easiest way to record and replay messages. As you know, Windows communicates with your program by sending messages to its main window function (and to any other child windows created by the program). Therefore, it is a relatively easy task to save each message that your program receives. Once a sequence of messages has been recorded, the messages can be replayed by sending them, in order, to your program using the **SendMessage( )** function.

While the approach to recording and replaying messages described in this section is the easiest to implement, it is also the most limited, because it will only record messages that are dispatched by your program's main message loop. It cannot be used to record messages sent to message boxes or modal dialog boxes. The reason for this is that these objects maintain their own message loops, which are beyond the control of your program. Later in this chapter, you will see one way around this restriction.

Since messages and the **SendMessage( )** function are fundamental to the implementation of the message recorder, let's review them now.

The MSG Structure

All messages sent to your program are stored in its *message queue* until they can be handled. When your program is ready to process another message, it retrieves it from the message queue and takes appropriate action. To obtain the next message, all programs use a message loop, similar to the one shown here:

```
while(GetMessage(&msg, NULL, 0, 0))
{
  if(!TranslateAccelerator(hwnd, hAccel, &msg)) {
    TranslateMessage(&msg);
    DispatchMessage(&msg);
  }
}
```

Each time **GetMessage( )** is called, it gets another message from your application's message queue. It puts this message into the structure pointed to by **msg**. All messages are structures of type **MSG**, which is defined like this:

```
typedef struct tagMSG {
  HWND hwnd;       // handle of window
  UINT message;    // message, itself
  WPARAM wParam;   // message-specific info
  LPARAM lParam;   // message-specific info
  DWORD time;      // time message posted
  POINT pt;        // position of mouse when message posted
} MSG
```

Here, **hwnd** is the handle of the window receiving the message. The actual message itself is contained in **message**. **wParam** and **lParam** contain any extra information associated with the message. The time the message was posted is contained in **time** and the coordinates of the mouse when the message was posted are in **pt**. For our purposes, only the first four fields (**hwnd**, **message**, **wParam**, and **lParam**) are of interest.

After a message is retrieved, accelerator keys and virtual key codes are translated. The message is then dispatched to the appropriate window using **DispatchMessage( )**. As you know, when a message is sent to one of your program's windows, it is passed to its window procedure. This function receives only the first four members of the **MSG** structure.

The SendMessage( ) Function

SendMessage( ) sends a message to a window. Most Windows programmers are familiar with this function and it is used by several of the other programs in this book. However, since it forms a crucial part of the message recorder, its use is summarized here. **SendMessage( )** has this prototype:

LRESULT SendMessage(HWND *hwnd*, UINT *msg*, WPARAM *wParam*,
     LPARAM *lParam*);

Here, *hwnd* is the handle of the window that will receive the message, *msg* is the message itself, and *wParam* and *lParam* contain any other values required by the message. Notice that the parameters to **SendMessage( )** are the same as the first four members of the **MSG** structure obtained by **GetMessage( )**. The value returned by **SendMessage( )** is the result generated by the message that it sends.

Using **SendMessage( )**, you can send a message to any window in your program. Thus, if you have a sequence of prerecorded messages, you can replay that sequence by sending each message to your program's main window using the function **SendMessage( )**.

Recording and Replaying Application Messages

The easiest way to record application messages is to add a step to your program's message loop. This extra step will record each message sent to your program. Keep in mind that this extra step will add overhead to your application. However, such overhead is unavoidable because it is part of the recording process.

As each message is received, it must be stored. For simple applications, such as the examples in this chapter, each message can be stored in an array. For the program that follows, messages will be stored in the following array of structures.

```
struct messages {
  UINT msg;
  WPARAM wParam;
```

```
    LPARAM lParam;
    HWND hwnd;
} MsgArray[MAXMESS];
```

For more demanding applications, you will need to either allocate space for each message dynamically or use a disk file for message storage.

When recording messages, it is important to understand that a Windows program receives a large number of messages. For example, every time you move the mouse, a message is sent. Not every message will be of interest to your program. Unwanted messages do not need to be recorded. Since you need to set aside storage for the messages that you record, recording only those of interest to your application helps reduce the amount of space required.

Once you have recorded a message sequence, it can be replayed by sending each message, in the order in which it was received, to the appropriate window. Since your program is in control during replay, prerecorded messages can be played back at varying speeds or, possibly, even in a different order than they were recorded.

SimpRec.cpp

Code

The **SimpRec.cpp** program, shown here, puts into practice the preceding discussion. It allows you to record and play back mouse, keyboard, and command messages that are received by the program's main window. Record and playback is controlled by the Record menu. To use the program, first select Start to begin recording messages. To stop recording, select Stop. To replay the sequence, select Run. You can replay the sequence as many times as you like. To record a new sequence, first select Reset, then select Start to record the new sequence.

The Options menu lets you clear the screen. It also lets you activate a slow play mode. As you will see, being able to slowly replay messages is useful in a variety of situations, including debugging and demonstrations. It can also prevent the message queue of your program from being overrun. Remember, you generate messages much more slowly than the program will when it replays them.

So that you can easily see the effects of the various messages, the program displays output each time a mouse button is pressed, at the location of the mouse at the time the button was pressed. The program also displays characters that you type. If you clear the window before replaying the messages, you will be able to more easily see your events replayed.

Here is the complete program listing for **SimpRec.cpp**. Sample output is shown in Figure 7-1.

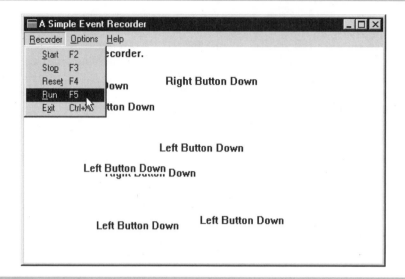

FIGURE 7-1. Sample output from **SimpRec.cpp**

```cpp
// A simple message recorder.

#include <windows.h>
#include <cstring>
#include <cstdio>
#include "rec.h"

#define MAXMESS 1000
#define ON 1
#define OFF 0
#define DELAY 200

struct messages {
  UINT msg;
  WPARAM wParam;
  LPARAM lParam;
  HWND hwnd;
} MsgArray[MAXMESS];

int lastmess = 0; // index one past last message
int record = OFF; // event recording on/off
int delay = 0;    // replay delay
HINSTANCE hInst;
```

```
HMENU hMenu;

LRESULT CALLBACK WindowFunc(HWND, UINT, WPARAM, LPARAM);

char szWinName[] = "MyWin";

int WINAPI WinMain(HINSTANCE hThisInst, HINSTANCE hPrevInst,
                   LPSTR lpszArgs, int nWinMode)
{
  HWND hwnd;
  MSG msg;
  WNDCLASSEX wcl;
  HACCEL hAccel;

  // Define a window class.
  wcl.cbSize = sizeof(WNDCLASSEX);
  wcl.hInstance = hThisInst;
  wcl.lpszClassName = szWinName;
  wcl.lpfnWndProc = WindowFunc;
  wcl.style = 0;
  wcl.hIcon = LoadIcon(NULL, IDI_APPLICATION); // large icon
  wcl.hIconSm = NULL; // use small version of large icon
  wcl.hCursor = LoadCursor(NULL, IDC_ARROW);
  wcl.hbrBackground = (HBRUSH) GetStockObject(WHITE_BRUSH);
  wcl.cbClsExtra = 0;
  wcl.cbWndExtra = 0;
  wcl.lpszMenuName = "RecorderMenu";

  // Register the window class.
  if(!RegisterClassEx(&wcl)) return 0;

  // Create a window.
  hwnd = CreateWindow(szWinName,
                      "A Simple Event Recorder",
                      WS_OVERLAPPEDWINDOW,
                      CW_USEDEFAULT, CW_USEDEFAULT,
                      CW_USEDEFAULT, CW_USEDEFAULT,
                      NULL, NULL, hThisInst, NULL);

  hInst = hThisInst; // save the current instance handle

  // Load accelerators.
  hAccel = LoadAccelerators(hThisInst, "RecorderMenu");
```

```
    hMenu = GetMenu(hwnd); // get handle to main menu

    // Display the window.
    ShowWindow(hwnd, nWinMode);
    UpdateWindow(hwnd);

    // The message loop.
    while(GetMessage(&msg, NULL, 0, 0))
    {
      if(record)
        switch(msg.message) { // filter messages
          case WM_CHAR:
          case WM_LBUTTONDOWN:
          case WM_RBUTTONDOWN:
          case WM_COMMAND:
            MsgArray[lastmess].hwnd = msg.hwnd;
            MsgArray[lastmess].msg = msg.message;
            MsgArray[lastmess].lParam = msg.lParam;
            MsgArray[lastmess].wParam = msg.wParam;
            lastmess++;
            if(lastmess == MAXMESS)
              MessageBox(hwnd, "Too Many Messages",
                     "Recorder Error", MB_OK);
        }
      if(!TranslateAccelerator(hwnd, hAccel, &msg)) {
        TranslateMessage(&msg);
        DispatchMessage(&msg);
      }
    }

    return msg.wParam;
}

// The window procedure.
LRESULT CALLBACK WindowFunc(HWND hwnd, UINT message,
                            WPARAM wParam, LPARAM lParam)
{
  HDC hdc;
  PAINTSTRUCT ps;

  int i, response;
  static unsigned j=0;
  char str[255];
  TEXTMETRIC tm;
```

```
SIZE size;

static int X=0, Y=0;    // current output location
static int maxX, maxY; // screen dimensions

static HDC memdc;       // store the virtual window handle
static HBITMAP hbit;   // store the virtual bitmap
HBRUSH hbrush;          // store the brush handle

switch(message) {
  case WM_CREATE:
    // create virtual window
    maxX = GetSystemMetrics(SM_CXSCREEN);
    maxY = GetSystemMetrics(SM_CYSCREEN);

    hdc = GetDC(hwnd);
    memdc = CreateCompatibleDC(hdc);
    hbit = CreateCompatibleBitmap(hdc, maxX, maxY);
    SelectObject(memdc, hbit);
    hbrush = (HBRUSH) GetStockObject(WHITE_BRUSH);
    SelectObject(memdc, hbrush);
    PatBlt(memdc, 0, 0, maxX, maxY, PATCOPY);

    ReleaseDC(hwnd, hdc);
    break;
  case WM_COMMAND:
    switch(LOWORD(wParam)) {
      case IDM_START:
        lastmess = 0;
        record = ON;
        SetWindowText(hwnd, "Recording");
        EnableMenuItem(hMenu, IDM_START, MF_GRAYED);
        EnableMenuItem(hMenu, IDM_RESET, MF_GRAYED);
        EnableMenuItem(hMenu, IDM_RUN, MF_GRAYED);
        EnableMenuItem(hMenu, IDM_EXIT, MF_GRAYED);
        break;
      case IDM_STOP:
        record = OFF;
        SetWindowText(hwnd, "A Simple Event Recorder");
        EnableMenuItem(hMenu, IDM_START, MF_ENABLED);
        EnableMenuItem(hMenu, IDM_RESET, MF_ENABLED);
        EnableMenuItem(hMenu, IDM_RUN, MF_ENABLED);
        EnableMenuItem(hMenu, IDM_EXIT, MF_ENABLED);
        break;
```

```
    case IDM_RESET:
      lastmess = 0;
      record = OFF;
      X = Y = 0;
      EnableMenuItem(hMenu, IDM_RUN, MF_GRAYED);
      break;
    case IDM_RUN:
      SetWindowText(hwnd, "Replaying");
      X = Y = 0;
      for(i=0; i<lastmess; i++) {
        SendMessage(MsgArray[i].hwnd,
                    MsgArray[i].msg,
                    MsgArray[i].wParam,
                    MsgArray[i].lParam);
        Sleep(delay);
      }
      SetWindowText(hwnd, "A Simple Event Recorder");
      break;
    case IDM_CLEAR:
      hdc = GetDC(hwnd);
      hbrush = (HBRUSH) GetStockObject(WHITE_BRUSH);
      SelectObject(memdc, hbrush);
      PatBlt(memdc, 0, 0, maxX, maxY, PATCOPY);
      SelectObject(hdc, hbrush);
      PatBlt(hdc, 0, 0, maxX, maxY, PATCOPY);
      ReleaseDC(hwnd, hdc);
      break;
    case IDM_SLOW:
      if(!delay) {
        CheckMenuItem(hMenu, IDM_SLOW, MF_CHECKED);
        delay = DELAY;
      }
      else {
        CheckMenuItem(hMenu, IDM_SLOW, MF_UNCHECKED);
        delay = 0;
      }
      break;
    case IDM_EXIT:
      response = MessageBox(hwnd, "Quit the Program?",
                            "Exit", MB_YESNO);
      if(response == IDYES) PostQuitMessage(0);
      break;
    case IDM_ABOUT:
      MessageBox(hwnd, "Simple Recorder V1.0",
```

```
                     "Message Recorder", MB_OK);
      break;
  }
  break;
case WM_CHAR:
  hdc = GetDC(hwnd);

  GetTextMetrics(hdc, &tm);

  sprintf(str, "%c", (char) wParam); // stringize character

  // output a carriage return, linefeed sequence
  if((char)wParam == '\r') {
    Y = Y + tm.tmHeight + tm.tmExternalLeading;
    X = 0; // reset to start of line
  }
  else {
    TextOut(memdc, X, Y, str, 1); // output to VW
    TextOut(hdc, X, Y, str, 1); // output to screen

    // compute length of character
    GetTextExtentPoint32(memdc, str, strlen(str), &size);
    X += size.cx; // advance to end of character
  }

  ReleaseDC(hwnd, hdc);
  break;
case WM_LBUTTONDOWN:
  hdc = GetDC(hwnd);
  strcpy(str, "Left Button Down");
  TextOut(memdc, LOWORD(lParam), HIWORD(lParam),
          str, strlen(str));
  TextOut(hdc, LOWORD(lParam), HIWORD(lParam),
          str, strlen(str));
  ReleaseDC(hwnd, hdc);
  break;
case WM_RBUTTONDOWN:
  hdc = GetDC(hwnd);
  strcpy(str, "Right Button Down");
  TextOut(memdc, LOWORD(lParam), HIWORD(lParam),
          str, strlen(str));
  TextOut(hdc, LOWORD(lParam), HIWORD(lParam),
          str, strlen(str));
  ReleaseDC(hwnd, hdc);
```

```
      break;
    case WM_PAINT:
      hdc = BeginPaint(hwnd, &ps);

      // copy virtual window onto screen
      BitBlt(hdc, ps.rcPaint.left, ps.rcPaint.top,
             ps.rcPaint.right-ps.rcPaint.left, // width
             ps.rcPaint.bottom-ps.rcPaint.top, // height
             memdc,
             ps.rcPaint.left, ps.rcPaint.top,
             SRCCOPY);

      EndPaint(hwnd, &ps);
      break;
    case WM_DESTROY:
      DeleteDC(memdc);
      DeleteObject(hbit);
      PostQuitMessage(0);
      break;
    default:
      return DefWindowProc(hwnd, message, wParam, lParam);
  }

  return 0;
}6
```

The program requires the **Rec.rc** resource file shown here:

```
// Event recorder resource file.
#include <windows.h>
#include "rec.h"

RecorderMenu MENU
{
  POPUP "&Recorder"
  {
    MENUITEM "&Start\tF2", IDM_START
    MENUITEM "Sto&p\tF3", IDM_STOP
    MENUITEM "Rese&t\tF4", IDM_RESET
    MENUITEM "&Run\tF5", IDM_RUN, GRAYED
    MENUITEM "E&xit\tCtrl+X", IDM_EXIT
  }
```

```
  POPUP "&Options"
  {
    MENUITEM "&Clear Window\tF6", IDM_CLEAR
    MENUITEM "&Slow Motion\tF7", IDM_SLOW
  }
  POPUP "&Help" {
    MENUITEM "&About\tF1", IDM_ABOUT
  }
}

RecorderMenu ACCELERATORS
{
  VK_F2, IDM_START, VIRTKEY
  VK_F3, IDM_STOP, VIRTKEY
  VK_F4, IDM_RESET, VIRTKEY
  VK_F5, IDM_RUN, VIRTKEY
  VK_F6, IDM_CLEAR, VIRTKEY
  VK_F7, IDM_SLOW, VIRTKEY
  "^X", IDM_EXIT
  VK_F1, IDM_ABOUT, VIRTKEY
}
```

The header file **Rec.h** is shown here:

```
#define IDM_EXIT     101
#define IDM_ABOUT    102
#define IDM_START    103
#define IDM_STOP     104
#define IDM_RESET    105
#define IDM_RUN      106
#define IDM_CLEAR    107
#define IDM_SLOW     108
```

ANNOTATIONS

Much of the code in the program will be familiar. The program uses the virtual window technology described in Chapter 2. It uses some of the text management techniques described in Chapter 3 to display characters in the main window. The parts of the program that relate to recording and replaying messages are described in detail in the following sections.

Global Declarations

The program begins with the following global **#define**s and declarations.

```
#define MAXMESS 1000
#define ON 1
#define OFF 0
#define DELAY 200

struct messages {
  UINT msg;
  WPARAM wParam;
  LPARAM lParam;
  HWND hwnd;
} MsgArray[MAXMESS];

int lastmess = 0; // index one past last message
int record = OFF; // event recording on/off
int delay = 0;    // replay delay


HINSTANCE hInst;
HMENU hMenu;
```

MAXMESS determines how many messages can be stored, **ON** and **OFF** are the values that specify whether event recording is on or off, and **DELAY** defines the number of milliseconds that will be delayed between messages during playback when the Delay option is selected.

The array **MsgArray** holds the messages as they are recorded. The index at which the next message will be stored is contained in **lastmess**. Whether recording is on or off is determined by the value in **record**. **delay** contains the delay interval. These variables do not necessarily have to be global in this version of the program; but they need to be global in the subsequent examples, so for convenience they are global here.

hInst holds the program's instance handle and **hMenu** holds a handle to the program's main menu.

The Message Loop

The most important part of the program (as it relates to recording messages) is the code that occurs within its message loop, shown here:

```
while(GetMessage(&msg, NULL, 0, 0))
{
  if(record)
    switch(msg.message) { // filter messages
      case WM_CHAR:
```

```
      case WM_LBUTTONDOWN:
      case WM_RBUTTONDOWN:
      case WM_COMMAND:
        MsgArray[lastmess].hwnd = msg.hwnd;
        MsgArray[lastmess].msg = msg.message;
        MsgArray[lastmess].lParam = msg.lParam;
        MsgArray[lastmess].wParam = msg.wParam;
        lastmess++;
        if(lastmess == MAXMESS)
          MessageBox(hwnd, "Too Many Messages",
                     "Recorder Error", MB_OK);
      }
   if(!TranslateAccelerator(hwnd, hAccel, &msg)) {
     TranslateMessage(&msg);
     DispatchMessage(&msg);
   }
}
```

The program records four types of messages: keyboard, left and right mouse button presses, and **WM_COMMAND** messages. Recall that **WM_COMMAND** messages are generated by such things as menu selections and dialog box actions. Of course, in your own application you can record all messages or any other set of messages that you desire. As mentioned, the global variable **record** governs the recording of messages. At the beginning of the program, it is set to **OFF** (zero). When Start is selected, it is set to **ON** (1). When Stop is selected, it is reset to **OFF**.

The index at which the next message will be stored (which is also the length of the current sequence) is contained in **lastmess**. This variable is incremented each time another message is recorded. The value of **lastmess** is also used when a prerecorded sequence is replayed.

Although **record** has only the values **ON** or **OFF** in the programs in this chapter, you might want to try defining other values for **record**. You could use them to indicate a subset of messages that you want to record. For example, you could define values that cause only mouse or only keyboard messages to be recorded.

Recording Messages

To record a message sequence, select Recorder | Start. This causes the **IDM_START** handler to execute. It is shown here:

```
case IDM_START:
  lastmess = 0;
  record = ON;
  SetWindowText(hwnd, "Recording");
  EnableMenuItem(hMenu, IDM_START, MF_GRAYED);
  EnableMenuItem(hMenu, IDM_RESET, MF_GRAYED);
```

```
EnableMenuItem(hMenu, IDM_RUN, MF_GRAYED);
EnableMenuItem(hMenu, IDM_EXIT, MF_GRAYED);
break;
```

Notice that **lastmess** is reset to 0. This allows a new message sequence to be recorded. Also, **record** is set to **ON**. Next, the title of the window is changed to Recording and all but the Stop selection in the Record menu is disabled.

Stopping Record

To stop recording, select Recorder | Stop. This causes the **IDM_STOP** handler, shown here, to execute:

```
case IDM_STOP:
  record = OFF;
  SetWindowText(hwnd, "A Simple Event Recorder");
  EnableMenuItem(hMenu, IDM_START, MF_ENABLED);
  EnableMenuItem(hMenu, IDM_RESET, MF_ENABLED);
  EnableMenuItem(hMenu, IDM_RUN, MF_ENABLED);
  EnableMenuItem(hMenu, IDM_EXIT, MF_ENABLED);
  break;
```

First, **record** is set to **OFF**. Then, the title to the window is restored. Finally, the Recorder menu items are enabled.

Replaying the Messages

After a message sequence has been recorded, it can be replayed by selecting Recorder | Run. When this is done, the **IDM_RUN** handler, shown here, is executed:

```
case IDM_RUN:
  SetWindowText(hwnd, "Replaying");
  X = Y = 0;
  for(i=0; i<lastmess; i++) {
    SendMessage(MsgArray[i].hwnd,
                MsgArray[i].msg,
                MsgArray[i].wParam,
                MsgArray[i].lParam);
    Sleep(delay);
  }
  SetWindowText(hwnd, "A Simple Event Recorder");
  break;
```

X and **Y** are static variables that store the location at which text will be displayed. They are reset to their starting values so that output will appear in the window in the same locations as it did when the events were recorded. Notice that after each call to **SendMessage( )**, **Sleep( )** is called. If **delay** is zero, then no delay takes place. Otherwise, the program will suspend for the specified number of milliseconds. Initially, **delay** is zero. However, if you have selected Options | Slow Motion, then a 200-millisecond delay will occur between each message.

During playback, the window title is changed to Replaying.

Resetting the Recorder

To record a new sequence, first select Recorder | Reset. This causes the following code to execute:

```
case IDM_RESET:
  lastmess = 0;
  record = OFF;
  X = Y = 0;
  EnableMenuItem(hMenu, IDM_RUN, MF_GRAYED);
  break;
```

This handler resets **lastmess**, **record**, **X**, and **Y** to their initial values, and disables the Run option. Thus, when you then select Reset, you will be effectively erasing any pre-existing sequence.

Clearing the Window and Delaying Playback

SimpRec.cpp includes two conveniences that make it easier to experiment with recording messages. First, you can erase the current contents of the window by selecting Options | Clear Window. Second, you can slow the speed of playback by selecting Options | Slow Motion. The handlers for these conveniences are shown here:

```
case IDM_CLEAR:
  hdc = GetDC(hwnd);
  hbrush = (HBRUSH) GetStockObject(WHITE_BRUSH);
  SelectObject(memdc, hbrush);
  PatBlt(memdc, 0, 0, maxX, maxY, PATCOPY);
  SelectObject(hdc, hbrush);
  PatBlt(hdc, 0, 0, maxX, maxY, PATCOPY);
  ReleaseDC(hwnd, hdc);
  break;
case IDM_SLOW:
  if(!delay) {
    CheckMenuItem(hMenu, IDM_SLOW, MF_CHECKED);
    delay = DELAY;
```

```
  }
  else {
    CheckMenuItem(hMenu, IDM_SLOW, MF_UNCHECKED);
    delay = 0;
  }
  break;
```

For **IDM_CLEAR**, the background brush is simply copied to the window, clearing all pre-existing content. For **IDM_SLOW**, when Slow Motion is checked, the global variable **delay** is set to **DELAY**; otherwise, it is set to 0.

Some Experiments

You will want to experiment with this program before moving on. For example, start recording and then select the Help main menu option. You will receive the Help message box. Press OK. Then, stop recording. When you play this sequence back, you will notice that the replay "hangs" when the Help message box is displayed and you must manually press OK. The reason for this is easy to understand: A message box (or a modal dialog box) creates its own message loop. Thus, events that occur within the message box are not sent to your program's main message loop and are, therefore, not recorded. In many situations, this is what you want to occur. That is, a message box is usually activated because user input is, indeed, required. (For example, a serious error may have occurred.) On the other hand, if this is not what you desire, then there are various ways around this problem. For example, during replay, you could simply not activate the message box. Another solution is presented later in this chapter, when a message journal is created.

Using Message Hook Functions

While there is nothing technically wrong with the preceding program, it is not generally the best way to implement a message recorder. First, most programmers will find the extra code inside the message loop to be unsettling. It is also potentially inefficient. For example, if you want to record or monitor only certain messages, you will be adding significant overhead to all messages—whether they are recorded or not. Fortunately, there is another method by which your program can tap into the message stream and this approach is built into Windows itself. The mechanism that allows this is the *hook function*. Hook functions allow you to "hook into" the message stream and monitor the flow of messages. Since hook functions operate under Windows' control and execute (more or less) at the operating system level, they provide a better approach to monitoring the message stream. They also provide capabilities beyond those available within the application program.

Before you can use hook functions to monitor and record messages, you will need to understand their theory of operation and learn about the API functions that support them.

Hook Theory

When you create a hook function, you are inserting a function into Windows' message handling chain. Once installed, the hook function can monitor messages. In some cases, it can even alter messages. The hook function is depicted in Figure 7-2.

There are two general types of hook functions: system wide and application specific. Using a system-wide hook function you can intercept all messages that enter the system. Using an application-specific hook function you can intercept only those messages directed at a specified window or application. Moreover, an application-specific hook will monitor only messages associated with a specific thread. This means that multithreaded programs may need to install additional hooks if each thread creates a window that must be monitored.

When using an application-specific hook, it is possible to select various categories of messages that the hook will receive. For example, it is possible to insert a hook that receives only keyboard messages. Another can receive only mouse messages. Since each hook impacts system performance, the ability to narrow the scope of a

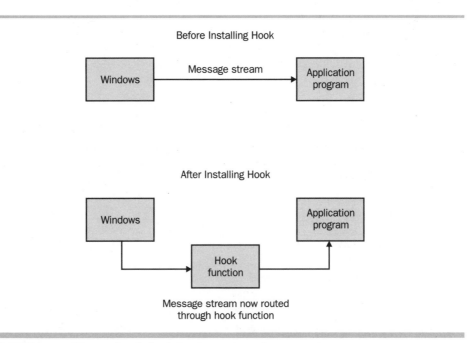

FIGURE 7-2. How a hook function intercepts the message stream

hook will be important in some applications. Of course, it is also possible to receive all messages associated with an application.

Windows implements hooks by maintaining a pointer to each hook function that has been installed in the system. Each hook function is called automatically by Windows when a message relating to that hook occurs in the input stream.

The General Form of a Hook Function

All hook functions have the following prototype:

LRESULT CALLBACK *Hook*(int *code*, WPARAM *wParam*, LPARAM *lParam*);

As you can see, all hooks are callback functions. The reason for this is obvious: they are called by Windows and not by your program. Here, *Hook* is the name of the hook function, which can be anything you like. Each time the hook function is called, the value of *code* determines what type of information is in the remaining two parameters and what action, if any, the hook function must take. The exact value of *code* depends upon the type of hook and the event that has occurred. The values of *wParam* and *lParam* also vary, depending upon the type of the hook, but usually *lParam* points to an object that describes the message. The return value of a hook function depends upon the nature of the hook and the action that has occurred.

Installing a Hook Function

To install a hook function, you must use **SetWindowsHookEx( )**. Its prototype is shown here:

HHOOK SetWindowsHookEx(int *type*, HOOKPROC *HookFunc*,
                   HINSTANCE *hInst*, DWORD *ThreadId*);

If successful, the function returns a handle to the hook, or **NULL** if an error occurs.

The type of hook being installed is specified by *type.* Here are its most commonly used values:

Hook Type	Purpose
WH_CALLWNDPROC	Monitors messages sent to your program's window procedure.
WH_CALLWNDPROCRET	Monitors messages after being sent to your program's window procedure.
WH_CBT	Monitors messages relating to computer-based training.
WH_DEBUG	Monitors all messages—used for debugging.

Hook Type	Purpose
WH_FOREGROUNDIDLE	Called when a foreground thread is going idle.
WH_GETMESSAGE	Monitors messages obtained by **GetMessage( )** or examined by **PeekMessage( )**.
WH_JOURNALPLAYBACK	Plays back mouse or keyboard messages.
WH_JOURNALRECORD	Records mouse or keyboard messages.
WH_KEYBOARD	Monitors keyboard messages.
WH_MOUSE	Monitors mouse messages.
WH_MSGFILTER	Monitors dialog, menu, scroll bar, or message box messages.
WH_SHELL	Monitors shell-related messages.
WH_SYSMSGFILTER	A global (system-wide) version of WH_MSGFILTER.

Of these, the **WH_JOURNALRECORD, WH_JOURNALPLAYBACK,** and **WH_SYSMSGFILTER** message hooks are always system-wide. The others may be system-wide or local to a specific thread.

HookFunc is a pointer to the hook function that will be installed. The instance handle of the DLL in which the hook function is defined is passed in *hInst.* However, if the hook function is defined within the current process and is monitoring a thread created by that process, then *hInst* must be **NULL.**

ThreadId is the ID of the thread being monitored. For a global hook function, *ThreadId* is zero.

Removing a Hook Function

Since hook functions negatively impact system performance, they should be removed as soon as they are no longer needed. To do this, call the **UnhookWindowsHookEx( )** function. Its prototype is shown here:

BOOL UnhookWindowsHookEx(HHOOK *HookFunc*);

Here, *HookFunc* is the handle of the hook function being removed. The function returns non-zero if successful and zero on failure.

Calling the Next Hook Function

Sometimes your hook function may be part of a chain of message hooks. Therefore, it is usually a good idea to pass along any message received by your hook to the next hook function. You do this by calling the **CallNextHookEx( )** function, shown here:

LRESULT CallNextHookEx(HHOOK *CurHook*, int *code*,
              WPARAM *wParam*, LPARAM *lParam*);

Here, *CurHook* is the handle of the currently executing hook. The values of *code*, *wParam*, and *lParam* must be those that are passed to the calling hook function. That is, the current hook function simply passes along the value of its parameters. The value returned is that returned by the next hook function.

Code

Recorder.cpp

Now that you understand the theory behind hooks and the functions required to support them, we can use a hook to improve the message recorder presented earlier. To use message hooks, your program will install a **WH_GETMESSAGE** hook. This hook is called whenever the application calls **GetMessage( )** or **PeekMessage( )**.

When a **WH_GETMESSAGE** hook function is called, the value of the *code* parameter determines what action the hook function must perform. If *code* is negative, then the function must immediately pass the message along to the next hook function by calling **CallNextHookEx( )**, returning its result.

If *code* is **HC_ACTION**, the function must handle the message. After processing the message, the hook function should pass the message along by calling **CallNextHookEx( )**. This ensures that other applications will also receive all appropriate messages. If for some reason you don't want to pass a message along, your hook function must return 0 after processing a message.

The value of *wParam* indicates whether the message has been removed from the message queue by a call to **GetMessage( )** or has only been examined because of a call to **PeekMessage( )**. If the message has been removed, *wParam* will contain **PM_REMOVE**. If it is still in the queue, *wParam* will contain **PM_NOREMOVE**. For the example in this book, the value of *wParam* can be ignored because all messages will be obtained by calling **GetMessage( )**.

The value of *lParam* points to a **MSG** structure that contains the message.

Here is the reworked message recorder program. This version uses a **WH_GETMESSAGE** hook function to monitor messages. It uses the same header and resource files as the previous version of the program.

```
// Recorder.cpp: Using a message hook function.

#include <windows.h>
#include <cstring>
#include <cstdio>
#include "rec.h"

#define MAXMESS 1000
#define ON 1
```

```
#define OFF 0
#define DELAY 200

LRESULT CALLBACK MsgHook(int code, WPARAM wParam,
                         LPARAM lParam);

struct messages {
  UINT msg;
  WPARAM wParam;
  LPARAM lParam;
  HWND hwnd;
} MsgArray[MAXMESS];

int lastmess = 0; // index one past last message
int record = OFF; // event recording on/off
int delay = 0;    // replay delay

HINSTANCE hInst;
HMENU hMenu;

HHOOK hHook; // message hook handle

HWND hwndglobal; // global window handle

LRESULT CALLBACK WindowFunc(HWND, UINT, WPARAM, LPARAM);
char szWinName[] = "MyWin";

int WINAPI WinMain(HINSTANCE hThisInst, HINSTANCE hPrevInst,
                   LPSTR lpszArgs, int nWinMode)
{
  HWND hwnd;
  MSG msg;
  WNDCLASSEX wcl;
  HACCEL hAccel;

  // Define a window class.
  wcl.cbSize = sizeof(WNDCLASSEX);
  wcl.hInstance = hThisInst;
  wcl.lpszClassName = szWinName;
  wcl.lpfnWndProc = WindowFunc;
  wcl.style = 0;
  wcl.hIcon = LoadIcon(NULL, IDI_APPLICATION); // large icon
  wcl.hIconSm = NULL; // use small version of large icon
```

```
   wcl.hCursor = LoadCursor(NULL, IDC_ARROW);
   wcl.hbrBackground = (HBRUSH) GetStockObject(WHITE_BRUSH);
   wcl.cbClsExtra = 0;
   wcl.cbWndExtra = 0;
   wcl.lpszMenuName = "RecorderMenu";

   // Register the window class.
   if(!RegisterClassEx(&wcl)) return 0;

   // Create a window.
   hwnd = CreateWindow(szWinName,
                       "Using a Message Hook",
                       WS_OVERLAPPEDWINDOW,
                       CW_USEDEFAULT, CW_USEDEFAULT,
                       CW_USEDEFAULT, CW_USEDEFAULT,
                       NULL, NULL, hThisInst, NULL);

   hInst = hThisInst; // save the current instance handle

   // Load accelerators.
   hAccel = LoadAccelerators(hThisInst, "RecorderMenu");

   hMenu = GetMenu(hwnd); // get handle to main menu

   hwndglobal = hwnd;

   // Display the window.
   ShowWindow(hwnd, nWinMode);
   UpdateWindow(hwnd);

   // The message loop.
   while(GetMessage(&msg, NULL, 0, 0))
   {
     if(!TranslateAccelerator(hwnd, hAccel, &msg)) {
       TranslateMessage(&msg);
       DispatchMessage(&msg);
     }
   }

   return msg.wParam;
}

// The window procedure.
```

```
LRESULT CALLBACK WindowFunc(HWND hwnd, UINT message,
                            WPARAM wParam, LPARAM lParam)
{
  HDC hdc;
  PAINTSTRUCT ps;

  int i, response;
  static unsigned j=0;
  char str[255];
  TEXTMETRIC tm;
  SIZE size;

  static int X=0, Y=0;    // current output location
  static int maxX, maxY; // screen dimensions

  static HDC memdc;      // store the virtual window handle
  static HBITMAP hbit; // store the virtual bitmap
  HBRUSH hbrush;         // store the brush handle

  switch(message) {
    case WM_CREATE:
      hHook = SetWindowsHookEx(WH_GETMESSAGE, (HOOKPROC) MsgHook,
                      NULL, GetCurrentThreadId());

      // create a virtual window
      maxX = GetSystemMetrics(SM_CXSCREEN);
      maxY = GetSystemMetrics(SM_CYSCREEN);

      hdc = GetDC(hwnd);
      memdc = CreateCompatibleDC(hdc);
      hbit = CreateCompatibleBitmap(hdc, maxX, maxY);
      SelectObject(memdc, hbit);
      hbrush = (HBRUSH) GetStockObject(WHITE_BRUSH);
      SelectObject(memdc, hbrush);
      PatBlt(memdc, 0, 0, maxX, maxY, PATCOPY);

      ReleaseDC(hwnd, hdc);
      break;
    case WM_COMMAND:
      switch(LOWORD(wParam)) {
        case IDM_START:
          lastmess = 0;
          record = ON;
```

```
        SetWindowText(hwnd, "Recording");
        EnableMenuItem(hMenu, IDM_START, MF_GRAYED);
        EnableMenuItem(hMenu, IDM_RESET, MF_GRAYED);
        EnableMenuItem(hMenu, IDM_RUN, MF_GRAYED);
        EnableMenuItem(hMenu, IDM_EXIT, MF_GRAYED);
        break;
    case IDM_STOP:
        record = OFF;
        SetWindowText(hwnd, "Using a Message Hook");
        EnableMenuItem(hMenu, IDM_START, MF_ENABLED);
        EnableMenuItem(hMenu, IDM_RESET, MF_ENABLED);
        EnableMenuItem(hMenu, IDM_RUN, MF_ENABLED);
        EnableMenuItem(hMenu, IDM_EXIT, MF_ENABLED);
        break;
    case IDM_RESET:
        lastmess = 0;
        record = OFF;
        X = Y = 0;
        EnableMenuItem(hMenu, IDM_RUN, MF_GRAYED);
        break;
    case IDM_RUN:
        SetWindowText(hwnd, "Replaying");
        X = Y = 0;
        for(i=0; i<lastmess; i++) {
            SendMessage(MsgArray[i].hwnd,
                        MsgArray[i].msg,
                        MsgArray[i].wParam,
                        MsgArray[i].lParam);
            Sleep(delay);
        }
        SetWindowText(hwnd, "Using a Message Hook");
        break;
    case IDM_CLEAR:
        hdc = GetDC(hwnd);
        hbrush = (HBRUSH)GetStockObject(WHITE_BRUSH);
        SelectObject(memdc, hbrush);
        PatBlt(memdc, 0, 0, maxX, maxY, PATCOPY);
        SelectObject(hdc, hbrush);
        PatBlt(hdc, 0, 0, maxX, maxY, PATCOPY);
        ReleaseDC(hwnd, hdc);
        break;
    case IDM_SLOW:
        if(!delay) {
```

```
          CheckMenuItem(hMenu, IDM_SLOW, MF_CHECKED);
          delay = DELAY;
        }
        else {
          CheckMenuItem(hMenu, IDM_SLOW, MF_UNCHECKED);
          delay = 0;
        }
        break;
      case IDM_EXIT:
        response = MessageBox(hwnd, "Quit the Program?",
                             "Exit", MB_YESNO);
        if(response == IDYES) PostQuitMessage(0);
        break;
      case IDM_ABOUT:
        MessageBox(hwnd, "Recorder V1.0",
                   "Message Hook Recorder", MB_OK);
        break;
    }
    break;
  case WM_CHAR:
    hdc = GetDC(hwnd);

    GetTextMetrics(hdc, &tm);

    sprintf(str, "%c", (char) wParam); // stringize character

    // output a carriage return, linefeed sequence
    if((char)wParam == '\r') {
      Y = Y + tm.tmHeight + tm.tmExternalLeading;
      X = 0; // reset to start of line
    }
    else {
      TextOut(memdc, X, Y, str, 1); // output to memory
      TextOut(hdc, X, Y, str, 1); // output to screen
      // compute length of character
      GetTextExtentPoint32(memdc, str, strlen(str), &size);
      X += size.cx; // advance to end of character
    }

    ReleaseDC(hwnd, hdc);
    break;
  case WM_LBUTTONDOWN:
    hdc = GetDC(hwnd);
```

```
            strcpy(str, "Left Button Down");
            TextOut(memdc, LOWORD(lParam), HIWORD(lParam),
                    str, strlen(str));
            TextOut(hdc, LOWORD(lParam), HIWORD(lParam),
                    str, strlen(str));
            ReleaseDC(hwnd, hdc);
            break;
        case WM_RBUTTONDOWN:
            hdc = GetDC(hwnd);
            strcpy(str, "Right Button Down");
            TextOut(memdc, LOWORD(lParam), HIWORD(lParam),
                    str, strlen(str));
            TextOut(hdc, LOWORD(lParam), HIWORD(lParam),
                    str, strlen(str));
            ReleaseDC(hwnd, hdc);
            break;
        case WM_PAINT:
            hdc = BeginPaint(hwnd, &ps);

            // copy virtual window onto screen
            BitBlt(hdc, ps.rcPaint.left, ps.rcPaint.top,
                    ps.rcPaint.right-ps.rcPaint.left, // width
                    ps.rcPaint.bottom-ps.rcPaint.top, // height
                    memdc,
                    ps.rcPaint.left, ps.rcPaint.top,
                    SRCCOPY);

            EndPaint(hwnd, &ps);
            break;
        case WM_DESTROY:
            UnhookWindowsHookEx(hHook);
            DeleteDC(memdc);
            DeleteObject(hbit);
            PostQuitMessage(0);
            break;
        default:
            return DefWindowProc(hwnd, message, wParam, lParam);
    }
    return 0;
}


// A WM_GETMESSAGE hook function.
LRESULT CALLBACK MsgHook(int code, WPARAM wParam, LPARAM lParam)
```

```
{
  MSG *msg;

  msg = (MSG *) lParam;

  if(code >= 0)
    if(record) {
      switch(msg->message) {
        case WM_CHAR:
        case WM_LBUTTONDOWN:
        case WM_RBUTTONDOWN:
        case WM_COMMAND:
          MsgArray[lastmess].hwnd = msg->hwnd;
          MsgArray[lastmess].msg = msg->message;
          MsgArray[lastmess].lParam = msg->lParam;
          MsgArray[lastmess].wParam = msg->wParam;
          lastmess++;
          if(lastmess == MAXMESS)
            MessageBox(hwndglobal, "Too Many Messages",
                       "Recorder Error", MB_OK);
      }
    }

  return CallNextHookEx(hHook, code, wParam, lParam);
}
```

ANNOTATIONS

Much of **Recorder.cpp** is similar to **SimpRec.cpp**. The main difference is that now messages are recorded by the **MsgHook( )** function and not by code within **WinMain( )**'s message loop. Therefore, the program's message loop has been returned to its standard form.

When the program begins, the first thing that its **WM_CREATE** handler does is register the message hook function using the line of code shown here:

```
hHook = SetWindowsHookEx(WH_GETMESSAGE, (HOOKPROC) MsgHook,
                         NULL, GetCurrentThreadId());
```

After this line executes, **MsgHook( )** is "wired" into the message stream. Notice that the fourth parameter is a call to **GetCurrentThreadID( )**. This function returns the ID associated with the calling thread.

When the program ends, the **WM_DESTROY** handler calls **UnhookWindowsHookEx( )** to unhook **MsgHook( )**. You must remember to unhook your hook functions because they have negative impact on performance.

Each message that is sent to the program is processed by **MsgHook( )**. It is shown here for your convenience:

```
// A WM_GETMESSAGE hook function.
LRESULT CALLBACK MsgHook(int code, WPARAM wParam, LPARAM lParam)
{
  MSG *msg;

  msg = (MSG *) lParam;

  if(code >= 0)
    if(record) {
      switch(msg->message) {
        case WM_CHAR:
        case WM_LBUTTONDOWN:
        case WM_RBUTTONDOWN:
        case WM_COMMAND:
          MsgArray[lastmess].hwnd = msg->hwnd;
          MsgArray[lastmess].msg = msg->message;
          MsgArray[lastmess].lParam = msg->lParam;
          MsgArray[lastmess].wParam = msg->wParam;
          lastmess++;
          if(lastmess == MAXMESS)
            MessageBox(hwndglobal, "Too Many Messages",
                    "Recorder Error", MB_OK);
      }
    }

  return CallNextHookEx(hHook, code, wParam, lParam);
}
```

If **code** is non-negative and **record** is **ON**, the message is recorded using the same general approach as that used by the preceding program. **MsgHook( )** ends by returning the result of a call to **CallNextHookEx( )**. As explained earlier, this ensures that any other message hooks in the system will also be called.

Keeping a System-Wide Message Journal

The preceding two example programs only recorded messages associated with the main window (or any child windows) of the application. This means that they did not keep a record of events that occurred outside of their windows. However, when creating macros or preparing demonstrations, it is often useful to be able to record all mouse and keyboard messages that occur, no matter what window generates them or what window they are for. A first, you might think that this is a difficult task. However, as you will see, support for such a job is built into Windows.

The facility that allows you to monitor, record, and replay system-wide input messages is the *journal hook*. Windows supports two journal hook functions that are specified by **WH_JOURNALRECORD** and **WH_JOURNALPLAYBACK** when **SetWindowsHookEx( )** is called. Using these hooks, you can maintain a system-wide journal of mouse and keyboard messages and, if you choose, replay those messages at a later time.

One word of warning is in order at the outset. Message journals record only mouse and keyboard input events. They cannot be used to record menu selections. You will have to add other facilities to handle this type of activity.

Before a system-wide journal can be created, you need to understand how to create the necessary record and playback hooks. Although they have the same general form as all other hook functions, they require some special handling on your part.

Creating a Journal Record Hook

Each time a **WH_JOURNALRECORD** hook is called, its *code* parameter determines what course of action the hook must follow. If *code* is negative, then the hook must simply pass the message along to the next hook function. It does so by calling **CallNextHookEx( )** and returning the result of this call. Otherwise, if *code* is **HC_ACTION**, the hook must record the message. Two other values can be contained in *code*: **HC_SYSMODALON** and **HC_SYSMODALOFF**. These values indicate that a system-modal dialog box was created or destroyed, respectively. Your hook function should not record messages that occur when a system-modal dialog box is active.

The *wParam* is always **NULL** and unused. The *lParam* parameter points to an **EVENTMSG** structure, which is defined like this:

```
typedef struct tagEVENTMSG {
  UINT message;
  UINT paramL;
  UINT paramH;
  DWORD time;
  HWND hwnd;
} EVENTMSG;
```

Each time your journal recorder function receives a message, it must store it. That is, your program must sequentially store all messages received by the recorder function. If you will be recording just a few messages, then you can use an array of type **EVENTMSG** for this purpose. Otherwise, you will need to either dynamically allocate storage or utilize a file for this purpose. It is important, however, that you store every message because all will be needed to ensure an accurate playback.

Except when *code* is negative, your record hook function must return either the result of a call to **CallNextHookEx( )**, or zero if you choose not to pass the message up the chain. As explained earlier, when *code* is negative, your function must terminate immediately by returning the value of a call to **CallNextHookEx( )**.

Since a journal records virtually all input events, a special means of signalling your program to stop the recording of journal entries is needed. To solve this problem, the key combination CTRL-BREAK is reserved as a stop signal during the recording process. This key combination generates a **WM_KEYDOWN** message with the **VK_CANCEL** key code contained within the *wParam* parameter. Your program must watch for this code and stop recording when it is received. Depending upon your application, you may or may not want to record the stop signal. If you do, then it can also be used to signal the end of a playback sequence. This is the approach used by the journal example that follows.

A **WH_JOURNALRECORD** hook begins receiving messages as soon as it is installed. Therefore, you will not want to install one until it is needed. Also, you will want to remove the hook as soon as you are done recording.

Creating a Journal Playback Function

Each time a **WH_JOURNALPLAYBACK** hook is called, its *code* parameter determines what course of action the hook must follow. If *code* is negative, then the hook must simply pass the message along to the next hook function. It does so by calling **CallNextHookEx( )** and returning the result of this call. If *code* is **HC_GETNEXT**, the hook must obtain the next message and copy it to the **EVENTMSG** structure pointed to by *lParam*. If *code* is **HC_SKIP**, the hook must prepare for the next **HC_GETNEXT** request. Thus, when **HC_GETNEXT** is received, your hook function copies the current message to the object pointed to by *lParam*, but it *does not* advance to the next message. The only time your hook function advances to the next message is when **HC_SKIP** is received. Therefore, two **HC_GETNEXT** requests without an intervening **HC_SKIP** request must return the same message.

The values **HC_SYSMODALON** and **HC_SYSMODALOFF** may also be contained in *code*. These values indicate that a system-modal dialog box was created or destroyed, respectively. Your hook function should not play back messages when a system-modal dialog box is active.

The return value of a playback hook is ignored unless *code* contains **HC_GETNEXT**. In this case, the return value indicates a delay interval that will be observed before the next message is processed. If the hook returns zero, the message is processed immediately. Otherwise, the specified delay will occur. The delay period is specified in terms of system clock ticks. You can use the delay feature to replay events at a faster or slower speed than they were recorded. It is also valuable as a means of preventing the input queue from being overrun. Remember, your program can replay input events far faster than you can enter them, manually. Thus, it is possible to overrun the input queue during playback if too many messages are dispatched.

To play back the journal recorded by a **WH_JOURNALRECORD** hook, you simply install a **WH_JOURNALPLAYBACK** hook. Once installed, it will automatically begin being called by Windows to obtain messages. That is, immediately upon its installation, the message stream will switch from your input to that produced by the **WH_JOURNALPLAYBACK** hook. In fact, while the journal playback hook is installed, mouse and keyboard input are disabled—except for a few special key combinations, such as CTRL-ALT-DEL. Therefore, before installing a playback hook, make sure that it is ready to provide messages. Also, you must remove the hook as soon as it has reached the end of the journal. Failure to do so will almost certainly lead to disaster.

Journals Are System-Wide Resources

As mentioned earlier, a journal is a system-wide feature. Thus, it will record events that happen in any active window. For example, using a journal you can also record mouse and keyboard events that occur within message boxes, modal dialog boxes, and even other programs.

Since a journal places itself into the system-wide message system, you must exercise care with its use. First, it will degrade the performance of all tasks. Second, you may create unforeseen side effects when a complex series of commands are replayed. For example, if you alter the shape or position of a window while recording and then play back those events without first returning the window to its former size and appearance, spurious messages may be sent to other applications that were previously under the original window. The point is that sometimes playing back a journal will not produce the precise results that you expect. Therefore, be careful.

There are three key combinations that cannot be recorded because they cancel journal hook functions. They are CTRL-ESC, ALT-ESC, and CTRL-ALT-DEL. These keys are especially useful if your application becomes "stuck" during record or playback. Pressing any of these keys will cancel the journal hooks.

Code

Journal.cpp

The following program implements a system-wide journal. You should have no trouble understanding its operation. It works much like the two preceding examples except that it will record all input events that occur within the system. Therefore, use it with care. Remember, to stop recording, press CTRL-BREAK. Sample output is shown in Figure 7-3.

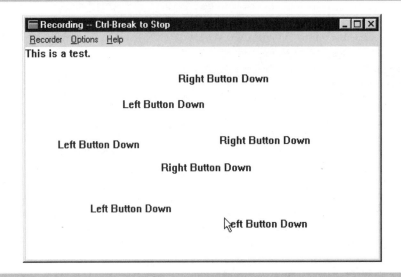

FIGURE 7-3. Sample output from **Journal.cpp**

When using the program, keep in mind that only mouse and keyboard events are recorded. Menu selections (which generate **WM_COMMAND** messages), for example, are not recorded. If you record a menu selection, then at playback the program will hang and you will need to press a system-key combination, such as CTRL-ESC, to regain control. If you want to record other messages you will need to add other hook functions.

```cpp
// Journal.cpp: Using a system journal.

#include <windows.h>
#include <cstring>
#include <cstdio>
#include "journal.h"

#define MAXMESS 2000
#define ON 1
#define OFF 0
#define DELAY 200

LRESULT CALLBACK RecHook(int, WPARAM, LPARAM);
LRESULT CALLBACK PlayHook(int, WPARAM, LPARAM);

EVENTMSG MsgArray[MAXMESS];
```

```
int record = OFF; // event recording on/off
int lastmess = 0; // index one past last message
int curmess = 0;  // index of current message
int delay = 1;    // replay delay

HINSTANCE hInst;

HHOOK hRecHook, hPlayHook;
HMENU hMenu;
HWND hwndglobal;

LRESULT CALLBACK WindowFunc(HWND, UINT, WPARAM, LPARAM);
char szWinName[] = "MyWin";

int WINAPI WinMain(HINSTANCE hThisInst, HINSTANCE hPrevInst,
                   LPSTR lpszArgs, int nWinMode)
{
  HWND hwnd;
  MSG msg;
  WNDCLASSEX wcl;
  HACCEL hAccel;

  // Define a window class.
  wcl.cbSize = sizeof(WNDCLASSEX);
  wcl.hInstance = hThisInst;
  wcl.lpszClassName = szWinName;
  wcl.lpfnWndProc = WindowFunc;
  wcl.style = 0;
  wcl.hIcon = LoadIcon(NULL, IDI_APPLICATION); // large icon
  wcl.hIconSm = NULL; // use small version of large icon
  wcl.hCursor = LoadCursor(NULL, IDC_ARROW);
  wcl.hbrBackground = (HBRUSH) GetStockObject(WHITE_BRUSH);
  wcl.cbClsExtra = 0;
  wcl.cbWndExtra = 0;
  wcl.lpszMenuName = "RecorderMenu";

  // Register the window class.
  if(!RegisterClassEx(&wcl)) return 0;

  // Create a window.
  hwnd = CreateWindow(szWinName,
                      "Using a Journal",
                      WS_OVERLAPPEDWINDOW,
```

```
                        CW_USEDEFAULT, CW_USEDEFAULT,
                        CW_USEDEFAULT, CW_USEDEFAULT,
                        NULL, NULL, hThisInst, NULL);

    hInst = hThisInst; // save the current instance handle
    hwndglobal = hwnd;

    // Load accelerators.
    hAccel = LoadAccelerators(hThisInst, "RecorderMenu");

    hMenu = GetMenu(hwnd); // get handle to main menu

    // Display the window.
    ShowWindow(hwnd, nWinMode);
    UpdateWindow(hwnd);

    // The message loop.
    while(GetMessage(&msg, NULL, 0, 0))
    {
      if(!TranslateAccelerator(hwnd, hAccel, &msg)) {
        TranslateMessage(&msg);
        DispatchMessage(&msg);
      }
    }

    return msg.wParam;
}

// The window procedure.
LRESULT CALLBACK WindowFunc(HWND hwnd, UINT message,
                            WPARAM wParam, LPARAM lParam)
{
  HDC hdc;
  PAINTSTRUCT ps;

  int response;
  char str[255];
  TEXTMETRIC tm;
  SIZE size;

  static int X=0, Y=0;    // current output location
  static int maxX, maxY; // screen dimensions
```

```
static HDC memdc;      // store the virtual window handle
static HBITMAP hbit;   // store the virtual bitmap
HBRUSH hbrush;         // store the brush handle

switch(message) {
  case WM_CREATE:
    // create virtual window
    maxX = GetSystemMetrics(SM_CXSCREEN);
    maxY = GetSystemMetrics(SM_CYSCREEN);

    hdc = GetDC(hwnd);
    memdc = CreateCompatibleDC(hdc);
    hbit = CreateCompatibleBitmap(hdc, maxX, maxY);
    SelectObject(memdc, hbit);
    hbrush = (HBRUSH) GetStockObject(WHITE_BRUSH);
    SelectObject(memdc, hbrush);
    PatBlt(memdc, 0, 0, maxX, maxY, PATCOPY);

    ReleaseDC(hwnd, hdc);
    break;
  case WM_COMMAND:
    switch(LOWORD(wParam)) {
      case IDM_START:
        lastmess = 0;
        record = ON;
        EnableMenuItem(hMenu, IDM_START, MF_GRAYED);
        EnableMenuItem(hMenu, IDM_RESET, MF_GRAYED);
        EnableMenuItem(hMenu, IDM_RUN, MF_GRAYED);
        EnableMenuItem(hMenu, IDM_EXIT, MF_GRAYED);
        SetWindowText(hwnd, "Recording -- Ctrl-Break to Stop");

        hRecHook = SetWindowsHookEx(WH_JOURNALRECORD,
                              (HOOKPROC) RecHook, hInst, 0);
        break;
      case IDM_RESET:
        X = Y = 0;
        lastmess = 0;
        curmess = 0;
        record = OFF;
        EnableMenuItem(hMenu, IDM_RUN, MF_GRAYED);
        break;
      case IDM_RUN:
        X = Y = 0;
```

```
            curmess = 0;
            SetWindowText(hwnd, "Replaying");
            hPlayHook = SetWindowsHookEx(WH_JOURNALPLAYBACK,
                                       (HOOKPROC) PlayHook, hInst, 0);
          break;
        case IDM_CLEAR:
          hdc = GetDC(hwnd);
          hbrush = (HBRUSH) GetStockObject(WHITE_BRUSH);
          SelectObject(memdc, hbrush);
          PatBlt(memdc, 0, 0, maxX, maxY, PATCOPY);
          SelectObject(hdc, hbrush);
          PatBlt(hdc, 0, 0, maxX, maxY, PATCOPY);
          ReleaseDC(hwnd, hdc);
          break;
        case IDM_SLOW:
          if(delay==1) {
            CheckMenuItem(hMenu, IDM_SLOW, MF_CHECKED);
            delay = DELAY;
          }
          else {
            CheckMenuItem(hMenu, IDM_SLOW, MF_UNCHECKED);
            delay = 1;
          }
          break;
        case IDM_EXIT:
          response = MessageBox(hwnd, "Quit the Program?",
                                "Exit", MB_YESNO);
          if(response == IDYES) PostQuitMessage(0);
          break;
        case IDM_ABOUT:
          MessageBox(hwnd, "Journal Recorder V1.0",
                     "Message Recorder", MB_OK);
          break;
      }
      break;
    case WM_KEYDOWN: // check for VK_CANCEL
      if(wParam == VK_CANCEL && record) {
        // stop recording
        UnhookWindowsHookEx(hRecHook);
        record = OFF;
        SetWindowText(hwnd, "Using a Journal");
        EnableMenuItem(hMenu, IDM_START, MF_ENABLED);
```

```
      EnableMenuItem(hMenu, IDM_RESET, MF_ENABLED);
      EnableMenuItem(hMenu, IDM_RUN, MF_ENABLED);
      EnableMenuItem(hMenu, IDM_EXIT, MF_ENABLED);
    }
    else if(wParam == VK_CANCEL && !record) {
      // stop playback
      UnhookWindowsHookEx(hPlayHook);
      record = OFF;
      SetWindowText(hwnd, "Using a Journal");
    }
    break;
  case WM_CHAR:
    hdc = GetDC(hwnd);

    GetTextMetrics(hdc, &tm);

    sprintf(str, "%c", (char) wParam); // stringize character

    // output a carriage return, linefeed sequence
    if((char)wParam == '\r') {
      Y = Y + tm.tmHeight + tm.tmExternalLeading;
      X = 0; // reset to start of line
    }
    else {
      TextOut(memdc, X, Y, str, 1); // output to memory
      TextOut(hdc, X, Y, str, 1); // output to memory
      // compute length of character
      GetTextExtentPoint32(memdc, str, strlen(str), &size);
      X += size.cx; // advance to end of character
    }

    ReleaseDC(hwnd, hdc);
    break;
  case WM_LBUTTONDOWN:
    hdc = GetDC(hwnd);
    strcpy(str, "Left Button Down");
    TextOut(memdc, LOWORD(lParam), HIWORD(lParam),
            str, strlen(str));
    TextOut(hdc, LOWORD(lParam), HIWORD(lParam),
            str, strlen(str));
    ReleaseDC(hwnd, hdc);
    break;
  case WM_RBUTTONDOWN:
```

```
        hdc = GetDC(hwnd);
        strcpy(str, "Right Button Down");
        TextOut(memdc, LOWORD(lParam), HIWORD(lParam),
                str, strlen(str));
        TextOut(hdc, LOWORD(lParam), HIWORD(lParam),
                str, strlen(str));
        ReleaseDC(hwnd, hdc);
        break;
      case WM_PAINT:
        hdc = BeginPaint(hwnd, &ps);

        // copy virtual window onto screen
        BitBlt(hdc, ps.rcPaint.left, ps.rcPaint.top,
                ps.rcPaint.right-ps.rcPaint.left, // width
                ps.rcPaint.bottom-ps.rcPaint.top, // height
                memdc,
                ps.rcPaint.left, ps.rcPaint.top,
                SRCCOPY);

        EndPaint(hwnd, &ps);
        break;
      case WM_DESTROY:
        DeleteDC(memdc);
        DeleteObject(hbit);
        PostQuitMessage(0);
        break;
      default:
        return DefWindowProc(hwnd, message, wParam, lParam);
  }

  return 0;
}

// Journal record hook.
LRESULT CALLBACK RecHook(int code, WPARAM wParam, LPARAM lParam)
{
  static bool recOK = true;

  if(code < 0)
    return CallNextHookEx(hRecHook, code, wParam, lParam);
  else if(code == HC_SYSMODALON)
    recOK = false;
  else if(code == HC_SYSMODALOFF)
    recOK = true;
```

```
  else if(recOK && record && (code == HC_ACTION)) {
    MsgArray[lastmess] = * (EVENTMSG *) lParam;
    lastmess++;
    if(lastmess == MAXMESS)
      MessageBox(hwndglobal, "Too Many Messages",
                 "Recorder Error", MB_OK);
  }
  return CallNextHookEx(hRecHook, code, wParam, lParam);
}

// Journal playback hook.
LRESULT CALLBACK PlayHook(int code, WPARAM wParam, LPARAM lParam)
{
  static bool s = false;
  static bool playOK = true;

  if(code < 0)
    return CallNextHookEx(hPlayHook, code, wParam, lParam);
  else if(code == HC_SYSMODALON)
    playOK = false;
  else if(code == HC_SYSMODALOFF)
    playOK = true;
  else if(playOK && (code == HC_GETNEXT)) {
    s = !s;
    if(s) return delay;
    * (EVENTMSG *)lParam = MsgArray[curmess];
  }
  else if(playOK && (code == HC_SKIP)) curmess++;

  return 0;
}
```

The program uses the following resource file, **Journal.rc**:

```
// Event recorder resource file.
#include <windows.h>
#include "journal.h"

RecorderMenu MENU
{
  POPUP "&Recorder"
  {
```

```
    MENUITEM "&Start\tF2", IDM_START
    MENUITEM "Rese&t\tF3", IDM_RESET
    MENUITEM "&Run\tF4", IDM_RUN, GRAYED
    MENUITEM "E&xit\tCtrl+X", IDM_EXIT
  }
  POPUP "&Options"
  {
    MENUITEM "&Clear Window\tF5", IDM_CLEAR
    MENUITEM "&Slow Motion\tF6", IDM_SLOW
  }
  POPUP "&Help" {
    MENUITEM "&About\tF1", IDM_ABOUT
  }
}

RecorderMenu ACCELERATORS
{
  VK_F2, IDM_START, VIRTKEY
  VK_F3, IDM_RESET, VIRTKEY
  VK_F4, IDM_RUN, VIRTKEY
  VK_F5, IDM_CLEAR, VIRTKEY
  VK_F6, IDM_SLOW, VIRTKEY
  "^X", IDM_EXIT
  VK_F1, IDM_ABOUT, VIRTKEY
}
```

The header file, **Journal.h**, is shown here:

```
#define IDM_EXIT    101
#define IDM_ABOUT   102
#define IDM_START   103
#define IDM_RESET   105
#define IDM_RUN     106
#define IDM_CLEAR   107
#define IDM_SLOW    108
```

ANNOTATIONS

While much of **Journal.cpp** is similar to **Recorder.cpp**, there are some important differences. The first thing to notice is that there is now no Stop option in the Recorder menu. Event recording can be stopped only by pressing CTRL-BREAK. Another difference is the addition of the global variables **curmess**, **hRecHook**, and **hPlayHook**. **curmess** holds the index of the current message, **hRecHook** stores the handle to the record function, and **hPlayHook** stores the handle to the playback function.

Other differences between **Journal.cpp** and **Recorder.cpp** are described in detail in the following sections.

The IDM_START Handler

The **IDM_START** handler is shown here. It is executed when the user starts recording a seqeunce.

```
case IDM_START:
  lastmess = 0;
  record = ON;
  EnableMenuItem(hMenu, IDM_START, MF_GRAYED);
  EnableMenuItem(hMenu, IDM_RESET, MF_GRAYED);
  EnableMenuItem(hMenu, IDM_RUN, MF_GRAYED);
  EnableMenuItem(hMenu, IDM_EXIT, MF_GRAYED);
  SetWindowText(hwnd, "Recording -- Ctrl-Break to Stop");

  hRecHook = SetWindowsHookEx(WH_JOURNALRECORD,
                              (HOOKPROC) RecHook, hInst, 0);
```

While much of it is the same as that used by the preceding two programs, it has one important difference: It inserts **RecHook( )** into the message stream. **RecHook( )** is the function that records messages. Since this function is registered using **WH_JOURNALRECORD**, it receives system-wide input messages. The handle to **RecHook( )** is stored in **hRecHook**. Remember, recording begins as soon as **RecHook( )** is installed.

Stopping Recording

To stop recording, the user must press CTRL-BREAK. This event is handled by the **WM_KEYDOWN** handler, shown here:

```
case WM_KEYDOWN: // check for VK_CANCEL
  if(wParam == VK_CANCEL && record) {
    // stop recording
    UnhookWindowsHookEx(hRecHook);
    record = OFF;
    SetWindowText(hwnd, "Using a Journal");
    EnableMenuItem(hMenu, IDM_START, MF_ENABLED);
    EnableMenuItem(hMenu, IDM_RESET, MF_ENABLED);
    EnableMenuItem(hMenu, IDM_RUN, MF_ENABLED);
    EnableMenuItem(hMenu, IDM_EXIT, MF_ENABLED);
  }
```

```
  else if(wParam == VK_CANCEL && !record) {
    // stop playback
    UnhookWindowsHookEx(hPlayHook);
    record = OFF;
    SetWindowText(hwnd, "Using a Journal");
  }
  break;
```

A **WM_KEYDOWN** message is generated whenever the user presses a non-system key. The virtual keycode associated with that message is contained in **wParam**. In this case, if **wParam** contains **VK_CANCEL**, then the user wants to stop the recording or playing back of a sequence. Depending upon the state of **record**, either **PlayHook( )** or **RecHook( )** is unhooked from the message stream by calling **UnhookWindowsHookEx( )**.

The IDM_RUN Handler

When the user selects Run, the **IDM_RUN** handler is executed.

```
case IDM_RUN:
  X = Y = 0;
  curmess = 0;
  SetWindowText(hwnd, "Replaying");
  hPlayHook = SetWindowsHookEx(WH_JOURNALPLAYBACK,
                              (HOOKPROC) PlayHook, hInst, 0);
  break;
```

In this case, the **PlayHook( )** function is inserted into the message stream and its handle is stored in **hPlayHook**. **PlayHook( )** replays the sequence by sending the messages in order, from start to finish. Playback begins as soon as **PlayHook( )** is installed.

The RecHook( ) Function

RecHook( ) is the hook function that records messages as they are generated. It is shown here:

```
// Journal record hook.
LRESULT CALLBACK RecHook(int code, WPARAM wParam, LPARAM lParam)
{
  static bool recOK = true;

  if(code < 0)
    return CallNextHookEx(hRecHook, code, wParam, lParam);
  else if(code == HC_SYSMODALON)
    recOK = false;
  else if(code == HC_SYSMODALOFF)
    recOK = true;
```

```
  else if(recOK && record && (code == HC_ACTION)) {
    MsgArray[lastmess] = * (EVENTMSG *) lParam;
    lastmess++;
    if(lastmess == MAXMESS)
      MessageBox(hwndglobal, "Too Many Messages",
                 "Recorder Error", MB_OK);
  }


  return CallNextHookEx(hRecHook, code, wParam, lParam);
}
```

It begins by declaring the static variable **recOK** and initializing it to **true**. Next, it checks the value of **code**. If it is negative, **RecHook( )** calls **CallNextHookEx( )** and returns. Otherwise, if **code** is **HC_SYSMODALON**, **recOK** is set to **false**. This indicates that a system-modal dialog box has been activated and no messages should be recorded. If **code** is **HC_SYSMODALOFF**, **recOK** is set to **true**, indicating that it is safe to record messages again. Otherwise, if **code** is **HC_ACTION** the message is recorded and stored in the **MsgArray** array.

The PlayHook( ) Function

To play back a prerecorded sequence, the **PlayHook( )** function, shown here, is inserted into the message stream.

```
// Journal playback hook.
LRESULT CALLBACK PlayHook(int code, WPARAM wParam, LPARAM lParam)
{
  static bool s = false;
  static bool playOK = true;

  if(code < 0)
    return CallNextHookEx(hPlayHook, code, wParam, lParam);
  else if(code == HC_SYSMODALON)
    playOK = false;
  else if(code == HC_SYSMODALOFF)
    playOK = true;
  else if(playOK && (code == HC_GETNEXT)) {
    s = !s;
    if(s) return delay;
    * (EVENTMSG *)lParam = MsgArray[curmess];
  }
  else if(playOK && (code == HC_SKIP)) curmess++;

  return 0;
}
```

It begins by declaring the static variables **s** (initialized to **false**) and **playOK** (initialized to **true**). Next, it checks the value of **code**. If it is negative, **PlayHook( )** calls **CallNextHookEx( )** and returns. Otherwise, if **code** is **HC_SYSMODALON**, **playOK** is set to **false**. This indicates that a system-modal dialog box has been activated and no message should be replayed. If **code** is **HC_SYSMODALOFF**, **playOK** is set to **true**, indicating that it is safe to replay messages again. If **code** is **HC_GETNEXT** the next message is obtained from the **MsgArray** array. This is performed by the following line:

```
* (EVENTMSG *)lParam = MsgArray[curmess];
```

Thus, when the function returns, the system has been given the next prerecorded message in the sequence. If **code** is **HC_SKIP** playback advances to the next message.

The static variable **s** controls when the delay interval is returned. To avoid an endless delay loop, the delay interval must be returned only every other time the next message is requested.

Some Things to Try

One of the first things that you might want to try is adding to each of the message recorder examples a dialog box that displays the messages that have been recorded. One way to do this is to use a list box. This addition will make it easy to see exactly what messages are recorded—and when.

With a little work, you could create a message editor that would let you add, delete, or modify messages in the list. In this way, you could create, edit, and replay your own message scripts.

Finally, you might find it an interesting challenge to create a macro facility that allows a number of different macros to be defined. You will need to provide some method of selecting among macros. One way is to allow the user to give each macro a name and then display the names of each macro in a list box. Use the index of each entry to select which macro sequence will be executed.

Tips for Working with MFC

All of the preceding event recorders can be adapted to MFC. In the case of the first, you will need to insert recording code into your message handlers. For the second two examples, just use **SetWindowsHookEx( )**, **UnhookWindowsHookEx( )**, and **CallNextHookEx( )** as the examples in this chapter do. MFC does not encapsulate these functions.

Print Utilities

Prior to Windows, sending output to a printer was a fairly mundane and simple-to-perform task. Most output was character oriented and the printer could be easily driven using only a few lines of code. However, because of Windows' device-independent philosophy, its multitasking, and the need to translate graphical screen images into their printed forms, printing under Windows presents the programmer with a bit more of a challenge. One of the best ways to meet that challenge is to have a collection of print utilities in your programmer's toolbox. Toward this end, this chapter develops two. The first prints the contents of a text file and the second prints the contents of a window. Each is useful as is, and each is easily adapted to other printing needs.

Printing Fundamentals

To print even the simplest document requires that your program perform a fairly complex sequence of steps. In general, to send output to the printer, you must

1. Obtain a printer-compatible device context.
2. Call various print-related API functions, which control the printer.
3. Create an Abort function and Cancel dialog box.

These steps are examined in detail by the following sections.

Obtaining a Printer DC

In the same way that a display device context describes and manages output to the screen, a printer device context describes and manages output to the printer. For this reason, you must obtain a printer device context before you can send output to the printer. There are two ways to obtain a device context: using **CreateDC( )** or using **PrintDlg( )**.

CreateDC( )

The first way to obtain a printer device context is to use **CreateDC( )**. Its prototype is shown here:

> HDC CreateDC(LPCSTR *lpszWhat*, LPCSTR *DevName*,
> LPCSTR *NotUsed*, CONST DEVMODE **DevMode*);

For printing under Windows 95/98, *lpszWhat* is not used and should be **NULL**. For printing under Windows NT/2000, *lpszWhat* must be **WINSPOOL** (to send output to the printer). *DevName* specifies the name of the printer as shown in the list of printers displayed by the Add Printer wizard or shown in the Printers window when you select Printers from the Windows Control Panel. *NotUsed* must be **NULL**. *DevMode* points to a **DEVMODE** structure that contains initialization information. To use the default initialization, *DevMode* must be **NULL**. **CreateDC( )** returns a handle to the device context if successful or **NULL** on failure. After your application is through printing, delete the device context by calling **DeleteDC( )**.

In some cases, your application will need to obtain the name of the currently selected printer. To do this, use **EnumPrinters( )** to obtain the names of available printers.

CreateDC( ) is most often used when printing does not involve interaction with the user. Although such situations are not common, they are not rare, either. For example, a system log might be printed after midnight, when no user is present. However, for most purposes (and for the examples in this chapter) you will acquire a printer DC using another of Windows API functions: **PrintDlg( )**.

PrintDlg( )

Most often, the easiest and best way to obtain a printer device context is to call **PrintDlg( )**. **PrintDlg( )** is one of Windows' common dialog boxes. As most readers know, common dialog boxes are system-defined dialog boxes that your application may use to perform various common input tasks, such as obtaining a filename, choosing a font, or setting a color. A common dialog box is activated by calling its API function.

PrintDlg( ) displays the standard Print common dialog box. You have certainly seen it in action because it is used by nearly all Windows applications. Its precise appearance varies, but it will look something like that shown in Figure 8-1. The advantage of using **PrintDlg( )** to obtain a device context is that it gives the user control over the printing operation. **PrintDlg( )** is both powerful and flexible. The following discussion describes its basic operation.

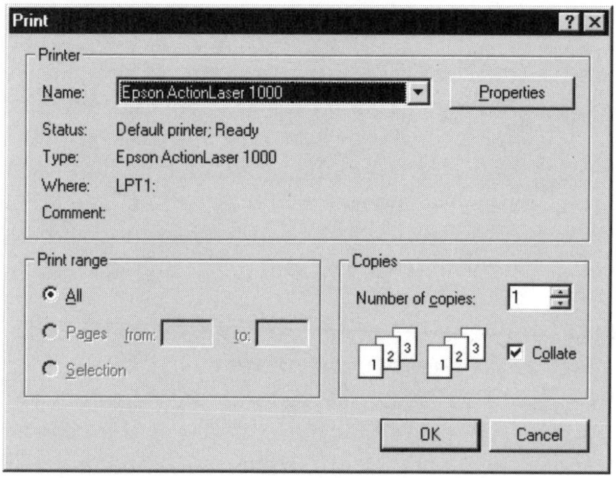

FIGURE 8-1. The Print common dialog box

PROGRAMMER'S NOTE   *For Windows 2000, the **PrintDlg( )** function has been superceded by **PrintDlgEx( )**. If you are writing exclusively for the Windows 2000 environment you will want to try substituting this function for **PrintDlg( )** in the print utilities.*

PrintDlg( ) has the following prototype:

BOOL PrintDlg(LPPRINTDLG *PrintDlg*);

It returns non-zero if the user terminates the dialog box by clicking OK. It returns zero if the user clicks Cancel (or presses ESC) or closes the box using the system menu. You must include **CommDlg.h** in your program in order to use this function.

The contents of the **PRINTDLG** structure pointed to by *PrintDlg* determine how **PrintDlg( )** operates. This structure is defined like this:

```
typedef struct tagPD {
  DWORD lStructSize;
```

```
  HWND hwndOwner;
  HGLOBAL hDevMode;
  HGLOBAL hDevNames;
  HDC hDC;
  DWORD Flags;
  WORD nFromPage;
  WORD nToPage;
  WORD nMinPage;
  WORD nMaxPage;
  WORD nCopies;
  HINSTANCE hInstance;
  LPARAM lCustData;
  LPPRINTHOOKPROC lpfnPrintHook;
  LPSETUPHOOKPROC lpfnSetupHook;
  LPCSTR lpPrintTemplateName;
  LPCSTR lpSetupTemplateName;
  HGLOBAL hPrintTemplate;
  HGLOBAL hSetupTemplate;
} PRINTDLG;
```

lStructSize contains the size of the **PRINTDLG** structure. **hwndOwner** specifies the handle of the window that owns **PrintDlg( )**.

hDevMode specifies the handle of a global **DEVMODE** structure that is used to initialize the dialog box controls prior to the call and contains the state of the controls after the call. This field may also be specified as **NULL**. In this case, **PrintDlg( )** allocates and initializes a **DEVMODE** structure and returns a handle to it in the **hDevMode** member. The **DEVMODE** structure is not used by the examples in this chapter.

hDevNames contains the handle of a global **DEVNAMES** structure. This structure specifies the name of the printer driver, the name of the printer, and the name of the port. These names are used to initialize the **PrintDlg( )** dialog box. After the call, they will contain the corresponding names entered by the user. This field may also be specified as **NULL**. In this case, **PrintDlg( )** allocates and initializes a **DEVNAMES** structure and returns a handle to it. The **DEVNAMES** structure is not used by the examples in this chapter. When both **hDevNames** and **hDevMode** are **NULL**, the default printer is used.

After the call, **hDC** will contain either the printer device context or information context, depending upon which value is specified in the **Flags** member. For the purposes of this chapter, **hDC** will contain a device context. (An information context simply contains information about a device context without actually creating one.)

nFromPage initializes the From edit box. On return, it will contain the starting page specified by the user. **nToPage** initializes the To edit box. On return, it will contain the ending page specified by the user.

nMinPage contains the minimum page number that can be selected in the From box. **nMaxPage** contains the maximum page number that can be selected in the To box.

nCopies initializes the Copies edit box. After the call, it will contain the number of copies to print as specified by the user. Your application must ensure that the number of copies requested by the user are actually printed.

hInstance contains the instance handle of an alternative dialog box specification if one is specified by the **lpPrintTemplateName** or **lpSetupTemplateName** members.

lCustData contains data that is passed to the optional functions pointed to by **lpfnPrintHook** or **lpfnSetupHook**.

lpfnPrintHook is a pointer to a function that preempts and processes messages intended for the Print dialog box. This element is only used if **Flags** contains the value **PD_ENABLEPRINTHOOK**. **lpfnSetupHook** is a pointer to a function that preempts and processes messages intended for the Print Setup dialog box. This element is only used if **Flags** contains the value **PD_ENABLESETUPHOOK**.

You can use a different layout (template) for the Print common dialog box. To do so, assign **lpPrintTemplateName** the address of the name of the dialog box resource that contains the new layout. **lpPrintTemplateName** is ignored unless **Flags** contains the value **PD_ENABLEPRINTTEMPLATE**.

You can use a different layout (template) for the Print Setup common dialog box. To do so, assign **lpSetupTemplateName** the address of the name of the dialog box resource that contains the new layout. **lpSetupTemplateName** is ignored unless **Flags** contains the value **PD_ENABLESETUPTEMPLATE**.

You can also use a different template for the Print common dialog box by specifying its handle in **hPrintTemplate** and specifying the **PD_ENABLEPRINTTEMPLATEHANDLE** flag. Similarly, you can use a different template for the Print Setup common dialog box by specifying its handle in **hSetupTemplate** and specifying the **PD_ENABLESETUPTEMPLATEHANDLE** flag. Otherwise, set these members to **NULL**.

PROGRAMMER'S NOTE   *The Print Setup common dialog box is obsolete. Use Page Setup instead.*

The **Flags** member contains values that determine precisely how the Print dialog box will behave and which fields will be active. On return, it will indicate the user's choices. It must be any valid combination of the values shown in Table 8-1.

As mentioned, on return, the **hDC** member will contain the printer's device context. Using this context, you can output to the printer using functions such as **TextOut( )** or **BitBlt( )** that operate on device contexts. After your application is through printing, delete the printer device context by calling **DeleteDC( )**.

Flag	Effect
PD_ALLPAGES	Checks the All radio button. (This is the default.) On return, this flag will be set if the All radio button is selected.
PD_COLLATE	Checks the Collate Copies check box. On return, this flag will be set if Collate Copies is checked and the selected printer driver does not provide collation. In this situation, your program must perform collation manually.
PD_DISABLEPRINTTOFILE	Deactivates the Print to File check box.
PD_ENABLEPRINTHOOK	Enables the **lpfnPrintHook** member.
PD_ENABLEPRINTTEMPLATE	Uses alternative dialog box template specified by **lpPrintTemplateName**.
PD_ENABLEPRINTTEMPLATEHANDLE	Uses alternative Print dialog box template specified by **hPrintTemplate**.
PD_ENABLESETUPHOOK	Enables the **lpfnSetupHook** member.
PD_ENABLESETUPTEMPLATE	Uses alternative dialog box template specified by **lpSetupTemplateName**.
PD_ENABLESETUPTEMPLATEHANDLE	Uses alternative Setup dialog box template specified by **hSetupTemplate**.
PD_HIDEPRINTTOFILE	Suppresses the Print to File check box.
PD_NONETWORKBUTTON	Suppresses Network button.
PD_NOPAGENUMS	Deactivates the Pages radio button.
PD_NOSELECTION	Deactivates the Selection radio button.
PD_NOWARNING	No warning message is displayed when there is no default printer.
PD_PAGENUMS	Selects the Pages radio button. On return, this flag is set if the Pages radio button is selected.
PD_PRINTSETUP	Print Setup rather than Print dialog box is displayed. This option is obsolete. Use the Page Setup common dialog box instead.
PD_PRINTTOFILE	Checks the Print to File check box. On return, indicates that user desires output directed to a file.
PD_RETURNDC	Causes a device context to be returned in **hDC**.

TABLE 8-1. The values for the **Flags** member of **PRINTDLG**

Flag	Effect
PD_RETURNDEFAULT	On return, **hDevMode** and **hDevNames** will contain values for the default printer. No dialog box is displayed. **hDevMode** and **hDevNames** must be **NULL** when **PrintDlg( )** is called.
PD_RETURNIC	Causes an information context to be returned in **hDC**.
PD_SELECTION	Selects the Selection radio button. On return, this flag will be set if the Selection radio button is selected.
PD_SHOWHELP	Help button is displayed.
PD_USEDEVMODECOPIESANDCOLLATE PD_USEDEVMODECOPIES	Deactivates Number of Copies spin control and/or Collate check box if the printer driver does not support multiple copies or collation, respectively. If not set, the number of copies is contained in the **nCopies** member and the **PD_COLLATE** flag will be set if collation is required.

TABLE 8-1.   The values for the **Flags** member of **PRINTDLG** *(continued)*

The Printer Functions

There are several functions that your program must use when printing. These functions are shown here:

> int EndDoc(HDC *hPrDC*);

> int EndPage(HDC *hPrDC*);

> int StartDoc(HDC *hPrDC*, CONST DOCINFO **Info*);

> int StartPage(HDC *hPrDC*);

In all cases, *hPrDC* is the handle of the printer device context. Also in all cases, the functions return a non-zero, positive value if successful. On failure they return zero or less.

To start printing, you must first call **StartDoc( )**. **StartDoc( )** performs two functions. First, it starts a print job. Second, its return value is the job ID. Although the examples in this chapter do not require print job IDs, some applications will because IDs are needed by some print-related functions. The *Info* parameter is a structure of type **DOCINFO**, which is defined like this:

```
typedef struct _DOCINFO {
  int cbSize;
  LPCSTR lpszDocName;
  LPCSTR lpszOutput;
  LPCSTR lpszDatatype;
  DWORD fwType;
} DOCINFO;
```

Here, **cbSize** must contain the size of the **DOCINFO** structure. **lpszDocName** is a pointer to the name of the print job. **lpszOutput** is a pointer to the name of the file that will receive printed output. However, to send output to the printer device context specified by *hPrDc*, **lpszOutput** must be **NULL**. **lpszDatatype** is a pointer to a string that identifies the type of data used to record the print job. This member can be **NULL**. **fwType** contains any additional data required by the print job.

To start printing, you must call **StartPage( )**. After each page is printed, you must call **EndPage( )**. **EndPage( )** advances the printer to a new page. Once your program is through printing, it must call **EndDoc( )**. Therefore, the following outline shows the sequence required to print a page:

StartDoc(dc, &info);

StartPage(dc);

   // print a page of data here

EndPage(dc);

EndDoc(dc);

Adding an Abort Function

Although it is possible to send output to the printer and forget about it, this is seldom adequate for real applications. Sometimes an error occurs while printing and a print job must be stopped. Sometimes the user will change his or her mind and want to cancel a print job. To handle such situations, your program must supply a printer abort function and a modeless dialog box that allows the user to cancel a print job before it is complete. According to standard Windows style, all programs must supply such a feature. In this section, you will see how to accomplish this.

SetAbortProc( )

To install an abort function, your program must call **SetAbortProc( )**. Its prototype is shown here:

int SetAbortProc(HDC *hPrDC*, ABORTPROC *AbortFunc*);

Here, *hPrDC* is the handle of the printer device context. *AbortFunc* is the name of the abort function that is being installed. The function returns a value that is greater than zero if successful or **SP_ERROR** on failure.

All abort functions have the following prototype:

BOOL CALLBACK *AbortFunc*(HDC *hPrDC*, int *Code*);

When called, *hPrDC* will contain the handle for the printer device context. *Code* will be zero unless an error has occurred. If desired, your application can watch this value and take appropriate action when an error is detected. The function must return non-zero to continue printing or zero to stop.

Inside the abort function, you must implement a message loop. However, instead of using **GetMessage( )** to retrieve messages, you must use **PeekMessage( )** with the **PM_REMOVE** option. The reason for this is that **GetMessage( )** waits for a message if one is not already in the message queue. **PeekMessage( )** does not. Thus, a skeletal abort function looks like this:

```
// Printer abort function.
BOOL CALLBACK AbortFunc(HDC hdc, int err)
{
  MSG message;

  while(PeekMessage(&message, NULL, 0, 0, PM_REMOVE)) {
    if(!IsDialogMessage(hDlg, &message)) {
      TranslateMessage(&message);
      DispatchMessage(&message);
    }
  }

  return printOK; // printOK is a global variable
}
```

The handle of the modeless dialog box, which is used to cancel the print job, must be stored in **hDlg**. The global variable **printOK** is a global variable, which must be initially set to non-zero. However, if the user cancels the print job, this variable will be set to zero. This action is accomplished by the Cancel dialog box, which is described next.

The Cancel Printing Dialog Box

After the abort function has been installed, your program must activate a modeless dialog box, which allows the user to cancel the print job. Although this dialog box can contain additional features and controls, it must contain at least one button, called Cancel, which cancels the print job. When the user clicks Cancel, the dialog box sets a global variable to zero. This global variable must be the same one returned by the abort function described in the preceding section.

A Text Printing Utility

The **PrntFile.cpp** program that follows allows the user to select a text file to be printed and then prints the file. Multiple copies may be printed. This example is a useful utility in its own right. It can also provide the foundation for your own file-printing tasks. Before a file can be printed, two pieces of information need to be known: the size of a page of paper and the name of the file.

Obtaining the Size of a Page

In order to print a multipage document, it is necessary to know how long a page is. Although not used by the following example, you may also need to know the width of a page. To obtain these dimensions, call the **GetDeviceCaps( )** function. To find the length of a printed page, use the **VERTRES** attribute. This causes the length of the page in pixels to be returned. To find the width of a page, use **HORZRES**. Using these dimensions, you can determine where one page ends and another begins. You can also determine when output exceeds the page width.

Obtaining a Filename

To obtain the name of the file to be printed, you can use another of Windows' common dialog boxes: Open. The Open dialog box is used to input the name of a file to be opened. It allows a user to select a filename either by typing it or choosing it from a list.

The user may also change directories or drives. The Open dialog box used by the following program is shown in Figure 8-2. The Open dialog box is activated by calling the **GetOpenFileName( )** API function. Its prototype is shown here:

    BOOL GetOpenFileName(LPOPENFILENAME *lpBuf*);

Here, *lpBuf* is a pointer to a structure of type **OPENFILENAME**. The function returns non-zero if a valid filename is specified by the user and zero otherwise.

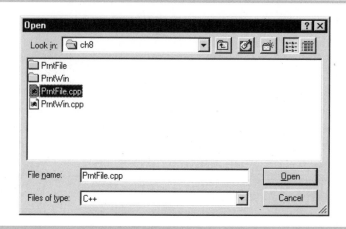

FIGURE 8-2.   The Open common dialog box

The **OPENFILENAME** structure pointed to by *lpBuf* must be initialized prior to calling **GetOpenFileName( )**. Upon return, the filename specified by the user, and several other pieces of information, will be contained in that structure. The **OPENFILENAME** structure is defined like this:

```
typedef struct tagOFN
{
  DWORD lStructSize;
  HWND hwndOwner;
  HINSTANCE hInstance;
  LPCSTR lpstrFilter;
  LPSTR lpstrCustomFilter;
  DWORD nMaxCustFilter;
  DWORD nFilterIndex;
  LPSTR lpstrFile;
  DWORD nMaxFile;
  LPSTR lpstrFileTitle;
```

```
    DWORD nMaxFileTitle;
    LPCSTR lpstrInitialDir;
    LPCSTR lpstrTitle;
    DWORD Flags;
    WORD nFileOffset;
    WORD nFileExtension;
    LPCSTR lpstrDefExt;
    LPARAM lCustData;
    LPOFNHOOKPROC lpfnHook;
    LPCSTR  lpTemplateName;
} OPENFILENAME;
```

Each element of **OPENFILENAME** is described here.

lStructSize must contain the size of the **OPENFILENAME** structure. **hwndOwner** must contain the handle of the window that owns the dialog box. If **Flags** contains either **OFN_ENABLETEMPLATE** or **OFN_ENABLETEMPLATEHANDLE**, then **hInstance** specifies a handle that defines an alternative dialog box template. Otherwise, **hInstance** is not used.

lpstrFilter must point to an array that contains pairs of strings that define a filename filter. The pairs of strings must be organized like this: *"description""mask"*, where the *description* identifies the type of files matched by the *mask*. For example, "C Files""C.*" specifies the description *C Files* and the mask *C.*. The last two strings in the array must be null in order to terminate the list. The names of the filters are displayed in a drop-down list from which the user may choose. If this element is **NULL**, then no filename filter is used.

lpstrCustomFilter points to a static array that will be used to store a file filter entered by the user. This array must initially contain a description and file filter using the format just described. However, after the user selects a filename, the new filter is copied into the array. If **lpstrCustomFilter** is **NULL**, then this element is ignored. The array must be 40 characters (or more) long.

nMaxCustFilter specifies the size of the array pointed to by **lpstrCustomFilter**. This value is needed only if **lpstrCustomFilter** is not **NULL**.

nFilterIndex specifies which pair of strings pointed to by **lpstrFilter** will provide the initial file filter and description when the dialog box is first displayed. The value 1 corresponds to the first pair. The second pair is specified by the value 2, and so on. This value is ignored if **lpstrFilter** is **NULL**. If **nFilterIndex** is zero, the strings pointed to by **lpstrCustomFilter** are used.

lpstrFile points to an array that will receive the complete file, path, and drive of the filename selected by the user. The array may contain an initial filename, which will be used to initialize the filename edit box or it may point to a null string.

nMaxFile specifies the size of the array pointed to by **lpstrFile**. The array should be at least 256 bytes long to accommodate the longest possible filename.

lpstrFileTitle points to an array that receives the filename (without path or drive information) of the file selected by the user. If the filename by itself is not needed, this field may be **NULL**.

nMaxFileTitle specifies the size of the array pointed to by **lpstrFileTitle**.

lpstrInitialDir points to an array that contains the directory that will first be used when the dialog box is activated. If **lpstrInitialDir** is **NULL**, then the current directory is used. However, if no files in the current directory match the specified file filter, then the user's personal files directory is used.

PROGRAMMER'S NOTE *In Windows 95 and Windows NT 4 and earlier, if **lpstrInitialDir** is **NULL**, then the current directory is used in all cases.*

lpstrTitle points to a string that will be used as the title for the dialog box. The default title is used if **lpstrTitle** is **NULL**. For the **GetOpenFileName( )** function, the default title is "Open".

The **Flags** element is used to set various options inside the dialog box. **GetOpenFilename( )** supports numerous options. Several of the most commonly used are shown here. You can OR together two or more flags if necessary.

Flags	Effect
OFN_ENABLEHOOK	Allows the function pointed to by **lpfnHook** to be used.
OFN_ENABLETEMPLATE	Allows alternative dialog box template to be used. In this case, **hInstance** specifies the instance handle of the module that contains the dialog box specified by **lpTemplateName**.
OFN_ENABLETEMPLATEHANDLE	Allows alternative dialog box template to be used. In this case, **hInstance** is the handle to a region of memory that contains the dialog box template.
OFN_FILEMUSTEXIST	User may only specify existent files.
OFN_HIDEREADONLY	Causes the read-only check box to be suppressed.
OFN_NOCHANGEDIR	Current directory remains unchanged by user selection.
OFN_PATHMUSTEXIST	User may only specify existent paths.

The **nFileOffset** element receives the index of the start of the filename within the string returned in the array pointed to by **lpstrFile**. (Remember, **lpstrFile** will contain drive and path information in addition to the filename.)

nFileExtension receives the index of the file extension within the string returned in the array pointed to by **lpstrFile**.

lpstrDefExt points to an array that contains a default extension that is appended to the filename entered by the user when no extension is included. (The extension should be specified without a leading period.) This field can be **NULL**.

lCustData contains data that is passed to the optional function pointed to by **lpfnHook**.

lpfnHook is a pointer to a function that preempts and processes messages intended for the dialog box. This element is used only if **Flags** contains the value **OFN_ENABLEHOOK**.

lpTemplateName points to the name of an alternative dialog box template. **hInstance** must be the handle to the module that contains the dialog box resource. **lpTemplateName** is ignored unless **Flags** contains the value **OFN_ENABLETEMPLATE**.

Although **OPENFILENAME** contains many members, several of them can be set either to zero or **NULL**. Others are ignored unless their associated flag is included. Thus, it is not as difficult to use **GetOpenFileName( )** as it may at first seem. One last point: The complement to **GetOpenFileName( )** is **GetSaveFileName( )**. It works in much the same way except that the standard Save As dialog box is displayed.

PROGRAMMER'S NOTE *For Windows 2000,* **OPENFILENAME** *adds these three fields:* ***rgpMonikers,*** ***cMonikers,*** *and* ***FlagsEx.*** *These add support for the* ***IMoniker*** *COM interface.*

PrntFile.cpp

Code

Here is the **PrntFile.cpp** file printing program. To print a file, select Print File | Print. You will then see the Open dialog box and can select the file to print. Once you have selected a file, the Print dialog box is displayed and your file will be printed. Remember, this program can only print plain text files. For example, it will print the source code files for the programs in this book, but it will not be able to print most word processor files, which include special format codes.

```cpp
// PrntFile.cpp -- Print a text file.

#include <windows.h>
#include <cstring>
#include <commdlg.h>
#include <cstdio>
#include "prntfile.h"

LRESULT CALLBACK WindowFunc(HWND, UINT, WPARAM, LPARAM);
void PrintInit(PRINTDLG *printdlg, HWND hwnd);
BOOL CALLBACK AbortFunc(HDC hdc, int err);
LRESULT CALLBACK KillPrint(HWND, UINT, WPARAM, LPARAM);

void PrintFile(HWND hwnd);

char szWinName[] = "MyWin";
```

```
HINSTANCE hInst;

int WINAPI WinMain(HINSTANCE hThisInst, HINSTANCE hPrevInst,
                   LPSTR lpszArgs, int nWinMode)
{
  HACCEL hAccel;
  HWND hwnd;
  MSG msg;
  WNDCLASSEX wcl;

  // Define a window class.
  wcl.cbSize = sizeof(WNDCLASSEX);
  wcl.hInstance = hThisInst;
  wcl.lpszClassName = szWinName;
  wcl.lpfnWndProc = WindowFunc;
  wcl.style = 0;
  wcl.hIcon = LoadIcon(NULL, IDI_APPLICATION); // large icon
  wcl.hIconSm = NULL; // use small version of large icon
  wcl.hCursor = LoadCursor(NULL, IDC_ARROW);
  wcl.hbrBackground = (HBRUSH) GetStockObject(WHITE_BRUSH);
  wcl.cbClsExtra = 0;
  wcl.cbWndExtra = 0;
  wcl.lpszMenuName = "PrintFile";

  // Register the window class.
  if(!RegisterClassEx(&wcl)) return 0;

  // Create a window.
  hwnd = CreateWindow(szWinName,
                      "Print a File",
                      WS_OVERLAPPEDWINDOW,
                      CW_USEDEFAULT, CW_USEDEFAULT,
                      CW_USEDEFAULT, CW_USEDEFAULT,
                      NULL, NULL, hThisInst, NULL);

  hInst = hThisInst; // save the current instance handle

  // Load accelerators.
  hAccel = LoadAccelerators(hThisInst, "PrintFile");

  // Display the window.
  ShowWindow(hwnd, nWinMode);
```

```
  UpdateWindow(hwnd);

  // The message loop.
  while(GetMessage(&msg, NULL, 0, 0))
  {
    if(!TranslateAccelerator(hwnd, hAccel, &msg)) {
      TranslateMessage(&msg);
      DispatchMessage(&msg);
    }
  }

  return msg.wParam;
}

// The window procedure.
LRESULT CALLBACK WindowFunc(HWND hwnd, UINT message,
                           WPARAM wParam, LPARAM lParam)
{
  int response;

  switch(message) {
    case WM_COMMAND:
      switch(LOWORD(wParam)) {
        case IDM_PRINTFILE:
          PrintFile(hwnd);
          break;
        case IDM_EXIT:
          response = MessageBox(hwnd, "Quit the Program?",
                                "Exit", MB_YESNO);
          if(response == IDYES) PostQuitMessage(0);
          break;
        case IDM_ABOUT:
          MessageBox(hwnd, "Print File V1.0",
                     "Print Text File", MB_OK);
          break;
      }
      break;
    case WM_DESTROY:
      PostQuitMessage(0);
      break;
    default:
      return DefWindowProc(hwnd, message, wParam, lParam);
```

```
  }
  return 0;
}


//////////////////////////////////////////////////////
//                                                    //
//  Print File Subsystem                              //
//                                                    //
//////////////////////////////////////////////////////

int printOK = 1;
HWND hDlg = NULL;

// Initialize PRINTDLG structure.
void PrintInit(PRINTDLG *printdlg, HWND hwnd)
{
  printdlg->lStructSize = sizeof(PRINTDLG);
  printdlg->hwndOwner = hwnd;
  printdlg->hDevMode = NULL;
  printdlg->hDevNames = NULL;
  printdlg->hDC = NULL;
  printdlg->Flags = PD_RETURNDC | PD_NOSELECTION |
                    PD_NOPAGENUMS | PD_HIDEPRINTTOFILE |
                    PD_COLLATE;
  printdlg->nFromPage = 0;
  printdlg->nToPage = 0;
  printdlg->nMinPage = 0;
  printdlg->nMaxPage = 0;
  printdlg->nCopies = 1;
  printdlg->hInstance = NULL;
  printdlg->lCustData = 0;
  printdlg->lpfnPrintHook = NULL;
  printdlg->lpfnSetupHook = NULL;
  printdlg->lpPrintTemplateName = NULL;
  printdlg->lpSetupTemplateName = NULL;
  printdlg->hPrintTemplate = NULL;
  printdlg->hSetupTemplate = NULL;
}

// Printer abort function.
BOOL CALLBACK AbortFunc(HDC hdc, int err)
```

```
{
  MSG message;

  while(PeekMessage(&message, NULL, 0, 0, PM_REMOVE)) {
    if(!IsDialogMessage(hDlg, &message)) {
      TranslateMessage(&message);
      DispatchMessage(&message);
    }
  }

  return printOK;
}

// Let user kill print process.
LRESULT CALLBACK KillPrint(HWND hdwnd, UINT message,
                           WPARAM wParam, LPARAM lParam)
{
  switch(message) {
    case WM_COMMAND:
      switch(LOWORD(wParam)) {
        case IDCANCEL:
          printOK = 0;
          DestroyWindow(hDlg);
          hDlg = NULL;
          return 1;
      }
      break;
  }
  return 0;
}

// Print a text file.
void PrintFile(HWND hwnd)
{
  OPENFILENAME fname;
  char filename[64];   // file name
  char fn[256] = "";   // full path name
  char filefilter[] = "Text\0*.TXT\0C\0*.C\0C++\0*.CPP\0\0\0";
  FILE *fp;
  int numlines;
  TEXTMETRIC tm;
  char str[250];
```

```
int i;
int copies;
int Y = 0;
PRINTDLG printdlg;
DOCINFO docinfo;

// first, get the name of the file to be printed

// initialize the OPENFILENAME struct
fname.lStructSize = sizeof(OPENFILENAME);
fname.hwndOwner = hwnd;
fname.lpstrFilter = filefilter;
fname.nFilterIndex = 1;
fname.lpstrFile = fn;
fname.nMaxFile = sizeof(fn);
fname.lpstrFileTitle = filename;
fname.nMaxFileTitle = sizeof(filename)-1;
fname.Flags = OFN_FILEMUSTEXIST | OFN_HIDEREADONLY;
fname.lpstrCustomFilter = NULL;
fname.lpstrInitialDir = NULL;
fname.lpstrTitle = NULL;
fname.lpstrDefExt = NULL;
fname.lCustData = 0;

if(!GetOpenFileName(&fname)) // get the file name
  return;

if((fp=fopen(fn, "r"))==NULL) {
  MessageBox(hwnd, fn, "Cannot Open File", MB_OK);
  return;
}

// initialize PRINTDLG struct
PrintInit(&printdlg, hwnd);

if(!PrintDlg(&printdlg)) return;

docinfo.cbSize = sizeof(DOCINFO);
docinfo.lpszDocName = "Printing File";
docinfo.lpszOutput = NULL;
docinfo.lpszDatatype = NULL;
docinfo.fwType = 0;
```

```
StartDoc(printdlg.hDC, &docinfo);

// get text metrics for printer
GetTextMetrics(printdlg.hDC, &tm);

// determine number of lines per page
numlines = GetDeviceCaps(printdlg.hDC, VERTRES);
numlines = numlines / (tm.tmHeight + tm.tmExternalLeading);

printOK = 1;
SetAbortProc(printdlg.hDC, (ABORTPROC) AbortFunc);
hDlg = CreateDialog(hInst, "PrCancel", hwnd, (DLGPROC) KillPrint);

// now, actually print the file
for(copies=0; copies < printdlg.nCopies; copies++) {
  StartPage(printdlg.hDC);
  Y = 0;
  i = 0;

  do {
    fgets(str, 80, fp); // get a line of text
    if(feof(fp)) break;

    if(str[strlen(str)-1] == '\n')
      str[strlen(str)-1] = 0; // remove cr-lf

    // send this line to the printer
    TextOut(printdlg.hDC, 0, Y, str, strlen(str));

    // advance to next line
    Y = Y + tm.tmHeight + tm.tmExternalLeading;
    i++;

    // see if at end of page
    if(numlines == i) {
      EndPage(printdlg.hDC);
      i = 0; Y = 0;
      StartPage(printdlg.hDC);
    }
  } while(!feof(fp));
```

```
    EndPage(printdlg.hDC);
    rewind(fp);
  }

  if(printOK) {
    DestroyWindow(hDlg);
    EndDoc(printdlg.hDC);
    hDlg = NULL;
  }

  DeleteDC(printdlg.hDC);
  fclose(fp);

}
```

The program uses the **PrntFile.rc** resource file shown here:

```
#include <windows.h>
#include "prntfile.h"

PrintFile MENU
{
  POPUP "&Print File"
  {
    MENUITEM "&Print\tF2", IDM_PRINTFILE
    MENUITEM "E&xit\tCtrl+X", IDM_EXIT
  }
  POPUP "&Help" {
    MENUITEM "&About\tF1", IDM_ABOUT
  }
}

PrintFile ACCELERATORS
{
  VK_F1, IDM_ABOUT, VIRTKEY
  VK_F2, IDM_PRINTFILE, VIRTKEY
  "^X", IDM_EXIT
}

PrCancel DIALOG 10, 10, 100, 40
CAPTION "Printing"
STYLE WS_CAPTION | WS_POPUP | WS_SYSMENU | WS_VISIBLE
```

```
{
  PUSHBUTTON "Cancel", IDCANCEL, 35, 12, 30, 14,
            WS_CHILD | WS_VISIBLE | WS_TABSTOP
}
```

The header file **PrntFile.h** is shown next:

```
#define IDM_PRINTFILE 100
#define IDM_EXIT      101
#define IDM_ABOUT     102
```

ANNOTATIONS

As it relates to printing a file, the interesting part of the program is contained within the Print File subsystem. It is examined in detail by the following sections.

PrintFile( )

To print a file, the program calls the **PrintFile( )** function. Here is its general operation. First, it sets up a call to **PrintDlg( )** to obtain a printer device context. Then it opens the file and begins a print job by calling **StartDoc( )**. Next, it obtains the text metrics for the printer DC. Then, it registers the abort procedure and creates the Cancel dialog box. Finally, the file is printed, using appropriate calls to **StartPage( )** and **EndPage( )**. Now, let's examine **PrintFile( )** line by line.

The function begins by defining a rather large number of variables, many of which are used when initializing the **OPENFILENAME**, **PRINTDLG**, and **DOCINFO** structures. Pay particular attention to the **filefilter** array, however. It is shown here:

```
char filefilter[] = "Text\0*.TXT\0C\0*.C\0C++\0*.CPP\0\0\0";
```

This string specifies the file filters available when the Open dialog box is created. Here, it is initialized to hold three file extensions—.TXT, .C, and .CPP—along with their descriptions. Remember, the array pointed to by **lpstrFilter** must contain *pairs of strings* and must end with two null strings.

Next, the **OPENFILENAME** structure, **fname**, is initialized and **GetOpenFileName( )** is called. When it returns, the select filename is used to open the file. These operations are shown here:

```
// first, get the name of the file to be printed

// initialize the OPENFILENAME struct
fname.lStructSize = sizeof(OPENFILENAME);
fname.hwndOwner = hwnd;
fname.lpstrFilter = filefilter;
fname.nFilterIndex = 1;
```

```
fname.lpstrFile = fn;
fname.nMaxFile = sizeof(fn);
fname.lpstrFileTitle = filename;
fname.nMaxFileTitle = sizeof(filename)-1;
fname.Flags = OFN_FILEMUSTEXIST | OFN_HIDEREADONLY;
fname.lpstrCustomFilter = NULL;
fname.lpstrInitialDir = NULL;
fname.lpstrTitle = NULL;
fname.lpstrDefExt = NULL;
fname.lCustData = 0;

if(!GetOpenFileName(&fname)) // get the file name
  return;

if((fp=fopen(fn, "r"))==NULL) {
  MessageBox(hwnd, fn, "Cannot Open File", MB_OK);
  return;
}
```

The **fname** structure is initialized as explained earlier when **OPENFILENAME** structure was described, but notice one thing: In the **Flags** field **OFN_FILEMUSTEXIST** and **OFN_HIDEREADONLY** are specified. This means that the user can open only existing files and that they need not be read-only. Once a filename has been obtained, it is used to open the file for printing. Observe that in this case, the entire drive, path, and filename contained in **fn** and pointed to by **lpstrFile** are used. If you wanted to restrict files to the current directory, then the contents of **filename** (pointed to by **lpstrFileTitle**) could have been used.

Next, the Print dialog box is displayed. This is accomplished by first calling **PrintInit( )**, discussed in the next section, to initialize a **PRINTDLG** structure.

```
// initialize PRINTDLG struct
PrintInit(&printdlg, hwnd);

if(!PrintDlg(&printdlg)) return;
```

Notice that if the user cancels the Print dialog box (or if an error occurs), then **PrintFile( )** returns without printing anything. Otherwise, on its return, the **hDC** field of **printdlg** will contain the handle of the printer device context.

Next, the following code initializes the **docinfo** structure and calls **StartDoc( )**. This starts a new print job.

```
docinfo.cbSize = sizeof(DOCINFO);
docinfo.lpszDocName = "Printing File";
docinfo.lpszOutput = NULL;
docinfo.lpszDatatype = NULL;
```

```
docinfo.fwType = 0;

StartDoc(printdlg.hDC, &docinfo);
```

Next, the text metrics of the printer must be obtained. Then the number of lines per page must be computed by obtaining the length of a page in pixels and then dividing that value by the height of a line of text. The code that handles these operations is shown here:

```
// get text metrics for printer
GetTextMetrics(printdlg.hDC, &tm);

// determine number of lines per page
numlines = GetDeviceCaps(printdlg.hDC, VERTRES);
numlines = numlines / (tm.tmHeight + tm.tmExternalLeading);
```

PrintFile( ) does not print page numbers. If you want to add this capability, remember to subtract a line or two from **numlines** to allow room for the page number.

Before printing can begin, the abort function must be registered and the Cancel dialog box must be created. These steps are handled by the following code.

```
printOK = 1;
SetAbortProc(printdlg.hDC, (ABORTPROC) AbortFunc);
hDlg = CreateDialog(hInst, "PrCancel", hwnd, (DLGPROC) KillPrint);
```

Notice the variable **printOK**. This is declared as global at the start of the Print File subsystem. It is used by the **KillPrint( )** and **AbortFunc( )** functions to cancel the printing of a file.

Now, the file can actually be printed. This operation is contained within a loop that iterates the number of times specified in **printdlg.nCopies**. Remember, this value will be the number of copies requested by the user if the printer does not support multiple copies on its own. The print-loop is shown here:

```
// now, actually print the file
for(copies=0; copies < printdlg.nCopies; copies++) {
  StartPage(printdlg.hDC);
  Y = 0;
  i = 0;

  do {
    fgets(str, 80, fp); // get a line of text
    if(feof(fp)) break;

    if(str[strlen(str)-1] == '\n')
      str[strlen(str)-1] = 0; // remove cr-lf
```

```
      // send this line to the printer
      TextOut(printdlg.hDC, 0, Y, str, strlen(str));

      // advance to next line
      Y = Y + tm.tmHeight + tm.tmExternalLeading;
      i++;

      // see if at end of page
      if(numlines == i) {
        EndPage(printdlg.hDC);
        i = 0; Y = 0;
        StartPage(printdlg.hDC);
      }
    } while(!feof(fp));

  EndPage(printdlg.hDC);
  rewind(fp);
}
```

Inside the print loop, lines of text are read from the file and sent to the printer. Each time a line is read, the line counter **i** is incremented. When a page full of text has been printed (that is, when **i** equals **numlines**) a new page is started and the various counters are reset. The actual printing of the file is straightforward. Notice, however, that carriage-return/linefeed sequences are stripped from the end of each line. Since the position of each line on the printed page is handled manually, these must be removed. Also note that each time the end of a page is reached, **EndPage( )** is called, the **X** and **Y** variables (which hold the current output location) are reset, and then **StartPage( )** is executed.

In this example, the length of a line is restricted to 80 characters and standard width paper is assumed. Thus, there is no need to obtain the width of a page. However, as an experiment you might want to try changing the program so that it automatically truncates long lines that exceed the page width.

If everything worked OK and the user did not cancel the print job, the Cancel dialog box is destroyed, the print job is terminated by calling **EndDoc( )**, and the Cancel dialog box handle, **hDlg**, is reset to **NULL**. Finally, the printer DC is destroyed and the file handle is closed. The code that handles these operations is shown here:

```
if(printOK) {
  DestroyWindow(hDlg);
  EndDoc(printdlg.hDC);
  hDlg = NULL;
}
```

```
DeleteDC(printdlg.hDC);
fclose(fp);
```

PrintInit( )

The **PrintInit( )** function initializes a **PRINTDLG** structure. Notice that the Selection radio button and the Pages edit boxes are disabled. The Print to File check box is also hidden. These controls are not needed by the program. The inclusion of the **PD_COLLATE** flag causes the Collate check box to be checked. The program always collates output. (Noncollated output is supported only if it is provided by the printer.)

AbortFunc( )

The abort function, **AbortFunc( )**, used for printing is essentially the same as the skeletal one described when the abort process was discussed earlier. The only point of interest is the message loop, shown here:

```
while(PeekMessage(&message, NULL, 0, 0, PM_REMOVE)) {
  if(!IsDialogMessage(hDlg, &message)) {
    TranslateMessage(&message);
    DispatchMessage(&message);
  }
}
```

Notice the variable **hDlg**. This is a global variable declared near the start of the Print File subsystem. It is initialized to **NULL** and is set by **KillPrint( )**, described in the next section. It holds the handle to the Cancel dialog box.

KillPrint( )

The modeless dialog box that allows the user to cancel printing is **KillPrint( )** and it is shown here:

```
// Let user kill print process.
LRESULT CALLBACK KillPrint(HWND hdwnd, UINT message,
                           WPARAM wParam, LPARAM lParam)
{
  switch(message) {
    case WM_COMMAND:
      switch(LOWORD(wParam)) {
        case IDCANCEL:
          printOK = 0;
          DestroyWindow(hDlg);
```

```
            hDlg = NULL;
            return 1;
        }
    break;
  }
  return 0;
}
```

KillPrint( ) follows the general outline described earlier. Notice that if the user cancels printing, **printOK** is set to 0, the dialog box is destroyed, **hDlg** is once again set to **NULL**, and 1 is returned. This signals that the printing must be stopped. Otherwise, 0 is returned, which means that printing can continue.

One last point: Don't be surprised if the Cancel dialog box appears for only a second or two. Because most systems use a print spooler, output will be interpreted by the printing functions as "printed" as soon as it has been sent to the spooler—not when it actually appears on a piece of paper.

Printing the Contents of a Window

Sending text output to the printer using **TextOut( )** as shown in the preceding **PrntFile.cpp** utility is the exception, not the rule. Most of the time, your program will need to render a printed version of a graphical image. Keep in mind that this image might contain text, but it will not be restricted to text. Since graphical images are stored in bitmaps, the problem of printing a graphical image becomes one of printing the contents of a bitmap. Here we will develop a utility that lets you print what is by far the most commonly used bitmap: the one that underlies a window. Using this utility, you will be able to print the contents of any window to which you have a handle.

Fortunately, printing a bitmap is not, in and of itself, a difficult task. However, two side issues need to be dealt with. First, before printing a bitmap, your program must determine whether the selected printer is capable of displaying graphical output. (Not all printers are.) Second, in order for the printed bitmap to have the same perspective that it does on the screen, some scaling of output might need to be performed. Let's examine each of these issues.

Determining Printer Raster Capabilities

Not all printers can print bitmaps. For example, some printers can only print text. In the language of Windows, a printer that can print a bitmap is capable of *raster operations*. The term *raster* originally referred to video display devices. However, it has been generalized. In its current usage, if a device has raster capabilities, then it can perform certain types of operations normally associated with a video display. In simple terms, if a printer has raster capabilities, then it can display graphical output.

Today, most commonly used printers have raster capabilities. However, since there are still many printers that do not have this capability, your program must check before attempting to print a bitmap. To do this, you will use the **GetDeviceCaps( )** function. Its prototype is shown here:

int GetDeviceCaps(HDC *hdc*, int *attribute*);

Here, *hdc* is the handle of the device context for which information is being obtained. The value of *attribute* determines precisely what attribute is retrieved. The function returns the requested information.

    GetDeviceCaps( ) can obtain a wide variety of attributes and most are not relevant to this chapter. The one that we will use to see if a printer is able to display a bitmap is **RASTERCAPS**. The return value will indicate what, if any, raster capabilities the printer has. It will be one or more of these values:

Value	Meaning
RC_BANDING	Printer DC requires banding support for graphics.
RC_BITBLT	Printer DC can be target of **BitBlt( )**.
RC_BITMAP64	Printer DC can handle bitmaps larger than 64K.
RC_DI_BITMAP	Printer DC supports device-independent bitmaps via the **SetDIBits( )** and **GetDIBits( )** functions.
RC_DIBTODEV	Printer DC supports **SetDIBitsToDevice( )**.
RC_FLOODFIL	Printer DC supports flood fills.
RC_PALETTE	Printer DC supports a palette.
RC_SCALING	Printer DC provides its own scaling capabilities.
RC_STRETCHBLT	Printer DC can be target of **StretchBlt( )**.
RC_STRETCHDIB	Printer DC can be target of **StretchDIBits( )**.

    For the purposes of this chapter, we are interested in only one of these values: **RC_STRETCHBLT**, which determines if the printer DC can be the target of a call to **StretchBlt( )**. As explained in the next section, the ability to use **StretchBlt( )** is required if the printed output is to be scaled properly.

Maintaining Perspective

If you want the bitmap to look the same when printed as it does when displayed on the screen, then you will need to scale the image appropriately when printing it. To accomplish this, you will need to know the resolution of both the screen and the printer. For this purpose, you will once again use the **GetDeviceCaps( )** function. To obtain the number of horizontal pixels-per-inch, specify **LOGPIXELSX** as the attribute. To retrieve the number of vertical pixels-per-inch, use **LOGPIXELSY**. For example, after these calls:

```
hres = GetDeviceCaps(hdc, LOGPIXELSX);
vres = GetDeviceCaps(hdc, LOGPIXELSY);
```

hres will contain the number of pixels-per-inch along the X axis and **vres** will contain the number of pixels-per-inch along the Y axis for the device context specified by **hdc**.

Once you have found the resolution of both the video DC and the printer DC, you can compute a scaling factor. You will use this scaling factor in a call to **StretchBlt( )** to render the bitmap, in its correct perspective, on the printer.

StretchBlt( )

StretchBlt( ) copies a bitmap and is related to the **BitBlt( )** function. However, in the process, **StretchBlt( )** expands or compresses the source bitmap so that it will fit and completely fill the target rectangle. Its prototype is

>BOOL StretchBlt(HDC *hDest*, int *DestX*, int *DestY*,
>   int *DestWidth*, int *DestHeight*,
>   HDC *hSource*, int *SourceX*, int *SourceY*,
>   int *SourceWidth*, int *SourceHeight*,
>   DWORD *dwHow*);

Here, *hDest* is the handle of the target device context, and *DestX* and *DestY* are the upper-left coordinates at which point the bitmap will be drawn. The width and height of the target bitmap are specified in *DestWidth* and *DestHeight*. The *hSource* parameter contains the handle of the source device context. The *SourceX* and *SourceY* specify the upper-left coordinates in the bitmap at which point the copy operation will begin. The width and height of the source bitmap are passed in *SourceWidth* and *SourceHeight*. **StretchBlt( )** automatically expands (that is, stretches) or contracts the source bitmap so that it will fit into the destination bitmap. This differs from **BitBlt( )**, which performs no stretching or compressing.

The value of *dwHow* determines how the bit-by-bit contents of the bitmap will actually be copied. It uses the same values as does the comparable parameter to **BitBlt( )**. Some of its most common values are shown here:

dwHow Macro	Effect
DSTINVERT	Inverts the bits in the destination bitmap.
SRCAND	ANDs bitmap with current destination.
SRCCOPY	Copies bitmap as is, overwriting previous contents.
SRCERASE	ANDs bitmap with the inverted bits of destination bitmap.
SRCINVERT	XORs bitmap with current destination.
SRCPAINT	ORs bitmap with current destination.

StretchBlt( ) is important when printing bitmaps because it allows you to scale the printed version. Remember, **StretchBlt( )** shrinks or enlarges the source bitmap, as needed, so that it fits the target rectangle. By applying the scaling factors to the dimensions of the target rectangle, you can use **StretchBlt( )** to scale the printed version of the bitmap. Of course, if no scaling is desired, your program can use **BitBlt( )** to copy a bitmap to the printer. It is just that the printed version will not have the same perspective as the screen image.

StretchBlt( ) returns non-zero if successful and zero on failure.

PrntWin.cpp

Code

The following program prints the contents of a window. It also allows you to enlarge the printed output. Using this option, you can set enlargement factors for the X and Y dimensions. By default, these factors are 1 and thus no enlargement takes place. However, they can be set anywhere between 1, and 10. Using these factors, you can print a window up to ten times as large as its original size. You can also enlarge only one dimension. Sample output from the program is shown in Figure 8-3.

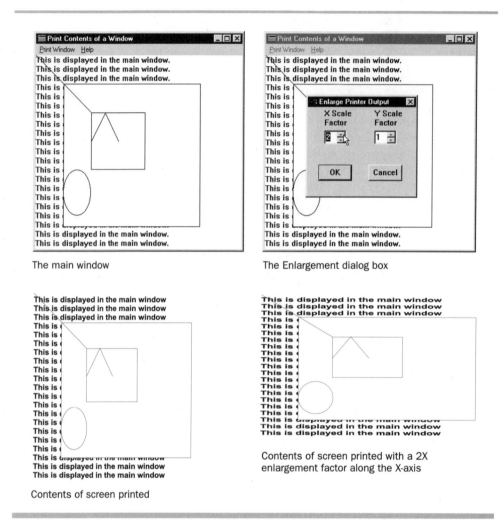

The main window

The Enlargement dialog box

Contents of screen printed

Contents of screen printed with a 2X
enlargement factor along the X-axis

FIGURE 8-3.   Sample output from **PrntWin.cpp**

PROGRAMMER'S NOTE   *PrntWin.cpp uses up/down common controls. This means that you must remember to include **ComCtl32.lib** in the link.*

```
// PrntWin.cpp -- Print the contents of a window.

#include <windows.h>
#include <cstring>
```

```c
#include <commdlg.h>
#include <commctrl.h>
#include "prntwin.h"

#define NUMLINES 25

LRESULT CALLBACK WindowFunc(HWND, UINT, WPARAM, LPARAM);
BOOL CALLBACK EnlargeDialog(HWND, UINT, WPARAM, LPARAM);
void PrintInit(PRINTDLG *printdlg, HWND hwnd);

BOOL CALLBACK AbortFunc(HDC hdc, int err);
LRESULT CALLBACK KillPrint(HWND, UINT, WPARAM, LPARAM);

void PrintWindow(HWND hwnd);

char szWinName[] = "MyWin";

HINSTANCE hInst;

int WINAPI WinMain(HINSTANCE hThisInst, HINSTANCE hPrevInst,
                   LPSTR lpszArgs, int nWinMode)
{
  HACCEL hAccel;
  HWND hwnd;
  MSG msg;
  WNDCLASSEX wcl;
  INITCOMMONCONTROLSEX cc;

  // Define a window class.
  wcl.cbSize = sizeof(WNDCLASSEX);
  wcl.hInstance = hThisInst;
  wcl.lpszClassName = szWinName;
  wcl.lpfnWndProc = WindowFunc;
  wcl.style = 0;
  wcl.hIcon = LoadIcon(NULL, IDI_APPLICATION); // large icon
  wcl.hIconSm = NULL; // use small version of large icon
  wcl.hCursor = LoadCursor(NULL, IDC_ARROW);
  wcl.hbrBackground = (HBRUSH) GetStockObject(WHITE_BRUSH);
  wcl.cbClsExtra = 0;
  wcl.cbWndExtra = 0;
  wcl.lpszMenuName = "PrintWin";
```

```
  // Register the window class.
  if(!RegisterClassEx(&wcl)) return 0;

  // Create a window.
  hwnd = CreateWindow(szWinName,
                      "Print Contents of a Window",
                      WS_OVERLAPPEDWINDOW,
                      CW_USEDEFAULT, CW_USEDEFAULT,
                      CW_USEDEFAULT, CW_USEDEFAULT,
                      NULL, NULL, hThisInst, NULL);

  hInst = hThisInst; // save the current instance handle

  // Load accelerators.
  hAccel = LoadAccelerators(hThisInst, "PrintWin");

  // Display the window.
  ShowWindow(hwnd, nWinMode);
  UpdateWindow(hwnd);

  // Initialize the common controls.
  cc.dwSize = sizeof(INITCOMMONCONTROLSEX);
  cc.dwICC = ICC_UPDOWN_CLASS;
  InitCommonControlsEx(&cc);

  // The message loop.
  while(GetMessage(&msg, NULL, 0, 0))
  {
    if(!TranslateAccelerator(hwnd, hAccel, &msg)) {
      TranslateMessage(&msg);
      DispatchMessage(&msg);
    }
  }

  return msg.wParam;
}

// The window procedure.
LRESULT CALLBACK WindowFunc(HWND hwnd, UINT message,
                            WPARAM wParam, LPARAM lParam)
{
  HDC hdc;
```

```
PAINTSTRUCT ps;
int response;
TEXTMETRIC tm;
char str[250];
int i;

int X = 0, Y = 0;   // current output location
int maxX, maxY;     // screen dimensions

static HDC memDC;    // virtual window handle
static HBITMAP hBit; // bitmap handle
HBRUSH hBrush;       // the brush handle

switch(message) {
  case WM_CREATE:
    // create a virtual window
    maxX = GetSystemMetrics(SM_CXSCREEN);
    maxY = GetSystemMetrics(SM_CYSCREEN);

    hdc = GetDC(hwnd);
    memDC = CreateCompatibleDC(hdc);
    hBit = CreateCompatibleBitmap(hdc, maxX, maxY);
    SelectObject(memDC, hBit);
    hBrush = (HBRUSH) GetStockObject(WHITE_BRUSH);
    SelectObject(memDC, hBrush);
    PatBlt(memDC, 0, 0, maxX, maxY, PATCOPY);

    // send some output to window
    GetTextMetrics(hdc, &tm);
    X = Y = 0;
    strcpy(str, "This is displayed in the main window.");
    for(i=0; i<NUMLINES; i++) {
      TextOut(memDC, X, Y, str, strlen(str));
      // advance to next line
      Y = Y + tm.tmHeight + tm.tmExternalLeading;
    }

    Rectangle(memDC, 50, 50, 300, 300);
    Rectangle(memDC, 100, 100, 200, 200);

    LineTo(memDC, 100, 100);
    MoveToEx(memDC, 150, 150, NULL);
```

```
  LineTo(memDC, 125, 100);
  LineTo(memDC, 100, 150);

  Ellipse(memDC, 50, 200, 100, 280);

  ReleaseDC(hwnd, hdc);
  break;
case WM_COMMAND:
  switch(LOWORD(wParam)) {
    case IDM_ENLARGE:
      DialogBox(hInst, "EnlargeDB",
                hwnd, (DLGPROC) EnlargeDialog);
      break;
    case IDM_PRINTWINDOW: // print contents of window
      PrintWindow(hwnd);
      break;
    case IDM_EXIT:
      response = MessageBox(hwnd, "Quit the Program?",
                           "Exit", MB_YESNO);
      if(response == IDYES) PostQuitMessage(0);
      break;
    case IDM_ABOUT:
      MessageBox(hwnd, "Print Window V1.0",
                "Print Window", MB_OK);
      break;
  }
  break;
case WM_PAINT:
  hdc = BeginPaint(hwnd, &ps);

  // copy virtual window to screen
  BitBlt(hdc, ps.rcPaint.left, ps.rcPaint.top,
         ps.rcPaint.right-ps.rcPaint.left, // width
         ps.rcPaint.bottom-ps.rcPaint.top, // height
         memDC,
         ps.rcPaint.left, ps.rcPaint.top,
         SRCCOPY);

  EndPaint(hwnd, &ps);
  break;
case WM_DESTROY:
  DeleteDC(memDC);
```

```
      DeleteObject(hBit);
      PostQuitMessage(0);
      break;
    default:
      return DefWindowProc(hwnd, message, wParam, lParam);
  }
  return 0;
}

///////////////////////////////////////////////////////
//                                                     //
//   Print Window Subsystem                            //
//                                                     //
///////////////////////////////////////////////////////

int printOK = 1;
HWND hDlg = NULL;

// Initialize PRINTDLG structure.
void PrintInit(PRINTDLG *printdlg, HWND hwnd)
{
  printdlg->lStructSize = sizeof(PRINTDLG);
  printdlg->hwndOwner = hwnd;
  printdlg->hDevMode = NULL;
  printdlg->hDevNames = NULL;
  printdlg->hDC = NULL;
  printdlg->Flags = PD_RETURNDC | PD_NOSELECTION |
                    PD_NOPAGENUMS | PD_HIDEPRINTTOFILE |
                    PD_COLLATE;
  printdlg->nFromPage = 0;
  printdlg->nToPage = 0;
  printdlg->nMinPage = 0;
  printdlg->nMaxPage = 0;
  printdlg->nCopies = 1;
  printdlg->hInstance = NULL;
  printdlg->lCustData = 0;
  printdlg->lpfnPrintHook = NULL;
  printdlg->lpfnSetupHook = NULL;
  printdlg->lpPrintTemplateName = NULL;
  printdlg->lpSetupTemplateName = NULL;
  printdlg->hPrintTemplate = NULL;
  printdlg->hSetupTemplate = NULL;
```

```
}

// Printer abort function.
BOOL CALLBACK AbortFunc(HDC hdc, int err)
{
  MSG message;

  while(PeekMessage(&message, NULL, 0, 0, PM_REMOVE)) {
    if(!IsDialogMessage(hDlg, &message)) {
      TranslateMessage(&message);
      DispatchMessage(&message);
    }
  }

  return printOK;
}

// Let user kill print process.
LRESULT CALLBACK KillPrint(HWND hdwnd, UINT message,
                           WPARAM wParam, LPARAM lParam)
{
  switch(message) {
    case WM_COMMAND:
      switch(LOWORD(wParam)) {
        case IDCANCEL:
          printOK = 0;
          DestroyWindow(hDlg);
          hDlg = NULL;
          return 1;
      }
    break;
  }
  return 0;
}

// These variables are used by both EnlargeDialog
// and by PrintWindow().
int Xenlarge = 1, Yenlarge = 1;

#define SCALEMAX 10

// Enlargement factor dialog function
```

```
BOOL CALLBACK EnlargeDialog(HWND hdwnd, UINT message,
                           WPARAM wParam, LPARAM lParam)
{
  static int tempX=1, tempY=1;

  static long temp;
  static HWND hEboxWnd1, hEboxWnd2;
  static HWND udWnd1, udWnd2;
  int low=1, high=SCALEMAX;


  switch(message) {
    case WM_INITDIALOG:
      hEboxWnd1 = GetDlgItem(hdwnd, IDD_EB1);
      hEboxWnd2 = GetDlgItem(hdwnd, IDD_EB2);
      udWnd1 = CreateUpDownControl(
                     WS_CHILD | WS_BORDER | WS_VISIBLE |
                     UDS_SETBUDDYINT | UDS_ALIGNRIGHT,
                     10, 10, 50, 50,
                     hdwnd,
                     IDD_UD1,
                     hInst,
                     hEboxWnd1,
                     SCALEMAX, 1, Xenlarge);

      udWnd2 = CreateUpDownControl(
                     WS_CHILD | WS_BORDER | WS_VISIBLE |
                     UDS_SETBUDDYINT | UDS_ALIGNRIGHT,
                     10, 10, 50, 50,
                     hdwnd,
                     IDD_UD2,
                     hInst,
                     hEboxWnd2,
                     SCALEMAX, 1, Yenlarge);

      tempX = Xenlarge;
      tempY = Yenlarge;
      return 1;
    case WM_VSCROLL: // process up-down control
      if(udWnd1==(HWND)lParam)
        tempX = GetDlgItemInt(hdwnd, IDD_EB1, NULL, 1);
      else if(udWnd2==(HWND)lParam)
```

```
          tempY = GetDlgItemInt(hdwnd, IDD_EB2, NULL, 1);
      return 1;
    case WM_COMMAND:
      switch(LOWORD(wParam)) {
        case IDOK:
          Xenlarge = tempX;
          Yenlarge = tempY;
        case IDCANCEL:
          EndDialog(hdwnd, 0);
          return 1;
        }
      break;
  }
  return 0;
}

// Print the contents of a window.
void PrintWindow(HWND hwnd)
{
  HDC hdc, memPrDC;
  HBITMAP hPrBit;
  int copies;
  double VidXPPI, VidYPPI, PrXPPI, PrYPPI;
  double Xratio, Yratio;
  RECT r;
  PRINTDLG printdlg;
  DOCINFO docinfo;

  hdc = GetDC(hwnd); // get device context of window

  GetClientRect(hwnd, &r); // get window's dimensions

  memPrDC = CreateCompatibleDC(hdc);
  hPrBit = CreateCompatibleBitmap(hdc, r.right, r.bottom);
  SelectObject(memPrDC, hPrBit);

  // save image in window for printing
  BitBlt(memPrDC, 0, 0, r.right, r.bottom, hdc, 0, 0, SRCCOPY);

  // initialize PRINTDLG struct
  PrintInit(&printdlg, hwnd);
```

```
if(!PrintDlg(&printdlg)) return;

docinfo.cbSize = sizeof(DOCINFO);
docinfo.lpszDocName = "Printing Window";
docinfo.lpszOutput = NULL;
docinfo.lpszDatatype = NULL;
docinfo.fwType = 0;

// obtain pixels-per-inch
VidXPPI = GetDeviceCaps(memPrDC, LOGPIXELSX);
VidYPPI = GetDeviceCaps(memPrDC, LOGPIXELSY);
PrXPPI = GetDeviceCaps(printdlg.hDC, LOGPIXELSX);
PrYPPI = GetDeviceCaps(printdlg.hDC, LOGPIXELSY);

// get scaling ratios
Xratio = PrXPPI / VidXPPI;
Yratio = PrYPPI / VidYPPI;

if(!(GetDeviceCaps(printdlg.hDC, RASTERCAPS)
   & RC_STRETCHBLT))
{
  MessageBox(hwnd, "Cannot Print Raster Images",
            "Error", MB_OK);
  return;
}

StartDoc(printdlg.hDC, &docinfo);

printOK = 1;
SetAbortProc(printdlg.hDC, (ABORTPROC) AbortFunc);
hDlg = CreateDialog(hInst, "PrCancel", hwnd, (DLGPROC) KillPrint);

for(copies=0; copies < printdlg.nCopies; copies++) {
  StartPage(printdlg.hDC);

  StretchBlt(printdlg.hDC, 0, 0,
            (int) (r.right*Xratio) * Xenlarge,
            (int) (r.bottom*Yratio) * Yenlarge,
            memPrDC, 0, 0,
            (int) r.right, (int) r.bottom,
            SRCCOPY);
```

```
    EndPage(printdlg.hDC);
  }

  if(printOK) {
    DestroyWindow(hDlg);
    EndDoc(printdlg.hDC);
    hDlg = NULL;
  }

  DeleteDC(printdlg.hDC);
  ReleaseDC(hwnd, hdc);
  ReleaseDC(hwnd, memPrDC);
  DeleteObject(hPrBit);
}
```

The **PrntWin.rc** resource file for the program is shown here:

```
#include <windows.h>
#include "prntwin.h"

PrintWin MENU
{
  POPUP "&Print Window"
  {
    MENUITEM "&Enlarge\tF2", IDM_ENLARGE
    MENUITEM "&Print\tF3", IDM_PRINTWINDOW
    MENUITEM "E&xit\tCtrl+X", IDM_EXIT
  }
  POPUP "&Help" {
    MENUITEM "&About\tF1", IDM_ABOUT
  }
}

PrintWin ACCELERATORS
{
  VK_F1, IDM_ABOUT, VIRTKEY
  VK_F2, IDM_ENLARGE, VIRTKEY
  VK_F3, IDM_PRINTWINDOW, VIRTKEY
  "^X", IDM_EXIT
}

EnlargeDB DIALOG 10, 10, 97, 77
CAPTION "Enlarge Printer Output"
```

```
STYLE WS_POPUP | WS_SYSMENU | WS_VISIBLE
{
  PUSHBUTTON "OK", IDOK, 10, 50, 30, 14,
             WS_CHILD | WS_VISIBLE | WS_TABSTOP
  PUSHBUTTON "Cancel", IDCANCEL, 55, 50, 30, 14,
             WS_CHILD | WS_VISIBLE | WS_TABSTOP
  LTEXT "X Scale Factor", IDD_TEXT1,  15, 1, 25, 20
  LTEXT "Y Scale Factor", IDD_TEXT2,  60, 1, 25, 20
  EDITTEXT IDD_EB1, 15, 20, 20, 12, ES_LEFT | WS_CHILD |
           WS_VISIBLE | WS_BORDER
  EDITTEXT IDD_EB2, 60, 20, 20, 12, ES_LEFT | WS_CHILD |
           WS_VISIBLE | WS_BORDER
}

PrCancel DIALOG 10, 10, 100, 40
CAPTION "Printing"
STYLE WS_CAPTION | WS_POPUP | WS_SYSMENU | WS_VISIBLE
{
  PUSHBUTTON "Cancel", IDCANCEL, 35, 12, 30, 14,
             WS_CHILD | WS_VISIBLE | WS_TABSTOP

}
```

The header file **PrntWin.h** is shown here:

```
#define IDM_EXIT          101
#define IDM_ABOUT         102
#define IDM_PRINTWINDOW   103
#define IDM_ENLARGE       104

#define IDD_EB1           200
#define IDD_EB2           201
#define IDD_UD1           202
#define IDD_UD2           203

#define IDD_TEXT1         210
#define IDD_TEXT2         211
```

ANNOTATIONS

Much of **PrntWin.cpp** is similar to **PrntFile.cpp**, described earlier. For example, **PrintInit( )**, **AbortFunc( )**, and **KillPrint( )** are unchanged. The program also uses the virtual window technology developed in Chapter 2. Here we will concentrate on those portions of **PrntWin.cpp** that are new.

PrintWindow( )

The **PrintWindow( )** function prints the contents of the window whose handle it is passed. It begins with the following declarations:

```
HDC hdc, memPrDC;
HBITMAP hPrBit;
int copies;
double VidXPPI, VidYPPI, PrXPPI, PrYPPI;
double Xratio, Yratio;
RECT r;
PRINTDLG printdlg;
DOCINFO docinfo;
```

The handle of the window's device context will be stored in **hdc**. **memPrDC** will hold the handle of a memory device context that will store the contents of the window for printing. The handle to a compatible bitmap will be stored in **hPrBit**. The pixels-per-inch for the screen and printer will be stored in **VidXPPI**, **VidYPPI**, **PrXPPI**, and **PrYPPI**. The ratios of these values will be stored in **Xratio**, **Yratio**. The size of the client area being printed is stored in **r**. The other variables perform the same functions as they did in the **PrntFile.cpp** program.

    PrintWindow( ) begins with the following sequence:

```
hdc = GetDC(hwnd); // get device context of window

GetClientRect(hwnd, &r); // get window's dimensions

memPrDC = CreateCompatibleDC(hdc);
hPrBit = CreateCompatibleBitmap(hdc, r.right, r.bottom);
SelectObject(memPrDC, hPrBit);

// save image in window for printing
BitBlt(memPrDC, 0, 0, r.right, r.bottom, hdc, 0, 0, SRCCOPY);
```

This code obtains a DC for the window being printed and retrieves the dimensions of its client area. It then creates a compatible DC and bitmap, and selects the bitmap into the DC. Finally, it copies the contents of the window into the memory DC. Thus, the DC referred to by **memPrDC** contains a copy of the contents of the window after this sequence executes. Shortly, you will see why this step is necessary.

    The next sequence of code activates the Print common dialog box and then initializes the **docinfo** structure.

```
// initialize PRINTDLG struct
PrintInit(&printdlg, hwnd);
```

```
if(!PrintDlg(&printdlg)) return;

docinfo.cbSize = sizeof(DOCINFO);
docinfo.lpszDocName = "Printing Window";
docinfo.lpszOutput = NULL;
docinfo.lpszDatatype = NULL;
docinfo.fwType = 0;
```

Next, the following code computes the scaling factors. Recall that in order for the printed output to look like the image shown on the screen, it is necessary to scale the image prior to printing.

```
// obtain pixels-per-inch
VidXPPI = GetDeviceCaps(memPrDC, LOGPIXELSX);
VidYPPI = GetDeviceCaps(memPrDC, LOGPIXELSY);
PrXPPI = GetDeviceCaps(printdlg.hDC, LOGPIXELSX);
PrYPPI = GetDeviceCaps(printdlg.hDC, LOGPIXELSY);

// get scaling ratios
Xratio = PrXPPI / VidXPPI;
Yratio = PrYPPI / VidYPPI;
```

First, the number of pixels-per-inch for both DCs are obtained by calling **GetDeviceCaps( )**. Then, the ratio of these values is computed for both the X and Y dimensions.

Next, the following code determines if the printer can support raster operations and **StretchBlt( )**.

```
if(!(GetDeviceCaps(printdlg.hDC, RASTERCAPS)
   & RC_STRETCHBLT))
{
  MessageBox(hwnd, "Cannot Print Raster Images",
            "Error", MB_OK);
  return;
}
```

As explained, in order to print graphical images, the printer must support raster operations. Support for **StretchBlt( )** is needed to allow the image to be properly scaled. It also enables the image to be enlarged.

Assuming that raster operations are supported, **PrintWindow( )** then starts a new print job, registers an abort function, and creates the Cancel dialog box using the following code:

```
StartDoc(printdlg.hDC, &docinfo);

printOK = 1;
```

```
SetAbortProc(printdlg.hDC, (ABORTPROC) AbortFunc);
hDlg = CreateDialog(hInst, "PrCancel", hwnd, (DLGPROC) KillPrint);
```

This sequence is the same as that used by the **PrntFile.cpp** program.

Next, the image in the window is printed using the following loop:

```
for(copies=0; copies < printdlg.nCopies; copies++) {
  StartPage(printdlg.hDC);

  StretchBlt(printdlg.hDC, 0, 0,
            (int) (r.right*Xratio) * Xenlarge,
            (int) (r.bottom*Yratio) * Yenlarge,
            memPrDC, 0, 0,
            (int) r.right, (int) r.bottom,
            SRCCOPY);

  EndPage(printdlg.hDC);
}
```

Notice how it takes only one call to **StretchBlt( )** to actually print the image. After the image is copied to the printer DC, the image will automatically be printed by the printer. Windows' device-independent architecture really shines in operations of this type.

The image is scaled by two values. The first is the pixel ratio of the screen to the printer that was computed earlier. The second is the factors contained in **Yenlarge** and **Xenlarge**. By default, these values are 1, which means that no enlargement takes place, but they can be set by the user. Values greater than 1 enlarge the printed image.

It is important to understand that it is technically possible to use **StretchBlt( )** to copy the contents of the window device context **hdc** directly to the printer device context without creating a compatible memory DC and bitmap (that is, without the use of **memPrDC** and **hPrBit**). However, the trouble with doing this is that the Cancel dialog box may show in the printed output! Remember, the window DC describes what is currently in the window. If, at the time of the call to **StretchBlt( )**, the window contains a dialog box, then that dialog box will also be copied to the printer. By saving the current contents of the window into **memPrDC** before the dialog box is displayed, this problem is avoided.

Assuming that the printing is successful, **PrintWindow( )** concludes by destroying the Cancel dialog box, terminating the print job, and resetting **hDlg**. Finally, the various handles are released. This code is shown here:

```
if(printOK) {
  DestroyWindow(hDlg);
  EndDoc(printdlg.hDC);
  hDlg = NULL;
}
```

```
DeleteDC(printdlg.hDC);
ReleaseDC(hwnd, hdc);
ReleaseDC(hwnd, memPrDC);
DeleteObject(hPrBit);
```

EnlargeDialog( )

To enlarge the printed image, the user selects Print Window | Enlarge. This causes
the Enlarge Printer Output dialog box to be displayed. Events from this box are
handled by the **EnlargeDialog( )** function. The main purpose of this dialog box is
to allow the user to set the X and/or Y enlargement factors. By default, these factors
are 1, but they can be set to values up to 10.

The dialog box uses up/down controls to set the enlargement factors and
their operation should be clear. Just remember that up/down controls generate
WM_VSCROLL messages. When the user clicks OK, the current values in the
up/down controls are copied into the global variables **Xenlarge** and **Yenlarge**. As
explained in the previous section, these values are used to enlarge an image when
it is printed by **PrintWindow( )**.

Tips for Using MFC

The common dialog functions, such as **GetOpenFileName( )** and **PrintDlg( )**, are
not encapsulated by MFC, so they are used as shown in this chapter. The printer
control functions, such as **StartDoc( )** and **EndDoc( )**, are encapsulated by the **CDC**
class. **GetDeviceCaps( )** is also encapsulated by **CDC**.

Two Screen Savers

ClockSav.cpp	A screen saver that shows the current time and date
AnimSav.cpp	An animated screen saver

I f you are like most programmers, then you have probably wanted to write your own screen saver. Indeed, it is rare to find a programmer who has not. While screen savers were initially invented to prevent phosphor burn on idle screens, they have taken on a life of their own. Today most screen savers provide an entertaining message, an interesting graphics display, a company logo, or a humorous animated sequence. As you will see, creating your own screen saver is one of the most interesting Windows programming tasks.

This chapter develops two simple screen savers. The first displays the current time and date in a moving pattern. The second animates a sprite, adapting some of the techniques developed in Chapter 4. Both screen savers support various configuration settings and these parameters are stored in the system registry. Therefore, a short overview of the system registry is also included in this chapter.

PROGRAMMER'S NOTE   *The instructions for creating a screen saver contained within this chapter apply only to Win32 environments.*

Screen Saver Fundamentals

A screen saver is actually one of the easiest Windows applications to program. One reason for this is that it does not create a main window. Instead, it uses the desktop (that is, the entire screen) as its window. It also does not contain a **WinMain( )** function or need to create a message loop. In fact, a screen saver requires only three functions, two of which may be empty placeholders.

When you create a screen saver, your program must include the header file **ScrnSave.h** and you must include **ScrnSave.lib** when linking. The screen saver library provides the necessary support for screen savers. This is why your screen saver code need only contain three functions; the rest of the details are handled by the library.

The Screen Saver Functions

The three functions that every screen saver must provide are shown here:

Function	Purpose
ScreenSaverProc( )	This is the screen saver's window procedure. It is passed messages and must respond appropriately.
ScreenSaverConfigureDialog( )	This is the dialog function for the screen saver's configuration dialog box. It can be empty if no configuration is supported.

Function	Purpose
RegisterDialogClasses( )	This function is used to register custom class types. It will be empty if no custom classes are used.

Although the names of these functions are defined by Windows, you must supply the functions themselves in the source code to your screen saver. (That is, they are not provided by Win32.) Let's take a closer look at these three functions now.

ScreenSaverProc( ) is a window procedure. Its prototype is shown here:

LRESULT WINAPI ScreenSaverProc(HWND *hwnd*, UINT *message*,
                              WPARAM *wParam*, LPARAM *lParam*);

It is passed messages in the same way as other window procedures. There is one important difference, however. If the function does not process a message, it must call **DefScreenSaverProc( )** rather than **DefWindowProc( )**. Also, the window handle passed to **ScreenSaverProc( )** in *hwnd* is the handle for the entire screen. That is, it is the handle of the desktop. Your screen saver will make use of this fact.

ScreenSaverConfigureDialog( ) is the dialog box function that handles the screen saver's configuration dialog box. It has the following prototype:

BOOL WINAPI ScreenSaverConfigureDialog(HWND *hdwnd*,
                              UINT *message*, WPARAM *wParam*,
                              LPARAM *lParam*);

If your screen saver does not require configuration, then the only thing this function must do is return zero. If the screen saver supports a configuration dialog box, then it must be defined in the screen saver's resource file and given the ID value of **DLG_SCRNSAVECONFIGURE**. This value is defined in **ScrnSave.h** as 2003.

RegisterDialogClasses( ) is used to register custom window classes. It has this prototype:

BOOL WINAPI RegisterDialogClasses(HANDLE *hInst*);

If your screen saver does not use custom window classes, simply return non-zero.

As mentioned, **ScreenSaverProc( )** will call **DefScreenSaverProc( )** if it does not process a message. The prototype for **DefScreenSaverProc( )** is shown here:

LRESULT WINAPI DefScreenSaverProc(HWND *hwnd*, UINT *message*,
                              WPARAM *wParam*, LPARAM *lParam*);

Two Screen Saver Resources

All screen savers must define two special resources: an icon and a string. The icon, whose ID must be **ID_APP**, identifies the screen saver. The string resource, whose identifier must be **IDS_DESCRIPTION**, contains a description of the screen saver. This string must be no more than 24 characters long. **ID_APP** and **IDS_DESCRIPTION** are defined in **ScrnSave.h**.

PROGRAMMER'S NOTE   *For Windows 95/98, the string defined by **IDS_DESCRIPTION** is not used within the Screen Saver panel of the Display Properties dialog box. Instead, the filename of the screen saver is shown. To show a longer description, give the screen saver a long filename. At the time of this writing, Microsoft's main documentation is in error about this point, but it is stated correctly in a technical bulletin dated December 23, 1998. The description string defined by **IDS_DESCRIPTION** is used correctly by Windows 2000.*

Other Programming Considerations

ScrnSave.h defines several global variables. The one of interest to us in this chapter is **hMainInstance**. This will contain the instance handle of the screen saver and will be needed if your screen saver creates a window, for example.

All screen savers are driven by a timer. Each time the timer goes off, the screen saver receives a **WM_TIMER** message. In response, the screen saver must update the screen display. A screen saver must start the timer when it is first activated and destroy the timer when it is destroyed.

After you have compiled the screen saver, you must rename it so that it has the .SCR extension rather than .EXE. Next, copy the renamed screen saver into the proper directory. For most Windows 95/98 users, the directory that holds screen savers will be WINDOWS\SYSTEM. For Windows NT/2000, the directory is usually WINNT\SYSTEM32. (The easiest way to determine which directory to use is to see which one holds the screen savers currently installed on your system.) Once you have renamed and copied the screen saver to the proper directory, you can select your new screen saver using the control panel.

Understanding the System Registry

The two screen savers described in this chapter, and most screen savers in general, need to store configuration information. For example, a screen saver will typically need to store a speed setting. The best place to store such settings is in the system registry. Although many readers will already be familiar with the registry and its use, a brief overview is presented here for those who are not.

The Registry Structure

The registry is a special, hierarchical database maintained by Windows that stores information related to three entities: the user, the machine, and the installed software.

The information stored in the registry is in binary form. For this reason there are only two ways by which you may alter or examine the contents of the registry: by using REGEDIT, the standard registry editor, or by using the registry management API functions. You cannot, for example, edit the registry using a text editor.

The registry consists of a set of keys structured as a tree. A *key* is, for practical purposes, a node in the tree. The name of a key is essentially the name of a node. A key may be empty, have subkeys, or contain values. Typically, these values consist of configuration information for a program. Thus, to use the registry, your program will create a key and store configuration information under that key. When the program needs this information, it will look up the key and then read the information. If the user changes the configuration settings, then your program will simply write those new values to the registry. Using the registry really is just this easy.

The Built-in Keys

The registry contains several built-in keys. Each key forms the root node for its own subtree of keys. The names of the built-in keys are shown here:

Key	Purpose
HKEY_CLASSES_ROOT	Holds information used by COM. Also defines associations between file extensions and applications.
HKEY_CURRENT_CONFIG	Holds current hardware configuration.
HKEY_CURRENT_USER	Holds information related to the current user. This is where user-related, application program configuration information is usually stored.
HKEY_LOCAL_MACHINE	Holds information about the system, including the installed software, network preferences, and other system-wide, hardware-related information.
HKEY_USERS	Holds the preferences for each user of the machine.
HKEY_DYN_DATA	Holds dynamic performance data. (Windows 95/98 only.)
HKEY_PERFORMANCE_DATA	Holds dynamic performance data. (Windows NT/2000 only.)

These keys are always open and may be used by your application. However, generally, an application will only use two of these keys: **HKEY_LOCAL_MACHINE**, which is used to store any system-wide configuration options relating to the machine, and **HKEY_CURRENT_USER**, which is used to store configuration options relating to the user.

Typically, an installation program will create a key under **HKEY_LOCAL_MACHINE** that contains the name and version number of an application package, plus the name of the company that created the application. Other application-related data may also be stored under **HKEY_LOCAL_MACHINE**. Under **HKEY_CURRENT_USER**, a program will store configuration options selected by the user. Default user configuration information may also be written under this key when the program is installed. Typically, the application will use this information when it begins execution. The configuration data for the screen saver will be stored under this key.

Since the screen savers in this chapter are quite simple, they don't require any special installation. Thus, we won't be using **HKEY_LOCAL_MACHINE**. However, the techniques used to read data from and write data to the registry using this key are the same as for **HKEY_CURRENT_USER**.

There are several standard subkeys that will normally be found in the registry. For example, under **HKEY_CURRENT_USER**, some of the standard subkeys are **Software** and **Control Panel**. When you add the configuration settings for a new program to the registry, you will typically do so under the **Software** subkey of **HKEY_CURRENT_USER**.

Since the registry is a set of hierarchical trees, you will need to specify a full path to the key that you want. Key paths are similar in concept to directory paths. Each key is separated from the one preceding it using a backslash (\) character. For example, if you access a key called **Screensaver** under the **Software** subkey of **HKEY_CURRENT_USER**, the key path will look like this:

HKEY_CURRENT_USER\Software\Screensaver

A key may also include a period.

Recall that in C/C++, the backslash character signals the start of an escape sequence when used in a string. Therefore, when specifying a string in a C/C++ program that contains a backslash, you must use two backslashes for each backslash character you need. For example, to specify the preceding path as a C/C++ string, use the following:

HKEY_CURRENT_USER\\Software\\Screensaver

If you forget to use the two backslashes, your registry functions will not work properly.

In Windows terminology, a *hive* is a key hierarchy that typically descends directly from either **HKEY_LOCAL_MACHINE** or **HKEY_USERS**. Some registry operations work on hives. For example, you can save or load a hive.

Registry Values

The registry allows several different types of data to be stored as values under a key. When you store or retrieve data, you must specify its name and its type. Table 9-1 shows the types of data supported by the registry. You will always add a value to the registry under a key that you have defined. There is no concept of simply adding a value to the registry by itself.

Data Type	Meaning
REG_BINARY	Generic type used to specify any binary data.
REG_DWORD	Long, unsigned integer.
REG_DWORD_LITTLE_ENDIAN	Long, unsigned integer stored with least significant byte first. This is called *little endian* format.
REG_DWORD_BIG_ENDIAN	Long, unsigned integer stored with most significant byte first. This is called *big endian* format.
REG_EXPAND_SZ	A string that contains unexpanded environmental variables.
REG_LINK	A Unicode symbolic link.
REG_MULTI_SZ	An array of strings. The last two strings must be null.
REG_NONE	Undefined type.
REG_QWORD	A quad-word value.
REG_QWORD_LITTLE_ENDIAN	A quad-word value stored with least significant byte first.
REG_RESOURCE_LIST	A resource list for a device driver.
REG_SZ	Normal, null-terminated string.

TABLE 9-1. The Data Types Supported by the registry

Creating and Opening a Key

All registry operations take place relative to an open key. The predefined keys described earlier are always open. Therefore, you will use one of the predefined keys as the starting point when opening any other key. To open an existing key, use **RegOpenKeyEx( )**. Its prototype is shown here:

LONG RegOpenKeyEx(HKEY *hKey*, LPCSTR *lpszSubKey*,
                  DWORD *NotUsed*, REGSAM *Access*,
                  PHKEY *Result*);

Here, *hKey* is the handle of an already open key, which may be one of the predefined keys. The key being opened must be a subkey of *hKey*. The name of the subkey is pointed to by *lpszSubKey*. *NotUsed* is reserved and must be zero. *Access* determines the access privileges for the subkey handle. This value can be any combination of the values shown in Table 9-2. *Result* is a pointer to a variable that, on return, contains the handle of the subkey.

The function returns **ERROR_SUCCESS** if successful. On failure, an error code is returned. The function fails if the specified key does not exist.

Access Value	Purpose
KEY_ALL_ACCESS	Allows all accesses.
KEY_CREATE_LINK	Allows the creation of a symbolic link.
KEY_CREATE_SUB_KEY	Allows the creation of subkeys.
KEY_ENUMERATE_SUB_KEYS	Allows the enumeration of subkeys.
KEY_EXECUTE	Allows read access.
KEY_NOTIFY	Allows change notification.
KEY_QUERY_VALUE	Allows read-access to subkey data.
KEY_READ	Allows all read accesses. This is the same as KEY_ENUMERATE_SUB_KEYS | KEY_NOTIFY | KEY_QUERY_VALUE.
KEY_SET_VALUE	Allows write-access to subkey data.
KEY_WRITE	Allows all write accesses. Same as KEY_CREATE_SUB_KEY | KEY_SET_VALUE.

TABLE 9-2. Key Access Privilege Values

Although you can use **RegOpenKeyEx( )** to open a registry key, you will probably find that more often you will use another registry function called **RegCreateKeyEx( )**. This function serves a dual purpose: It will open an already existing key or, if the specified key does not exist, it will create it. Its prototype is shown here:

LONG RegCreateKeyEx(HKEY *hKey*, LPCSTR *lpszSubKey*,
　　　　　　　　　　DWORD *NotUsed*, LPSTR *lpszClass*,
　　　　　　　　　　DWORD *How*, REGSAM *Access*,
　　　　　　　　　　LPSECURITY_ATTRIBUTES *SecAttr*,
　　　　　　　　　　PHKEY *Result*, LPDWORD *WhatHappened*);

Here, *hKey* is the handle of an open key. *lpszSubKey* is a pointer to the name of the key to open or create. *NotUsed* is reserved and must be zero. *lpszClass* is a pointer to the class type for the key. This value is only used for keys being created and, at the time of this writing, this string should be null.

For the use with a screen saver, the value of *How* should be

REG_OPTION_NON_VOLATILE

This creates a nonvolatile key that is stored on disk. This is the default.

Access determines the access privileges of the key. It may be any valid combination of the values shown in Table 9-2.

SecAttr is a pointer to a **SECURITY_ATTRIBUTES** structure that defines the security descriptor for the key. For our purposes, this value can be **NULL**.

On return, the variable pointed to by *Result* will contain the handle of the key that has just been created or opened. *WhatHappened* is a pointer to a variable that, on return, describes which action took place. It will either be **REG_CREATED_ NEW_KEY**, if a new key was created, or **REG_OPENED_EXISTING_KEY**, if an already existing key was opened.

The function returns **ERROR_SUCCESS** if successful. On failure, an error code is returned.

Storing Values

Once you have obtained an open key, you can store values under it. To do this, use **RegSetValueEx( )**. Its prototype is shown here:

```
LONG RegSetValueEx(HKEY hKey, LPCSTR lpszName,
                   DWORD NotUsed, DWORD DataType,
                   CONST LPBYTE lpValue, DWORD SizeOfValue);
```

hKey is the handle of an open key that has been opened with **KEY_SET_VALUE** access rights. *lpszName* is a pointer to the name of the value. If this name does not already exist, it is added to the key. *NotUsed* is currently reserved and must be set to zero.

DataType specifies the type of data that is being stored. It must be one of the values specified in Table 9-1. *lpValue* is a pointer to the data being stored. *SizeOfValue* specifies the size of this data (in bytes). For string data, the null-terminator must also be counted.

RegSetValueEx( ) returns **ERROR_SUCCESS** if successful. On failure, it returns an error code.

Retrieving Values

Once you have stored a value in the registry, it can be retrieved at any time by your program (or by any other program). To do so, use the **RegQueryValueEx( )** function, shown here:

```
LONG RegQueryValueEx(HKEY hKey, LPSTR lpszName,
                     LPDWORD NotUsed, LPDWORD DataType,
                     LPBYTE Value, LPDWORD SizeOfData);
```

hKey is the handle of an open key, which must have been opened with **KEY_QUERY_VALUE** access privileges. *lpszName* is a pointer to the name of the value desired. This value must already exist under the specified key. *NotUsed* is currently reserved and must be set to **NULL**.

DataType is a pointer that, on return, contains the type of the value being retrieved. This will be one of the values shown in Table 9-1. *Value* is a pointer to a buffer that, on return, contains the data associated with the specified value. *SizeOfData* is a pointer to a variable that contains the size of the buffer in bytes. On return, *SizeOfData* will point to the number of bytes stored in the buffer.

RegQueryValueEx( ) returns **ERROR_SUCCESS** if successful. On failure, it returns an error code.

Closing a Key

To close a key, use **RegCloseKey( )**, shown here:

LONG RegCloseKey(HKEY *hKey*);

Here, *hKey* is the handle of the key being closed. The function returns **ERROR_SUCCESS** if successful. On failure, an error code is returned.

REGEDIT

Your program interacts with the registry using the registry API functions. However, if you want to examine (or even alter) the contents of the registry, you may do so using REGEDIT. REGEDIT displays the registry, including all keys and values. You can add, delete, and modify both keys and values. Normally, you will not want to manually change the registry. If you do so incorrectly, your computer might stop working! However, using REGEDIT to view the structure and contents of the registry is completely safe and it will give you a concrete understanding of the registry's organization. It also will allow you to see how the screen savers store their configuration data.

A Clock Screen Saver

The clock screen saver displays the current time and date. This information moves about the screen. This screen saver allows you to

- ◆ Set the timing interval between updates.
- ◆ Set the time format.
- ◆ Set the date format.
- ◆ Turn the date on or off.

The major advantage of this screen saver is that the time and date are always visible, even when the computer is otherwise idle. Put differently, when using this screen saver, you won't have to move the mouse to see the time display in the task bar when you want to know the time!

PROGRAMMER'S NOTE *The following program uses a spin control, which is a common control. You will need to include **ComCtl32.lib** when linking.*

Code

The **ClockSav.cpp** program is shown here. Figure 9-1 shows how this screen saver appears in the Display Properties dialog box.

ClockSav.cpp

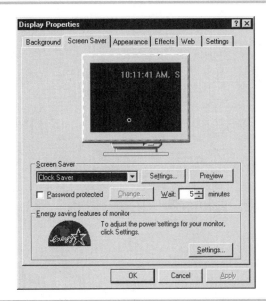

FIGURE 9-1. The clock screen saver

```
// ClockSav.cpp: A screen saver that displays
//               the time and date.
#include <windows.h>
#include <scrnsave.h>
#include <commctrl.h>
#include <cstring>
#include <ctime>
#include "clocksav.h"
```

```
#define DELAYMAX 999

long delay;             // timer delay.
long twelve_hour;       // set for 12-hour mode
long long_date_format;  // set for long date format
long date_on;           // set to show date

// Screen Saver Function
LRESULT WINAPI ScreenSaverProc(HWND hwnd, UINT message,
                                WPARAM wParam, LPARAM lParam)
{
  static HDC hdc;
  static unsigned int timer;
  static RECT scrdim;
  static SIZE size;
  static int X = 0, Y = 0;
  static HBRUSH hBlkBrush;
  unsigned long result;
  char timestr[80], datestr[80];
  time_t t_t;
  tm *t;

  HKEY hRegKey; // registry key
  unsigned long datatype, datasize; // registry types and sizes

  switch(message) {
    case WM_CREATE:
      // open screen saver key or create, if necessary
      RegCreateKeyEx(HKEY_CURRENT_USER,
        "Software\\HSPrograms\\ClockSaver",
        0, "", 0, KEY_ALL_ACCESS,
        NULL, &hRegKey, &result);

      // if key was created
      if(result==REG_CREATED_NEW_KEY) {
        // set its initial values
        delay = 100;
        RegSetValueEx(hRegKey, "delay", 0,
          REG_DWORD, (LPBYTE) &delay, sizeof(DWORD));

        date_on = BST_CHECKED;
```

```
      RegSetValueEx(hRegKey, "date_on", 0,
         REG_DWORD, (LPBYTE) &date_on, sizeof(DWORD));

      twelve_hour = BST_CHECKED;
      RegSetValueEx(hRegKey, "twelve_hour", 0,
         REG_DWORD, (LPBYTE) &twelve_hour, sizeof(DWORD));

      long_date_format = BST_CHECKED;
      RegSetValueEx(hRegKey, "long_date", 0,
         REG_DWORD, (LPBYTE) &long_date_format, sizeof(DWORD));
   }
   else { // key was already in registry
      // get values
      datasize = sizeof(DWORD);
      RegQueryValueEx(hRegKey, "delay", NULL,
         &datatype, (LPBYTE) &delay, &datasize);

      RegQueryValueEx(hRegKey, "date_on", NULL,
         &datatype, (LPBYTE) &date_on, &datasize);

      RegQueryValueEx(hRegKey, "twelve_hour", NULL,
         &datatype, (LPBYTE) &twelve_hour, &datasize);

      RegQueryValueEx(hRegKey, "long_date", NULL,
         &datatype, (LPBYTE) &long_date_format, &datasize);
   }


   RegCloseKey(hRegKey);

   timer = SetTimer(hwnd, 1, delay, NULL);
   hBlkBrush = (HBRUSH) GetStockObject(BLACK_BRUSH);
   break;
case WM_ERASEBKGND:
   hdc = GetDC(hwnd);

   // get coordinates of screen
   GetClientRect(hwnd, &scrdim);

   // erase the screen
   SelectObject(hdc, hBlkBrush);
   PatBlt(hdc, 0, 0, scrdim.right, scrdim.bottom, PATCOPY);
```

```
        ReleaseDC(hwnd, hdc);
        break;
    case WM_TIMER:
        hdc = GetDC(hwnd);

        // get current system time
        t_t = time(NULL);
        t = localtime(&t_t);

        // erase previous output
        SelectObject(hdc, hBlkBrush);
        PatBlt(hdc, X, Y, X + size.cx, Y + size.cy, PATCOPY);

        // move string to new location
        X += 10; Y += 10;
        if(X > scrdim.right) X = 0;
        if(Y > scrdim.bottom) Y = 0;

        // setup colors
        SetBkColor(hdc, RGB(0, 0, 0));
        SetTextColor(hdc, RGB(0, 255, 255));

        // format time and date
        if(twelve_hour)
            strftime(timestr, 79, "%I:%M:%S %p", t);
        else
            strftime(timestr, 79, "%H:%M:%S", t);

        if(long_date_format)
            strftime(datestr, 79, ",  %A %B %d, %Y", t);
        else
            strftime(datestr, 79, ",  %m/%d/%Y", t);

        // add date string if requested
        if(date_on)
            strcat(timestr, datestr);

        // output time and date
        TextOut(hdc, X, Y, timestr, strlen(timestr));
```

```
      // save length of this string
      GetTextExtentPoint32(hdc, timestr, strlen(timestr), &size);

      ReleaseDC(hwnd, hdc);
      break;
    case WM_DESTROY:
      KillTimer(hwnd, timer);
      break;
    default:
      return DefScreenSaverProc(hwnd, message, wParam, lParam);
  }

  return 0;
}

// Configuration Dialog Box Function
BOOL WINAPI ScreenSaverConfigureDialog(HWND hdwnd, UINT message,
                WPARAM wParam, LPARAM lParam)
{
  static HWND hEboxWnd;
  static HWND udWnd;
  INITCOMMONCONTROLSEX cc;
  unsigned long result;
  static HKEY hRegKey; // registry key
  unsigned long datatype, datasize; // registry types and sizes


  switch(message) {
    case WM_INITDIALOG:
      // initialize common controls
      cc.dwSize = sizeof(INITCOMMONCONTROLSEX);
      cc.dwICC = ICC_UPDOWN_CLASS;
      InitCommonControlsEx(&cc);

      // open screen saver key or create, if necessary
      RegCreateKeyEx(HKEY_CURRENT_USER,
        "Software\\HSPrograms\\ClockSaver",
        0, "", 0, KEY_ALL_ACCESS,
        NULL, &hRegKey, &result);
```

```
// if key was created
if(result==REG_CREATED_NEW_KEY) {
  // set its initial values
  delay = 100;
  RegSetValueEx(hRegKey, "delay", 0,
    REG_DWORD, (LPBYTE) &delay, sizeof(DWORD));

  date_on = BST_CHECKED;
  RegSetValueEx(hRegKey, "date_on", 0,
    REG_DWORD, (LPBYTE) &date_on, sizeof(DWORD));

  twelve_hour = BST_CHECKED;
  RegSetValueEx(hRegKey, "twelve_hour", 0,
    REG_DWORD, (LPBYTE) &twelve_hour, sizeof(DWORD));

  long_date_format = BST_CHECKED;
  RegSetValueEx(hRegKey, "long_date", 0,
    REG_DWORD, (LPBYTE) &long_date_format, sizeof(DWORD));
}
else { // key was already in registry
  // get values
  datasize = sizeof(DWORD);
  RegQueryValueEx(hRegKey, "delay", NULL,
    &datatype, (LPBYTE) &delay, &datasize);
  RegQueryValueEx(hRegKey, "date_on", NULL,
    &datatype, (LPBYTE) &date_on, &datasize);
  RegQueryValueEx(hRegKey, "twelve_hour", NULL,
    &datatype, (LPBYTE) &twelve_hour, &datasize);
  RegQueryValueEx(hRegKey, "long_date", NULL,
    &datatype, (LPBYTE) &long_date_format, &datasize);
}

// create delay spin control
hEboxWnd = GetDlgItem(hdwnd, IDD_EB1);
udWnd = CreateUpDownControl(
            WS_CHILD | WS_BORDER | WS_VISIBLE |
            UDS_SETBUDDYINT | UDS_ALIGNRIGHT,
            20, 10, 50, 50,
            hdwnd,
            IDD_UPDOWN,
            hMainInstance,
            hEboxWnd,
```

```
                      DELAYMAX, 1, delay);

    // set checkboxes
    SendDlgItemMessage(hdwnd, IDD_CB1, BM_SETCHECK,
                        date_on, 0);
    SendDlgItemMessage(hdwnd, IDD_CB2, BM_SETCHECK,
                        twelve_hour, 0);
    SendDlgItemMessage(hdwnd, IDD_CB3, BM_SETCHECK,
                        long_date_format, 0);

    return 1;
  case WM_COMMAND:
    switch(LOWORD(wParam)) {
      case IDOK:
        // set values
        delay = GetDlgItemInt(hdwnd, IDD_EB1, NULL, 1);
        date_on =  SendDlgItemMessage(hdwnd, IDD_CB1,
                        BM_GETCHECK, 0, 0);
        twelve_hour = SendDlgItemMessage(hdwnd, IDD_CB2,
                          BM_GETCHECK, 0, 0);
        long_date_format = SendDlgItemMessage(hdwnd, IDD_CB3,
                            BM_GETCHECK, 0, 0);

        // update registry
        RegSetValueEx(hRegKey, "delay", 0,
          REG_DWORD, (LPBYTE) &delay, sizeof(DWORD));
        RegSetValueEx(hRegKey, "date_on", 0,
          REG_DWORD, (LPBYTE) &date_on, sizeof(DWORD));
        RegSetValueEx(hRegKey, "twelve_hour", 0,
          REG_DWORD, (LPBYTE) &twelve_hour, sizeof(DWORD));
        RegSetValueEx(hRegKey, "long_date", 0,
          REG_DWORD, (LPBYTE) &long_date_format, sizeof(DWORD));

        // fall through to next case ...
      case IDCANCEL:
        RegCloseKey(hRegKey);
        EndDialog(hdwnd, 0);
        return 1;
    }
    break;
}
return 0;
```

```
}

// No classes to register.
BOOL WINAPI RegisterDialogClasses(HANDLE hInst)
{
  return 1;
}
```

The resource file **ClockSav.rc** is shown here:

```
// Dialog box for clock screen saver.
#include <windows.h>
#include <scrnsave.h>
#include "clocksav.h"

ID_APP ICON SCRICON.ICO

STRINGTABLE
{
  IDS_DESCRIPTION "Clock Saver"
}

DLG_SCRNSAVECONFIGURE DIALOGEX 18, 18, 110, 80
CAPTION "Set Screen Saver Options"
STYLE DS_MODALFRAME | WS_POPUP | WS_VISIBLE | WS_CAPTION |
      WS_SYSMENU
{
  PUSHBUTTON "OK", IDOK, 20, 62, 30, 14,
            WS_CHILD | WS_VISIBLE | WS_TABSTOP
  PUSHBUTTON "Cancel", IDCANCEL, 60, 62, 30, 14,
            WS_CHILD | WS_VISIBLE | WS_TABSTOP
  EDITTEXT IDD_EB1, 5, 5, 24, 12, ES_LEFT | WS_CHILD |
          WS_VISIBLE | WS_BORDER
  LTEXT "Delay in milliseconds", IDD_TEXT1, 35, 7, 100, 12
  AUTOCHECKBOX "Show Date", IDD_CB1 5, 20, 60, 14
  AUTOCHECKBOX "Use 12 Hour Time", IDD_CB2, 5, 32, 84, 14
  AUTOCHECKBOX "Use Long Date Format", IDD_CB3, 5, 44, 84, 14
}
```

The header file **ClockSav.h** is shown next:

```
#define IDD_EB1     200
#define IDD_UPDOWN  201
```

```
#define IDD_TEXT1     202
#define IDD_CB1       203
#define IDD_CB2       204
#define IDD_CB3       205
```

ANNOTATIONS

ClockSav.cpp begins by defining **DELAYMAX**, which determines the maximum update interval. Next, four global variables are declared. The length of the update-interval is stored in **delay**. If 12-hour format is used, then **twelve_hour** will be set to non-zero; otherwise, the time is displayed using a 24-hour format. If **long_date_format** is non-zero, then the date string is spelled out; otherwise, a short-form date is used. The date will be shown only if **date_on** is non-zero. These variables are global because they need to be accessed by both **ScreenSaverProc( )** and **ScreenSaverConfigureDialog( )**.

Since there are no custom window classes used by **ClockSav.cpp**, **RegisterDialogClasses( )** simply returns non-zero. The remainder of the program is contained in **ScreenSaverProc( )** and **ScreenSaverConfigureDialog( )**, which are examined by the following sections.

ScreenSaverProc( )

As explained, **ScreenSaverProc( )** is the window procedure for a screen saver. Thus, it receives messages passed to the screen saver. **ScreenSaverProc( )** declares several variables that are used by the various message handlers. Each message handler is examined here.

WM_CREATE   Each time a screen saver is activated, it receives two messages. The first is **WM_CREATE**. A screen saver uses this message to perform any initializations it requires and to start the timer. The **WM_CREATE** handler for **ClockSav.cpp** begins with the following call to **RegCreateKeyEx( )**.

```
// open screen saver key or create, if necessary
RegCreateKeyEx(HKEY_CURRENT_USER,
   "Software\\HSPrograms\\ClockSaver",
   0, "", 0, KEY_ALL_ACCESS,
   NULL, &hRegKey, &result);
```

RegCreateKeyEx( ) either opens or creates the registry key **ClockSaver**, which is a subkey of **HSPrograms**, which, in turn, is a subkey of **Software** under the built-in key **HKEY_CURRENT_USER**. That is, the key path being opened (or created) is

HKEY_CURRENT_USER\Software\HSPrograms\ClockSaver

If the specified key does not already exist in the registry (as it won't when you first run the screen saver), then **RegCreateKeyEx( )** creates it for you. If it does already exist, then the key path is opened. The registry path created by the program (as displayed by REGEDIT) is shown in Figure 9-2.

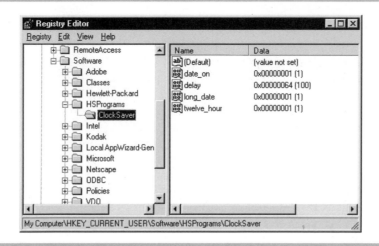

FIGURE 9-2.   The registry path created by the screen saver

After **RegCreateKeyEx( )** returns, the contents of **result** are examined to determine whether the key was created or opened. If the key was created, then the registry is given initial, default values for **delay**, **twelve_hour**, **long_date_format**, and **date_on**. These values are set by calling **RegSetValueEx( )**, as shown here:

```
// if key was created
if(result==REG_CREATED_NEW_KEY) {
  // set its initial values
  delay = 100;
  RegSetValueEx(hRegKey, "delay", 0,
     REG_DWORD, (LPBYTE) &delay, sizeof(DWORD));

  date_on = BST_CHECKED;
  RegSetValueEx(hRegKey, "date_on", 0,
     REG_DWORD, (LPBYTE) &date_on, sizeof(DWORD));

  twelve_hour = BST_CHECKED;
  RegSetValueEx(hRegKey, "twelve_hour", 0,
     REG_DWORD, (LPBYTE) &twelve_hour, sizeof(DWORD));
```

```
    long_date_format = BST_CHECKED;
    RegSetValueEx(hRegKey, "long_date", 0,
        REG_DWORD, (LPBYTE) &long_date_format, sizeof(DWORD));
}
```

As you can see, each attribute is stored as a double word value of type **REG_DWORD**. The delay value is initially set to 100 milliseconds. The values of **date_on**, **long_date**, and **twelve_hour** determine the state of the three check boxes and are set to **BST_CHECKED**.

If the key already existed, then the various parameters are read from the registry by calling **RegQueryValueEx( )**, using the following sequence:

```
else { // key was already in registry
  // get values
  datasize = sizeof(DWORD);
  RegQueryValueEx(hRegKey, "delay", NULL,
      &datatype, (LPBYTE) &delay, &datasize);

  RegQueryValueEx(hRegKey, "date_on", NULL,
      &datatype, (LPBYTE) &date_on, &datasize);

  RegQueryValueEx(hRegKey, "twelve_hour", NULL,
      &datatype, (LPBYTE) &twelve_hour, &datasize);

  RegQueryValueEx(hRegKey, "long_date", NULL,
      &datatype, (LPBYTE) &long_date_format, &datasize);
}
```

Before ending, the **WM_CREATE** handler closes the registry key, starts the refresh timer, and stores a handle to a black brush, which is used to repaint the screen. The code that does this is shown here:

```
RegCloseKey(hRegKey);

timer = SetTimer(hwnd, 1, delay, NULL);
hBlkBrush = (HBRUSH) GetStockObject(BLACK_BRUSH);
break;
```

WM_ERASEBKGND   After **WM_CREATE** has been processed, the next message received by your screen saver is **WM_ERASEBKGND**. When this message is received, the screen saver must clear the entire screen. The **WM_ERASEBCKGND** handler for **ClockSav.cpp** is shown here:

```
case WM_ERASEBKGND:
  hdc = GetDC(hwnd);
```

```
// get coordinates of screen
GetClientRect(hwnd, &scrdim);

// erase the screen
SelectObject(hdc, hBlkBrush);
PatBlt(hdc, 0, 0, scrdim.right, scrdim.bottom, PATCOPY);

ReleaseDC(hwnd, hdc);
break;
```

There are, of course, several ways to erase the screen. The method employed by the screen savers in this chapter is to obtain the coordinates of the screen, select the black brush, and then use **PatBlt( )** to fill the specified region with black (that is, nothing). Remember, *hwnd* contains the handle of the desktop, so the call to **GetClientRect( )** returns the dimensions of the entire screen.

WM_TIMER   At the end of each timing interval, **WM_TIMER** is sent to the screen saver. In response, the screen saver first erases the time and date from its current location, obtains the new time, advances the location counters, and then redisplays the time and date in the new location. Let's look at this process step by step.

    WM_TIMER begins with the following sequence:

```
hdc = GetDC(hwnd);

// get current system time
t_t = time(NULL);
t = localtime(&t_t);
```

First, the device context of the screen is obtained and stored in **hdc**. Then the current system time and date are obtained by using the standard C time function, **time( )**. This is converted into the local time by calling another standard function: **localtime( )**.

    Then, the portion of the screen that held the previous output is erased, and the next output location is computed.

```
// erase previous output
SelectObject(hdc, hBlkBrush);
PatBlt(hdc, X, Y, X + size.cx, Y + size.cy, PATCOPY);

// move string to new location
X += 10; Y += 10;
if(X > scrdim.right) X = 0;
if(Y > scrdim.bottom) Y = 0;
```

When the first **WM_TIMER** message occurs, there will be no previous time and date string to erase and **size.cx** and **size.cy** will be 0. (They are 0 because **size** is a static variable and all static variables are initialized to 0 by default.) On subsequent invocations, **size.cx** and **size.cy** will hold the extents of the region to erase. With each timing interval, the coordinates at which the time and date string is displayed are advanced 10 units. If either coordinate exceeds the dimension of the screen, it is reset to 0.

The time and date string is displayed in turquoise. The precise format of the time and date, and whether the date is shown, is determined by the values of **twelve_hour**, **long_date_format**, and **date_on**. The time and date are formatted by the standard C library function, **strftime( )**. These operations are performed by the following code:

```
// setup colors
SetBkColor(hdc, RGB(0, 0, 0));
SetTextColor(hdc, RGB(0, 255, 255));

// format time and date
if(twelve_hour)
  strftime(timestr, 79, "%I:%M:%S %p", t);
else
  strftime(timestr, 79, "%H:%M:%S", t);

if(long_date_format)
  strftime(datestr, 79, ",  %A %B %d, %Y", t);
else
  strftime(datestr, 79, ",  %m/%d/%Y", t);

// add date string if requested
if(date_on)
  strcat(timestr, datestr);

// output time and date
TextOut(hdc, X, Y, timestr, strlen(timestr));
```

Finally, the dimensions of the current time and date string are stored in **size** by calling **GetTextExtentPoint32( )**, and then **hdc** is released.

```
// save length of this string
GetTextExtentPoint32(hdc, timestr, strlen(timestr), &size);

ReleaseDC(hwnd, hdc);
```

The values stored in **size** will be used when the next **WM_TIMER** message is handled to erase the previous string.

WM_DESTROY   When the user presses a key or moves the mouse, the screen saver receives a **WM_DESTROY** message. When this occurs, the screen saver cancels the timer.

ScreenSaverConfigureDialog( )

The **ScreenSaverConfigureDialog( )** function allows four items to be configured: the delay period, the format of the time, the format of the date, and whether the date is included in the display. When this dialog function is executed, it produces the dialog box shown in Figure 9-3.

FIGURE 9-3.   The clock screen saver configuration dialog box

When the dialog box is first executed, it receives the standard **WM_INITDIALOG** message. First, the common controls are initialized. This step is necessary because a spin control is used to set the delay interval. Next, the **ClockSaver** registry key is either created or opened using the same mechanism as described for **ScreenSaverProc( )**.

Once the initialization information has been obtained, the dialog box creates the delay-length spin control. It also initializes three check boxes, which are used to specify the state of the **date_on**, **twelve_hour**, and **long_date_format** variables.

The configuration dialog box contains two pushbuttons: Cancel and OK. If the user selects Cancel, then any changes made by the user are ignored. If the user clicks OK, then the contents of the spin control and edit box are used to update the registry.

An Animated Screen Saver

AnimSav.cpp creates a screen saver that animates a series of bitmaps across the screen. It adapts the animation techniques described in Chapter 4, showing how they can be applied to a screen saver. While this example is quite simple—it just animates a single sprite—the same general techniques can be used to create a more sophisticated graphical screen saver.

AnimSav.cpp allows three attributes to be set: the delay interval between screen refreshes and the amount the image moves in the X and Y directions with each refresh cycle. These three values give you control over the apparent speed and direction of the sprite.

Before examining the code, one important point needs to be made. When you create a bitmap using an image editor, such as the one supplied with Visual C++, then by default the bitmap uses a white background. However, the background color used by most screen savers (including those in this chapter) is black. Since it is easiest to animate a sprite that is contained within a bitmap that uses the same background color as that of the screen, **AnimSav.cpp** inverts the image of the bitmaps that it animates. Thus, a white background becomes black. This technique allows the screen saver to work with bitmaps that you already have. If you want to construct bitmaps in which the background is black, then the bitmap should not be inverted. (You will see how to make this change in the annotations for **AnimSav.cpp**.)

AnimSav.cpp

Code

The code for **AnimSav.cpp** is shown here. It animates the cat bitmaps developed in Chapter 4. Figure 9-4 shows how this screen saver appears in the Display Properties dialog box.

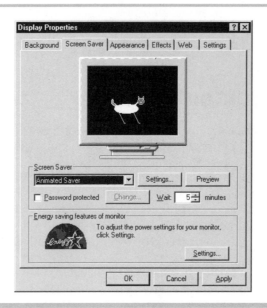

FIGURE 9-4. The animated screen saver

```
// AnimSav.cpp: An animated screen saver.
#include <windows.h>
#include <scrnsave.h>
#include <commctrl.h>
#include <cstring>
#include "animsav.h"

#define DELAYMAX 999
#define INCMAX 50
#define BITMAPSIZE 64

long delay;        // timer delay
long xInc, yInc; // animation increments

HBITMAP hAnBit1, hAnBit2, hAnBit3; // animation bitmaps

// Screen Saver Function
LRESULT WINAPI ScreenSaverProc(HWND hwnd, UINT message,
                       WPARAM wParam, LPARAM lParam)
{
```

```
static HDC hdc;
static unsigned int timer;
static RECT scrdim;
static int X = 0, Y = 0;
static HBRUSH hBlkBrush;
unsigned long result;

HKEY hRegKey; // registry key
unsigned long datatype, datasize; // registry types and sizes

static int map = 0;
static HDC bmpdc;

switch(message) {
  case WM_CREATE:
    // open screen saver key or create, if necessary
    RegCreateKeyEx(HKEY_CURRENT_USER,
      "Software\\HSPrograms\\AnimatedSaver",
      0, "", 0, KEY_ALL_ACCESS,
      NULL, &hRegKey, &result);

    // if key was created
    if(result==REG_CREATED_NEW_KEY) {
      // set its initial values
      delay = 100;
      RegSetValueEx(hRegKey, "delay", 0,
        REG_DWORD, (LPBYTE) &delay, sizeof(DWORD));

      xInc = 5;
      RegSetValueEx(hRegKey, "xInc", 0,
        REG_DWORD, (LPBYTE) &xInc, sizeof(DWORD));

      yInc = 2;
      RegSetValueEx(hRegKey, "yInc", 0,
        REG_DWORD, (LPBYTE) &yInc, sizeof(DWORD));
    }
    else { // key was already in registry
      // get values
      datasize = sizeof(DWORD);
      RegQueryValueEx(hRegKey, "delay", NULL,
        &datatype, (LPBYTE) &delay, &datasize);
      RegQueryValueEx(hRegKey, "xInc", NULL,
```

```
            &datatype, (LPBYTE) &xInc, &datasize);
      RegQueryValueEx(hRegKey, "yInc", NULL,
            &datatype, (LPBYTE) &yInc, &datasize);
   }

   RegCloseKey(hRegKey);

   // load the bitmaps
   hAnBit1 = LoadBitmap(hMainInstance, "MYBP1");
   hAnBit2 = LoadBitmap(hMainInstance, "MYBP2");
   hAnBit3 = LoadBitmap(hMainInstance, "MYBP3");

   // create a DC for the bitmaps
   bmpdc = CreateCompatibleDC(hdc);

   timer = SetTimer(hwnd, 1, delay, NULL);
   hBlkBrush = (HBRUSH) GetStockObject(BLACK_BRUSH);
   break;
case WM_ERASEBKGND:
   hdc = GetDC(hwnd);

   // get coordinates of screen
   GetClientRect(hwnd, &scrdim);

   // erase the screen
   SelectObject(hdc, hBlkBrush);
   PatBlt(hdc, 0, 0, scrdim.right, scrdim.bottom, PATCOPY);

   ReleaseDC(hwnd, hdc);
   break;
case WM_TIMER:
   hdc = GetDC(hwnd);

   // erase previous image
   SelectObject(hdc, hBlkBrush);
   PatBlt(hdc, X, Y, X + BITMAPSIZE, Y + BITMAPSIZE, PATCOPY);

   // get size of client area
   GetClientRect(hwnd, &scrdim);

   // move to next location
   X += xInc;
```

```
        Y += yInc;
        if(X > scrdim.right) X = 0;
        if(Y > scrdim.bottom) Y = 0;


        map++;
        if(map>2) map = 0;


        // switch between sprites
        switch(map) {
          case 0:
            SelectObject(bmpdc, hAnBit1);
            break;
          case 1:
            SelectObject(bmpdc, hAnBit2);
            break;
          case 2:
            SelectObject(bmpdc, hAnBit3);
            break;
        }


        // copy bitmap to screen
        BitBlt(hdc, X, Y, BITMAPSIZE, BITMAPSIZE,
               bmpdc, 0, 0, NOTSRCCOPY);


        ReleaseDC(hwnd, hdc);
        break;
      case WM_DESTROY:
        DeleteObject(hAnBit1);
        DeleteObject(hAnBit2);
        DeleteObject(hAnBit3);
        DeleteDC(bmpdc);
        KillTimer(hwnd, timer);
        break;
      default:
        return DefScreenSaverProc(hwnd, message, wParam, lParam);
  }

  return 0;
}


// Configuration Dialog Box Function
BOOL WINAPI ScreenSaverConfigureDialog(HWND hdwnd, UINT message,
```

```
                    WPARAM wParam, LPARAM lParam)
{
  static HWND hEboxWndDelay, hEboxWndXinc, hEboxWndYinc;
  static HWND udWndDelay, udWndXinc, udWndYinc;
  INITCOMMONCONTROLSEX cc;
  unsigned long result;

  static HKEY hRegKey; // registry key
  unsigned long datatype, datasize; // registry types and sizes

  switch(message) {
    case WM_INITDIALOG:
      // initialize common controls
      cc.dwSize = sizeof(INITCOMMONCONTROLSEX);
      cc.dwICC = ICC_UPDOWN_CLASS;
      InitCommonControlsEx(&cc);

      // open screen saver key or create, if necessary
      RegCreateKeyEx(HKEY_CURRENT_USER,
        "Software\\HSPrograms\\AnimatedSaver",
        0, "", 0, KEY_ALL_ACCESS,
        NULL, &hRegKey, &result);

      // if key was created
      if(result==REG_CREATED_NEW_KEY) {
        // set its initial values
        delay = 100;
        RegSetValueEx(hRegKey, "delay", 0,
          REG_DWORD, (LPBYTE) &delay, sizeof(DWORD));

        xInc = 5;
        RegSetValueEx(hRegKey, "xInc", 0,
          REG_DWORD, (LPBYTE) &xInc, sizeof(DWORD));

        yInc = 2;
        RegSetValueEx(hRegKey, "yInc", 0,
          REG_DWORD, (LPBYTE) &yInc, sizeof(DWORD));
      }
      else { // key was already in registry
        // get values
        datasize = sizeof(DWORD);
        RegQueryValueEx(hRegKey, "delay", NULL,
```

```
            &datatype, (LPBYTE) &delay, &datasize);
    RegQueryValueEx(hRegKey, "xInc", NULL,
            &datatype, (LPBYTE) &xInc, &datasize);
    RegQueryValueEx(hRegKey, "yInc", NULL,
            &datatype, (LPBYTE) &yInc, &datasize);
}


// create delay spin control
hEboxWndDelay = GetDlgItem(hdwnd, IDD_EB1);
udWndDelay = CreateUpDownControl(
                WS_CHILD | WS_BORDER | WS_VISIBLE |
                UDS_SETBUDDYINT | UDS_ALIGNRIGHT,
                20, 10, 50, 50,
                hdwnd,
                IDD_UPDOWN1,
                hMainInstance,
                hEboxWndDelay,
                DELAYMAX, 1, delay);


// create X-increment spin control
hEboxWndXinc = GetDlgItem(hdwnd, IDD_EB2);
udWndXinc = CreateUpDownControl(
                WS_CHILD | WS_BORDER | WS_VISIBLE |
                UDS_SETBUDDYINT | UDS_ALIGNRIGHT,
                20, 50, 50, 50,
                hdwnd,
                IDD_UPDOWN2,
                hMainInstance,
                hEboxWndXinc,
                INCMAX, 0, xInc);


// create Y-increment spin control
hEboxWndYinc = GetDlgItem(hdwnd, IDD_EB3);
udWndYinc = CreateUpDownControl(
                WS_CHILD | WS_BORDER | WS_VISIBLE |
                UDS_SETBUDDYINT | UDS_ALIGNRIGHT,
                20, 90, 50, 50,
                hdwnd,
                IDD_UPDOWN3,
                hMainInstance,
                hEboxWndYinc,
                INCMAX, 0, yInc);
```

```
        return 1;
   case WM_COMMAND:
     switch(LOWORD(wParam)) {
       case IDOK:
         // set values
         delay = GetDlgItemInt(hdwnd, IDD_EB1, NULL, 1);
         xInc = GetDlgItemInt(hdwnd, IDD_EB2, NULL, 1);
         yInc = GetDlgItemInt(hdwnd, IDD_EB3, NULL, 1);

         // update registry
         RegSetValueEx(hRegKey, "delay", 0,
           REG_DWORD, (LPBYTE) &delay, sizeof(DWORD));
         RegSetValueEx(hRegKey, "xInc", 0,
           REG_DWORD, (LPBYTE) &xInc, sizeof(DWORD));
         RegSetValueEx(hRegKey, "yInc", 0,
           REG_DWORD, (LPBYTE) &yInc, sizeof(DWORD));

         // fall through to next case ...
       case IDCANCEL:
         RegCloseKey(hRegKey);
         EndDialog(hdwnd, 0);
         return 1;
     }
     break;
 }
 return 0;
}

// No classes to register.
BOOL WINAPI RegisterDialogClasses(HANDLE hInst)
{
 return 1;
}
```

The **AnimSav.rc** resource file is shown next:

```
// Dialog box for screen saver.
#include <windows.h>
#include <scrnsave.h>
#include "animsav.h"
```

```
MYBP1 BITMAP BP1.BMP
MYBP2 BITMAP BP2.BMP
MYBP3 BITMAP BP3.BMP

ID_APP ICON SCRICON.ICO

STRINGTABLE
{
  IDS_DESCRIPTION "Animated Saver"
}

DLG_SCRNSAVECONFIGURE DIALOGEX 18, 18, 110, 90
CAPTION "Set Screen Saver Options"
STYLE DS_MODALFRAME | WS_POPUP | WS_VISIBLE | WS_CAPTION |
     WS_SYSMENU
{
  PUSHBUTTON "OK", IDOK, 20, 70, 30, 14,
            WS_CHILD | WS_VISIBLE | WS_TABSTOP
  PUSHBUTTON "Cancel", IDCANCEL, 60, 70, 30, 14,
            WS_CHILD | WS_VISIBLE | WS_TABSTOP
  EDITTEXT IDD_EB1, 5, 5, 24, 12, ES_LEFT | WS_CHILD |
          WS_VISIBLE | WS_BORDER
  EDITTEXT IDD_EB2, 5, 25, 24, 12, ES_LEFT | WS_CHILD |
          WS_VISIBLE | WS_BORDER
  EDITTEXT IDD_EB3, 5, 45, 24, 12, ES_LEFT | WS_CHILD |
          WS_VISIBLE | WS_BORDER
  LTEXT "Delay in milliseconds", IDD_TEXT1, 35, 7, 100, 12
  LTEXT "X Increment", IDD_TEXT2, 35, 27, 100, 12
  LTEXT "Y Increment", IDD_TEXT3, 35, 47, 100, 12
}
```

The header **AnimSav.h** is shown here:

```
#define IDD_EB1      200
#define IDD_EB2      201
#define IDD_EB3      202

#define IDD_UPDOWN1  203
#define IDD_UPDOWN2  204
#define IDD_UPDOWN3  205

#define IDD_TEXT1    206
#define IDD_TEXT2    207
#define IDD_TEXT3    208
```

ANNOTATIONS

Much of **AnimSav.cpp** is the same as **ClockSav.cpp** described earlier and, as mentioned, the animation code is adapted from Chapter 4. Here we will concentrate on the new elements.

AnimSav.cpp begins by defining the values **INCMAX** and **BITMAPSIZE**. **INCMAX** determines the maximum increment that can be applied to the animation mechanism between cycles. The size of the bitmap being animated is specified by **BITMAPSIZE**.

The global variables **xInc** and **yInc** store the horizontal and vertical increments applied to the bitmap during each animation cycle. The greater these values, the faster the sprite appears to move.

ScreenSaverProc( )

Most of **ScreenSaverProc( )** is the same as the one defined by **ClockSav.cpp**. Notice, however, that two new static variables are declared: **map**, which governs bitmap switching, and **bmpdc**, which holds the bitmap DC.

As before, when **WM_CREATE** is received, the registry key is created or opened and its values initialized or obtained. Notice, however, that the bitmaps to be animated are also loaded. As the program is written, you must provide three bitmaps, which will be cycled through, one after the other. As explained in Chapter 4, using multiple bitmaps helps create the illusion of motion. The bitmap DC is also created and its handle is assigned to **bmpdc**.

Each time **WM_TIMER** is received, the previous image is erased, the location for the next image is computed, and the next bitmap is selected. Finally, the selected bitmap is copied to the screen using this call to **BitBlt( )**:

```
BitBlt(hdc, X, Y, BITMAPSIZE, BITMAPSIZE,
       bmpdc, 0, 0, NOTSRCCOPY);
```

Notice that **NOTSRCCOPY**, which inverts the source image, is used to copy the bitmap. As explained at the start of this section, the default background color for bitmaps is white. Thus, if such a bitmap is copied as is to a blank screen, then its rectangle will stand out as white against the black background of the screen. While it is possible to create bitmapped images that are drawn on a black background, it is a simple matter to invert a standard bitmap while it is being copied by specifying **NOTSRCCOPY**. This causes white to become black. If you choose to use bitmaps that are drawn on a black background, then substitute **SRCCOPY** for **NOTSRCCOPY** in the call to **BitBlt( )**.

ScreenSaverConfigureDialog( )

The **ScreenSaverConfigureDialog( )** used by **AnimSav.cpp** works the same as the one defined for **ClockSav.cpp**. The main difference is that **AnimSav.cpp** uses three spin controls, which are used to set the delay, the X increment, and the Y increment.

Tips for Using MFC

It is possible to create a screen saver using MFC, but the specifics are different than described in this chapter. Frankly, most screen savers are so simple that there often is little or no gain from using MFC.

CHAPTER 10

Three Easy TAPI Programs

SimpDial.cpp	A simple dialing program
AutoDial.cpp	A more sophisticated dialing program
ListDial.cpp	A program that dials a list of telephone numbers

For being such a simple concept in principle, managing telephone calls via your computer can be a daunting task. The subsystem that helps you manage calls is TAPI, which stands for Telephony Application Programming Interface. To put it bluntly, one of the first things that you learn about TAPI is that it is one complicated system. In fact, if you examine some of the sample TAPI code provided by Microsoft you will see that it runs to several hundred lines of code! Because of its complexity, many programmers have avoided putting telephone support into their applications. One reason that TAPI is so complex is that it can be used to create a sophisticated telephone system, with all types of advanced features. However, if you limit your use of TAPI to voice-only calls and assume a POTS (Plain Old Telephone Service) environment, most of the complexity falls away.

In this chapter we will examine three simple TAPI applications. The first shows the easiest way that you can use your computer to dial a number. The second shows how to dial a number with a bit more control and oversight given to your program. The third shows how to dial a list of numbers. All three examples are voice-only and assume a POTS environment. While these programs are useful in their own right, their main purpose is to serve as clear examples that are easy to understand. Once you understand the TAPI essentials, you can easily build your own sophisticated TAPI applications.

Before beginning, it is important to state that TAPI controls only the telephone system, not the information flowing through a telephone connection. If you want to transfer digital data, you will need to use other API functions.

TAPI Basics

TAPI is a *very large* subject. One could easily fill a book with its complete description. Fortunately, for simple applications you need understand only a few basic concepts and terms.

What Does TAPI Do?

The TAPI subsystem helps your program manage telephone calls. It provides a convenient interface between your program and the Telephony Service Provider (TSP). When using TAPI functions, each function call is passed along to **Tapisrv.exe**. **Tapisrv.exe** contains the TAPI functions and provides the interface to the TSP. The TSP implements the Telephony Service Provider Interface (TSPI). The TSP interacts with the hardware and is (more or less) a device driver. Fortunately, we don't need to worry about service providers to use TAPI.

Service Levels

TAPI defines four levels of telephony service: assisted, basic, supplementary, and extended. Assisted telephony is a limited, but easy-to-use mechanism, which makes it possible to add dialing capabilities to nearly any application. It can be used to make only outgoing calls and does not provide fine-grained control over a call. Basic telephony allows your application to take full control over the placing and monitoring of a call. Supplementary telephony allows your application to do such things as hold a call, create a conference call, or transfer a call. Extended telephony allows extensions that are supplied by service providers. This chapter uses only assisted and basic telephony.

Versions of TAPI

One of the most troubling aspects of TAPI is that several different versions exist. For Win32 applications, the earliest version that can be used is 1.4. The newest version is currently 2.1. When using assisted telephony, you need not worry about TAPI versions; but, for the other service modes, your application must determine the version of the TAPI library installed on the computer. You will see how to do this later in this chapter.

The TAPI Header and Library

To use TAPI, your program must include **tapi.h**. It must also include **tapi32.lib** in the link process. You can add **tapi32.lib** to a Visual C++ project by selecting Project | Settings. This opens the Project Settings dialog box. Next, select the Link tab and add **tapi32.lib** to the link list.

Canonical Versus Dialable Numbers

When placing a call, the number you are dialing must be in a *dialable format*. All "normal" telephone numbers, such as 555-4322, are already in dialable format. Dialable numbers also can contain additional pieces of information, but they are not needed for the purposes of this chapter. Sometimes an application will store a number in *canonical format*. The canonical format starts with a plus sign (+) and includes a country code, an optional area code, and other pieces of information followed by the number. TAPI includes a function called **lineTranslateAddress( )**, which converts canonical numbers into dialable ones.

In the language of TAPI, a number is called an *address*. Thus, addresses may be either canonical or dialable. This chapter will continue to use the term *telephone number* since this is the most commonly used term.

Asynchronous Behavior

TAPI includes both synchronous and asynchronous functions. Synchronous functions do not return until they have completely accomplished their tasks. Asynchronous functions initiate their tasks, but then return. The reason for asynchronous functions is that some time lags occur naturally with certain operations, such as waiting for a dial tone when dialing a call. When an asynchronous function executes, it returns the success or failure of the initiation of the operation. The final determination of success or failure is confirmed when TAPI sends your application a **LINE_REPLY** message. For the simple TAPI applications shown in this chapter, we won't need to worry about asynchronous behavior, but more sophisticated programs will need to.

A Simple Dialing Program

The easiest way to add dialing capabilities to an application is to use TAPI's assisted telephony function, **tapiRequestMakeCall( )**. This function dials the number that you pass to it and works only for voice calls. With **tapiRequestMakeCall( )**, you need not deal with any of the underlying details; TAPI automates the entire process.

The prototype for **tapiRequestMakeCall( )** is shown here:

LONG tapiRequestMakeCall(LPCSTR *lpszPhNum*, LPCSTR *lpszCaller*,
                 LPCSTR *lpszCalled*, LPCSTR *lpszRemark*);

Here, *lpszPhNum* is the pointer to a string that contains the number that you want to dial. This number can be in either a dialable or a canonical format. If it is in a canonical format, it will be automatically converted into a dialable format. A pointer to the name of the application that is issuing the request is passed in *lpszCaller*. *lpszCalled* is a pointer to the name of the person that you are calling. *lpszRemark* is a pointer to a remark that describes the call. Any or all of *lpszCaller*, *lpszCalled*, and *lpszRemark* can be **NULL**. The function returns 0 if successful or one of the following errors:

Value	Meaning
TAPIERR_NOREQUESTRECIPIENT	No call-control application available.
TAPIERR_INVALIDESTADDRESS	Invalid number.
TAPIERR_REQUESTQUEUEFULL	Queue is full.
TAPIERR_INVALPOINTER	Pointer error. (A pointer may be pointing to an invalid address.)

tapiRequestMakeCall( ) relies upon a call-control manager. Notice the error **TAPIERR_NOREQUESTRECIPIENT**. This error occurs if there is no call-control manager that can handle the call request. A call-control manager is provided automatically by all Win32 environments, so not having one is usually not a problem. For example, Windows 98 provides the Phone Dialer utility. Multiple call requests are queued until they can be handled by the call manager.

To use **tapiRequestMakeCall( )**, simply pass the appropriate strings. The call-control manager takes over from there. This is why assisted telephony is so valuable. You can include dialing capabilities into nearly any application with almost no overhead, as the following program demonstrates.

Code

SimpDial.cpp

The **SimpDial.cpp** program dials a number using **tapiRequestMakeCall( )**. This is the simplest way that a program can dial a number, but it can only be used to place voice calls. The program includes a File menu and a Help menu. To dial a number, select File | Dial. This activates the Dial dialog box, which allows you to enter the number you want. After entering the number, click the Dial pushbutton. Your number is then dialed. At this point, the call-control manager takes over and you are shown a dialog box that allows you to pick up the telephone handset or hang up the call. Sample output is shown in Figure 10-1. Remember, you must include **tapi32.lib** in the link when you compile the program.

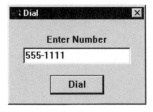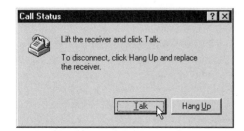

FIGURE 10-1.   Sample output from **SimpDial.cpp**

The code for **SimpDial.cpp** is shown here:

```
// SimpDial.cpp: Using assisted telephony.

#include <windows.h>
#include <tapi.h>
#include "simpdial.h"

LRESULT CALLBACK WindowFunc(HWND, UINT, WPARAM, LPARAM);
```

```
BOOL CALLBACK DialDialog(HWND hdwnd, UINT message,
                         WPARAM wParam, LPARAM lParam);

char szWinName[] = "MyWin"; // name of window class

HINSTANCE hInst;

int WINAPI WinMain(HINSTANCE hThisInst, HINSTANCE hPrevInst,
                   LPSTR lpszArgs, int nWinMode)
{
  MSG msg;
  WNDCLASSEX wcl;
  HWND hwnd;
  HACCEL hAccel;

  // Define a window class.
  wcl.cbSize = sizeof(WNDCLASSEX);
  wcl.hInstance = hThisInst;
  wcl.lpszClassName = szWinName;
  wcl.lpfnWndProc = WindowFunc;
  wcl.style = 0; // default style
  wcl.hIcon = LoadIcon(NULL, IDI_APPLICATION); // large icon
  wcl.hIconSm = NULL; // use small version of large icon
  wcl.hCursor = LoadCursor(NULL, IDC_ARROW);
  wcl.hbrBackground = (HBRUSH) GetStockObject(WHITE_BRUSH);
  wcl.cbClsExtra = 0;
  wcl.cbWndExtra = 0;
  wcl.lpszMenuName = "DialMenu";

  // Register the window class.
  if(!RegisterClassEx(&wcl)) return 0;

  // Create a window.
  hwnd = CreateWindow(szWinName,
                      "Using Assisted Telephony",
                      WS_OVERLAPPEDWINDOW,
                      CW_USEDEFAULT, CW_USEDEFAULT,
                      CW_USEDEFAULT, CW_USEDEFAULT,
                      NULL, NULL, hThisInst, NULL);

  hInst = hThisInst;

  // Load accelerators.
  hAccel = LoadAccelerators(hThisInst, "DialMenu");
```

```
  // Display the window.
  ShowWindow(hwnd, nWinMode);
  UpdateWindow(hwnd);

  // The message loop.
  while(GetMessage(&msg, NULL, 0, 0))
  {
    if(!TranslateAccelerator(hwnd, hAccel, &msg)) {
      TranslateMessage(&msg);
      DispatchMessage(&msg);
    }
  }

  return msg.wParam;
}

// The window procedure.
LRESULT CALLBACK WindowFunc(HWND hwnd, UINT message,
                            WPARAM wParam, LPARAM lParam)
{
  int response;

  switch(message) {
    case WM_COMMAND:
      switch(LOWORD(wParam)) {
        case IDM_DIAL: // activate Dial dialog box
          // get name of font
          response = DialogBox(hInst, "DialDB", hwnd,
                               (DLGPROC) DialDialog);
          if(!response)
            MessageBox(hwnd, "Dialing Cancelled",
                       "Cancelled", MB_OK);
          break;
        case IDM_EXIT:
          response = MessageBox(hwnd, "Quit the Program?",
                                "Exit", MB_YESNO);
          if(response == IDYES) PostQuitMessage(0);
          break;
        case IDM_ABOUT:
          MessageBox(hwnd, "Assisted Telephony\n",
                     "About", MB_OK);
          break;
      }
```

```
    break;

  case WM_DESTROY:
    PostQuitMessage(0);
    break;
  default:
    return DefWindowProc(hwnd, message, wParam, lParam);
  }
  return 0;
}


// Dial number.
BOOL CALLBACK DialDialog(HWND hdwnd, UINT message,
                         WPARAM wParam, LPARAM lParam)
{
  char number[80];
  long result;

  switch(message) {
    case WM_COMMAND:
      switch(LOWORD(wParam)) {
        case IDCANCEL:
          EndDialog(hdwnd, 0);
          return 1;
        case IDD_DIAL:
          GetDlgItemText(hdwnd, IDD_EB1, number, 79);
          result = tapiRequestMakeCall(number, "SimpDial",
                      "Test Call",
                      "Testing assisted telephony.");

          if(result) {
            MessageBox(hdwnd, "Cannot place call.", "Error",
                      MB_OK);
            EndDialog(hdwnd, 0);
          }

          EndDialog(hdwnd, 1);
          return 1;
      }
      break;
  }
  return 0;
}
```

The program requires the **SimpDial.rc** resource file, shown next:

```
#include <windows.h>
#include "simpdial.h"

DialMenu MENU
{
  POPUP "&File" {
    MENUITEM "&Dial\tF2", IDM_DIAL
    MENUITEM "E&xit\tCtrl+X", IDM_EXIT
  }
  POPUP "&Help" {
    MENUITEM "&About", IDM_ABOUT
  }
}

DialMenu ACCELERATORS
{
  VK_F2, IDM_DIAL, VIRTKEY
  "^X", IDM_EXIT
  VK_F1, IDM_ABOUT, VIRTKEY
}

DialDB DIALOG 10, 10, 100, 60
CAPTION "Dial"
STYLE WS_POPUP | WS_CAPTION | WS_SYSMENU | WS_VISIBLE
{
  CTEXT "Enter Number", 300, 10, 10, 80, 12
  EDITTEXT IDD_EB1, 10, 20, 80, 12, ES_LEFT |
           WS_VISIBLE | WS_BORDER | ES_AUTOHSCROLL |
           WS_TABSTOP
  DEFPUSHBUTTON "Dial" IDD_DIAL, 30, 40, 40, 14,
           WS_CHILD | WS_VISIBLE | WS_TABSTOP
}
```

The header file **SimpDial.h** is shown here:

```
#define IDM_DIAL      100
#define IDM_EXIT      101
#define IDM_ABOUT     102

#define IDD_EB1       200
#define IDD_DIAL      201
```

ANNOTATIONS

The first thing to notice is that the header **tapi.h** is included in the program. This defines the prototypes and macros required by the telephony subsystem. Most of **WinMain( )** is standard skeletal code. However, notice that the program loads the DialMenu menu and accelerator table from the resource file. Also, the global variable **hInst** is assigned the instance handle from the application. This handle is needed when the Dial dialog box is created.

In **WindowFunc( )**, if the user selects File | Dial, the Dial dialog box is activated. Notice that a return value of 0 from the call to **DialogBox( )** indicates that the user did not place a call.

The Dial dialog box includes an edit box and a pushbutton. The number to be dialed is entered into the edit box. To dial the number, click the Dial pushbutton. This dialog box is managed by the **DialDialog( )** function. It handles two commands. First, if the user closes the box by clicking the close icon, the system-defined **IDCANCEL** command is sent. This is processed by the following code.

```
case IDCANCEL:
  EndDialog(hdwnd, 0);
```

The call to **EndDialog( )** causes the dialog box to be closed. Notice that its second argument is 0. This value becomes the return value of the call to **DialogBox( )** that opened the dialog box. A return value of 0 indicates that the user did not place a call.

If the user clicks the Dial pushbutton, then the following code executes:

```
case IDD_DIAL:
  GetDlgItemText(hdwnd, IDD_EB1, number, 79);
  result = tapiRequestMakeCall(number, "SimpDial",
              "Test Call",
              "Testing assisted telephony.");

  if(result) {
    MessageBox(hdwnd, "Cannot place call.", "Error",
              MB_OK);
    EndDialog(hdwnd, 0);
  }

  EndDialog(hdwnd, 1);
```

First, the number entered by the user in the edit box is obtained by calling **GetDlgItemText( )**. This function copies the contents of the specified control into a character array. In this case, it copies the number into the **number** array. Next, the call to **tapiRequestMakeCall( )** is made. This causes the dialing sequence to be initiated. The call to **tapiRequestMakeCall( )** returns immediately even though the call itself takes several seconds to dial. If the call to **tapiRequestMakeCall( )** fails, it is reported and **EndDialog( )** is called with the value 0 as its second argument. Otherwise, **EndDialog( )** is called with the value 1 as its second argument. This value indicates that the dialing sequence was successfully begun. It is important to understand that when **tapiRequestMakeCall( )** returns without an error it does not mean that the call has actually been placed or connected. It simply means that the dialing sequence has been started successfully.

Autodialing with Low-Level TAPI Functions

Although using **tapiRequestMakeCall( )** is by far the easiest way to add dialing capabilities to an application, it is by no means the only way. If you want more detailed control over a call and more detailed status information about a call, then you will need to use the low-level TAPI functions. While the use of the low-level functions can be very complicated for many types of calls and environments, if you restrict your calls to POTS and voice-only, then the low-level functions are not difficult to master.

To dial a call using the low-level functions requires that your application follow these steps.

1. Initialize the TAPI subsystem by calling **lineInitializeEx( )**.

2. Obtain the version of TAPI that both the application and the system can support by calling **lineNegotiateAPIVersion( )**.

3. Obtain the device capabilities of the system by calling **lineGetDevCaps( )**. For POTS-based, voice-only calls, this step can be skipped. (Since we are placing only voice calls, we won't be using this function in this chapter.)

4. A line must be opened via a call to **lineOpen( )**.

5. The call is dialed by calling **lineMakeCall( )**.

6. When the call is over, the functions **lineDrop( )** and **lineDeallocateCall( )** are executed.

7. When you are done using TAPI, **lineClose( )** and **lineShutdown( )** should be called.

Next, each of these functions is examined in detail.

lineInitializeEx( )

Before you can use TAPI, you must initialize it by calling **lineInitializeEx( )**. This function requires that TAPI version 2.0 or greater be supported by your compiler.

(Earlier versions of TAPI require the use of **lineInitialize( )**.) The prototype for **lineInitializeEx( )** is shown here:

LONG lineInitializeEx(LPHLINEAPP *lphLineAppHandle*, HINSTANCE *hInst*,
    LINECALLBACK *tapiFunc*, LPCSTR *lpszProgName*,
    LPDWORD *lpNumLines*, LPDWORD *lpVersion*,
    LPLINEINITIALIZEEXPARAMS *lpExParams*);

Here, *lphLineAppHandle* is a pointer to an **HLINEAPP** object that receives the application's TAPI handle. *hInst* specifies the instance handle for the calling application. The function pointed to by *tapiFunc* receives TAPI messages for the calling application. The application name is passed in *lpszProgName*. You can also pass **NULL** for this parameter. *lpNumLines* is a pointer to a long integer that upon return will contain the number of lines available to the application. Prior to the call, the number of the newest version of TAPI that is supported by the application must be in the long integer pointed to by *lpVersion*. On return, this variable contains the number of the newest version of TAPI supported by the system. The high-order word contains the major version number and the low-order word contains the minor version number. At the time of this writing, you should initialize the version number to 0x00020000. The value pointed to by *lpExParams* specifies what type of event notification mechanism is used. The function returns 0 if successful. A negative value indicates an error.

Starting with TAPI version 2.0, you can use one of three different ways to be notified about events: hidden window, event handle, or completion port. The method is determined by the values contained in the **LINEINITIALIZEEXPARAMS** structure pointed to by *lpExparams*. This structure is shown here:

```
typedef struct lineinitializeexparams_tag {
  DWORD dwTotalSize;   // total size of structure
  DWORD dwNeededSize;  // number of bytes required
  DWORD dwUsedSize;    // number of bytes containing data
  DWORD dwOptions;     // event notification method
  union {
    HANDLE hEvent;     // contains event handle
    HANDLE hCompletionPort; // contains completion port handle
  } Handles;
  DWORD dwCompletionKey; // completion key
} LINEINTIALIZEEXPARAMS;
```

The notification method that we will use is hidden window. It is also the only mechanism supported by earlier versions of TAPI. When using the hidden window method, TAPI notifies your application about events by calling the function specified by *tapiFunc* in the call to **lineInitializeEx( )**. To specify the hidden window method, you must initialize the **dwOptions** field of the structure pointed to by *lpExParams* to this value:

LINEINITIALIZEEXOPTION_USEHIDDENWINDOW

You must also initialize **dwTotalSize**, **dwNeededSize**, and **dwUsedSize** appropriately.

When using the hidden window event notification method, events are sent as messages to the function specified by *tapiFunc*. This is a callback function that must have this prototype:

void CALLBACK tapiFunc(DWORD *hDev*, DWORD *mess*, DWORD *data*,
                          DWORD *arg1*, DWORD *arg2*, DWORD *arg3*);

When called, *hDev* will contain a line handle or a call handle, depending upon the message. The message, itself, is passed in *mess*. The *data* parameter receives application-defined data. The *arg1*, *arg2*, and *arg3* parameters receive information related to the message.

TAPI defines several messages. The only one we need to handle for the example in this chapter is **LINE_CALLSTATE**. More sophisticated applications will need to handle other messages, such as **LINE_REPLY**, **LINE_REQUEST**, and **LINE_CLOSE**.

When a **LINE_CALLSTATE** message is received, *hDev* contains the handle of the call, and *data* contains application-defined data. The state of the call is passed in *arg1*. Here are a few of its possible values:

Value	Meaning
LINECALLSTATE_IDLE	No call in progress.
LINECALLSTATE_DIALTONE	Dial tone acquired.
LINECALLSTATE_DIALING	Number is being dialed.
LINECALLSTATE_RINGBACK	Dialed number is ringing.
LINECALLSTATE_BUSY	Dialed number is busy.
LINECALLSTATE_CONNECTED	Call is connected.
LINECALLSTATE_DISCONNECTED	Call is disconnected.

It is important to understand that not all of these messages will be received by all types of calls.

The values of *arg2* and *arg3* contain extended state information for certain states. They are not needed by the example in this chapter.

lineNegotiateAPIVersion( )

Once TAPI has been initialized, you must "negotiate" which version of TAPI your program is going to use. There are several versions of TAPI and your program must use the version that is available on the machine in which it is running. To do this, use **lineNegotiateAPIVersion( )**, shown here:

```
LONG lineNegotiateAPIVersion(HLINEAPP hLineAppHandle,
                    DWORD LineNum,
                    DWORD OldestVer, DWORD NewestVer,
                    LPDWORD lpNegVer,
                    LPLINEEXTENSIONID lpExID);
```

Here, *hLineAppHandle* is the line handle obtained from **lineInitializeEx( )**. The number of the line (also called the device ID) is passed in *LineNum*. The first line in the system has an ID of 0. The oldest version of TAPI that the program can support is passed in *OldestVer* and the newest version that is supported is passed in *NewestVer*. The newest version supported by your compiler will be contained in the macro **TAPI_CURRENT_VERSION**. On return, the agreed-upon version is contained in the variable pointed to by *lpNegVer*. If the TSP provides extensions, they will be returned in *lpExID*. If you don't care about extensions, then this parameter can be ignored, as it is by the example in this chapter. The function returns 0 if successful and a negative value on failure.

    At the time of this writing, many TAPI applications restrict their operation to the features supported by TAPI 1.4 to ensure that they can run in the widest range of execution environments. For simple programs, such as those shown in this book, TAPI 1.4 is fully sufficient and the oldest version of TAPI that is required is 1.4. You can change this to 2.0 or later if you desire.

PROGRAMMER'S NOTE: *If you want to build a version of your program that explicitly specifies TAPI 1.4, you should define **TAPI_CURRENT_VERSION** as 0x00010004 before including **tapi.h**.*

lineOpen( ) and lineMakeCall( )

Once TAPI has been intialized and a version has been agreed to, you can open a line by calling **lineOpen( )**, shown here:

```
LONG lineOpen(HLINEAPP hLineAppHandle, DWORD LineNum,
            LPHLINE hOpenLine, DWORD TapiVer,
            DWORD ExtVer, DWORD data,
            DWORD Privileges, DWORD MediaMode,
            LPLINECALLPARAMS const lpLCP);
```

Here, *hLineAppHandle* is the handle obtained from **lineInitializeEx( )**. The line ID you want to dial out on is passed in *LineNum*. A pointer to an **HLINE** object is passed in *hOpenLine*. It receives the line handle upon successfully opening the line. The version of TAPI you negotiated is passed in *TapiVer*. The version of the TAPI extensions (if any) is passed in *ExtVer*. This should be 0 when no TAPI extensions are used. User-defined data is passed in *data*. The privileges requested are passed in *Privileges*. For out-going only calls, pass **LINECALLPRIVILEGE_NONE**. (You can use TAPI to answer calls, too, but we won't be doing so here.) The *MediaMode* parameter is not used by outgoing calls and can be 0. The *lpLCP* parameter is used only under special circumstances and can be **NULL** for our purposes. The function returns 0 if successful and a negative value on failure.

Once a line has been opened, you are now ready to make a call by calling **lineMakeCall( )**. Its prototype is shown here:

```
LONG lineMakeCall(HLINE hOpenLine, LPHCALL lphCall,
                  LPCSTR lpszNumber, DWORD CountryCode,
                  LPLINECALLPARAMS const lpLCP);
```

Here, *hOpenLine* is the handle to an open line. The handle to the call is returned in the object pointed to by *lphCall*. The number to be dialed is pointed to by *lpszNumber*. This number must be in a dialable format (not canonical). The country code, if any, is passed in *CountryCode*. Pass 0 to use the default country code. *lpLCP* specifies the parameters of the call. **LINECALLPARAMS** is a very large structure. Fortunately, if you are making a voice call, then *lpLCP* can be **NULL** (which causes the default voice settings to be used). The function returns a positive value if successful and a negative value on failure.

PROGRAMMER'S NOTE: *lineMakeCall( ) is an asynchronous function. The handle pointed to by* lphCall *is not valid until a* **LINE_REPLY** *message is received with the value 0 in the arg2 parameter.*

lineDrop( ) and lineDeallocateCall( )

Once a call is over you must disconnect by calling **lineDrop( )**. Its prototype is shown here:

```
LONG lineDrop(HCALL hCall, LPCSTR lpszRemark, DWORD Len);
```

Here, *hCall* is the handle of the call being dropped. The string pointed to in *lpszRemark* is sent to the called party and can be **NULL**. The length of the string is passed in *Len*. This value is not used if *lpszRemark* is **NULL**. The function returns a positive value if successful and a negative value on failure. **lineDrop( )** is an asynchronous function and a value of 0 in the *arg2* parameter of a **LINE_REPLY** message indicates success.

Once a call has been disconnected, its handle can be freed by calling
lineDeallocateCall( ), shown here:

> LONG lineDeallocateCall(HCALL *hCall*);

Here, *hCall* is the handle being freed. The function returns 0 if successful and a
negative value on failure.

lineClose( ) and lineShutDown( )

Once you are done with a line and will be making no further calls on it, the line can
be closed by calling **lineClose( )**. Its prototype is shown here:

> LONG lineClose(HLINE *hOpenLine*);

Here, *hOpenLine* is the handle to the open line that is being closed. The function
returns 0 if successful and a negative value on failure.

When you are done using TAPI, call **lineShutdown( )**, shown here:

> LONG lineShutdown(HLINEAPP *hLineAppHandle*);

Here, *hLineAppHandle* is the handle obtained from **lineIntializeEx( )**. The function
returns 0 if successful and a negative value on failure.

AutoDial.cpp

Code

The **AutoDial.cpp** program, shown next, modifies the previous dialing program so
that it uses the low-level TAPI functions rather than relying on
tapiRequestMakeCall( ).

```
// AutoDial.cpp: Demonstrate TAPI functions for phone connections.

#include <windows.h>
#include <tapi.h>
#include "autodial.h"

LRESULT CALLBACK WindowFunc(HWND, UINT, WPARAM, LPARAM);
void CALLBACK PhFunc(DWORD hDev, DWORD mess, DWORD data,
                     DWORD arg1, DWORD arg2, DWORD arg3);
BOOL CALLBACK DialDialog(HWND hdwnd, UINT message,
                         WPARAM wParam, LPARAM lParam);

char szWinName[] = "MyWin"; // name of window class
```

```
HINSTANCE hInst;

char number[80];

int WINAPI WinMain(HINSTANCE hThisInst, HINSTANCE hPrevInst,
                   LPSTR lpszArgs, int nWinMode)
{
  MSG msg;
  WNDCLASSEX wcl;
  HACCEL hAccel;
  HWND hwnd;

  // Define a window class.
  wcl.cbSize = sizeof(WNDCLASSEX);
  wcl.hInstance = hThisInst;
  wcl.lpszClassName = szWinName;
  wcl.lpfnWndProc = WindowFunc;
  wcl.style = 0; // default style
  wcl.hIcon = LoadIcon(NULL, IDI_APPLICATION); // large icon
  wcl.hIconSm = NULL; // use small version of large icon
  wcl.hCursor = LoadCursor(NULL, IDC_ARROW);
  wcl.hbrBackground = (HBRUSH) GetStockObject(WHITE_BRUSH);
  wcl.cbClsExtra = 0;
  wcl.cbWndExtra = 0;
  wcl.lpszMenuName = "DialMenu";

  // Register the window class.
  if(!RegisterClassEx(&wcl)) return 0;

  hInst = hThisInst;

  // Create a window.
  hwnd = CreateWindow(szWinName,
                      "Autodialing with TAPI",
                      WS_OVERLAPPEDWINDOW,
                      CW_USEDEFAULT, CW_USEDEFAULT,
                      CW_USEDEFAULT, CW_USEDEFAULT,
                      NULL, NULL, hThisInst, NULL);

  hInst = hThisInst;

  // Load accelerators.
  hAccel = LoadAccelerators(hThisInst, "DialMenu");
```

```
  // Display the window.
  ShowWindow(hwnd, nWinMode);
  UpdateWindow(hwnd);

  // The message loop.
  while(GetMessage(&msg, NULL, 0, 0))
  {
    if(!TranslateAccelerator(hwnd, hAccel, &msg)) {
      TranslateMessage(&msg);
      DispatchMessage(&msg);
    }
  }

  return msg.wParam;
}

// The window procedure.
LRESULT CALLBACK WindowFunc(HWND hwnd, UINT message,
                            WPARAM wParam, LPARAM lParam)
{
  static HLINEAPP hLineAppHandle;  // handle to line app
  static HLINE hOpenLine = NULL;   // handle to open line
  static HCALL hCall = NULL;       // handle to call
  LINEINITIALIZEEXPARAMS exParams; // specifies TAPI mode
  LINEEXTENSIONID extensions;      // not used
  unsigned long lines;             // number of lines
  static unsigned long version = 0x00020000; // TAPI version
  long int result;  // results of TAPI functions
  int response;

  switch(message) {
    case WM_CREATE:
      exParams.dwTotalSize = sizeof(exParams);
      exParams.dwNeededSize = sizeof(exParams);
      exParams.dwUsedSize = sizeof(exParams);
      exParams.dwOptions =
                LINEINITIALIZEEXOPTION_USEHIDDENWINDOW;

      // initialize TAPI phone subsystem
      result = lineInitializeEx(&hLineAppHandle, hInst,
                                PhFunc, "My Dialer", &lines,
                                &version, &exParams);
```

```
   if(result) {
     MessageBox(hwnd, "Cannot initialize TAPI.",
                      "Error", MB_OK);
     break;
   }

   if(lines == 0) {
     MessageBox(hwnd, "No lines.", "Error", MB_OK);
     break;
   }

   // negotiate a version
   result = lineNegotiateAPIVersion(hLineAppHandle, 0,
                      0x00010004,
                      TAPI_CURRENT_VERSION,
                      &version, &extensions);
   if(result) MessageBox(hwnd,
                      "Version negotiation failed.",
                      "Error", MB_OK);

   break;
case WM_COMMAND:
   switch(LOWORD(wParam)) {
     case IDM_DIAL: // activate Dial dialog box
       // get name of font
       result = DialogBox(hInst, "DialDB", hwnd,
               (DLGPROC) DialDialog);
       if(!result) break; // user cancelled call

       if(hCall) { // shut down any open call
         lineDrop(hCall, NULL, 0);
         lineDeallocateCall(hCall);
       }

       // open a line
       result = lineOpen(hLineAppHandle, 0, &hOpenLine,
                      version, 0, 0,
                      LINECALLPRIVILEGE_NONE, 0, NULL);

       if(result) {
         MessageBox(hwnd, "Cannot open line.",
                      "Error", MB_OK);
         break;
```

```
            }

            // dial the number
            result = lineMakeCall(hOpenLine, &hCall,
                                   number, 0, NULL);

            if(result <=0) MessageBox(hwnd, "Can't dial.",
                                       "Error", MB_OK);
            break;
          case IDM_EXIT:
            response = MessageBox(hwnd, "Quit the Program?",
                                   "Exit", MB_YESNO);
            if(response == IDYES) PostQuitMessage(0);
            break;
          case IDM_ABOUT:
            MessageBox(hwnd, "Using TAPI\n",
                             "About", MB_OK);
            break;
        }
      break;
    case WM_DESTROY:
      lineClose(hOpenLine);
      lineShutdown(hLineAppHandle);
      PostQuitMessage(0);
      break;
    default:
      return DefWindowProc(hwnd, message, wParam, lParam);
  }
  return 0;
}


// TAPI response function.
void CALLBACK PhFunc(DWORD hDev, DWORD mess, DWORD data,
                     DWORD arg1, DWORD arg2, DWORD arg3)
{
  switch(mess) {
    // you can check for other messages here
    case LINE_CALLSTATE:
      switch(arg1) {
        // check for other states, here
        case LINECALLSTATE_DISCONNECTED:
          lineDrop((HCALL) hDev, NULL, 0);
          lineDeallocateCall((HCALL) hDev);
          MessageBox(HWND_DESKTOP, "Disconnected",
```

```
                          "Call Status", MB_OK);
          break;
      }
      break;
  }
}


// Dialing dialog.
BOOL CALLBACK DialDialog(HWND hdwnd, UINT message,
                         WPARAM wParam, LPARAM lParam)
{
  switch(message) {
    case WM_COMMAND:
      switch(LOWORD(wParam)) {
        case IDCANCEL:
          EndDialog(hdwnd, 0);
          return 1;
        case IDD_DIAL:
          GetDlgItemText(hdwnd, IDD_EB1, number, 79);
          EndDialog(hdwnd, 1);
          return 1;
      }
      break;
  }
  return 0;
}
```

The resource file for the program, **AutoDial.rc**, is shown here:

```
#include <windows.h>
#include "autodial.h"

DialMenu MENU
{
  POPUP "&File" {
    MENUITEM "&Dial\tF2", IDM_DIAL
    MENUITEM "E&xit\tCtrl+X", IDM_EXIT
  }
  POPUP "&Help" {
    MENUITEM "&About", IDM_ABOUT
  }
}
```

```
DialMenu ACCELERATORS
{
  VK_F2, IDM_DIAL, VIRTKEY
  "^X", IDM_EXIT
  VK_F1, IDM_ABOUT, VIRTKEY
}

DialDB DIALOG 10, 10, 100, 60
CAPTION "Dial"
STYLE WS_POPUP | WS_CAPTION | WS_SYSMENU | WS_VISIBLE
{
  CTEXT "Enter Number", 300, 10, 10, 80, 12
  EDITTEXT IDD_EB1, 10, 20, 80, 12, ES_LEFT |
            WS_VISIBLE | WS_BORDER | ES_AUTOHSCROLL |
            WS_TABSTOP
  DEFPUSHBUTTON "Dial" IDD_DIAL, 30, 40, 40, 14,
            WS_CHILD | WS_VISIBLE | WS_TABSTOP
}
```

The header file **AutoDial.h** is shown next:

```
#define IDM_DIAL       100
#define IDM_EXIT       101
#define IDM_ABOUT      102

#define IDD_EB1        200
#define IDD_DIAL       201
```

ANNOTATIONS

While **AutoDial.cpp** performs the same function (it dials a number) as the preceding **SimpDial.cpp** program, it is much more complex. This is because we are handling all of the TAPI calls manually. Let's begin its examination with the declarations that occur within **WindowFunc( )**.

```
static HLINEAPP hLineAppHandle;  // handle to line app
static HLINE hOpenLine = NULL;    // handle to open line
static HCALL hCall = NULL;        // handle to call
LINEINITIALIZEEXPARAMS exParams;  // specifies TAPI mode
LINEEXTENSIONID extensions;       // not used
unsigned long lines;              // number of lines
static unsigned long version = 0x00020000; // TAPI version
```

```
long int result; // results of TAPI functions
int response;     // message box result
```

First are declared the various TAPI handles and structures that are used by the TAPI functions. The **lines** variable will receive the number of available lines and **version** specifies the TAPI version. The version is initially set to 2.0. The **result** variable will receive the result of a TAPI function call.

When the program receives a **WM_CREATE** message, it initializes the TAPI system. The **WM_CREATE** handler is shown here:

```
case WM_CREATE:
  exParams.dwTotalSize = sizeof(exParams);
  exParams.dwNeededSize = sizeof(exParams);
  exParams.dwUsedSize = sizeof(exParams);
  exParams.dwOptions =
            LINEINITIALIZEEXOPTION_USEHIDDENWINDOW;

  // initialize TAPI phone subsystem
  result = lineInitializeEx(&hLineAppHandle, hInst,
                            PhFunc, "My Dialer", &lines,
                            &version, &exParams);

  if(result) {
    MessageBox(hwnd, "Cannot initialize TAPI.",
                     "Error", MB_OK);
    break;
  }

  if(lines == 0) {
    MessageBox(hwnd, "No lines.", "Error", MB_OK);
    break;
  }

  // negotiate a version
  result = lineNegotiateAPIVersion(hLineAppHandle, 0,
                     0x00010004,
                     TAPI_CURRENT_VERSION,
                     &version, &extensions);
  if(result) MessageBox(hwnd,
                     "Version negotiation failed.",
                     "Error", MB_OK);
  break;
```

The handler begins by initializing **exParams** and setting its **dwOptions** field so that TAPI uses the hidden window method of reporting events. Next, it calls

lineInitializeEx( ) to initialize the TAPI subsystem. A failure to initialize is reported. Notice that **PhFunc( )** is specified as the callback function for telephone events. (We will look at it in a moment.) On return, the **lines** variable will contain the number of available lines. If this value is zero, then no calls can be made and this fact is reported.

After a successful initialization, the TAPI version is negotiated by calling **lineNegotiateAPIVersion( )**. Upon a successful return, the agreed-upon version will be contained in **version**.

To place a call, the user selects File | Dial. This causes the following handler to execute:

```
case IDM_DIAL: // activate Dial dialog box
  // get name of font
  result = DialogBox(hInst, "DialDB", hwnd,
                     (DLGPROC) DialDialog);
  if(!result) break; // user cancelled call

  if(hCall) { // shut down any open call
    lineDrop(hCall, NULL, 0);
    lineDeallocateCall(hCall);
  }

  // open a line
  result = lineOpen(hLineAppHandle, 0, &hOpenLine,
                    version, 0, 0,
                    LINECALLPRIVILEGE_NONE, 0, NULL);

  if(result) {
    MessageBox(hwnd, "Cannot open line.",
               "Error", MB_OK);
    break;
  }

  // dial the number
  result = lineMakeCall(hOpenLine, &hCall,
                        number, 0, NULL);

  if(result <=0) MessageBox(hwnd, "Can't dial.",
                            "Error", MB_OK);
  break;
```

First, the Dial dialog box is displayed. This allows the user to enter a number. To dial the number, the user must click the Dial pushbutton. If the user cancels the dialog box without clicking Dial, then the rest of the handler is ignored. Next, if there is currently an open call, it is shut.

Once the number has been obtained, a line is opened by calling **lineOpen( )**. If this is successful, then the number is dialed by calling **lineMakeCall( )**. If the number cannot be dialed, the failure is reported. Notice that the last parameter to **lineMakeCall( )** is **NULL**. This causes a standard voice call to be placed.

Before moving on, it must be pointed out that more sophisticated applications will need to call **lineGetDevCaps( )** to obtain the capabilities of the system before opening a line. We can skip this step here because we are assuming the crudest system—POTS—and are placing a voice-only call.

All TAPI events are sent to the **PhFunc( )** callback function, shown here:

```
// TAPI response function.
void CALLBACK PhFunc(DWORD hDev, DWORD mess, DWORD data,
                     DWORD arg1, DWORD arg2, DWORD arg3)
{
  switch(mess) {
    // you can check for other messages here
    case LINE_CALLSTATE:
      switch(arg1) {
        // check for other states, here
        case LINECALLSTATE_DISCONNECTED:
          lineDrop((HCALL) hDev, NULL, 0);
          lineDeallocateCall((HCALL) hDev);
          MessageBox(HWND_DESKTOP, "Disconnected",
                     "Call Status", MB_OK);
          break;
      }
      break;
  }
}
```

As you can see, it handles only one message and within that message, one event. The message stream generated by a voice call that is handled by the default call-control manager is very thin. Since voice calls are ultimately under the control of the user, few messages are generated and even fewer need to be handled explicitly. For example, the user decides when to hang up.

The one event that is handled is **LINECALLSTATUS_DISCONNECTED**, which is passed as part of a **LINE_CALLSTATE** message. When this is received, the program drops the line and deallocates the call handle. It also reports that a disconnection has occurred. The program will only receive this message prior to the user picking up the handset. Once control passes to the user, the message stream stops.

If you compare the code for this version of the dialing program with that shown earlier, it is easy to see why **tapiRequestMakeCall( )** is so valuable. By using assisted telephony, your program can auto-dial numbers for a user without incurring the rather heavy overhead associated with TAPI's low-level functions. Of course, if you want to use TAPI for anything other than voice-only calls, then you have no choice but to use the full TAPI subsystem.

A Phone List Dialer

To conclude this chapter, we will use TAPI to create a simple but useful function called **DialList( )** that automatically dials a list of telephone numbers, one after the other. This function is useful when you need to make calls to several people. For example, such a function will be especially useful for tasks such as managing political-action phone trees. Since only voice calls are supported, we will be using **tapiRequestMakeCall( )** to simplify the coding. Of course, you might want to try adapting the program to use the low-level TAPI functions if you want finer-grained control over the dialing process.

Code

ListDial.cpp

The **ListDial.cpp** program allows you to place a single telephone call or dial a list of numbers. For a single number, it uses the same mechanism as that employed by **SimpDial.cpp,** described earlier. To dial a list of numbers, you will select File | Dial List. This causes the **DialList( )** function to be called with a list of phone numbers. Each number in the list is dialed sequentially, until the list is empty. Before each number is dialed, you have a chance to cancel, skipping the remaining numbers in the list. The code for **ListDial.cpp** is shown here:

```cpp
// ListDial.cpp: Dial a number of a list of numbers.

#include <windows.h>
#include <tapi.h>
#include "listdial.h"

LRESULT CALLBACK WindowFunc(HWND, UINT, WPARAM, LPARAM);
BOOL CALLBACK DialDialog(HWND hdwnd, UINT message,
                         WPARAM wParam, LPARAM lParam);

bool DialList(char *plist[][2]);

char szWinName[] = "MyWin"; // name of window class

HINSTANCE hInst;

// a list of fake numbers
char *phonebook[][2] = {
```

```
  "Tom",  "555-1111",
  "Rex",  "555-2222",
  "Mary",  "555-3333",
  "Tod",  "555-4444",
  "",  ""
};


int WINAPI WinMain(HINSTANCE hThisInst, HINSTANCE hPrevInst,
                   LPSTR lpszArgs, int nWinMode)
{
  MSG msg;
  WNDCLASSEX wcl;
  HWND hwnd;
  HACCEL hAccel;

  // Define a window class.
  wcl.cbSize = sizeof(WNDCLASSEX);
  wcl.hInstance = hThisInst;
  wcl.lpszClassName = szWinName;
  wcl.lpfnWndProc = WindowFunc;
  wcl.style = 0; // default style
  wcl.hIcon = LoadIcon(NULL, IDI_APPLICATION); // large icon
  wcl.hIconSm = NULL; // use small version of large icon
  wcl.hCursor = LoadCursor(NULL, IDC_ARROW);
  wcl.hbrBackground = (HBRUSH) GetStockObject(WHITE_BRUSH);
  wcl.cbClsExtra = 0;
  wcl.cbWndExtra = 0;
  wcl.lpszMenuName = "DialMenu";

  // Register the window class.
  if(!RegisterClassEx(&wcl)) return 0;

  // Create a window.
  hwnd = CreateWindow(szWinName,
                      "Dial Phone List",
                      WS_OVERLAPPEDWINDOW,
                      CW_USEDEFAULT, CW_USEDEFAULT,
                      CW_USEDEFAULT, CW_USEDEFAULT,
                      NULL, NULL, hThisInst, NULL);

  hInst = hThisInst;
```

```
// Load accelerators.
hAccel = LoadAccelerators(hThisInst, "DialMenu");

// Display the window.
ShowWindow(hwnd, nWinMode);
UpdateWindow(hwnd);

// The message loop.
while(GetMessage(&msg, NULL, 0, 0))
{
  if(!TranslateAccelerator(hwnd, hAccel, &msg)) {
    TranslateMessage(&msg);
    DispatchMessage(&msg);
  }
}

return msg.wParam;
}

// The window procedure.
LRESULT CALLBACK WindowFunc(HWND hwnd, UINT message,
                            WPARAM wParam, LPARAM lParam)
{
  int response;

  switch(message) {
   case WM_COMMAND:
      switch(LOWORD(wParam)) {
        case IDM_DIAL: // activate Dial dialog box
          // Get a number to Dial
          response = DialogBox(hInst, "DialDB", hwnd,
                     (DLGPROC) DialDialog);
          if(!response)
            MessageBox(hwnd, "Dialing Cancelled",
                       "Cancelled", MB_OK);
          break;
        case IDM_DIALLIST:
          response = MessageBox(hwnd, "Dial Phone list?",
                                "Dial List", MB_YESNO);
          if(response == IDYES) DialList(phonebook);

          break;
        case IDM_EXIT:
```

```
              response = MessageBox(hwnd, "Quit the Program?",
                                    "Exit", MB_YESNO);
              if(response == IDYES) PostQuitMessage(0);
              break;
            case IDM_ABOUT:
              MessageBox(hwnd, "Dial Numbers\n",
                         "About", MB_OK);
              break;
          }
          break;

        case WM_DESTROY:
          PostQuitMessage(0);
          break;
        default:
          return DefWindowProc(hwnd, message, wParam, lParam);
    }
    return 0;
}

// Dial a number.
BOOL CALLBACK DialDialog(HWND hdwnd, UINT message,
                         WPARAM wParam, LPARAM lParam)
{
  char number[80];
  long result;

  switch(message) {
    case WM_COMMAND:
      switch(LOWORD(wParam)) {
        case IDCANCEL:
          EndDialog(hdwnd, 0);
          return 1;
        case IDD_DIAL:
          GetDlgItemText(hdwnd, IDD_EB1, number, 79);
          result = tapiRequestMakeCall(number, "ListDial",
                       "Outgoing",
                       "Assisted dialing.");

          if(result)
            MessageBox(hdwnd, "Cannot place call.", "Error",
                       MB_OK);

          EndDialog(hdwnd, 1);
```

```
        return 1;
      }
      break;
  }
  return 0;
}

// Dial a list of numbers.
bool DialList(char *plist[][2])
{
  long result;
  int i = 0;

  // dial the list
  while(*plist[i][0]) {
    result = tapiRequestMakeCall(phonebook[i][1],
                "ListDial", phonebook[i][0],
                "Dialing a list.");

    if(result) {
      MessageBox(HWND_DESKTOP, phonebook[i][0],
                "Error Dialing", MB_OK);
      return false;
    }

    i++;

    if(*plist[i][0]) {
      result = MessageBox(HWND_DESKTOP, "Next?",
                        "Dial Next Call", MB_YESNO);
      if(result == IDNO) return true;
    }
  }

  return true;
}
```

The resource file, **ListDial.rc**, required by the program is shown here:

```
#include <windows.h>
#include "listdial.h"
```

```
DialMenu MENU
{
  POPUP "&File" {
    MENUITEM "&Dial\tF2", IDM_DIAL
    MENUITEM "Dial &List\tF3", IDM_DIALLIST
    MENUITEM "E&xit\tCtrl+X", IDM_EXIT
  }
  POPUP "&Help" {
    MENUITEM "&About", IDM_ABOUT
  }
}


DialMenu ACCELERATORS
{
  VK_F2, IDM_DIAL, VIRTKEY
  VK_F3, IDM_DIALLIST, VIRTKEY
  "^X", IDM_EXIT
  VK_F1, IDM_ABOUT, VIRTKEY
}


DialDB DIALOG 10, 10, 100, 60
CAPTION "Dial"
STYLE WS_POPUP | WS_CAPTION | WS_SYSMENU | WS_VISIBLE
{
  CTEXT "Enter Number", 300, 10, 10, 80, 12
  EDITTEXT IDD_EB1, 10, 20, 80, 12, ES_LEFT |
          WS_VISIBLE | WS_BORDER | ES_AUTOHSCROLL |
          WS_TABSTOP
  DEFPUSHBUTTON "Dial" IDD_DIAL, 30, 40, 40, 14,
          WS_CHILD | WS_VISIBLE | WS_TABSTOP
}
```

The **ListDial.h** header file is shown here:

```
#define IDM_DIAL        100
#define IDM_DIALLIST    101
#define IDM_EXIT        102
#define IDM_ABOUT       103

#define IDD_EB1         200
#define IDD_DIAL        201
```

ANNOTATIONS

Because the parts of the program that dial a single number are the same as in **SimpDial.cpp**, shown earlier, the main area of interest is the **DialList( )** function, which dials a list of numbers. The prototype for **DialList( )** is

bool DialList(char *_plist_[][2]);

Here, _plist_ is a pointer to the list of numbers to dial. The function returns **true** if successful and **false** on failure.

The number list pointed to by _plist_ must consist of a two-dimensional array of **char *** pointers. For each row, the first pointer must point to the name of the person being dialed and the second pointer must point to a dialable number. The list must be terminated by two pointers to null-strings. Here is the way the list used by the program is initialized:

```
// a list of fake numbers
char *phonebook[][2] = {
  "Tom", "555-1111",
  "Rex", "555-2222",
  "Mary", "555-3333",
  "Tod", "555-4444",
  "", ""
};
```

As the comment states, these are fake numbers. You will need to create your own call list.

When **DialList( )** begins, it declares two variables. The first is **result**, which holds the result returned by **tapiRequestMakeCall( )** and **MessageBox( )**. The second is **i**, which holds the current index into the call list. This variable is incremented after each call.

The following loop actually dials the list of numbers. Its operation is straightforward.

```
// dial the list
while(*plist[i][0]) {
  result = tapiRequestMakeCall(phonebook[i][1],
             "ListDial", phonebook[i][0],
             "Dialing a list.");

  if(result) {
    MessageBox(HWND_DESKTOP, phonebook[i][0],
               "Error Dialing", MB_OK);
    return false;
  }
```

```
  i++;

  if(*plist[i][0]) {
    result = MessageBox(HWND_DESKTOP, "Next?",
                        "Dial Next Call", MB_YESNO);
    if(result == IDNO) return true;
  }
}
```

Notice that after each number is dialed, a message box is displayed, giving the user a chance to stop the process. If the user chooses to continue calling, then the next number is dialed.

Tips for Using MFC

Currently, MFC does not encapsulate the TAPI subsystem. To use TAPI in an MFC program, simply call the TAPI functions directly, as shown in the examples in this chapter.

Creating DLLs

A s you know, the Windows API is stored as a dynamic link library (DLL). This means that when your application program uses an API function, the code for that function is not actually included in your program's object file. Instead, loading instructions are supplied. When your program is loaded for execution, the dynamically linked API function is added. It is possible for you to create your own dynamic link libraries, which work in the same way. This chapter explains how to create a DLL and then converts two of the utilities presented earlier in this book into DLLs.

Dynamic Linking Versus Static Linking

Windows supports two types of linking: static and dynamic. Static linking occurs at compile time. The code for a statically linked function is physically added to your program's .EXE file. Functions that will be statically linked are usually stored in either .OBJ or .LIB files. For example, when you write a large program, consisting of several separate compilation units (files), the linker will combine the .OBJ files for each module when it creates the .EXE file. In this case, the resulting .EXE file will contain all of the code found in all of the .OBJ files. Static linking is also the way that C/C++ runtime library functions, which are stored in .LIB files, are included in your programs.

In contrast, dynamic linking takes place when your program is executed rather than when it is compiled, and the code for dynamically linked functions does not appear in your program's .EXE file. Dynamically linked functions are stored in a .DLL file that is separate from the rest of your program. The contents of the DLL are added to your program when it is run.

Two Varieties of Dynamic Linking

There are two varieties of dynamic linking: *load-time* and *runtime*. Load-time dynamic linking is the most common and it is the type of dynamic linking that will be used in the first part of this chapter. When using load-time dynamic linking, DLL-based functions that are called by your program are automatically loaded when your program is loaded into memory for execution. An *import library* that contains loading instructions for the DLL is required and this library must be included in the link when you compile a program that uses the DLL.

Runtime dynamic linking allows you to manually load a dynamic link library during the execution of your program. To do this, you will use a function such as **LoadLibrary( )**. Because you are manually loading the DLL, no import library is required. Runtime dynamic linking is useful when a program needs to call functions that are known only at runtime. For most dynamic linking situations, however, load-time DLLs are a better option. An example that uses runtime dynamic linking concludes this chapter.

Whether you use load-time or runtime dynamic linking, the DLL is built in the same way. It is only how that library is loaded that changes. Furthermore, this is determined by the programs that use the DLL, and not the DLL itself.

Remember: If your program explicitly calls a DLL-based function, then that function will be dynamically loaded automatically at load-time. No further action on the part of your program is required. Runtime dynamic linking is needed only when your program wants to load a DLL function that is not explicitly called.

Why Create a DLL?

You might be wondering why you would want to create your own dynamic link library. Frankly, for small programs there are no advantages. It is just easier to link all of the functions used by your program at compile time. However, for large software systems, involving several components that share a custom function library, the advantages can be enormous. For example:

◆ Placing functions in a DLL reduces the size of each component because the functions are not duplicated in each program when stored on disk. Although disk space is currently plentiful and cheap, it is still wrong to waste it.

◆ Using DLLs makes upgrades easier. When a function stored in a normal library is changed, each program that uses that function must be relinked. When using dynamic linking, only the DLL file must be recompiled. All applications that use that DLL will automatically use the new version of the function the next time they are executed.

◆ Using DLLs can make it easier to fix code "in the field." For example, if you have a misbehaving, mission-critical program, it is far easier to download a repaired dynamic link library than it is to download the entire application. This is quite important for programs used in remote environments, such as spacecraft, unmanned monitoring posts, and the like.

Of course, nothing is without its costs. The downside to using your own DLLs is that your program is now in two (or more) pieces. This makes the management of that program harder and does open up some failure paths. For example, if the dynamic link library is out of sync with the application, trouble is sure to follow. That said, when building large software systems, the benefits of dynamic linking exceed its negatives.

DLL Basics

There are a few rules that apply to building and using DLLs with which you need to be familiar. First, any function contained in a DLL that will be called by code outside the DLL must be *exported*. Second, in order for a program to call a function contained in a DLL, the program must *import* it. When using C/C++, export is accomplished using the **dllexport** keyword and import is done with **dllimport**. **dllexport** and **dllimport** are extended keywords supported by both Microsoft Visual C++ and Borland C++.

PROGRAMMER'S NOTE: *In Windows 3.1, functions exported from DLLs had to be specified in the EXPORTS section of the .DEF file associated with the DLL. Although this is still allowed, **dllexport** provides a more convenient alternative.*

The **dllexport** and **dllimport** keywords cannot be used by themselves. Instead, they need to be preceded by another extended keyword: _ _**declspec**. Its general form is shown here:

_ _declspec(*specifier*)

where *specifier* is a storage class specifier. For DLLs, *specifier* will be either **dllexport** or **dllimport**. For example, to export a function called **MyFunc( )**, you would use a line like this:

```
__declspec(dllexport) void MyFunc(int a)
```

To simplify the syntax of declaring imported and exported functions, most programmers create a macro name that can be substituted for the rather long _ _**declspec** specification. For example:

```
#define DllExport __declspec (dllexport)
```

Now, **MyFunc( )** can be exported using this simpler statement:

```
DllExport void MyFunc(int a)
```

If your DLL is compiled as a C++ program and you want it to also be able to be used by C programs, then you will need to add the "C" linkage specification, as shown here:

```
#define DllExport extern "C" __declspec (dllexport)
```

This prevents the standard C++ name mangling (also called *name decoration*) from taking place. Name mangling is the process by which the name of a function is modified to include type-related information. This process is used to distinguish between different forms of overloaded functions, between member functions of different classes, functions in different name spaces, and so on. We will include the C linkage specification for the examples in this book to avoid any possible troubles in this regard. (If you are compiling C programs, then do not add **extern "C"** since it isn't needed and it will not be accepted by the compiler.)

As it must for any other library function that your program uses, your program must include the prototypes to functions contained in a DLL. This is why you must include **windows.h** in all Windows programs, for example. The easiest way to include prototypes for the functions in your DLL is to create a companion header file.

When compiling a DLL, you must tell the compiler that a DLL is being created. To do this, simply specify that you are creating a DLL when creating a new project. If you are unsure about what compiler options to set, refer to your compiler's documentation. (Instructions for Visual C++ are given for the programs in this book.)

After you have compiled a DLL, two files will be present. One will contain the DLL functions and will use the .DLL extension. The other will contain loading information for the functions and it will use the .LIB extension. This is the import library that is required for load-time dynamic linking. You must link this library file with any program that will be calling functions contained within your DLL.

The .DLL file must be in a directory where it will be found when your application is loaded. Windows searches for DLLs in the following sequence. It first searches the directory that held the application. Next, it looks in the current working directory. Then it examines the standard DLL directory. Next, it searches the Windows directory. Finally, it searches any directories specified in the PATH variable. It is strongly suggested that when you are experimenting with DLLs, you keep them in the same directory as the application and not in any of the standard directories. This way, you avoid any chance of accidentally overwriting a DLL that is used by your system's software.

If a program requires a DLL that cannot be found, the program will not be executed and a message box will be displayed on the screen.

Using DllMain( )

Some DLLs will require special startup or shutdown code. To allow for this, all DLLs have a function called **DllMain( )** that is called when the DLL is being initialized or terminated. This function is defined by you, in your dynamic link library source file. However, if you don't define this function, then a default version is automatically provided by the compiler.

DllMain( ) has the following prototype:

BOOL WINAPI DllMain(HINSTANCE *hInstance*, ULONG *What*,
                    LPVOID *NotUsed*);

When this function is called by Windows, *hInstance* is the instance handle of the DLL, *What* specifies what action is occurring, and *NotUsed* is reserved. The function must return non-zero if successful and zero on failure.

The value in *What* will be one of the following:

Value	Meaning
DLL_PROCESS_ATTACH	Process is beginning use of DLL.
DLL_PROCESS_DETACH	Proccess is releasing DLL.
DLL_THREAD_ATTACH	Process has created a new thread.
DLL_THREAD_DETACH	Process has destroyed a thread.

When *What* contains **DLL_PROCESS_ATTACH**, it means that a process has loaded the DLL. (In technical terms, it means that the library has been mapped into the process' address space.) If **DllMain( )** returns zero in response to this action, the process attempting to attach to the DLL is terminated. For each process that uses the DLL, **DllMain( )** will only be called once with **DLL_PROCESS_ATTACH**.

When *What* contains **DLL_PROCESS_DETACH**, the process no longer needs the DLL. This typically occurs when the process itself terminates. It also occurs when a DLL is being explicitly released.

When a process that has already attached a DLL creates a new thread, then **DllMain( )** will be called with **DLL_THREAD_ATTACH**. When a thread is destroyed, **DllMain( )** is called with **DLL_THREAD_DETACH**. Multiple thread attach and detach messages can be generated by a single process.

In general, your implementation of **DllMain( )** must take appropriate action, based upon the contents of *What*, whenever it is called. Of course, such appropriate action may be to do nothing other than return non-zero.

Creating a DLL Version of WinPrintf( )

In Chapter 3 we developed several text-based output functions, including **WinPrintf( )**, a Windows version of **printf( )**. Here we will transform that function into a DLL. The principal advantage to putting **WinPrintf( )** into a DLL is that it will be available to any program that wants to use it without having to duplicate its code in each program's .EXE file. Of course, the **WinPrntf.dll** file must be present on the system.

PROGRAMMER'S NOTE: *You might want to try converting the other text-output functions described in Chapter 3 into DLLs. Just follow the same approach as that used here.*

Code

WinPrntf.cpp

Here is the code to the DLL version of **WinPrintf( )**. To compile this code, create a DLL project. For Visual C++, select Win32 Dynamic-Link Library in the Projects tab of the New dialog box. Next, compile the library. This will result in these two files being created: **WinPrntf.dll** and **WinPrntf.lib**. As explained, the .DLL file will contain the dynamic link library, itself. The .LIB file will contain the import library that must be linked with any application that calls **WinPrintf( )**.

```cpp
// WinPrntf.cpp - A DLL version of WinPrintf()
#include <windows.h>
#include <cstring>
#include <cstdio>

#define DllExport extern "C" __declspec (dllexport)

/* WinPrintf() is a general-purpose, window-based
   output function.

   HDC: specifies the device context in which output
        will occur.
   str: String containing characters and format codes.
*/

DllExport int WinPrintf(HDC hdc, char *str, ...)
{
  /* The following is needed to force floating-point
     support to be loaded. */
  double fp = 0.01;

  TEXTMETRIC tm;
  SIZE size;

  char result[1024]; // formatted text
  char chstr[2];     // string-ized character for output
  char *p;           // pointer to result

  int retval;      // holds return value
  int tabwidth;    // width in tab for current font
  int lineheight;  // height of a line of text
  static int X=0, Y=0; // current output location

  if(hdc == NULL) { // reset X and Y
    X = Y = 0;
    return 0;
  }

  va_list ptr; // get arg pointer
```

```
// point ptr to the first arg after str
va_start(ptr, str);

// pass args to vsprintf()
retval = vsprintf(result, str, ptr);

// get text metrics
GetTextMetrics(hdc, &tm);
tabwidth = 8 * tm.tmMaxCharWidth;
lineheight = tm.tmHeight + tm.tmExternalLeading;

chstr[1] = 0; // put a null at end of chstr

// now, output the string
p = result;
while(*p) {
  if(*p == '\n') { // advance to next line
    Y += lineheight;
    X = 0;
    p++;
  }
  else if(*p == '\t') { // process a tab
    X = ((X / tabwidth) * tabwidth) + tabwidth;
    p++;
  }
  else { // handle a normal char
    chstr[0] = *p;
    p++;

    TextOut(hdc, X, Y, chstr, 1); // output each char

    // advance to next character position
    GetTextExtentPoint32(hdc, chstr, 1, &size);
    X += size.cx;
  }
}

return retval;
}
```

The header file, **WinPrntf.h**, which must be included by any program that calls **WinPrintf( )**, is shown here:

```
#define DllImport extern "C" __declspec (dllimport)

DllImport void WinPrintf(HDC hdc, char *str, ...);
```

ANNOTATIONS

The code to **WinPrintf( )** itself was described in Chapter 3 and, with one exception, is unchanged. The exception is the following addition that occurs at the start of the function:

```
/* The following is needed to force floating-point
   support to be loaded. */
double fp = 0.01;
```

As the comment suggests, this code is needed to force the floating-point library to be loaded. Although **WinPrintf( )** does not itself use the floating-point library, it is needed if you use **WinPrintf( )** to output a floating-point value. Without this line (or something similar), the floating-point library is not available and you will receive a runtime error. This problem occurs with Visual C++, and it might occur with other compilers.

To make **WinPrintf( )** into a DLL is a simple matter: It must be exported. This is accomplished by first defining the macro **DllExport**, as shown here:

```
#define DllExport extern "C" __declspec (dllexport)
```

Next, **DllExport** is added to the declaration for **WinPrintf( )**, as shown next:

```
DllExport int WinPrintf(HDC hdc, char *str, ...)
```

Once this change has been made, the file **WinPrntf.cpp** can be compiled as a DLL.

Since **WinPrintf( )** requires no special initialization, there is no need to define **DllMain( )**; the default version is sufficient.

Demonstrating the WinPrintf( ) DLL

Here is the **WinPrintf( )** demonstration program from Chapter 3 that has been reworked to use **WinPrntf.dll**. It no longer contains the code for **WinPrintf( )** inline. Instead, only the header **WinPrntf.h** is included. The code for **WinPrintf( )** is loaded dynamically when the program is loaded.

WPDemo.cpp

Code

Here is the code to **WPDemo.cpp** that demonstrates the **WinPrintf( )** DLL. Since **WPDemo.cpp** explicitly calls **WinPrintf( )**, the program uses load-time dynamic linking. This means that you will need to include **WinPrntf.lib** in the link. Also, be sure that a copy of **WinPrntf.dll** is available in the current working directory.

```cpp
// WPDemo.cpp - Demonstrates the WinPrintf() DLL.

#include <windows.h>
#include <cstring>
#include "winprntf.h"

LRESULT CALLBACK WindowFunc(HWND, UINT, WPARAM, LPARAM);

char szWinName[] = "MyWin"; // name of window class

int WINAPI WinMain(HINSTANCE hThisInst, HINSTANCE hPrevInst,
                   LPSTR lpszArgs, int nWinMode)
{
  MSG msg;
  WNDCLASSEX wcl;
  HWND hwnd;

  // Define a window class.
  wcl.cbSize = sizeof(WNDCLASSEX);
  wcl.hInstance = hThisInst;
  wcl.lpszClassName = szWinName;
  wcl.lpfnWndProc = WindowFunc;
  wcl.style = 0; // default style
  wcl.hIcon = LoadIcon(NULL, IDI_APPLICATION); // large icon
  wcl.hIconSm = NULL; // use small version of large icon
  wcl.hCursor = LoadCursor(NULL, IDC_ARROW);
  wcl.hbrBackground = (HBRUSH) GetStockObject(WHITE_BRUSH);
  wcl.cbClsExtra = 0;
  wcl.cbWndExtra = 0;
  wcl.lpszMenuName = NULL; // no menu

  // Register the window class.
  if(!RegisterClassEx(&wcl)) return 0;

  // Create a window.
  hwnd = CreateWindow(szWinName,
```

```
                      "Demonstrating the WinPrintf DLL",
                      WS_OVERLAPPEDWINDOW,
                      CW_USEDEFAULT, CW_USEDEFAULT,
                      CW_USEDEFAULT, CW_USEDEFAULT,
                      NULL, NULL, hThisInst, NULL);


  // Display the window.
  ShowWindow(hwnd, nWinMode);
  UpdateWindow(hwnd);

  // The message loop.
  while(GetMessage(&msg, NULL, 0, 0))
  {
    TranslateMessage(&msg);
    DispatchMessage(&msg);
  }
  return msg.wParam;
}

// The window procedure.
LRESULT CALLBACK WindowFunc(HWND hwnd, UINT message,
                            WPARAM wParam, LPARAM lParam)

{
  HDC hdc;
  PAINTSTRUCT ps;

  switch(message) {
    case WM_PAINT:
      hdc = BeginPaint(hwnd, &ps);

      WinPrintf(NULL, ""); // reset X and Y

      WinPrintf(hdc, "%d + %d = %d\n", 8, 9, 8+9);
      WinPrintf(hdc, "Current balance is: $%7.2f\n", 42343.79);
      WinPrintf(hdc, "This is a test. ");
      WinPrintf(hdc, "This is on the same line.\n");
      WinPrintf(hdc, "Tabs\tare \tnow\texpanded.\n");
      WinPrintf(hdc, "Some\tmore\ttab\texamples.\n");

      EndPaint(hwnd, &ps);
      break;
    case WM_DESTROY:
      PostQuitMessage(0);
```

```
      break;
   default:
     return DefWindowProc(hwnd, message, wParam, lParam);
   }
   return 0;
}
```

ANNOTATIONS

This program demonstrates **WinPrntf.dll**. In order to call **WinPrintf( )**, **WPDemo.cpp** includes the header **WinPrntf.h**, which contains the **WinPrintf( )** import declaration. When the program is loaded for execution, **WinPrintf( )** is automatically loaded from its DLL. Once this has been done, **WinPrintf( )** is called in the normal fashion.

Creating a Mouse Manager DLL

In Chapter 6 we created a mouse manager subsystem that let you set the number of mouse trails and the double-click speed and swap the mouse buttons. Here we will transform that subsystem into a DLL. This requires a bit more work than that required to make **WinPrintf( )** into a DLL because the mouse manager activates a dialog box and processes messages from that box. We will also be making use of **DllMain( )**.

PROGRAMMER'S NOTE: *You might want to try converting the keyboard control panel described in Chapter 6 into a DLL. Just follow the same approach as that used here.*

Code

MouseMan.cpp

Here is the code to **MouseMan.cpp**, the DLL-based mouse manager. It contains three functions, **DllMain( )**, **MouseManager( )**, and **MousePanel( )**. To activate the mouse control panel, a program will call **MouseManager( )**, which activates the mouse control panel, using **MousePanel( )** as the dialog box window function.

To compile **MouseMan.cpp** using Visual C++, create a DLL program by selecting Win32 Dynamic Link Library in the Projects tab of the New dialog box. Next, compile the library. This will result in these two files being created: **MouseMan.dll** and **MouseMan.lib**. As explained, the .DLL file will contain the dynamic link library itself. The .LIB file contains the import library that must be linked with any application that calls **MouseManager( )**.

PROGRAMMER'S NOTE: *Because MouseMan.cpp uses the trackbar common control, you must include ComCtl32.lib in the link.*

```
// MouseMan.cpp - A mouse manager DLL.
#include <windows.h>
#include <commctrl.h>
#include <cstring>
#include <cstdio>
#include "mmanager.h"

#define DllExport extern "C" __declspec (dllexport)
BOOL CALLBACK MousePanel(HWND hdwnd, UINT message,
                         WPARAM wParam, LPARAM lParam);


HINSTANCE hInst;

// Use DllMain() to save the instance handle.
BOOL WINAPI DllMain(HINSTANCE hInstance, ULONG what,
                    LPVOID Notused)
{

  if(what == DLL_PROCESS_ATTACH)
    hInst = hInstance; // save instance handle

  return 1;
}

/* MouseManager manages the mouse

   hwnd: Window handle of calling application.

*/
DllExport void MouseManager(HWND hwnd)
{
  INITCOMMONCONTROLSEX cc;

  // Initialize the common controls.
  cc.dwSize = sizeof(INITCOMMONCONTROLSEX);
  cc.dwICC = ICC_BAR_CLASSES;
  InitCommonControlsEx(&cc);

  DialogBox(hInst, "MouseDB", hwnd,
            (DLGPROC) MousePanel);
}

// Mouse Manager dialog box.
```

```
BOOL CALLBACK MousePanel(HWND hdwnd, UINT message,
                         WPARAM wParam, LPARAM lParam)
{
  char str[80];
  HDC hdc;
  PAINTSTRUCT paintstruct;

  static unsigned orgDblClk;
  static unsigned orgTrails;
  static int orgBswap;

  static HWND hTrackTrails;
  static HWND hTrackDblClk;

  unsigned trackpos;
  int low=1, high=10;

  switch(message) {
    case WM_INITDIALOG:
      // create double-click track bar
      orgDblClk = GetDoubleClickTime();
      hTrackDblClk = CreateWindow(TRACKBAR_CLASS,
                  "",
                  WS_CHILD | WS_VISIBLE | WS_TABSTOP |
                  TBS_AUTOTICKS | WS_BORDER,
                  2, 2,
                  200, 28,
                  hdwnd,
                  NULL,
                  hInst,
                  NULL
      );
      SendMessage(hTrackDblClk, TBM_SETRANGE,
                  1, MAKELONG(low, high));
      SendMessage(hTrackDblClk, TBM_SETPOS,
                  1, orgDblClk / 100);


      // create mouse trails track bar
      SystemParametersInfo(SPI_GETMOUSETRAILS,
                        NULL, &orgTrails, 0);
      if(orgTrails==0) orgTrails = 1;
      hTrackTrails = CreateWindow(TRACKBAR_CLASS,
```

```
                "",
                WS_CHILD | WS_VISIBLE | WS_TABSTOP |
                TBS_AUTOTICKS | WS_BORDER,
                2, 62,
                200, 28,
                hdwnd,
                NULL,
                hInst,
                NULL
    );
    SendMessage(hTrackTrails, TBM_SETRANGE,
            1, MAKELONG(low, high));
    SendMessage(hTrackTrails, TBM_SETPOS,
            1, orgTrails);


    // set double-click time in edit box
    SetDlgItemInt(hdwnd, IDD_EB1, orgDblClk, 1);

    // set mouse trails in edit box
    SetDlgItemInt(hdwnd, IDD_EB2, orgTrails-1, 1);

    // determine original swap-state of buttons
    orgBswap = SwapMouseButton(false);
    SwapMouseButton(orgBswap);

    // set button swap check box
    SendDlgItemMessage(hdwnd, IDD_CB1, BM_SETCHECK,
                    orgBswap, 0);

    return 1;
case WM_HSCROLL: // a track bar was activated
    if(hTrackTrails == (HWND)lParam) {
      switch(LOWORD(wParam)) {
        case TB_TOP:
        case TB_BOTTOM:        // For this example
        case TB_LINEUP:        // all messages will be
        case TB_LINEDOWN:      // processed in the same
        case TB_THUMBPOSITION: // way.
        case TB_THUMBTRACK:
        case TB_PAGEUP:
        case TB_PAGEDOWN:
          trackpos = SendMessage(hTrackTrails,
```

```
                                    TBM_GETPOS, 0, 0);
          SetDlgItemInt(hdwnd, IDD_EB2, trackpos-1, 1);
          SystemParametersInfo(SPI_SETMOUSETRAILS,
                                   trackpos, 0, 0);
          return 1;
      }
    }
    else if(hTrackDblClk == (HWND)lParam) {
      switch(LOWORD(wParam)) {
        case TB_TOP:
        case TB_BOTTOM:         // For this example
        case TB_LINEUP:         // all messages will be
        case TB_LINEDOWN:       // processed in the same
        case TB_THUMBPOSITION: // way.
        case TB_THUMBTRACK:
        case TB_PAGEUP:
        case TB_PAGEDOWN:
          trackpos = SendMessage(hTrackDblClk,
                         TBM_GETPOS, 0, 0);
          SetDlgItemInt(hdwnd, IDD_EB1,
                         trackpos * 100, 1);
          SetDoubleClickTime(trackpos * 100);
          return 1;
      }
    }
    break;
  case WM_COMMAND:
    switch(LOWORD(wParam)) {
      case IDOK:
        EndDialog(hdwnd, 0);
        return 1;
      case IDCANCEL:
        SystemParametersInfo(SPI_SETMOUSETRAILS,
                                 orgTrails, 0, 0);
        SetDoubleClickTime(orgDblClk);

        if(orgBswap)
          SwapMouseButton(true);
        else
          SwapMouseButton(false);

        EndDialog(hdwnd, 1);
        return 1;
```

```
        case IDD_CB1:
          if(SendDlgItemMessage(hdwnd,
              IDD_CB1, BM_GETCHECK, 0, 0) == BST_CHECKED)
            SwapMouseButton(true);
          else
            SwapMouseButton(false);

          return 1;
        case IDD_EB1:
          // update double-click trackbar
          trackpos = GetDlgItemInt(hdwnd, IDD_EB1, NULL, 1) / 100;
          SendMessage(hTrackDblClk, TBM_SETPOS, 1, trackpos);
          SetDoubleClickTime(trackpos * 100);
          return 1;
        case IDD_EB2:
          // update mouse trails trackbar
          trackpos = GetDlgItemInt(hdwnd, IDD_EB2, NULL, 1);
          SendMessage(hTrackTrails, TBM_SETPOS, 1, trackpos+1);
          SystemParametersInfo(SPI_SETMOUSETRAILS,
                                trackpos+1, 0, 0);

          return 1;
      }
      break;
    case WM_PAINT:
      hdc = BeginPaint(hdwnd, &paintstruct);
      SetBkMode(hdc, TRANSPARENT);

      sprintf(str, "Set Double-Click Time");
      TextOut(hdc, 30, 34, str, strlen(str));

      sprintf(str, "Set Number of Trails");
      TextOut(hdc, 30, 92, str, strlen(str));

      EndPaint(hdwnd, &paintstruct);
      return 1;
  }
  return 0;
}
```

The **MouseMan.rc** resource file is shown here:

```
#include <windows.h>
#include "mmanager.h"
```

```
MouseDB DIALOG 18, 18, 126, 100
CAPTION "Mouse Manager"
STYLE DS_MODALFRAME | WS_POPUP | WS_CAPTION | WS_SYSMENU
{
  PUSHBUTTON "OK", IDOK, 30, 80, 30, 14,
           WS_CHILD | WS_VISIBLE | WS_TABSTOP
  PUSHBUTTON "Cancel", IDCANCEL, 70, 80, 30, 14,
           WS_CHILD | WS_VISIBLE | WS_TABSTOP
  EDITTEXT IDD_EB1, 105, 2, 20, 12, ES_LEFT | WS_CHILD |
         WS_VISIBLE | WS_BORDER
  EDITTEXT IDD_EB2, 105, 31, 12, 12, ES_LEFT | WS_CHILD |
         WS_VISIBLE | WS_BORDER
  AUTOCHECKBOX "Swap Buttons", IDD_CB1, 1, 60, 60, 10
}
```

The header file **MManager.h** is shown next:

```
#define IDD_CB1    400
#define IDD_EB1    500
#define IDD_EB2    501
```

Here is the **MouseMan.h** header file. This file must be included by any program that calls the **MouseManager( )** function.

```
#define DllImport extern "C" __declspec (dllimport)

DllImport void MouseManager(HWND hwnd);
```

ANNOTATIONS

The mouse manager uses the **MousePanel( )** dialog box function and the **MouseDB** dialog box resource template. These are the same as described in Chapter 6. Since **MousePanel( )** is not called from outside the DLL, it is not exported.

To activate the mouse control panel, your program calls **MouseManager( )**. This function does two things. First, it initializes the common controls by calling **InitCommonControlsEx( )**. This step is necessary because the mouse control panel uses trackbars, which are common controls. Second, **MouseManager( )** calls **DialogBox( )**, specifying the **MouseDB** resource template and the **MousePanel( )** dialog box function. This causes the mouse control panel to be displayed. Since **MouseManager( )** is called from outside the DLL, it must be exported.

MouseMan.cpp defines its own **DllMain( )**, which performs one important function: It saves the instance handle passed in **hInstance** into the global handle **hInst**. The instance handle is needed by **DialogBox( )** when creating the mouse control panel. Since no other messages are important to the mouse manager, they are ignored.

Demonstrating the Mouse Manager DLL

The **MMDemo.cpp** program demonstrates the mouse manager DLL by reworking the original code from Chapter 6.

MMDemo.cpp

Code

Here is the code for **MMDemo.cpp**. This program also uses load-time dynamic linking and you must include the import library **MouseMan.lib** in the link. Also, be sure that a copy of **MouseMan.dll** is available in the current working directory.

```
// MMDemo.cpp - Demonstrate the mouse manager DLL.

#include <windows.h>
#include "mmdemo.h"
#include "mouseman.h"

LRESULT CALLBACK WindowFunc(HWND, UINT, WPARAM, LPARAM);

char szWinName[] = "MyWin";

int WINAPI WinMain(HINSTANCE hThisInst, HINSTANCE hPrevInst,
                   LPSTR lpszArgs, int nWinMode)
{
  MSG msg;
  HWND hwnd;
  WNDCLASSEX wcl;
  HACCEL hAccel;

  // Define a window class.
  wcl.cbSize = sizeof(WNDCLASSEX);
  wcl.hInstance = hThisInst;
  wcl.lpszClassName = szWinName;
  wcl.lpfnWndProc = WindowFunc;
  wcl.style = CS_DBLCLKS; // enable double-clicks
  wcl.hIcon = LoadIcon(NULL, IDI_APPLICATION); // large icon
```

```
      wcl.hIconSm = NULL; // use small version of large icon
      wcl.hCursor = LoadCursor(NULL, IDC_ARROW);
      wcl.hbrBackground = (HBRUSH) GetStockObject(WHITE_BRUSH);
      wcl.cbClsExtra = 0;
      wcl.cbWndExtra = 0;
      wcl.lpszMenuName = "MouseMenu";

      // Register the window class.
      if(!RegisterClassEx(&wcl)) return 0;

      // Create a window.
      hwnd = CreateWindow(szWinName,
                          "Using The Mouse Control Panel DLL",
                          WS_OVERLAPPEDWINDOW,
                          CW_USEDEFAULT, CW_USEDEFAULT,
                          CW_USEDEFAULT, CW_USEDEFAULT,
                          NULL, NULL, hThisInst, NULL);

      // Load accelerators.
      hAccel = LoadAccelerators(hThisInst, "MouseMenu");

      // Display the window.
      ShowWindow(hwnd, nWinMode);
      UpdateWindow(hwnd);

      // The message loop.
      while(GetMessage(&msg, NULL, 0, 0))
      {
        if(!TranslateAccelerator(hwnd, hAccel, &msg)) {
          TranslateMessage(&msg);
          DispatchMessage(&msg);
        }
      }

      return msg.wParam;
}

// The window procedure.
LRESULT CALLBACK WindowFunc(HWND hwnd, UINT message,
                            WPARAM wParam, LPARAM lParam)
{
  int response;
```

```
HDC hdc;
char str[80];
switch(message) {
  case WM_COMMAND:
    switch(LOWORD(wParam)) {
      case IDM_DIALOG: // launch mouse manager
        MouseManager(hwnd);
        break;
      case IDM_EXIT:
        response = MessageBox(hwnd, "Quit the Program?",
                             "Exit", MB_YESNO);
        if(response == IDYES) PostQuitMessage(0);
        break;
      case IDM_ABOUT:
        MessageBox(hwnd, "Mouse Control Panel, V1.0",
                  "Mouse Control Panel", MB_OK);
        break;
    }
    break;
  case WM_LBUTTONDBLCLK:
    hdc = GetDC(hwnd);

    strcpy(str, "double-click");
    TextOut(hdc, 1, 1, str, strlen(str));

    ReleaseDC(hwnd, hdc);
    break;
  case WM_LBUTTONDOWN:
    hdc = GetDC(hwnd);

    strcpy(str, "single-click ");
    TextOut(hdc, 1, 1, str, strlen(str));

    ReleaseDC(hwnd, hdc);
    break;
  case WM_DESTROY:
    PostQuitMessage(0);
    break;
  default:
    return DefWindowProc(hwnd, message, wParam, lParam);
}
return 0;
}
```

Here is the **MMDemo.rc** resource file:

```
#include <windows.h>
#include "mmdemo.h"

MouseMenu MENU
{
  POPUP "&Options"
  {
    MENUITEM "&Mouse Manager\tF2", IDM_DIALOG
    MENUITEM "&Exit\tF3", IDM_EXIT
  }
  POPUP "&Help" {
    MENUITEM "&About\tF1", IDM_ABOUT
  }
}

MouseMenu ACCELERATORS
{
  VK_F2, IDM_DIALOG, VIRTKEY
  VK_F3, IDM_EXIT, VIRTKEY
  VK_F1, IDM_ABOUT, VIRTKEY
}
```

Here is the **MMDemo.h** header file:

```
#define IDM_DIALOG    100
#define IDM_EXIT      101
#define IDM_ABOUT     102
```

ANNOTATIONS

MMDemo.cpp works the same as the mouse control panel demonstration program described in Chapter 6. There are only slight differences. First, the header **MouseMan.h**, which contains the **MouseManager( )** import statement, is included. Second, a call to **MouseManager( )** is made when the user selects Options | Mouse Manager. In the previous version, a call to **DialogBox( )** was used to activate the mouse control panel directly.

Using Runtime Dynamic Linking

The foregoing programs have used load-time dynamic linking and this is the most common type of dynamic linking. As explained, with load-time dynamic linking, your program calls a DLL function by name and the DLL that contains that function is automatically loaded when the application is loaded.

Runtime dynamic linking works differently because the process of loading the DLL and calling a function contained within that DLL is handled manually by you. Runtime dynamic linking applies only to situations in which you do not know in advance what function you want to call. For example, you might have a program that calls a utility function that is specified by the user while the program is running. In such a situation, your program must manually load the DLL, obtain a pointer to the function that it wishes to use, and then call that function through the pointer. For runtime dynamic linking, no import library or import header file is needed.

At the core of runtime dynamic linking are these three functions:

HMODULE LoadLibrary(LPCSTR *DllName*);
BOOL FreeLibrary(HMODLUE *hMod*);
FARPROC GetProcAddress(HMODULE *hMod*, LPCSTR *FuncName*);

LoadLibrary( ) loads the DLL specified by *DllName* and returns a handle to it. **NULL** is returned on failure. **FreeLibrary( )** frees the DLL when it is no longer needed. It returns non-zero if successful and zero on failure. **GetProcAddress( )** returns a pointer to the function named by *FuncName* that is contained in the DLL specified by *hMod*. Using this pointer, you can then call the desired function. If the function is not found, a null pointer is returned. Be careful, though. The name of the function must match exactly the name specified within the DLL. C++ name mangling may distort function names. You might want to avoid this by using the C linkage specification when you create your DLL functions.

RTDemo.cpp

Code

To try runtime dynamic linking, run this version of the mouse manager demonstration program from the preceding section. It uses the **MMDemo.rc** resource file and the **MMDemo.h** header file shown earlier. It does not require **MouseMan.h**, however, and you no longer need to include **MouseMan.lib** in the link.

```
// RTDemo.cpp - Loading the mouse manager DLL at runtime.

#include <windows.h>
#include "mmdemo.h"
```

```
LRESULT CALLBACK WindowFunc(HWND, UINT, WPARAM, LPARAM);

char szWinName[] = "MyWin";

int WINAPI WinMain(HINSTANCE hThisInst, HINSTANCE hPrevInst,
                   LPSTR lpszArgs, int nWinMode)
{
  MSG msg;
  HWND hwnd;
  WNDCLASSEX wcl;
  HACCEL hAccel;

  // Define a window class.
  wcl.cbSize = sizeof(WNDCLASSEX);
  wcl.hInstance = hThisInst;
  wcl.lpszClassName = szWinName;
  wcl.lpfnWndProc = WindowFunc;
  wcl.style = CS_DBLCLKS; // enable double-clicks
  wcl.hIcon = LoadIcon(NULL, IDI_APPLICATION); // large icon
  wcl.hIconSm = NULL; // use small version of large icon
  wcl.hCursor = LoadCursor(NULL, IDC_ARROW);
  wcl.hbrBackground = (HBRUSH) GetStockObject(WHITE_BRUSH);
  wcl.cbClsExtra = 0;
  wcl.cbWndExtra = 0;
  wcl.lpszMenuName = "MouseMenu";

  // Register the window class.
  if(!RegisterClassEx(&wcl)) return 0;

  // Create a window.
  hwnd = CreateWindow(szWinName,
                      "Using The Mouse Control Panel DLL",
                      WS_OVERLAPPEDWINDOW,
                      CW_USEDEFAULT, CW_USEDEFAULT,
                      CW_USEDEFAULT, CW_USEDEFAULT,
                      NULL, NULL, hThisInst, NULL);

  // Load accelerators.
  hAccel = LoadAccelerators(hThisInst, "MouseMenu");

  // Display the window.
```

```
  ShowWindow(hwnd, nWinMode);
  UpdateWindow(hwnd);

  // The message loop.
  while(GetMessage(&msg, NULL, 0, 0))
  {
    if(!TranslateAccelerator(hwnd, hAccel, &msg)) {
      TranslateMessage(&msg);
      DispatchMessage(&msg);
    }
  }


  return msg.wParam;
}

// The window procedure.
LRESULT CALLBACK WindowFunc(HWND hwnd, UINT message,
                            WPARAM wParam, LPARAM lParam)
{
  int response;
  HDC hdc;
  char str[80];

  HMODULE hlib;    // handle to DLL
  void (*f)(HWND); // pointer to MouseManager()

  switch(message) {
    case WM_COMMAND:
      switch(LOWORD(wParam)) {
        case IDM_DIALOG: // launch mouse manager
          hlib = LoadLibrary("MouseMan.dll");
          if(!hlib) {
            MessageBox(hwnd, "Cannot load library.",
                             "Error", MB_OK);
            break;
          }

          // get pointer to MouseManager()
          f = (void (*)(HWND)) GetProcAddress(hlib, "MouseManager");
          if(!f) {
            MessageBox(hwnd, "Cannot load function.",
                             "Error", MB_OK);
            break;
```

```
        }

        // call MouseManager() through f
        f(hwnd);

        // free the DLL
        FreeLibrary(hlib);
        break;
      case IDM_EXIT:
        response = MessageBox(hwnd, "Quit the Program?",
                              "Exit", MB_YESNO);
        if(response == IDYES) PostQuitMessage(0);
        break;
      case IDM_ABOUT:
        MessageBox(hwnd, "Mouse Control Panel, V1.0",
                   "Mouse Control Panel", MB_OK);
        break;
    }
    break;
  case WM_LBUTTONDBLCLK:
    hdc = GetDC(hwnd);

    strcpy(str, "double-click");
    TextOut(hdc, 1, 1, str, strlen(str));

    ReleaseDC(hwnd, hdc);
    break;
  case WM_LBUTTONDOWN:
    hdc = GetDC(hwnd);

    strcpy(str, "single-click ");
    TextOut(hdc, 1, 1, str, strlen(str));

    ReleaseDC(hwnd, hdc);
    break;
  case WM_DESTROY:
    PostQuitMessage(0);
    break;
  default:
    return DefWindowProc(hwnd, message, wParam, lParam);
  }
  return 0;
}
```

ANNOTATIONS

In **RTDemo.cpp**, the **MouseManager( )** function is not called by name in the program. Instead, its DLL is manually loaded and the function is called via a pointer. The first change to notice is that the header **MouseMan.h** is no longer included. Since **MouseManager( )** is not called explicitly, there is no need to include its import declaration.

The other changes necessary to load the **MouseMan.dll** at runtime are in **WindowFunc( )**. First, notice the addition of these two variables.

```
HMODULE hlib;      // handle to DLL
void (*f)(HWND); // pointer to MouseManager()
```

The handle to the DLL will be stored in **hlib**, and **f** will point to **MouseManager( )** after it has been loaded.

The library is loaded and **MouseManager( )** is called when the user selects Options | Mouse Manager. This is processed by the **IDM_DIALOG** handler shown here:

```
case IDM_DIALOG: // launch mouse manager
  hlib = LoadLibrary("MouseMan.dll");
  if(!hlib) {
    MessageBox(hwnd, "Cannot load library.",
                     "Error", MB_OK);
    break;
  }

  // get pointer to MouseManager()
  f = (void (*)(HWND)) GetProcAddress(hlib, "MouseManager");
  if(!f) {
    MessageBox(hwnd, "Cannot load function.",
                     "Error", MB_OK);
    break;
  }

  // call MouseManager() through f
  f(hwnd);

  // free the DLL
  FreeLibrary(hlib);
  break;
```

As you can see, this version of **IDM_DIALOG** is substantially different than the one in **MMDemo.cpp**. First, the **MouseMan.dll** library is loaded by the call to **LoadLibrary( )**. If the library cannot be found, the error is reported. Next, the address of **MouseManager( )** is obtained by calling **GetProcAddress( )**, and this address is assigned to **f**. If the function cannot be found, an error is reported. Then, **MouseManager( )** is called through **f**. Finally, the library is released by calling **FreeLibrary( )**.

As this program illustrates, through the use of runtime dynamic linking it is possible to load and execute any function contained within any DLL. This makes runtime dynamic linking quite powerful. It also makes it a bit dangerous when the consequences of executing a function are unknown!

Tips for Using MFC

DLLs are easily produced using MFC. There is one important difference to be aware of, however. You must not declare your own **DllMain( )** function. Instead, perform initialization and shutdown operations in **CWinApp::InitInstance( )** and **CWinApp::ExitInstance( )**. MFC handles **DllMain( )** for you.

CHAPTER 12

Odds and Ends

This book ends with three simple, yet useful utilities that don't fit into any of the preceding chapters. They are

◆ A memory usage monitor

◆ An alarm clock

◆ A multiple-monitor demonstrator

Although each utility provides a function that is available in one form or another through more sophisticated accessories, each offers the advantages of being lightweight, readily adaptable, and convenient. In programming, one often finds that the best tools are those that are the easiest to use.

A Memory Monitor

When debugging or optimizing programs it is common to employ a performance analyzer that shows how your program uses various system resources. While such an analyzer is very useful, sometimes all you want to know is how your program is using memory. For example, you might want to see how memory is impacted when various functions execute, when certain resources are used, or when checking for memory leaks. For these and other situations, the memory monitor developed in this section is a perfect solution. Because it is so small, its impact on your system is slight—you can just let it run in a corner of the screen while you test your programs.

Information about memory and its current usage is obtained by calling **GlobalMemoryStatus( )**, shown here:

VOID GlobalMemoryStatus(MEMORYSTATUS *MemStat);

MemStat is a pointer to a structure of type **MEMORYSTATUS** that will be filled with information about the state of the system memory.

MEMORYSTATUS is defined like this:

```
typedef struct _MEMORYSTATUS {
  DWORD dwLength;
  DWORD dwMemoryLoad;
  DWORD dwTotalPhys;
  DWORD dwAvailPhys;
  DWORD dwTotalPageFile;
  DWORD dwAvailPageFile;
  DWORD dwTotalVirtual;
  DWORD dwAvailVirtual;
} MEMORYSTATUS;
```

The length of **MEMORYSTATUS** is contained in **dwLength** after the call to **GlobalMemoryStatus( )** returns. Its value before the call is ignored and it does not need to be set in advance.

The percentage of physical memory currently in use is returned in **dwMemoryLoad**. The amount of physical memory installed in the computer is returned in **dwTotalPhys**. The amount of that memory that is free is returned in **dwAvailPhys**.

The largest possible size of the paging file is returned in **dwTotalPageFile**. The amount of the paging file that is free is returned in **dwAvailPageFile**.

The amount of virtual memory is returned in **dwTotalVirt**. The amount of that memory that is free is returned in **dwAvailVirt**.

MemMon.cpp

Code

Here is the code for **MemMon.cpp**. To use the program, just execute it. It displays the current memory usage, updated every quarter-second. By default, it displays information about the physical memory; but, if you check Show Virtual Memory in the Options menu, then virtual memory usage is also shown. Sample output is shown in Figure 12-1.

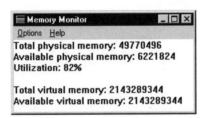

FIGURE 12-1. Sample output from **MemMon.cpp**

```
// MemMon.cpp -- A memory monitor.

#include <windows.h>
#include <cstdio>
#include "memmon.h"

LRESULT CALLBACK WindowFunc(HWND, UINT, WPARAM, LPARAM);
int WinPrintf(HDC hdc, char *str, ...);
```

```
char szWinName[] = "MyWin";

int WINAPI WinMain(HINSTANCE hThisInst, HINSTANCE hPrevInst,
                   LPSTR lpszArgs, int nWinMode)
{
  MSG msg;
  HWND hwnd;
  WNDCLASSEX wcl;
  HACCEL hAccel;

  // Define a window class.
  wcl.cbSize = sizeof(WNDCLASSEX);
  wcl.hInstance = hThisInst;
  wcl.lpszClassName = szWinName;
  wcl.lpfnWndProc = WindowFunc;
  wcl.style = 0; // default style
  wcl.hIcon = LoadIcon(NULL, IDI_APPLICATION); // large icon
  wcl.hIconSm = NULL; // use small version of large icon
  wcl.hCursor = LoadCursor(NULL, IDC_ARROW);
  wcl.hbrBackground = (HBRUSH) GetStockObject(WHITE_BRUSH);
  wcl.cbClsExtra = 0;
  wcl.cbWndExtra = 0;
  wcl.lpszMenuName = "MemoryMenu";

  // Register the window class.
  if(!RegisterClassEx(&wcl)) return 0;

  // Create a window.
  hwnd = CreateWindow(szWinName,
                      "Memory Monitor",
                      WS_OVERLAPPEDWINDOW,
                      CW_USEDEFAULT, CW_USEDEFAULT,
                      275, 100,
                      NULL, NULL, hThisInst, NULL);

  // Load accelerators.
  hAccel = LoadAccelerators(hThisInst, "MemoryMenu");

  // Display the window.
  ShowWindow(hwnd, nWinMode);
  UpdateWindow(hwnd);

  // The message loop.
```

```
  while(GetMessage(&msg, NULL, 0, 0))
  {
    if(!TranslateAccelerator(hwnd, hAccel, &msg)) {
      TranslateMessage(&msg);
      DispatchMessage(&msg);
    }
  }

  return msg.wParam;
}

// The window procedure.
LRESULT CALLBACK WindowFunc(HWND hwnd, UINT message,
                           WPARAM wParam, LPARAM lParam)
{
  int response;
  RECT r;
  HMENU hmenu, hsubmenu;
  HDC hdc;
  MEMORYSTATUS mem;
  static unsigned int timer;
  static bool virtmem = false;

  switch(message) {
    case WM_CREATE:
      timer = SetTimer(hwnd, 1, 250, NULL);
      break;
    case WM_COMMAND:
      switch(LOWORD(wParam)) {
        case IDM_SHOWVIRT:
          virtmem = !virtmem; // reverse state of flag
          GetWindowRect(hwnd, &r); // get current location

          // get handle to 1st submenu
          hmenu = GetMenu(hwnd);
          hsubmenu = GetSubMenu(hmenu, 0);

          // set or clear virtual memory option and adjust size of window
          if(virtmem) {
            CheckMenuItem(hsubmenu, IDM_SHOWVIRT, MF_CHECKED);
            MoveWindow(hwnd, r.left, r.top, 275, 150, 1);
          }
          else {
```

```
        CheckMenuItem(hsubmenu, IDM_SHOWVIRT, MF_UNCHECKED);
        MoveWindow(hwnd, r.left, r.top, 275, 100, 1);
      }

      break;
    case IDM_EXIT:
      response = MessageBox(hwnd, "Quit the Program?",
                            "Exit", MB_YESNO);
      if(response == IDYES) PostQuitMessage(0);
      break;
    case IDM_ABOUT:
      MessageBox(hwnd, "Memory Monitor, V1.0",
                "Memory Monitor", MB_OK);
      break;
  }
  break;
case WM_TIMER:
  hdc = GetDC(hwnd);

  // get current memory status
  GlobalMemoryStatus(&mem);

  WinPrintf(NULL, ""); // reset output

  WinPrintf(hdc, "Total physical memory: %ld\n",
          mem.dwTotalPhys);
  WinPrintf(hdc, "Available physical memory: %ld\n",
          mem.dwAvailPhys);
  WinPrintf(hdc, "Utilization: %ld%%\n\n", mem.dwMemoryLoad);

  if(virtmem) {
    WinPrintf(hdc, "Total virtual memory: %ld\n",
            mem.dwTotalVirtual);
    WinPrintf(hdc, "Available virtual memory: %ld\n",
            mem.dwTotalVirtual);
  }

  ReleaseDC(hwnd, hdc);
  break;
case WM_DESTROY:
  KillTimer(hwnd, timer);
  PostQuitMessage(0);
  break;
```

```
    default:
      return DefWindowProc(hwnd, message, wParam, lParam);
  }
  return 0;
}

// A general-purpose, window-based output function.
int WinPrintf(HDC hdc, char *str, ...)
{
  TEXTMETRIC tm;
  SIZE size;

  char result[1024]; // formatted text
  char chstr[2];     // string-ized character for output
  char *p;           // pointer to result

  int retval;        // holds return value
  int tabwidth;      // width in tab for current font
  int lineheight;    // height of a line of text
  static int X=0, Y=0; // current output location

  if(hdc == NULL) { // reset X and Y
    X = Y = 0;
    return 0;
  }

  va_list ptr; // get arg pointer

  // point ptr to the first arg after str
  va_start(ptr, str);

  // pass args to vsprintf()
  retval = vsprintf(result, str, ptr);

  // get text metrics
  GetTextMetrics(hdc, &tm);
  tabwidth = 8 * tm.tmMaxCharWidth;
  lineheight = tm.tmHeight + tm.tmExternalLeading;

  chstr[1] = 0; // put a null at end of chstr

  // now, output the string
  p = result;
```

```
while(*p) {
  if(*p == '\n') { // advance to next line
    Y += lineheight;
    X = 0;
    p++;
  }
  else if(*p == '\t') { // process a tab
    X = ((X / tabwidth) * tabwidth) + tabwidth;
    p++;
  }
  else { // handle a normal char
    chstr[0] = *p;
    p++;

    TextOut(hdc, X, Y, chstr, 1); // output each char

    // advance to next character position
    GetTextExtentPoint32(hdc, chstr, 1, &size);
    X += size.cx;
  }
}

return retval;
}
```

The **MemMon.rc** resource file is shown here:

```
#include <windows.h>
#include "memmon.h"

MemoryMenu MENU
{
  POPUP "&Options"
  {
    MENUITEM "Show Virtual Memory\tF2", IDM_SHOWVIRT
    MENUITEM "&Exit\tCtrl+X", IDM_EXIT
  }
  POPUP "&Help" {
    MENUITEM "&About\tF1", IDM_ABOUT
  }
}

MemoryMenu ACCELERATORS
```

```
{
  "^X", IDM_EXIT
  VK_F2, IDM_SHOWVIRT, VIRTKEY
  VK_F1, IDM_ABOUT, VIRTKEY
}
```

The header file **MemMon.h** is shown next:

```
#define IDM_EXIT      100
#define IDM_ABOUT     101
#define IDM_SHOWVIRT  102
```

ANNOTATIONS

MemMon.cpp is straightforward. It starts a timer with a period of 250 milliseconds. (You can use a shorter timing interval if you like.) At the end of each period, it obtains and displays the current memory usage. Notice that the program utilizes the **WinPrintf( )** function developed in Chapter 3. (See Chapter 3 for a description.) Whether or not the virtual memory is displayed is determined by the state of the **virtmem** variable. The main action of the program takes place in the **WM_TIMER** and **IDM_SHOWVIRT** handlers. Each is examined in detail next.

The WM_TIMER Handler

At the end of each timing interval, the **WM_TIMER** handler, shown here, executes.

```
case WM_TIMER:
  hdc = GetDC(hwnd);

  // get current memory status
  GlobalMemoryStatus(&mem);

  WinPrintf(NULL, ""); // reset output

  WinPrintf(hdc, "Total physical memory: %ld\n",
          mem.dwTotalPhys);
  WinPrintf(hdc, "Available physical memory: %ld\n",
          mem.dwAvailPhys);
  WinPrintf(hdc, "Utilization: %ld%%\n\n", mem.dwMemoryLoad);

  if(virtmem) {
    WinPrintf(hdc, "Total virtual memory: %ld\n",
            mem.dwTotalVirtual);
    WinPrintf(hdc, "Available virtual memory: %ld\n",
```

```
                    mem.dwTotalVirtual);
  }


  ReleaseDC(hwnd, hdc);
  break;
```

First, a handle to the device context is obtained and the current memory status is retrieved. Next, **WinPrintf( )** is called with **NULL** as the first argument. As explained in Chapter 3, this causes **WinPrintf( )** to reset its output coordinates to the upper-left corner of the window. Next, the total and available physical memory is displayed, followed by the usage percentage. If the user has requested virtual memory information, then **virtmem** will be **true** and the total and available amount of virtual memory will also be displayed. Finally, the device context is released.

The IDM_SHOWVIRT Handler

When the user selects Show Virtual Memory from the Options menu, an **IDM_SHOWVIRT** command message is sent. It is handled by the following code:

```
case IDM_SHOWVIRT:
  virtmem = !virtmem; // reverse state of flag
  GetWindowRect(hwnd, &r); // get current location

  // get handle to 1st submenu
  hmenu = GetMenu(hwnd);
  hsubmenu = GetSubMenu(hmenu, 0);

  // set or clear virtual memory option and adjust size of window
  if(virtmem) {
    CheckMenuItem(hsubmenu, IDM_SHOWVIRT, MF_CHECKED);
    MoveWindow(hwnd, r.left, r.top, 275, 150, 1);
  }
  else {
    CheckMenuItem(hsubmenu, IDM_SHOWVIRT, MF_UNCHECKED);
    MoveWindow(hwnd, r.left, r.top, 275, 100, 1);
  }

  break;
```

Show Virtual Memory is handled as a toggled check menu item. Each time it is selected, its state changes. When the program begins, it is unchecked (off). The state of this item is reflected by the **virtmem** variable. Initially, **virtmem** is **false**. Each time the user selects Show Virtual Memory, the state of **virtmen** is reversed. Thus, when the user checks Show Virtual Memory, **virtmen** will be **true**.

Next, the current location (in screen coordinates) of the window is obtained by calling **GetWindowRect( )**. This information is needed because the size of the window will need to be adjusted. **GetWindowRect( )** has the following prototype:

BOOL GetWindowRect(HWND *hwnd*, RECT **rect*);

Here, *hwnd* specifies the window in question, and *rect* receives the coordinates of the upper-left and lower-right corners.

Next, a handle to the Options submenu is obtained. (The management of menus and submenus is described in detail in Chapter 1.) Then, depending upon the state of **virtmen**, the Show Virtual Memory menu item is either checked or cleared. Also, the size of the window is either enlarged (to show the virtual memory) or reduced (when the virtual memory is not wanted).

The window size is changed by calling **MoveWindow( )**, which allows you to specify a new position and dimensions for an existing window. Its prototype is shown here:

BOOL MoveWindow(HWND *hwnd*, int *UpX*, int *UpY*,
      int *width*, int *height*, BOOL *redraw*);

Here, *hwnd* is the handle of the window being moved. The window will be repositioned with its upper-left corner at the location specified by *UpX* and *UpY*. These coordinates are screen-relative. The new width and height are passed in *width* and *height*. If *redraw* is non-zero, then the contents of the window are repainted.

In the program, **MoveWindow( )** is called with the coordinates of the upper-left corner that were obtained from **GetWindowRect( )**. This ensures that the location of the window on the screen does not change. Only the height of the window is adjusted.

A Variation to Try

Here is a variation that you might want to try: Have the memory monitor update the display each time the memory usage changes, rather than relying on a timer. For some situations, this might prove beneficial.

Tips for Using MFC

The memory monitor can be easily converted to MFC. **GlobalMemoryStatus( )** is not encapsulated by MFC. **GetWindowRect( )** and **MoveWindow( )** are encapsulated by the **CWnd** class. **SetTimer( )** and **KillTimer( )** are also members of **CWnd**.

An Alarm Clock

If you have ever missed an important meeting, forgotten to make a conference call, or neglected to go to lunch, then you will find the alarm clock utility described in this section especially helpful!

The alarm clock program is very simple. It displays the current time and lets you set a target time. When the target time is reached, a bell is rung. If the alarm clock was minimized, its window is also restored when the alarm goes off. Only one option is supported: You can use either 12-hour or 24-hour time. Despite its simplicity, this simple utility has proven itself to be quite useful on a number of occasions.

AlarmClk.cpp

Code

Here is the code for **AlarmClk.cpp**. The program displays the current time. To set a target time, choose Alarm | Set Alarm. To switch between 12-hour and 24-hour times, use the Options menu. Sample output is shown in Figure 12-2.

FIGURE 12-2. Sample output from **AlarmClk.cpp**

```
// AlarmClk: A simple alarm clock program.

#include <windows.h>
#include <ctime>
#include <cstdio>
#include "alarmclk.h"

LRESULT CALLBACK WindowFunc(HWND, UINT, WPARAM, LPARAM);
BOOL CALLBACK SetAlarm(HWND hdwnd, UINT message,
                       WPARAM wParam, LPARAM lParam);

char szWinName[] = "MyWin"; // name of window class
```

```
char target[80] = "Not Set"; // target time
bool twelve_hour = true;

HINSTANCE hInst;

int WINAPI WinMain(HINSTANCE hThisInst, HINSTANCE hPrevInst,
                   LPSTR lpszArgs, int nWinMode)
{
  HWND hwnd;
  MSG msg;
  WNDCLASSEX wcl;
  HACCEL hAccel;

  // Define a window class.
  wcl.cbSize = sizeof(WNDCLASSEX);
  wcl.hInstance = hThisInst;
  wcl.lpszClassName = szWinName;
  wcl.lpfnWndProc = WindowFunc;
  wcl.style = 0; // default style
  wcl.hIcon = LoadIcon(NULL, IDI_APPLICATION); // large icon
  wcl.hIconSm = NULL; // use small version of large icon
  wcl.hCursor = LoadCursor(NULL, IDC_ARROW);
  wcl.hbrBackground = (HBRUSH) GetStockObject(WHITE_BRUSH);
  wcl.cbClsExtra = 0;
  wcl.cbWndExtra = 0;
  wcl.lpszMenuName = "AlarmMenu"; // specify class menu

  // Register the window class.
  if(!RegisterClassEx(&wcl)) return 0;

  hInst = hThisInst; // save instance handle

  // Create a window.
  hwnd = CreateWindow(szWinName, "Alarm Clock",
                      WS_OVERLAPPEDWINDOW,
                      CW_USEDEFAULT, CW_USEDEFAULT,
                      250, 100,
                      NULL, NULL, hThisInst, NULL);

  // Load keyboard accelerators.
  hAccel = LoadAccelerators(hThisInst, "AlarmMenu");
```

```
    // Display the window.
    ShowWindow(hwnd, nWinMode);
    UpdateWindow(hwnd);

    // The message loop.
    while(GetMessage(&msg, NULL, 0, 0))
    {
      if(!TranslateAccelerator(hwnd, hAccel, &msg)) {
        TranslateMessage(&msg);
        DispatchMessage(&msg);
      }
    }
    return msg.wParam;
}

// The window procedure.
LRESULT CALLBACK WindowFunc(HWND hwnd, UINT message,
                            WPARAM wParam, LPARAM lParam)
{
  HDC hdc;
  PAINTSTRUCT ps;
  HMENU hmenu, hsubmenu;
  int response;
  char timestr[80];
  time_t t_t;

  static tm *t;

  switch(message) {
    case WM_CREATE:
      // start timer
      SetTimer(hwnd, 1, 1000, NULL);

      // get current system time
      t_t = time(NULL);
      t = localtime(&t_t);
      break;
    case WM_TIMER: // update time
      t_t = time(NULL);
      t = localtime(&t_t);

      if(twelve_hour)
        strftime(timestr, 79, "%I:%M:%S %p", t);
```

```
    else
      strftime(timestr, 79, "%H:%M:%S", t);

  // see if target time has come
  if(!strcmp(target, timestr)) {
    MessageBeep(MB_OK);
    ShowWindow(hwnd, SW_RESTORE);
  }

  InvalidateRect(hwnd, NULL, 1);
  break;
case WM_COMMAND:
  switch(LOWORD(wParam)) {
    case IDM_EXIT:
      response = MessageBox(hwnd, "Quit the Program?",
                            "Exit", MB_YESNO);
      if(response == IDYES) PostQuitMessage(0);
      break;
    case IDM_12HOUR: // use 12 hour clock
      twelve_hour = true;

      // switch enabled states for Time menu
      hmenu = GetMenu(hwnd);
      hsubmenu = GetSubMenu(GetSubMenu(hmenu, 1), 0);

      // activate the 24-hour option
      EnableMenuItem(hsubmenu, IDM_24HOUR,
                  MF_BYCOMMAND | MF_ENABLED);

      // deactivate the 12-hour option
      EnableMenuItem(hsubmenu, IDM_12HOUR,
                  MF_BYCOMMAND | MF_GRAYED);

      InvalidateRect(hwnd, NULL, 1);
      break;
    case IDM_24HOUR: // use 24 hour clock
      twelve_hour = false;
        // switch enabled states for Time menu
      hmenu = GetMenu(hwnd);
```

```
          hsubmenu = GetSubMenu(GetSubMenu(hmenu, 1), 0);

          // activate the 12-hour option
          EnableMenuItem(hsubmenu, IDM_12HOUR,
                        MF_BYCOMMAND | MF_ENABLED);

          // deactivate the 24-hour option
          EnableMenuItem(hsubmenu, IDM_24HOUR,
                        MF_BYCOMMAND | MF_GRAYED);

          InvalidateRect(hwnd, NULL, 1);
          break;
        case IDM_SETTIME:
          DialogBox(hInst, "AlarmDB", hwnd, (DLGPROC) SetAlarm);
          break;
        case IDM_ABOUT:
          MessageBox(hwnd, "Alarm Clock V1.0",
                     "About", MB_OK);
          break;
      }
      break;
    case WM_PAINT:
      if(twelve_hour)
        strftime(timestr, 79, "Current time: %I:%M:%S %p", t);
      else
        strftime(timestr, 79, "Current time: %H:%M:%S", t);

      hdc = BeginPaint(hwnd, &ps);

      TextOut(hdc, 10, 10, timestr, strlen(timestr));

      strcpy(timestr, "Target time:");
      TextOut(hdc, 10, 30, timestr, strlen(timestr));

      strcpy(timestr, target);
      TextOut(hdc, 97, 30, timestr, strlen(timestr));

      EndPaint(hwnd, &ps);
      break;
    case WM_DESTROY:
      KillTimer(hwnd, 1);
      PostQuitMessage(0);
      break;
```

```
      default:
        return DefWindowProc(hwnd, message, wParam, lParam);
  }
  return 0;
}

// Set alarm dialog box.
BOOL CALLBACK SetAlarm(HWND hdwnd, UINT message,
                       WPARAM wParam, LPARAM lParam)
{
  int h, m, s;
  int ok;
  static int hmax = 12, hmin = 1;
  int pm;
  HWND hCB;

  switch(message) {
    case WM_INITDIALOG:
      SetDlgItemText(hdwnd, IDD_EB1, "00");
      SetDlgItemText(hdwnd, IDD_EB2, "00");
      SetDlgItemText(hdwnd, IDD_EB3, "00");

      hCB = GetDlgItem(hdwnd, IDD_CB1);
      if(twelve_hour) {
        hmax = 12;
        hmin = 1;
        EnableWindow(hCB, 1); // enable PM check box
      }
      else {
        hmax = 23;
        hmin = 0;
        EnableWindow(hCB, 0); // disable PM check box
      }

      return 1;
    case WM_COMMAND:
      switch(LOWORD(wParam)) {
        case IDCANCEL:
          EndDialog(hdwnd, 1);
          return 1;
        case IDOK:
          // get hour
          h = GetDlgItemInt(hdwnd, IDD_EB1, &ok, 0);
```

```
        if(!ok || h > hmax || h < hmin) {
            MessageBox(hdwnd, "Invalid Hour",
                        "Error", MB_OK);
            return 1;
        }

        // get minutes
        m = GetDlgItemInt(hdwnd, IDD_EB2, &ok, 0);
        if(!ok || m > 59) {
          MessageBox(hdwnd, "Invalid Minutes",
                        "Error", MB_OK);
            return 1;
        }

        // get seconds
        s = GetDlgItemInt(hdwnd, IDD_EB3, &ok, 0);
        if(!ok || s > 59) {
          MessageBox(hdwnd, "Invalid Seconds",
                        "Error", MB_OK);
            return 1;
        }

        // construct target time string
        sprintf(target, "%02d:%02d:%02d", h, m, s);

        // add AM or PM if needed
        if(twelve_hour) {
          pm = SendDlgItemMessage(hdwnd, IDD_CB1,
                                    BM_GETCHECK, 0, 0);
          if(pm == BST_CHECKED) strcat(target, " PM");
          else strcat(target, " AM");
        }

        EndDialog(hdwnd, 0);
        return 1;
      }
    }
  return 0;
}
```

The **AlarmClk.rc** resource file is shown next:

```
#include <windows.h>
#include "alarmclk.h"

AlarmMenu MENU
{
  POPUP "&Alarm"
  {
    MENUITEM "&Set Alarm\tF2", IDM_SETTIME
    MENUITEM "E&xit\tCtrl+X", IDM_EXIT
  }
  POPUP "&Options"
  {
    POPUP "&Time" {
      MENUITEM "&12 Hour\tF3", IDM_12HOUR, GRAYED
      MENUITEM "&24 Hour\tF4", IDM_24HOUR
    }
  }
  POPUP "&Help" {
    MENUITEM "&About\tF1", IDM_ABOUT
  }
}


AlarmMenu ACCELERATORS
{
  "^X",  IDM_EXIT
  VK_F2, IDM_SETTIME, VIRTKEY
  VK_F3, IDM_12HOUR, VIRTKEY
  VK_F4, IDM_24HOUR, VIRTKEY
  VK_F1, IDM_ABOUT, VIRTKEY
}


AlarmDB DIALOG 10, 10, 100, 80
CAPTION "Set Alarm"
STYLE DS_MODALFRAME | WS_POPUP | WS_CAPTION | WS_SYSMENU
{
  EDITTEXT IDD_EB1, 10, 12, 14, 12, ES_LEFT | WS_CHILD |
           WS_BORDER | WS_VISIBLE | WS_TABSTOP
  EDITTEXT IDD_EB2, 40, 12, 14, 12, ES_LEFT | WS_CHILD |
           WS_BORDER | WS_VISIBLE | WS_TABSTOP
  EDITTEXT IDD_EB3, 70, 12, 14, 12, ES_LEFT | WS_CHILD |
           WS_BORDER | WS_VISIBLE | WS_TABSTOP
  LTEXT "Enter Target Time", IDD_TEXT1, 20, 26, 80, 14,
```

```
 LTEXT "Hour", IDD_TEXT2, 10, 2, 20, 10,
 LTEXT "Min.", IDD_TEXT3, 40, 2, 20, 10,
 LTEXT "Sec.", IDD_TEXT4, 70, 2, 20, 10,
 AUTOCHECKBOX "PM", IDD_CB1, 10, 40, 30, 14,
 PUSHBUTTON "OK", IDOK, 34, 60, 30, 14,
         WS_CHILD | WS_VISIBLE | WS_TABSTOP
}
```

The **AlarmClk.h** header file is shown here:

```
#define IDM_EXIT        100
#define IDM_12HOUR      101
#define IDM_24HOUR      102
#define IDM_SETTIME     103
#define IDM_ABOUT       104

#define IDD_EB1         200
#define IDD_EB2         201
#define IDD_EB3         202
#define IDD_TEXT1       203
#define IDD_TEXT2       204
#define IDD_TEXT3       205
#define IDD_TEXT4       206
#define IDD_CB1         207
```

ANNOTATIONS

The operation of the alarm clock is straightforward. First, a timer is created with a period of one second. At the end of each interval, the current time is obtained and displayed. If the current time matches the target time, the alarm goes off. The time is set by the AlarmDB dialog box, which is handled by the **SetAlarm( )** function. This program reworks some of the menus from **DynMenu.cpp** in Chapter 1, which allow you to select either 12-hour or 24-hour time. Let's examine the key pieces of the utility individually.

The WM_TIMER Handler

At the end of each timing period a **WM_TIMER** message is sent and is handled by the following code:

```
case WM_TIMER: // update time
  t_t = time(NULL);
  t = localtime(&t_t);

  if(twelve_hour)
```

```
    strftime(timestr, 79, "%I:%M:%S %p", t);
  else
    strftime(timestr, 79, "%H:%M:%S", t);

  // see if target time has come
  if(!strcmp(target, timestr)) {
    MessageBeep(MB_OK);
    ShowWindow(hwnd, SW_RESTORE);
  }

  InvalidateRect(hwnd, NULL, 1);
  break;
```

First, the current time is obtained via the standard C/C++ time functions. Next, a string version of the time is created by calling **strftime( )**. The precise format of this string depends upon whether 12-hour or 24-hour time is being used.

The current time string is then compared against the target time string. If they match, the bell is sounded and the window is restored. Restoring the window allows you to run the clock in the background until the alarm goes off. Finally, the call to **InvalidateRect( )** updates the current time in the main window.

IDM_12HOUR and IDM_24HOUR Handlers

The **IDM_12HOUR** and **IDM_24HOUR** handlers process the user's time format selection in the Time menu. These handlers are the same as those used in Chapter 1. Refer there for details. In brief, here is what they do: The 12-Hour and 24-Hour menu items are mutually exclusive. Thus, the currently selected option is grayed. When the user selects the other time format, that menu item is grayed and the other is enabled. In both cases, the **twelve_hour** variable is set appropriately, with the value **true** meaning that a 12-hour clock has been selected.

SetAlarm( )

When the user sets the alarm, the Set Alarm dialog box is displayed. Messages from this box are processed by the **SetAlarm( )** dialog box function. Each message handler is described below.

WM_INITDIALOG   When the Set Alarm dialog box is first activated, its **WM_INITDIALOG** handler, shown here, is executed.

```
case WM_INITDIALOG:
  SetDlgItemText(hdwnd, IDD_EB1, "00");
  SetDlgItemText(hdwnd, IDD_EB2, "00");
  SetDlgItemText(hdwnd, IDD_EB3, "00");
```

```
hCB = GetDlgItem(hdwnd, IDD_CB1);
if(twelve_hour) {
  hmax = 12;
  hmin = 1;
  EnableWindow(hCB, 1); // enable PM check box
}
else {
  hmax = 23;
  hmin = 0;
  EnableWindow(hCB, 0); // disable PM check box
}

return 1;
```

This handler begins by initializing the hour, minutes, and seconds edit boxes to 00. This is done as a courtesy to the user and is not technically necessary. Next, the handle of the PM check box is obtained and stored in **hCB**. Then, the values of **hmax** and **hmin** are set, depending upon whether 12-hour or 24-hour time is being used. These values are used later to determine if the user has entered an appropriate value for the hour. Next, if 12-hour time is in effect, the PM check box is enabled; otherwise, it is disabled. When using 12-hour time, check the PM box to indicate that the target time is in the afternoon.

IDOK   When the user presses OK, the **IDOK** handler, shown here, executes.

```
case IDOK:
  // get hour
  h = GetDlgItemInt(hdwnd, IDD_EB1, &ok, 0);
  if(!ok || h > hmax || h < hmin) {
    MessageBox(hdwnd, "Invalid Hour",
               "Error", MB_OK);
    return 1;
  }

  // get minutes
  m = GetDlgItemInt(hdwnd, IDD_EB2, &ok, 0);
  if(!ok || m > 59) {
    MessageBox(hdwnd, "Invalid Minutes",
               "Error", MB_OK);
    return 1;
  }
```

```
// get seconds
s = GetDlgItemInt(hdwnd, IDD_EB3, &ok, 0);
if(!ok || s > 59) {
  MessageBox(hdwnd, "Invalid Seconds",
             "Error", MB_OK);
  return 1;
}

// construct target time string
sprintf(target, "%02d:%02d:%02d", h, m, s);

// add AM or PM if needed
if(twelve_hour) {
  pm = SendDlgItemMessage(hdwnd, IDD_CB1,
                          BM_GETCHECK, 0, 0);
  if(pm == BST_CHECKED) strcat(target, " PM");
  else strcat(target, " AM");
}

EndDialog(hdwnd, 0);
return 1;
```

First, the time the user entered is obtained from the edit boxes. In the process, the range of each value is checked. If any value is out of range, an error is reported and the Set Alarm dialog box is not closed. Otherwise, the values are used to construct the target-time string, which will include an AM/PM designation when 12-hour time is in effect. This string is put into the **target** array. Finally, the dialog box is closed.

IDCANCEL   If the user cancels the Set Alarm dialog box, **IDCANCEL** is sent. In this case, the dialog box is closed, but the string in **target** is not changed.

Some Variations

Here are some variations on the alarm clock that you might want to try. First, add the ability to include a message that will be displayed when the alarm goes off. For example, you might use a message such as "Production meeting in conference room." Expanding on this concept, you might want to allow up to, say, ten target times, each with its own message. This way, you could start the alarm clock in the morning and it would remind you of events as the day progressed.

Tips for Using MFC

The alarm clock is easily converted to MFC. Tips for converting the menu handlers were presented in Chapter 1. **SetTimer( )** and **KillTimer( )** are members of **CWnd** as are **GetDlgItemInt( )**, **SetDlgItemText( )**, and **SendDlgItemMessage( )**. **EnableWindow( )** is also a member of **CWnd**.

Using Multiple Monitors

First provided by Windows 98, and then supported by Windows 2000, the ability to use more than one monitor is an important Windows enhancement that many users (and most programmers!) find helpful. With Windows 98/2000, it is possible to connect up to nine monitors to a single system. The additional monitors add to the display area, acting as one big screen. For example, when you put a second video card in your system and attach a monitor to it, you can use both monitors as a single large display surface. You can drag applications between the monitors and even split a window between the two. The more monitors you add, the more screen area you have. This offers some very pleasing options for developers. For example, you could move the debug window of your compiler to a second monitor. This would free up all of the primary monitor's workspace for your source code editor. Or, if you like to work online, you could have your browser on one monitor and your application development environment on another. Frankly, the potential for this capability is unlimited.

This section develops a simple utility that demonstrates the multiple monitor capability of Windows 98/2000. It also shows the programming techniques necessary to manage and utilize this exciting capability.

Virtual Display Space

When your system contains more than one monitor, a virtual display space is created that spans the monitors. This is also called the *virtual desktop* or the *virtual screen*. The size and shape of the virtual desktop is determined by how the monitors are arranged. For example, if you have two monitors and each has a resolution of 640 by 480, and the two monitors are side by side, the size of the virtual desktop is 1280 by 480. If one monitor is directly over the other, the size of the virtual desktop is 640 by 960. It is important to understand that the virtual display space is a continuum that spans the monitors. Thus, it is possible to have windows that are larger than any single monitor.

The monitor arrangement is under user control and is accomplished using the Settings tab in the Display Properties property sheet. Figure 12-3 shows how this window appears when two monitors are used.

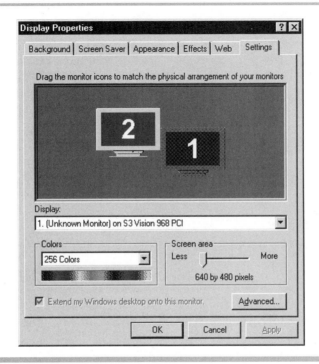

FIGURE 12-3. Setting the position of two monitors

In all cases, the first (or primary) monitor is always located with its origin at 0, 0. (If it weren't, existing programs could not run right.) Since the primary monitor always has its origin at 0, 0, this implies that monitors positioned to the left or above the primary one will use negative coordinates; and this implication is correct. For example, if you have two monitors and the second monitor is directly to the left of the primary monitor and if both have resolutions of 640 by 480, then the origin of the virtual desktop is at –640, 0. The fact that virtual screen coordinates can potentially be negative must be taken into account by any code that uses screen coordinates for positioning windows.

To obtain the origin, width, and height of the virtual screen, use the **GetSystemMetrics( )** function with the following values:

SM_XVIRTUALSCREEN	Left coordinate of origin.
SM_YVIRTUALSCREEN	Top coordinate of origin.
SM_CXVIRTUALSCREEN	Width of virtual screen.
SM_CYVIRTUALSCREEN	Height of virtual screen.

To obtain the number of monitors attached to the system, pass the value **SM_CMONITORS**.

One last point: The monitors do not need to be directly side by side or directly over one another. They may be staggered. Thus, you cannot make simplistic assumptions about what will be visible just because you know the resolution of the monitors installed in a system.

The Multiple Monitor APIs

The multiple-monitor subsystem is supported by the five API functions shown in Table 12-1. Of these, we will be using **EnumDisplayMonitors( )**, **GetMonitorInfo( )**, and **MonitorFromWindow( )**. Each is examined next.

EnumDisplayMonitors( )

EnumDisplayMonitors( ) obtains information about the monitors in the system. Its prototype is shown here:

> BOOL EnumDisplayMonitors(HDC *hdc*, RECT **rect*,
> MONITORENUMPROC *enumFunc*,
> LPARAM *extra*);

Here, *hdc* contains either the DC of a specific region or **NULL**. If a device context is passed, then only those monitors that contain a portion of the DC are enumerated. If *hdc* is **NULL**, the entire virtual screen is used. The *rect* parameter specifies a clipping region within *hdc*. It can also be **NULL**. To enumerate all monitors, both *hdc* and *rect*

Function	Description
EnumDisplayMonitors( )	Enumerates information about the monitors installed in the computer.
GetMonitorInfo( )	Obtains information about a monitor given its handle.
MonitorFromPoint( )	Given a screen location, this function returns a handle to the monitor that contains the point.
MonitorFromRect( )	Given a rectangular region, this function returns a handle to the monitor that contains the largest portion of that region.
MonitorFromWindow( )	Given a window handle, this function returns a handle to the monitor that contains the largest portion of that window.

TABLE 12-1. The Multiple-Monitor API Functions

should be **NULL**. *enumFunc* is a pointer to a callback function that will be called once for each monitor. The value of *extra* is passed to *enumFunc*. The function returns non-zero if successful and zero on failure.

The function pointed to by *enumFunc* is automatically called one time for each monitor enumerated. This callback function has the following prototype. (Of course, the name of the function may differ.)

BOOL CALLBACK *enumFunc*(HMONITOR *hmon*, HDC *hdc*,
RECT **rect*, LPARAM *extra*);

Here, *hmon* is the handle to the monitor being enumerated and *hdc* contains the DC. The *hdc* parameter will be **NULL** if the *hdc* parameter to **EnumDisplayMonitors( )** was **NULL**. The coordinates in *rect* represent the dimensions of the enumerated monitor if *hdc* is **NULL**. Otherwise, it contains the portion of the region specified by the *rect* parameter to **EnumDisplayMonitors( )** that lies within the monitor. The value in *extra* contains the value that was specified in the call to **EnumDisplayMonitors( )**. Your function must return non-zero to continue the enumeration or zero to stop it.

GetMonitorInfo( )

GetMonitorInfo( ) obtains information about a specific monitor. Its prototype is shown here:

BOOL GetMonitorInfo(HMONITOR *hmon*, MONITORINFOEX **mi*);

Here, *hmon* is the handle to the monitor about which you wish to obtain information. The information about the monitor is returned in the **MONITORINFOEX** structure pointed to by *mi*. The function returns non-zero if successful and zero on failure.

The **MONITORINFOEX** structure is defined like this:

```
typedef struct tagMONITORINFOEX {
  DWORD cbSize;
  RECT rcMonitor;
  RECT rcWork;
  DWORD dwFlags;
  CHAR szDevice[CCJDEVICENAME];
} MONITORINFOEX;
```

Here, **cbSize** contains the size of the structure. This field must be set prior to calling **GetMonitorInfo( )**.

rcMonitor describes the bounding rectangle for the specified monitor in terms of virtual screen coordinates. Thus, if the monitor in question is directly left of the primary monitor and it has a resolution of 640 by 480, then the left, top coordinates in **rcMonitor** will be –640, 0 and its right, bottom coordinates will be 0, 480.

rcWork describes the work area of the monitor in terms of virtual screen coordinates.

If **dwFlags** contains **MONITORINFOF_PRIMARY,** then the monitor is the primary monitor.

The name of the monitor is found in **szDevice.**

PROGRAMMER'S NOTE: *You can use a MONITORINFO structure in place of a MONITORINFOEX structure, if you like. The only difference between the two is that MONITORINFO does not contain the szDevice field.*

MonitorFromWindow( )

You can obtain the handle of the monitor that is displaying a window by calling **MonitorFromWindow( ).** Its prototype is shown here:

HMONITOR MonitorFromWindow(HWND *hwnd*, DWORD *retval*);

Here, *hwnd* is the handle of the window. The value passed in *retval* determines what the function returns if the specified window is not currently in any monitor. It can be one of these values:

MONITOR_DEFAULTTONEAREST
MONITOR_DEFAULTTONULL
MONITOR_DEFAULTTO PRIMARY

Code

MultMon.cpp

The **MultMon.cpp** program demonstrates the use of multiple monitors. For the sake of simplicity, the example assumes a system with two monitors, but you can easily change this. The program allows you to enumerate information about the monitors, position the program's window to either monitor, and obtain information about the current monitor. Sample output is shown in Figure 12-4.

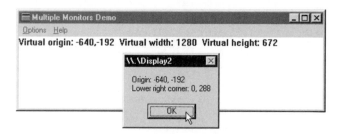

FIGURE 12-4.   Sample output from **MultMon.cpp**

```
// MultMon.cpp --  Using multiple monitors.
#define WINVER 0x0500

#include <windows.h>
#include <cstring>
#include <cstdio>
#include "MultMon.h"

LRESULT CALLBACK WindowFunc(HWND, UINT, WPARAM, LPARAM);

char szWinName[] = "MyWin"; // name of window class

BOOL CALLBACK MonInfo(HMONITOR hMon, HDC hdc,
                      LPRECT rect, LPARAM extra);
BOOL CALLBACK DisplayMonInfo(HMONITOR hMon, HDC hdc,
                             LPRECT rect, LPARAM extra);

int monOrg[9][2]; // max of 9 monitors
int numMon = 0;

int WINAPI WinMain(HINSTANCE hThisInst, HINSTANCE hPrevInst,
                   LPSTR lpszArgs, int nWinMode)
{
  HWND hwnd;
  MSG msg;
  WNDCLASSEX wcl;
  HACCEL hAccel;

  // Define a window class.
  wcl.cbSize = sizeof(WNDCLASSEX);
  wcl.hInstance = hThisInst;
  wcl.lpszClassName = szWinName;
  wcl.lpfnWndProc = WindowFunc;
  wcl.style = 0; // default style
  wcl.hIcon = LoadIcon(NULL, IDI_APPLICATION); // large icon
  wcl.hIconSm = NULL; // use small version of large icon
  wcl.hCursor = LoadCursor(NULL, IDC_ARROW);
  wcl.hbrBackground = (HBRUSH) GetStockObject(WHITE_BRUSH);
  wcl.cbClsExtra = 0;
```

```
  wcl.cbWndExtra = 0;
  wcl.lpszMenuName = "MultMon"; // specify class menu

  // Register the window class.
  if(!RegisterClassEx(&wcl)) return 0;

  // Create a window.
  hwnd = CreateWindow(szWinName, "Multiple Monitors Demo",
                      WS_OVERLAPPEDWINDOW,
                      CW_USEDEFAULT, CW_USEDEFAULT,
                      CW_USEDEFAULT, CW_USEDEFAULT,
                      NULL, NULL, hThisInst, NULL);

  // Load keyboard accelerators.
  hAccel = LoadAccelerators(hThisInst, "MultMon");

  // Display the window.
  ShowWindow(hwnd, nWinMode);
  UpdateWindow(hwnd);

  // The message loop.
  while(GetMessage(&msg, NULL, 0, 0))
  {
    if(!TranslateAccelerator(hwnd, hAccel, &msg)) {
      TranslateMessage(&msg);
      DispatchMessage(&msg);
    }
  }


  return msg.wParam;
}

// The window procedure.
LRESULT CALLBACK WindowFunc(HWND hwnd, UINT message,
                            WPARAM wParam, LPARAM lParam)
{
  HDC hdc;
  static char str1[255];
  char str2[255];
  PAINTSTRUCT paintstruct;
  int response;
  MONITORINFOEX mi;
  HMONITOR hMon;
```

```
static int vTop, vLeft, vRight, vBottom;

switch(message) {
  case WM_CREATE:
    vTop = GetSystemMetrics(SM_YVIRTUALSCREEN);
    vLeft = GetSystemMetrics(SM_XVIRTUALSCREEN);
    vRight = GetSystemMetrics(SM_CXVIRTUALSCREEN);
    vBottom = GetSystemMetrics(SM_CYVIRTUALSCREEN);

    EnumDisplayMonitors(NULL, NULL, MonInfo, 0);

    sprintf(str1,
            "%s%d,%d  %s%d  %s%d",
            "Virtual origin: ", vLeft, vTop,
            "Virtual width: ", vRight,
            "Virtual height: ", vBottom);

    break;
  case WM_COMMAND:
    switch(LOWORD(wParam)) {
      case IDM_ENUM:
        EnumDisplayMonitors(NULL, NULL, DisplayMonInfo,
                            (LPARAM) hwnd);

        sprintf(str2, "%d", numMon);
        MessageBox(hwnd, str2, "Monitors in System",
                   MB_OK);
        break;
      case IDM_MON1: // move to primary monitor
        // monitor 1 is always located at 0, 0
        MoveWindow(hwnd, 100, 100, 450, 200, 1);
        break;
      case IDM_MON2: // move to monitor 2
        MoveWindow(hwnd, monOrg[1][0]+100,
                   monOrg[1][1]+100, 450, 200, 1);
        break;
      case IDM_CURMON:
        hMon = MonitorFromWindow(hwnd,
                                 MONITOR_DEFAULTTOPRIMARY);
        mi.cbSize = sizeof(MONITORINFOEX);
        GetMonitorInfo(hMon, &mi);
        sprintf(str2,
                "%s\nOrigin: %d, %d\nLower right corner: %d, %d",
```

```
                        mi.szDevice,
                        mi.rcMonitor.left, mi.rcMonitor.top,
                        mi.rcMonitor.right, mi.rcMonitor.bottom);
              MessageBox(hwnd, str2, "Current Monitor", MB_OK);
              break;
          case IDM_EXIT:
              response = MessageBox(hwnd, "Quit the Program?",
                                "Exit", MB_YESNO);
              if(response == IDYES) PostQuitMessage(0);
              break;
          case IDM_ABOUT:
              MessageBox(hwnd, "Multiple Monitor Demonstrator V1.0",
                        "Multiple Monitors", MB_OK);
              break;
        }
        break;
      case WM_PAINT:
        hdc = BeginPaint(hwnd, &paintstruct);
        TextOut(hdc, 0, 0, str1, strlen(str1));
        EndPaint(hwnd, &paintstruct);
        break;
      case WM_DESTROY:
        PostQuitMessage(0);
        break;
      default:
        return DefWindowProc(hwnd, message, wParam, lParam);
    }
    return 0;
}


// Enumerate monitors and store origins.
BOOL CALLBACK MonInfo(HMONITOR hMon, HDC hdc,
                        LPRECT rect, LPARAM extra)
{
  MONITORINFOEX mi;

  mi.cbSize = sizeof(MONITORINFOEX);
  GetMonitorInfo(hMon, &mi);

  monOrg[numMon][0] = mi.rcMonitor.left;
  monOrg[numMon][1] = mi.rcMonitor.top;
  numMon++;
```

```
  return TRUE;
}

// Show info on all monitors in system.
BOOL CALLBACK DisplayMonInfo(HMONITOR hMon, HDC hdc,
                              LPRECT rect, LPARAM hwnd)
{
  MONITORINFOEX mi;
  char str[255];

  mi.cbSize = sizeof(MONITORINFOEX);
  GetMonitorInfo(hMon, &mi);

  sprintf(str,
          "Origin: %d, %d\nLower right corner: %d, %d",
          mi.rcMonitor.left, mi.rcMonitor.top,
          mi.rcMonitor.right, mi.rcMonitor.bottom);
  MessageBox((HWND)hwnd, str, mi.szDevice, MB_OK);

  return TRUE;
}
```

The **MultMon.rc** resource file is shown here:

```
// Use Multiple Monitors
#include <windows.h>
#include "MultMon.h"

MultMon MENU
{
  POPUP "&Options"
  {
    MENUITEM "&Enumerate\tF2", IDM_ENUM
    MENUITEM "&Primary Monitor\tF3", IDM_MON1
    MENUITEM "&Secondary Monitor\tF4", IDM_MON2
    MENUITEM "&Show Info\tF5", IDM_CURMON
    MENUITEM "E&xit\tCtrl+X", IDM_EXIT
  }
  POPUP "&Help" {
    MENUITEM "&About\tF1", IDM_ABOUT
  }
}
```

```
// Define menu accelerators
MultMon ACCELERATORS
{
  VK_F1, IDM_ABOUT, VIRTKEY
  VK_F2, IDM_ENUM, VIRTKEY
  VK_F3, IDM_MON1, VIRTKEY
  VK_F4, IDM_MON2, VIRTKEY
  VK_F5, IDM_CURMON, VIRTKEY
  "^X", IDM_EXIT
}
```

The header file **MultMon.h** is shown here:

```
#define IDM_MON1    101
#define IDM_MON2    102
#define IDM_CURMON  103
#define IDM_EXIT    104
#define IDM_ENUM    105
#define IDM_ABOUT   106
```

ANNOTATIONS

To begin, notice that the program defines **WINVER** with the value 0x0500. Since multiple monitors are fairly new, your compiler may require this definition in order to compile the multiple-monitor APIs.

The program declares two global variables: **monOrg** and **numMon**. **monOrg** is a two-dimensional array that will be used to hold the origin of each monitor. **numMon** will hold the number of monitors installed in the host computer. This program has several pieces and each will be examined separately.

WindowFunc( )

Much of the action takes place in **WindowFunc( )**. It begins by declaring several variables. Notice in particular **mi**, which is a structure of type **MONITORINFOEX** and **hMon**, which is monitor handle of type **HMONITOR**.

THE WM_CREATE HANDLER   When **WindowFunc( )** receives a **WM_CREATE** message, it obtains information about the virtual desktop. This handler is shown here:

```
case WM_CREATE:
  vTop = GetSystemMetrics(SM_YVIRTUALSCREEN);
  vLeft = GetSystemMetrics(SM_XVIRTUALSCREEN);
  vRight = GetSystemMetrics(SM_CXVIRTUALSCREEN);
  vBottom = GetSystemMetrics(SM_CYVIRTUALSCREEN);
```

```
EnumDisplayMonitors(NULL, NULL, MonInfo, 0);

sprintf(str1,
        "%s%d,%d  %s%d  %s%d",
        "Virtual origin: ", vLeft, vTop,
        "Virtual width: ", vRight,
        "Virtual height: ", vBottom);

break;
```

First, the coordinates of the virtual desktop are retrieved and stored in the static variables **vTop**, **vLeft**, **vRight**, and **vBottom**. Next, the monitors are enumerated, using the callback function **MonInfo( )**. **MonInfo( )** counts the monitors and stores their origins for later use. Finally, the origin, width, and height of the virtual desktop are displayed.

THE IDM_ENUM HANDLER   When you select Options | Enumerate, the **IDM_ENUM** handler shown here executes. It displays information about each monitor.

```
case IDM_ENUM:
  EnumDisplayMonitors(NULL, NULL, DisplayMonInfo,
                             (LPARAM) hwnd);

  sprintf(str2, "%d", numMon);
  MessageBox(hwnd, str2, "Monitors in System",
             MB_OK);
  break;
```

Here, the monitors are enumerated using the **DisplayMonInfo( )** function, which displays information about each monitor.

THE IDM_MON1 AND IDM_MON2 HANDLERS   When you choose Options | Secondary Monitor, the main window is moved to the second monitor. To move back, select Primary Monitor. These actions are performed by the **IDM_MON1** and **IDM_MON2** handlers, shown here:

```
case IDM_MON1: // move to primary monitor
  // monitor 1 is always located at 0, 0
  MoveWindow(hwnd, 100, 100, 450, 200, 1);
  break;
case IDM_MON2: // move to monitor 2
  MoveWindow(hwnd, monOrg[1][0]+100,
             monOrg[1][1]+100, 450, 200, 1);
  break;
```

The window is moved using the **MoveWindow( )** function, described earlier in this chapter. Notice that the primary monitor is always located at 0, 0. Thus, the coordinates to **MoveWindow( )** are "normal." However, the second monitor (and all others) must have its coordinates adjusted relative to the origin of the monitor. This is why the origin of the enumerated monitors was stored when the program started running.

THE IDM_CURMON HANDLER   To obtain the coordinates of the monitor that the window is currently on, choose Show Info. This causes the **IDM_CURMON** handler, shown here, to execute.

```
case IDM_CURMON:
  hMon = MonitorFromWindow(hwnd,
                      MONITOR_DEFAULTTOPRIMARY);
  mi.cbSize = sizeof(MONITORINFOEX);
  GetMonitorInfo(hMon, &mi);
  sprintf(str2,
          "%s\nOrigin: %d, %d\nLower right corner: %d, %d",
          mi.szDevice,
          mi.rcMonitor.left, mi.rcMonitor.top,
          mi.rcMonitor.right, mi.rcMonitor.bottom);
  MessageBox(hwnd, str2, "Current Monitor", MB_OK);
  break;
```

The handler begins by obtaining the handle to the current monitor by calling **MonitorFromWindow( )**. Notice that the second argument is **MONITOR_DEFAULTTOPRIMARY**. This means that if the program's window is not currently shown on any monitor, then information about the primary monitor is displayed. The monitor information is obtained by calling **GetMonitorInfo( )**.

MonInfo( )

MonInfo( ), shown here, is the callback function used by **EnumDisplayMonitors( )** inside the **WM_CREATE** handler. It counts the monitors and stores the origin (in virtual screen coordinates) of each.

```
// Enumerate monitors and store origins.
BOOL CALLBACK MonInfo(HMONITOR hMon, HDC hdc,
                      LPRECT rect, LPARAM extra)
{
  MONITORINFOEX mi;
```

```
    mi.cbSize = sizeof(MONITORINFOEX);
    GetMonitorInfo(hMon, &mi);

    monOrg[numMon][0] = mi.rcMonitor.left;
    monOrg[numMon][1] = mi.rcMonitor.top;
    numMon++;

    return TRUE;
}
```

Each time this function is called, the coordinates of the monitor whose handle is passed in **hMon** are obtained by calling **GetMonitorInfo( )**. Although the program demonstrates only the first two monitors, this function will store the origins of all monitors in the system.

Recall that **numMon** is a global variable that is initialized to 0. It is incremented each time **MonInfo( )** is called. After the monitors have been enumerated, **numMon** will contain a value equal to the number of monitors installed on the host computer.

DisplayMonInfo( )

DisplayMonInfo( ) is the callback function used by **EnumDisplayMonitors( )** inside the **IDM_ENUM** handler. It displays the coordinates of the upper-left and lower-right corners of each monitor, and the name of each monitor.

```
// Show info on all monitors in system.
BOOL CALLBACK DisplayMonInfo(HMONITOR hMon, HDC hdc,
                             LPRECT rect, LPARAM hwnd)
{
  MONITORINFOEX mi;
  char str[255];

  mi.cbSize = sizeof(MONITORINFOEX);
  GetMonitorInfo(hMon, &mi);

  sprintf(str,
          "Origin: %d, %d\nLower right corner: %d, %d",
          mi.rcMonitor.left, mi.rcMonitor.top,
          mi.rcMonitor.right, mi.rcMonitor.bottom);
  MessageBox((HWND)hwnd, str, mi.szDevice, MB_OK);

  return TRUE;
}
```

Information about each monitor is obtained by calling **GetMonitorInfo( )**, using the monitor handle passed to it in **hMon**.

Tips for Using MFC

Currently, MFC does not wrap the multiple-monitor API functions. However, this situation may change in the future.

APPENDIX
A

The Windows
Skeleton

All Windows programs have certain things in common. These elements can be assembled into a skeleton that forms the starting point from which programs can be written. In the world of Windows programming, application skeletons are frequently employed because there is a substantial "price of admission" when creating a Windows program. Unlike DOS programs, for example, in which a minimal program is about five lines long, a minimal Windows program is approximately 50 lines long. Therefore, application skeletons save time and typing, and are quite helpful when developing Windows applications.

This appendix has two purposes. First, it describes in detail the skeleton upon which most of the code in this book is built. Not all programmers write code the same way. This obviously true statement is even "more true" in the world of Windows programming. Because of this, an in-depth discussion of the framework that underpins the programs will be useful to many readers.

The second purpose of this appendix is to review the fundamental elements that comprise any API-based Windows application and how Windows interacts with these elements. While most readers will already be familiar with this material, some may not. Since an understanding of the architecture of a Windows program is necessary for successful Windows programming, it is included here.

How Windows and Your Program Interact

When you write a program for many operating systems, it is your program that initiates interaction with the operating system. For example, in a DOS program, it is the program that requests such things as input and output. Put differently, programs written in the "traditional way" call the operating system. The operating system does not call your program. However, in a large measure, Windows works in the opposite way. It is Windows that calls your program. The process works like this: A program waits until it is sent a *message* by Windows. The message is passed to your program through a special function that is called by Windows. Once a message is received, your program is expected to take an appropriate action. While your program may call one or more Windows API functions when responding to a message, it is still Windows that initiates the activity. More than anything else, it is the message-based interaction with Windows that dictates the general form of all Windows programs.

There are many different types of messages that Windows may send to your program. For example, each time the mouse is clicked on a window belonging to your program, a mouse-clicked message will be sent. Another type of message is sent each time a window belonging to your program must be redrawn. Still another message is sent each time the user presses a key when your program is the focus of input. Keep one fact firmly in mind: As far as your program is concerned, messages arrive randomly. This is why Windows programs resemble interrupt-driven programs. You can't know what message will be next.

Windows Application Basics

Before examining the Windows application skeleton, some basic concepts common to all Windows programs need to be discussed.

WinMain( )

All Windows programs begin execution with a call to **WinMain( )**. (Windows programs do not have a **main( )** function.) **WinMain( )** has some special properties that differentiate it from other functions in your application. First, it must be compiled using the **WINAPI** calling convention. (You will see **APIENTRY** used as well. They both mean the same thing.) By default, functions in your C or C++ programs use the C calling convention, but it is possible to compile a function so that it uses a different calling convention. For example, a common alternative is to use the Pascal calling convention. For various technical reasons, the calling convention Windows uses to call **WinMain( )** is **WINAPI**. The return type of **WinMain( )** should be **int**.

The Window Procedure

All Windows programs must contain a special function that is *not* called by your program, but is called by Windows. This function is generally referred to as the *window procedure* or *window function*. The window function is called by Windows when it needs to pass a message to your program. It is through this function that Windows communicates with your program. The window function receives the message in its parameters. All window functions must be declared as returning type **LRESULT CALLBACK**. The type **LRESULT** is a 32-bit integer. The **CALLBACK** calling convention is used with those functions that will be called by Windows. In Windows terminology, any function that is called by Windows is referred to as a *callback* function.

In addition to receiving the messages sent by Windows, the window function must initiate any actions indicated by a message. Typically, a window function's body consists of a **switch** statement that links a specific response to each message to which the program will respond. Your program need not respond to every message that Windows will send. For messages that your program doesn't care about, you can let Windows provide default processing. Since there are hundreds of different messages that Windows can generate, it is common for most messages to be processed by Windows and not your program.

All messages are 32-bit integer values. Further, all messages are linked with any additional information that the message requires.

Window Classes

When a Windows program first begins execution, it will need to define and register a *window class*. (Here, the word *class* is not being used in its C++ sense. Rather, it means *style* or *type*.) When you register a window class, you are telling Windows about the form and function of the window. However, registering the window class does not cause a window to come into existence. To actually create a window requires additional steps.

The Message Loop

As explained earlier, Windows communicates with your program by sending it messages. All Windows applications must establish a *message loop* inside the **WinMain( )** function. This loop reads any pending message from the application's message queue and then dispatches that message back to Windows, which then calls your program's window function with that message as a parameter. This may seem to be an overly complex way of passing messages, but it is, nevertheless, the way that all Windows programs must function. (Part of the reason for this is to return control to Windows so that the scheduler can allocate CPU time as it sees fit rather than waiting for your application's time slice to end.)

Windows Data Types

The Windows API functions do not make extensive use of standard C/C++ data types, such as **int** or **char ***. Instead, many data types used by Windows have been **typdef**ed within the WINDOWS.H file and/or its related files. This file is supplied by Microsoft (and any other company that makes a Windows C++ compiler) and must be included in all Windows programs. Some of the most common types are **HANDLE**, **HWND**, **UINT**, **BYTE**, **WORD**, **DWORD**, **LONG**, **BOOL**, **LPSTR**, and **LPCSTR**. **HANDLE** is a 32-bit integer that is used as a handle. There are a number of handle types, but they all are the same size as **HANDLE**. A *handle* is simply a value that identifies some resource. For example, **HWND** is a 32-bit integer that is used as a window handle. Also, all handle types begin with an "H." **BYTE** is an 8-bit unsigned character. **WORD** is a 16-bit unsigned short integer. **DWORD** is an unsigned 32-bit integer. **UINT** is an unsigned 32-bit integer. **LONG** is a signed 32-bit integer. **BOOL** is an integer. This type is used to indicate values that are either true or false, but it differs from the standard C++ **bool** type in that **BOOL** can store any integer value. **LPSTR** is a pointer to a string and **LPCSTR** is a **const** pointer to a string.

In addition to the basic types described above, Windows defines several structures. The two that are used by the skeleton program are **MSG** and **WNDCLASSEX**. The **MSG** structure holds a Windows message and **WNDCLASSEX** is a structure that defines a window class.

A Windows Skeleton

A minimal Windows program (that is, a skeleton) must contain two functions: **WinMain( )** and the window function. The **WinMain( )** function must perform the following general steps:

1. Define a window class.
2. Register that class with Windows.
3. Create a window of that class.
4. Display the window.
5. Begin running the message loop.

The window function must respond to all relevant messages. Since the skeleton program does nothing but display its window, the only message that it must respond to is the one that tells the application that the user has terminated the program.

The following program defines a minimal Windows skeleton that serves as a starting point for the programs in this book. It creates a standard window that includes a title. The window also contains the system menu and is, therefore, capable of being minimized, maximized, moved, resized, and closed. It also contains the standard minimize, maximize, and close boxes.

```
// Application Skeleton
#include <windows.h>

LRESULT CALLBACK WindowFunc(HWND, UINT, WPARAM, LPARAM);

char szWinName[] = "MyWin"; // name of window class

int WINAPI WinMain(HINSTANCE hThisInst, HINSTANCE hPrevInst,
                   LPSTR lpszArgs, int nWinMode)
{
  HWND hwnd;
  MSG msg;
  WNDCLASSEX wcl;

  // Define a window class.
  wcl.cbSize = sizeof(WNDCLASSEX);

  wcl.hInstance = hThisInst;      // handle to this instance
  wcl.lpszClassName = szWinName;  // window class name
  wcl.lpfnWndProc = WindowFunc;   // window function
```

```
  wcl.style = 0; // default style

  wcl.hIcon = LoadIcon(NULL, IDI_APPLICATION); // large icon
  wcl.hIconSm = NULL; // use small version of large icon
  wcl.hCursor = LoadCursor(NULL, IDC_ARROW); // cursor

  wcl.lpszMenuName = NULL; // no class menu

  wcl.cbClsExtra = 0; // no extra memory needed
  wcl.cbWndExtra = 0;

  // Make the window white.
  wcl.hbrBackground = (HBRUSH) GetStockObject(WHITE_BRUSH);

  // Register the window class.
  if(!RegisterClassEx(&wcl)) return 0;

  // Create a window.
  hwnd = CreateWindow(
    szWinName,      // name of window class
    "Windows Skeleton",  // title
    WS_OVERLAPPEDWINDOW, // window style - normal
    CW_USEDEFAULT, // X coordinate - let Windows decide
    CW_USEDEFAULT, // Y coordinate - let Windows decide
    CW_USEDEFAULT, // width - let Windows decide
    CW_USEDEFAULT, // height - let Windows decide
    NULL,          // no parent window
    NULL,          // no override of class menu
    hThisInst,     // handle for this instance
    NULL           // no additional arguments
  );

  // Display the window.
  ShowWindow(hwnd, nWinMode);
  UpdateWindow(hwnd);

  // Create the message loop.
  while(GetMessage(&msg, NULL, 0, 0))
  {
    TranslateMessage(&msg); // translate keyboard messages
    DispatchMessage(&msg);  // send message to window function
  }
  return msg.wParam;
}
```

```
// The window procedure.
LRESULT CALLBACK WindowFunc(HWND hwnd, UINT message,
                            WPARAM wParam, LPARAM lParam)
{
  switch(message) {
    case WM_DESTROY: // terminate the program
      PostQuitMessage(0);
      break;
    default:
      /* Let Windows process any messages not specified in
         the preceding switch statement. */
      return DefWindowProc(hwnd, message, wParam, lParam);
  }
  return 0;
}
```

Let's go through this program step by step.

First, all Windows programs must include the header file WINDOWS.H. As stated, this file (along with its support files) contains the API function prototypes and various types, macros, and definitions used by Windows. For example, the data types **HWND** and **WNDCLASSEX** are defined in WINDOWS.H.

The window function used by the program is called **WindowFunc( )**. It is declared as a callback function because this is the function that Windows calls to communicate with the program.

As explained, program execution begins with **WinMain( )**. **WinMain( )** is passed four parameters. **hThisInst** and **hPrevInst** are handles. **hThisInst** refers to the current instance of the program. Remember, Windows is a multitasking system, so it is possible that more than one instance of your program may be running at the same time. **hPrevInst** will always be **NULL**. The **lpszArgs** parameter is a pointer to a string that holds any command line arguments specified when the application was begun. The **nWinMode** parameter contains a value that determines how the window will be displayed when your program begins execution.

Inside the function, three variables are created. The **hwnd** variable will hold the handle to the program's window. The **msg** structure variable will hold window messages, and the **wcl** structure variable will be used to define the window class.

PROGRAMMER'S NOTE: *As mentioned above, the **hPrevInst** parameter will always be **NULL** for Win32 programs. But, in a 16-bit, Windows 3.1 program, **hPrevInst** will be non-zero if there are other instances of the program currently executing. This reflects a fundamental difference between Windows 3.1 and 32-bit versions of Windows. In Windows 3.1, multiple instances of a program share window classes and various other bits of data. Therefore, it was important for an application to know if another version of itself was running in the system. However, in 32-bit versions of Windows each process is isolated from the next and there is no automatic sharing of window classes and the like. The only reason that the **hPrevInst** exists in 32-bit Windows is for the sake of compatibility.*

Defining the Window Class

The first two actions that **WinMain( )** takes is to define a window class and then register it. A window class is defined by filling in the fields defined by the **WNDCLASSEX** structure. Its fields are shown here:

```
UINT cbSize;             // size of the WNDCLASSEX structure
UINT style;              // type of window
WNDPROC lpfnWndProc;     // address to window procedure
int cbClsExtra;          // extra class memory
int cbWndExtra;          // extra window memory
HINSTANCE hInstance;     // handle of this instance
HICON hIcon;             // handle of standard icon
HICON hIconSm;           // handle of small icon
HCURSOR hCursor;         // handle of mouse cursor
HBRUSH hbrBackground;    // background color
LPCSTR lpszMenuName;     // name of main menu
LPCSTR lpszClassName;    // name of window class
```

As you can see by looking at the program, **cbSize** is assigned the size of the **WNDCLASSEX** structure. The **hInstance** member is assigned the current instance handle as specified by **hThisInst**. The name of the window class is pointed to by **lpszClassName**, which points to the string **"MyWin"** in this case. The address of the window function is assigned to **lpfnWndProc**. No default style is specified. No extra memory is needed.

All Windows applications need to define a default shape for the mouse cursor and for the application's icons. An application can define its own custom version of these resources or it may use one of the built-in styles, as the skeleton does. In either case, handles to these resources must be assigned to the appropriate members of the **WNDCLASSEX** structure. To see how this is done, let's begin with icons.

For all modern versions of Windows, an application has two icons associated with it: one large size and one small. (Windows 3.1 and early versions of Windows NT only supported the standard icon.) The small icon is used when the application is minimized and it is also the icon that is used for the system menu. The large icon (also called the standard icon) is displayed when you move or copy an application to the desktop. Large icons are 32 by 32 bitmaps and small icons are 16 by 16 bitmaps. The large icon is loaded by the API function **LoadIcon( )**, whose prototype is shown here:

HICON LoadIcon(HINSTANCE *hInst*, LPCSTR *lpszName*);

This function returns a handle to an icon. Here, *hInst* specifies the handle of the module that contains the icon and its name is specified in *lpszName*. However, to use one of the built-in icons, you must use **NULL** for the first parameter and the name of a built-in icon for the second. Here are the names of some of the built-in icons:

Icon Macro	Shape
IDI_APPLICATION	Default icon
IDI_ERROR	Error symbol
IDI_INFORMATION	Information
IDI_QUESTION	Question mark
IDI_WARNING	Exclamation point
IDI_WINLOGO	Windows logo

Here are two important points about loading icons. First, if your application does not specify a small icon, the standard icon's resource file is examined. If it contains a small icon, then this icon is used. Otherwise, the standard icon is simply shrunk when the small icon is needed. If you don't want to specify a small icon, assign **hIconSm** the value **NULL**, as the skeleton does. Second, in general, **LoadIcon( )** can only be used to load the large size icon. You can use **LoadImage( )** to load icons of differing sizes.

To load the mouse cursor, use the API **LoadCursor( )** function. This function has the following prototype:

HCURSOR LoadCursor(HINSTANCE *hInst*, LPCSTR *lpszName*);

This function returns a handle to a cursor resource. Here, *hInst* specifies the handle of the module that contains the mouse cursor and its name is specified in *lpszName*. However, to use one of the built-in cursors, you must use **NULL** for the first parameter and specify one of the built-in cursors using its macro for the second parameter. Some of the most common built-in cursors are shown here:

Cursor Macro	Shape
IDC_ARROW	Default arrow pointer
IDC_CROSS	Cross hairs
IDC_IBEAM	Vertical I-beam
IDC_WAIT	Hourglass

The background color of the window created by the skeleton is specified as white and a handle to this brush is obtained using the API function **GetStockObject( )**. A *brush* is a resource that paints the screen using a predetermined size, color, and pattern. The function **GetStockObject( )** obtains a handle to a number of standard display objects, including brushes, pens (which draw lines), and character fonts. It has this prototype:

HGDIOBJ GetStockObject(int *object*);

The function returns a handle to the object specified by *object*. (The type **HGDIOBJ** is a GDI handle.) Here are some of the built-in brushes available to your program:

Macro Name	Background Type
BLACK_BRUSH	Black
DKGRAY_BRUSH	Dark gray
HOLLOW_BRUSH	See-through window
LTGRAY_BRUSH	Light gray
WHITE_BRUSH	White

You may use these macros as parameters to **GetStockObject( )** to obtain a brush.

Once the window class has been fully specified, it is registered with Windows using the API function **RegisterClassEx( )**, whose prototype is shown here:

ATOM RegisterClassEx(CONST WNDCLASSEX *lpWClass*);

The function returns a value that identifies the window class. **ATOM** is a **typedef** that means **WORD**. Each window class is given a unique value. *lpWClass* must be the address of a **WNDCLASSEX** structure.

Creating a Window

Once a window class has been defined and registered, your application can actually create a window of that class using the API function **CreateWindow( )**, whose prototype is shown here:

```
HWND CreateWindow(
  LPCSTR lpClassName,    // name of window class
  LPCSTR lpWinName,      // title of window
  DWORD dwStyle,         // type of window
  int X, int Y,          // upper-left coordinates
  int Width, int Height, // dimensions of window
  HWND hParent,          // handle of parent window
  HMENU hMenu,           // handle of main menu
  HINSTANCE hThisInst,   // handle of creator
  LPVOID lpszAdditional  // pointer to additional info
);
```

Index

About the CD-ROM

The source code for the programs contained in this book are found on the companion CD-ROM. The code for each chapter is stored within its own directory. Within each directory, the file names match those shown in the book. To compile the programs you must use a Windows-compatible compiler, following the instructions supplied with that compiler. The files are marked as Read-Only on the CD-ROM. You will want to clear this attribute after copying the files to your hard drive.

For the convenience of those readers using Visual C++ 6 or later, the Visual C++-compatible project files for each program are also included. The project files are located within their respective subdirectories. If you are using Visual C++, you can simply load the desired project file and then select Build to compile. Remember to clear the Read-Only attribute from the files before compiling. If you don't, you will see a message stating that the ClassView information file cannot be accessed when you load a project.

Slight differences between Windows NT, 2000, 95, and 98 exist, and some programs will execute slightly differently when run on different platforms. This is to be expected. One other point: To run the **Rotate.cpp** program described in Chapter 3 under Windows NT/2000, you will need to remove the comment symbol from the beginning of the line that calls **SetGraphicsMode( )**.

If you have a question about the programs in this book, you can call Herb Schildt's consulting office at 217.586.4683.